Colonialism & Violence in Zimbabwe

Colonialism & Violence in Zimbabwe

A History of Suffering

HEIKE I. SCHMIDT

Research Associate
African Studies Centre
University of Oxford

 JAMES CURREY

James Currey
is an imprint of Boydell & Brewer Ltd
PO Box 9, Woodbridge, Suffolk IP12 3DF, GB
www.jamescurrey.com

and of

Boydell & Brewer Inc.
668 Mt Hope Avenue, Rochester, NY 14620-2731, US
www.boydellandbrewer.com

Distributed in Zimbabwe by
Weaver Press
PO Box A1922
Avondale
Harare
Zimbabwe
www.weaverpresszimbabwe.com

The publisher has no responsibility for the continued existence
or accuracy of URLs for external or third-party internet websites
referred to in this book, and does not guarantee that any content
on such websites is, or will remain, accurate or appropriate.

British Library Cataloguing in Publication Data
A catalogue record for this book is available from the British Library

ISBN 978-1-84701-051-3 (James Currey Cloth)

Papers used by Boydell & Brewer are natural, recyclable products
made from wood grown in sustainable forests

Typeset in 10.5/11.5 Monotype Ehrhardt
by forzalibro designs, Harare
Printed and bound in Great Britain by CPI Group Ltd, Croydon, CR0 4YY

Mr T

Contents

Contents

7

Epilogue

List of Illustrations

MAPS

FIGURES

List of Acronyms

ADA	Agricultural Development Authority
ADF	African Development Fund
ARDA	Agricultural Rural Development Authority
BSAC	British South Africa Company
BSAP	British South Africa Police
CCJP	Catholic Commission of Justice and Peace
CID	Criminal Investigation Department
CL	Communal Land
CNC	Chief Native Comissioner (here Manyikaland)
CSO	Central Statistical Office (now ZIMSTAT)
CT	Communist Terrorist
DA	District Administrator
DAO	District Administrator's Office (here Mutasa)
DC	District Commissioner
DERUDE	Department of Rural Development
EEC	European Economic Community
EHTE	Eastern Highlands Tea Estates
FRELIMO	Front for the Liberation of Mozambique
JOC	Joint Operations Command
LAA	Land Apportionment Act
LDO	Land Development Officer
MNR	Mozambique National Resistance Movement; also RENAMO
MP	Member of Parliament
NAZ	National Archives of Zimbabwe, Harare
NC	Native Commissioner
NDP	National Democratic Party
NLHA	Native Land Husbandry Act of 1951
NRC	National Records Centre, Harare
OMMA	Old Mutare Mission
PAO	Provincial Administrator's Office Archives, Chere, Mutare
PC	Provincial Commissioner (here Manyikaland)
PNC	Provincial Native Commissioner (here Manyikaland)
PP	Private Papers
PTSD	Post Traumatic Stress Disorder
PV	Protected Village
PVS	Planned Village Settlement
RAR	Rhodesian African Rifles
RENAMO	National Resistance Movement Mozambique; also MNR
SNA	Special Native Area
SON	Superintendant of Natives (here Manyikaland)

TILCOR	Tribal Trust Land Development Corporation
TTL	Tribal Trust Land
UDI	Unilateral Declaration of Independence
ZANLA	Zimbabwe African National Liberation Army
ZANU	Zimbabwe African National Union
ZANU(PF)	Zimbabwe African National Union (Patriotic Front)
ZAOGA	Zimbabwe Assembly of God
ZAPU	Zimbabwe African People's Union
ZIMCORD	Zimbabwe Conference on Reconstruction and Development
ZIPRA	Zimbabwe People's Revolutionary Army
ZNA	Zimbabwe National Army

Glossary

Binga Guru	Mutasa's spiritual and political centre and royal burial ground
chimbwido	girl or young woman who assisted the guerrilla fighters during the Liberation war
ishe	chief
keep	vernacular term for Protected Village; fortified centre of a Protected Village
lobola	also *roora*; bride-price, bride-wealth
madzviti	invaders, raiding warriors
mainini	junior co-wife in a polygynous marriage
mambo	paramount ruler of the Manyika people; king
mbuya	polite address of older woman
mhondoro	senior or royal spirit medium
mtengesi	sell-out
mujibha	boy or young man who assisted the guerrilla fighters during the Liberation war
mutopo	totem
muzvare	daughter of a chief; here chieftainess
ñ'anga	healer; ritual expert
ngozi	avenging spirit
pungwe	nightly meeting for rituals, Christian prayer or politicisation
sabhuku	village headman; 'kraalhead'
sadza	mealie meal porridge; staple food
Security Forces	Rhodesian army
sekuru	polite address of older man
svikiro	ancestral spirit medium
zunde	chiefly fields, cultivated for communal purposes such as rituals or drought relief

1. *Honde Valley, 1992. View from the south-east towards the escarpment, with Mount Njangani on the horizon to the right* (Source: Heike I. Schmidt)

Acknowledgements

Words do not suffice to thank those who accompanied over time or briefly connected with my research project and whose insight and support were crucial to bring this undertaking to fruition. Researching and writing about violence and suffering in particular ask much of those who are part of the process, whether sharing, listening, or commenting. Most humbling were the tremendous patience and kindness of the women and men in Zimbabwe who were willing to talk to me about the past and present of the Honde Valley and about their lives. This project would not have been possible without their help. As we agreed, most will remain anonymous in the narrative that follows. Amongst those who supported my research in Zimbabwe, I wish to mention the late Mambo Abishai Chimbadzwa Mutasa, Ishe Chikomba and his father, Ishe Zindi, Phillippa Mukanganwa, Josephine Chiinze, Onea Chizana, Mbuya Kwenje, and Geoff Baxter. Nomsa Ncube kept me on my toes by carefully probing why anybody should do research on Manicaland when there is so much to be done on Matabeleland. In addition, the deWolf family, Hiltrud and Detlev Lubjahn, Mai Makunike, Jane Muomba, Nyasha Murphree, Joachim Murat, and the late Mister Gnanamuthu Sathiagnanan were most gracious hosts. I owe special thanks to Mai Phyllis and Mister Munjoma.

Oral research was facilitated by the interpretation, translation, and transcription of interviews by Mai Munjoma, Mister Munjoma, Jane Muomba, Mona Lisa Sakarombe, David Mubaira, Osmas Mubaira, Temba Bvute, Mai Makunike, and Simba Handiseni. Without exception, the staff at the archives and offices whom I consulted were extremely helpful. I would like to especially thank Sheila Ndlovu and Mister Nyamangodo at the National Archives of Zimbabwe, Blessing Muringapasi at the National Records Centre, the Provincial Administrator Manicaland and his staff, the District Administrator Mutasa and his staff, and Mike Auret. Thanks also to Victor Machingaidze.

I am grateful to the Zimbabwe Research Council for granting my research permit and the Department of Economic History at the University of Zimbabwe for hosting me as Research Associate. Researching and writing this book were furthermore made possible by grants from the Economic and Social Research Council, the German Historical Institute London, the German Academic Exchange Service, and the Committee for Graduate Studies, the Raymond Carr Fund, Beit Fund Grants, an APM Read Scholarship in History, all of which were granted through the University of Oxford, as well as a Mellon Foundation Sawyer Post-Doctoral Fellowship at Emory University. Julia Wigg did a tremendous job in copy-editing an earlier version of the manuscript and my editor Lynn Taylor has been a pleasure to work with.

It took a long time to decide whether and if so how to write this book. During the process that resulted in this study, I incurred many debts, not least through constructive criticism at conferences and seminars. First and foremost, I have learned a great deal from my students, their critical insights, unrelenting questioning of concepts, and probing of problems which has altered my sense of what it means to be a historian and how I wish to explore the past in my research. Thanks among many to Victoria Penziner Hightower, Sean McCafferty, Marianne Sarkis, and Peter Hoesing.

The 'old Zimbabwe cluster' made me feel at home when I first arrived in Oxford: Jocelyn Alexander, Jeremy Brickhill, Marieke Clarke, David Maxwell, JoAnn McGregor and Ken Wilson, as well as Bella Mukonyora, Elspeth Robson, and Margaret Hall. Phyllis Ferguson introduced me to the art of surviving the alma mater. Since then, I have had most supportive colleagues at a range of departments. My gratitude to the late Albert Wirz, Aimee Lee and Bill Cheek, Peter Garretson, and Walter Sauer. Thanks also to Marcia Wright, Steve Feierman, and Betsy Schmidt for supporting my academic pursuits and believing in me, as well as to John Lonsdale, both a pillar and an inspiration for historical argument and intellectual elegance. Some friends were there when it mattered. Donald Moore encouraged me to listen. Terry Ranger has shown tremendous patience with my ongoing confusion over the finer theological differences between the many churches in Zimbabwe. He also gracefully accepted my defection to Tanzania. Finally, Georg Deutsch saw this project through thick and thin. While developing an at times annoying, albeit healthy habit of tuning out all things Honde Valley, he was always there when a helping hand was needed. Thank you.

The most formidable challenge in writing this book was a process of intellectual and personal transformation that turned a passion for Zimbabwe and its past and present into the quest for composing an academic narrative that does justice to the lives of those African men and women who shared their experiences with me. Politically, intellectually, emotionally, psychologically, morally, suffering is 'A Problem We all Live with', as Norman Rockwell so brilliantly portrayed in his 1964 painting of little Ruby Bridges and the struggle over school integration in the American South. The wider purpose of this study is to connect the reader to suffering in one particular place and hence to reflect on its significance in this world's past and present. Whether this microhistory of the Honde Valley and social history of suffering has succeeded in doing so is for the reader to decide. None of this would have been possible without the support by others, but the full responsibility for what follows lies solely with the author.

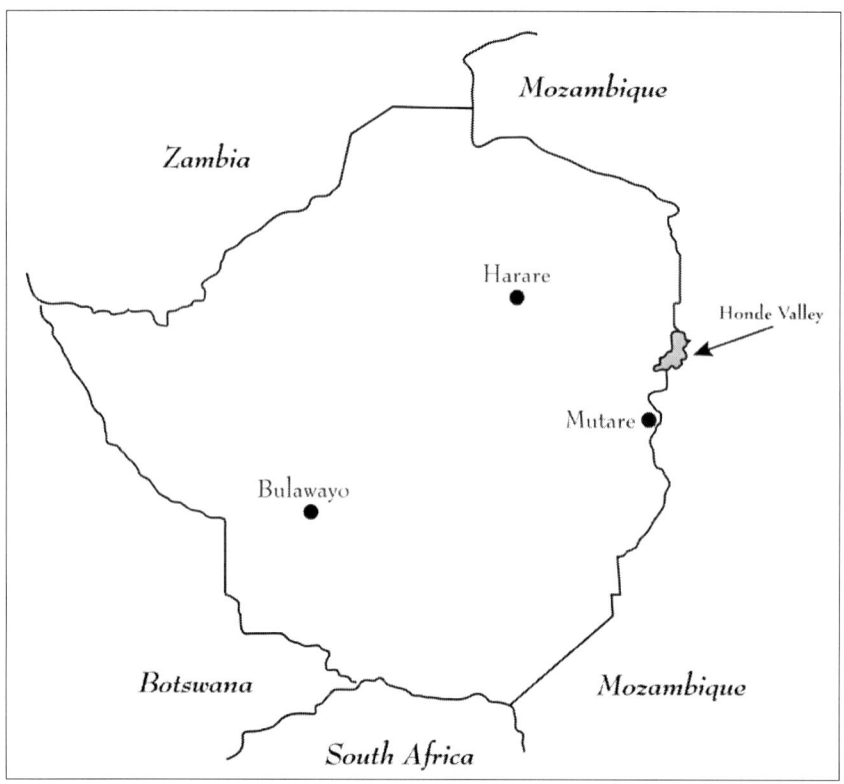

Map 1 Honde Valley in Zimbabwe

1
Introduction

Probably the most famous work of art portraying suffering and violence is Picasso's painting *Guernica* (1937). Many readings of this painting are possible; one would be that in the face of utter destruction, *Guernica* depicts an affirmation of personhood.[1] This is the *leitmotif* of this book. It is the voice breaking the silence of violation, without romanticising it or assuming its authenticity that this book is listening out for. The purpose of this study is to examine historical phenomena such as colonialism, nationalism, and decolonisation, with the human condition as the starting point of the historical examination, not its by-product or determinant in the shape of resistance or coping strategies. Spatial practices such as forced displacement will be looked at through the lens of desire, that is, the purposeful choice to negotiate the boundaries of one's lifeworld individually or communally.[2] From such a perspective, violence and suffering are seen as central to the understanding of Africa's past, yet not reduced to mere dislocation, disruption, and destruction. Violence aims at victimising and silencing those who are violated, but it does not always succeed in doing so. One of the most overlooked aspects in the study of violence has been the potential disconnect between the intent to violate and the perception of being violated. This is a void which this study aims to fill.

An elder from the Honde Valley explained in reference to the early twentieth century: 'When war rages hot, much death occurs – and many people flee.'[3] This book examines the intersection of identity, experience, and community against the backdrop of such heat, a vernacular term that signifies a time of danger to physical, social, and spiritual wellbeing due to war. It raises the question when violence causes suffering and how such experiences are made sense of in everyday life, while at the same time acknowledging that the heat of war causes death, flight, and the disruption of communities, as the elder emphasised. The main argument of this study is two-fold. First, across the disciplines, violation and suffering are usually treated as phenomena of crisis and exception. Here, on the contrary, the starting point is to acknowledge that violence in its various forms is existential and accordingly part of everyday life. Therefore, the book traces the making and unmaking of community and belonging through violence. It also follows that even actions, with at times significant political

1

consequences such as opposition against intervention by the settler state and support for the liberation armies, might have been carried by a radically local agenda of defending a frontier mode of life instead of nationalist mobilisation. Secondly, in the process of creating memory, those who suffer violence invest experiences of violation with meaning. They thus break the enforced silence and assert personhood. Spiritual healing and landscape practices provide important arenas for such processes.

Political identity and the sense of community and belonging in rural African societies are usually articulated in moral terms. This study employs Cambridge historian John Lonsdale's theorem of 'moral ethnicity', which refers to what he calls the inner architecture of community. This identity is constituted through the perception of 'civic virtue' in a constant debate over what makes someone a valuable member of the community. Lonsdale privileges debate over discourse in part because the concept includes land use practices and, one may add, performative enactments. While thus historically constructed, civic virtue is often perceived as tradition, an unchanging given. An understanding of civic virtue is specific to each society and differs by age, gender, and social status.[4] Personal and social memory as much as individual and communal actions play an important role in reflecting and shaping a person's standing and claim to be part of this moral ethnicity.

This book is a social history of suffering and a micro-history of one particular area in Eastern Zimbabwe, the Honde Valley. It scrutinises violence through episodes of violent conflict, in particular warrior raids in the nineteenth century, the Makombe War (1917–1920), the Second Chimurenga, Zimbabwe's liberation war (1972–1980), and the Mozambican RENAMO war (1975–1992), named after the insurgents, the National Resistance Movement of Mozambique. Violence is here understood in a broader sense than military conflict, however, and includes aspects of imperial practices such as land alienation, enforced agricultural policies, and also the othering gaze of self-perceived pioneers.

Major themes running through this study are the frontier character of the valley that has made it both an area of opportunity and danger; insurgency and counter-insurgency, including mobilisation and villagisation; communal violation and spiritual healing; and gendered and age-specific responses to the challenges as well as life chances violence offered to the valley's inhabitants. The temporal scope of the book reaches back beyond the more recent episodes of conflict because people's memories and historical narratives craft the meaning of war through past events. Thus, this book roughly covers the period from the 1850s to the 1990s.

This study contributes to three fields of investigation: violence, memory, and landscape. It shows how valley inhabitants made sense of violence through mediating negotiations of the present, imaginations of the future, and memories of the past. Violence is thus interpreted as a social process, the meaning of which is made and unmade in personal and social memory. The same historical trajectory can be found elsewhere, yet the way in which local identities have been shaped by its frontier character is specific to this area.[5] The inhabitants have perceived the valley not only as a place of refuge and opportunity, but also of danger. The close examination of why people chose to take the risk of living in a location that any time could turn 'hot', and the analysis of how violence has impacted the historical trajectory of the area, allows for the dismantling of simplifying nationalist and post-nationalist treatments of political violence, such as Zimbabwe's war of liberation, that still frame conflict merely in terms of resistance. The book focuses on the making of meaning and identity in relation to violence rather than restricting itself to politicisation, mobilisation, and victimisation. In short, this study calls for a re-examination of the concept of violence in historical perspective and insists on its creativity as a means of articulating personhood and belonging.

The Debate

The purpose of this history of suffering is to contribute to three bodies of literature. It engages the regional and local historiography on liberation wars by employing violence as a category of historical analysis. In addition, it adds the crucial element of violence and resistance, central topics of African history since its beginnings as an academic discipline, to the new colonial history of Africa. This volume also questions some of the prevailing assumptions about violence in cross-disciplinary debate.

First, the extensive historiography on liberation wars in southern Africa has significantly pushed forward the wider field of resistance studies.[6] Groundbreaking early works such as Terence Ranger's *Revolt in Southern Rhodesia 1896-7*, published in 1967,[7] influenced the Zimbabwean nationalists' understanding of mobilisation and anti-colonial resistance when their liberation war of the twentieth century was on its way, and Ranger's accompanying articles introduced the theorem of primary resistance on the same topic, albeit in comparative perspective.[8] Ranger's *Peasant Consciousness*, which was published much later, added to his earlier nationalist history by posing the simplifying, yet at the time important and new argument, that Zimbabwe's peasants had been politicised before the freedom fighters arrived in the 1970s, and that together they formed a 'composite peasant–guerrilla ideology', a 'liberation ideology with peasant aspirations'.[9] Decades of work on Mozambique by Allen and Barbara Isaacman have encompassed many aspects of violence such as banditry, labour resistance, the liberation war of the 1970s, and, through a recent return to their earlier research, a new understanding of ethnicity and masculinity in relation to changing landscapes of violence, with a focus on the nineteenth century. They have significantly informed the understanding of conflict in southern Africa and beyond by connecting questions of violence, personhood, identity, and labour that go far beyond class analysis or a peasant resistance approach.[10] Meanwhile, studies on urban South Africa during and after the apartheid era have made a major contribution to the perception of urban (counter-)insurgency, youth and political violence, and the horrors of a supremacist authoritarian state.[11]

Despite this rich historiography, two major problems can be observed, ones that afflict Zimbabwean violence and resistance studies in particular. First, much of the literature is empiricist to a point where even central concepts are not defined.[12] The imprudent use of concepts as ambiguous as violence and memory severely impede any critical reading of such works.[13] Secondly, along similar lines, Zimbabwe's historiography, while providing a detailed mapping of the past for Zimbabweanists, suffers from narrow introversion: district case studies are compiled, adding new material without significantly altering the understanding of conflict in that country and without being obviously relevant in comparative perspective.[14] Rare exceptions are among the early contributions, especially David Lan's *Guns and Rain* and Norma Kriger's *Peasant Voices*.[15]

Lan was first in breaking Zimbabwe's nationalist narrative when he proposed that mobilisation for the liberation war was rooted in the guerrilla fighters presenting themselves to the rural population as sons of the soil, children of the local elders, but imbued with authority and legitimacy by the ancestors, the return of whose land they were fighting for.[16] Kriger's study of the Second Chimurenga has had a major impact on the study of insurgencies. She provocatively observed that mobilisation was rooted in intra-African inequality in its colonial manifestations, that peasant agendas tended to be more radical than those of the guerrillas during the war, and that the presence of young men with guns provided the opportunity to settle internal struggles within peasant communities.[17] She also showed guerrilla coercion vis-à-vis the civilian population, an argument for which she has been viciously attacked. In the early 1990s, Zimbabwean historian Kenneth Manungo even accused her of being a bourgeois traitor to the peasant class for pointing out that guerrilla fighters and youths at times abused the power they gained to inflict violence on civilians and elders respectively.[18]

Somewhat surprisingly, the district studies that Kriger, Lan, and Ranger researched in the early 1980s still largely present the most insightful interpretative frame for the Second Chimurenga.[19] Ranger has pointed out that a new, patriotic history has recently come to dominate politics, the media, school books, and even some academic treatments of the past in Zimbabwe.[20] Seen as part of the 'Third Chimurenga' proclaimed by President Robert Mugabe in the context of the 2000 parliamentary elections, which focused on land reform and on 'resisting imperialists and their local agents',[21] patriotic history mirrors that struggle by focusing on colonial violence and British imperialism. What emerges is a portrayal of the past that reflects contemporary hyper-nationalist concerns rather than insights into history.

Kriger, Lan, and Ranger's arguments differ – quite significantly so in part – yet read together they provide a detailed understanding of insurgent civilian relations. These contrasting models do not simply represent three different district studies by a political scientist, an anthropologist, and a historian; but jointly they also illustrate an important point that is often overlooked. By its very nature guerrilla war, with small, mobile military units who usually fight for a political agenda, necessitates strategic adjustments to local conditions and the ability of combatants to form bonds with the local population to gain their support. Consequently, in contrast to conventional war, the patterns of interaction have to be highly localised and adaptive. A generalised model of insurgencies is necessarily an oversimplification. While geographically small, the Honde Valley, having been the most contested area during Zimbabwe's liberation war and due to its specific terrain – with dense vegetation, hills and granite peaks breaking up the valley bottom, and a steep and partially heavily forested escarpment towards the west – is an ideal area to map such complexity. Hence, this study provides considerable insight into guerrilla tactics, guerrilla–civilian relations, and the settler regime's response. It offers an unusually detailed understanding of the rural insurgency and counter-insurgency campaigns, while attempting conceptual clarity and applying a micro-historical approach. This book thus contributes directly to the extensive historiography on southern Africa's liberation wars, yet also seeks wider applicability across time and space regarding the study of political violence and (counter-)insurgency warfare.

Second, this study contributes to Africa's new colonial history which has set into motion a vibrant discussion of Africa's past from the mid-1990s onwards. Frederick Cooper and others took a decided step away from the oversimplifying resistance paradigm that had shaped the field of African history since the 1950s and that still frames much of historical writing today. Cooper poignantly insists that African life-worlds during the colonial period can neither be summarised as merely caught in a choice between resistance and collaboration, nor necessarily shaped entirely by colonialism.[22] Frederik Cooper and Ann Laura Stoler's call for examining the mutual flows of influence between metropole and colony and the internal contradictions of colonialism as an exploitative system of political domination imposed by the government of a nation state supposedly committed to the ideas of the Enlightenment[23] has not been fully answered yet for Africa. However, an emphasis on African thought, creativity, and vernacular knowledge has become visible in recent work,[24] although there has also been a clear danger of an uncritical return to the African agency paradigm that proclaims Africans were not mere victims under colonial rule and that they too had the ability to act.[25] Paradoxically, with the important historiographic turn towards a new colonial history, it is the study of conflict that often remains caught up in the resistance paradigm.[26] This book attempts to break ground by presenting a complex and layered argument about conflict in Zimbabwe under minority rule, one that is further enriched by reaching back into the past, before colonialism, and into the decade after independence, for while the colonial period brought much change it does not present a discrete era of experience, identity, and the making of meaning.

Finally, this study questions assumptions that prevail in the cross-disciplinary debate about war and violence. These widespread notions include an Africa lost in what influential Oxford economist Paul Collier recently called the 'conflict trap',[27] the apparent dichotomy between victim and perpetrator; and the universality of trauma. This brief discussion will begin with the connection between conflict and the economy.

Collier is undoubtedly correct in identifying Africa as the world region most affected by poverty and conflict in today's world. According to him, seven hundred million Africans are part of the 'bottom billion', that is, people and governments who cannot help themselves and that are in turn part of the world's five billion poor facing one billion rich people.[28] His claim that 'seventy-three percent of people in the societies of the bottom billion have recently been through a civil war or are still in one'[29] seems a problematic generalisation to uphold for Africa, as it depends on quantifying conflict and its effects. His criterion for the definition of civil war is that of scale, that is, the rate and distribution of combat deaths, while most Zimbabweans – and historians – would have difficulty identifying, for example, any of the violent conflicts in Zimbab-we in the past one hundred years as civil war.[30] More importantly, Collier's 'agenda for action'[31] emphasises that the rich need finally to engage in helping the bottom billion to escape the traps of conflict, bad governance, environ-mental resources, and political geography through 'change from within', not by outside imposition. Nevertheless, he emphasises the importance of the experi-ence of the most developed countries and admonishes the bottom billion that 'They will need to learn.'[32]

Anthropologist Carolyn Nordstrom has taken a very different approach to regions of poverty and conflict. She has shown the potential of 'shadow econ-omies', informal economic networks that connect legal and other spheres of economic activity, especially in conflict areas, with global flows of capital and consumption.[33] She argues convincingly that dismissing shadow economies as subverting the national market or as mere criminal activity denies their impor-tance to the global economy. Moreover, they are crucial for survival in crisis regions with a failing or absent state where they represent entrepreneurial initi-ative and skills. Somewhat ironically, she also points out that they are grounded in 'cultures of trust'.[34]

Nordstrom's 'cultures of trust' in the economic sphere are paralleled by Paul Richards' concept of 'war talk', an equally paradoxical discursive understand-ing of insurgent tactics and ideology. From his study of Sierra Leone's war of the 1990s, Richards suggests that in order to understand conflict and violence, and to further peace, it is important to listen for the meaning of war to all involved. He understands war as text, as a discursive practice, and thus provides an approach that allows the identification of meaning even in what appear to be meaningless acts of terror.[35] Violence committed by African actors is usually dismissed as barbaric atavism of an Africa trapped in chaos and destruction, as in Kaplan's influential and notorious barbarism thesis of the early 1990s that proclaimed some conflict areas, such as Africa, should just be left alone because they simply could not be helped.[36] Published not long after the US debacle in Mogadishu in 1993 and two months before the Rwandan genocide of 1994, Kaplan was inspired by Samuel Huntington's *Clash of Civilizations*.[37] His work contributed to the US government's decision to veto – together with France – the United Nations Security Council's declaration of the conflict in Rwanda as genocide, thereby significantly contributing to the failure to prevent and then stop the killing of around 800,000 Rwandans.[38]

This book proposes that economists' insights can indeed bring about posi-tive change, but the onus is not primarily upon the so-called 'bottom billion', the vast majority of whom are African, to learn from 'the rich'. Instead, the rest can learn from the experience of conflict in Africa. Vernacular knowledge is all too often marginalised or even dismissed as scientific knowledge takes centre stage. However, what might appear from the outside as a society or commu-nity trapped in crisis, with local discourse relevant only insofar as it hampers modernisation efforts, may well disguise localised strategies and vernacu-lar understanding and decision-making. Relearning the local, as others have pointed out, is of importance, and here the argument is that it might indeed add to broader understandings of crisis, conflict, and violence. This study is not primarily concerned with economic developments, even though cash crop production did play an important role in how the Second Chimurenga unfolded in the Honde Valley. But Nordstrom's suggestion of understanding the creative quality of 'shadow economies' and their moral nature is a most useful approach to examining local identities and experiences in a frontier area, rather than dismissing the periods of conflict as mere disruption. In addition, following Richards' suggestion of treating war as text, it is possible to locate meaning in what might otherwise appear silencing terror. The focus is on the valley's frontier people, those who take risks because they seek opportunities.

The second violence argument this book takes issue with is the apparent dichotomy between victim and perpetrator.[39] It is problematic for two main reasons. The experience of violence and the perception of being violated can be disconnected. South African philosopher Johan Degenaar gives the example of a drowning woman who is knocked out by her rescuer. For the purpose of his argument, he points out that even though great force was used, in the normative sense, there was no intention of violation, hence this is not an example of violence.[40] One can add another aspect to this discussion. What if the drowning person was trying to commit suicide? She might well feel violated, even though this was not the rescuer's intention. As shown above, the opposite might also be the case: intent of violation, but no such perception on part of the person who experiences the violence. Degenaar further explains the potential disconnect when pointing to the difference in a normative and metaphorical definition of violence, with the former being the intentional application of force by one person against another. A metaphorical definition on the other hand allows for two important ambiguities: violence comes in many forms and guises, not only as physical force; it can be psychological, verbal, sexual, or structural. Also, even the application of extreme force does not necessarily make for an experience of violation on the part of the person who is impacted by it, nor does the lack of intention necessarily prevent violation.[41]

Another argument against any assumed clear cut distinction between perpetrator and victim lies in the nature of insurgencies themselves. Central tactics of Maoist guerrilla warfare include the indistinguishability of combatants and civilians in the eyes of the enemy and, at the same time, the focus on so-called soft targets, that is, primarily attacking infrastructure and civilians rather than core military installations and combat troops. This tactical consideration against the backdrop of political violence hugely complicates the question of victim and perpetrator. One example from the Second Chimurenga is the single largest massacre of civilians, when 27 tea workers were killed in the Honde Valley in 1976. The local ZANLA unit might well have been responsible, acting with the intention of setting an example when the men refused to listen to the liberation fighters' appeals to cease working for the settler economy. Another example is provided by David Caute's *Under the Skin*, with its rich testimony from white settlers during the Second Chimurenga. He shows that many felt violated – betrayed by their ungrateful servants and labourers in a 'country [with] the best race relations in the world'.[42] The settler experience of betrayal and violation was underpinned by government publicity. The Rhodesian Department of Information published the army magazine *Rhodesian Fighting Forces*. At the height of the liberation war they ran the motto 'Then as now … co-operation is a feature of Rhodesian life' with reference to the

First Chimurenga of 1896–1897 and continued to claim that 'there may not be another country where relations between the races … are as harmonious as in Rhodesia'.[43] Such blatant propaganda does not contradict the fact that many Rhodesians saw the liberation war as illegitimate terror. Yet both examples illustrate that in order to understand how insurgencies are fought and to examine violence in general, it is crucial to consider the elements of intent and violation, even if it raises epistemological problems and complicates argument and analysis.

The third aspect in cross-disciplinary studies of violence which this volume critically engages is the concept of trauma. War and violence-related psychological trauma only became a topic of historical study as late as the 1980s, and in the context of Holocaust studies. Even in the fields of psychiatry and psychology it was only in 1980 that post-traumatic stress disorder (PTSD) was officially recognised by the American Psychiatric Association.[44] The casualties of the Vietnam War finally saw the profession pay full attention to researching the anxiety disorder that displays symptoms such as flashbacks. Historians subsequently began to understand the importance of the concept for interpreting past suffering, especially that of Holocaust survivors.[45]

The difficulty of transporting this psychiatric concept, or indeed any scientific knowledge, into the realm of historical interpretation is that such transfer is based on the assumption of universality. More so, as the psychiatrist Matthew Friedman points out in the official definition provided by the United States Department of Veteran Affairs, PTSD is 'unique among psychiatric diagnoses' for its focus on the 'traumatic stressor'.[46] According to biomedical understanding, PTSD can only be understood through the episode of violation that caused it; the disorder is universal; and it appears to be connected with the notion of individuality originating in western society in the late eighteenth century.[47] The psychiatric definition of PTSD allows that not all but most people will suffer from certain symptoms after a traumatic experience and that not everybody develops full PTSD. Nevertheless, encountering individuals or communities who underwent comparable violent experiences and finding that some do not display the symptoms of PTSD while those of the western ilk do opens up the dangerous possibility of dismissing vernacular cosmologies or even re-opening a stereotypical discourse of Africa's otherness. A return to Africa's marginalisation and to a view of African men, women, and children as the civilised individual's other must be avoided because othering and generalisation reduce Africa to one-dimensionality. Instead, one may argue that social healing and the constitution of moral community present opportunities for the rest to learn from Africa, which is what this book suggests.

Violence, Memory, & Landscape

The three themes running through this book are violence, memory, and landscape. Violence is the centre of the study, because the main concern is to enhance the understanding of its experiences and practices in the context of insurgency and counter-insurgency. In this discussion, memory has a dual role. It serves as a methodological tool through the application of oral history in order to access the past and is itself also the object of study, given that memory plays a crucial role in accommodating experiences of violence individually or socially. In addition, the concept of violence is opaque and varied. Linking it to perceptions of landscape grounds violence in notions of belonging and identity. As a significant and signifying phenomenon, landscape opens a complex view of violence and power, be it hegemonic state power or the power of guns in the hands of young men. More generally, landscape imagination and practices facilitate the historian's task of populating the past[48] and thus to bring the experience and memory of violence to the foreground. What follows is a brief discussion of violence, memory, and landscape as categories of historical analysis.

VIOLENCE

Violence, in contrast to most concepts of historical analysis, raises particular epistemological challenges, not least for the reason that it implicates researcher and reader morally, ethically, and politically. Violence is a concept that is ambiguous, universal, and uncomfortable to study, because it leaves no neutral ground to the participant or observer. The difficulty in employing the concept is further complicated by a body of literature that more often than not does not provide even a working definition, and by the range of uses one finds within and across the disciplines, from a narrow understanding of the application of physical force to Kleinman's all encompassing perspective of 'everyday violences'.[49] The latter is an elaboration of Johan Galtung's structural violence to move beyond inequality intrinsic in the structures of society, such as customs and normativity, and to include all experiences of suffering. With social relations being inherently unequal, to Kleinman 'everyday violences' are essentially existential.[50] This opens the door to inflationary use, while at the same time pointing to the crucial insight that violation is subjective and quotidian and hence does not ordinarily constitute a crisis.[51]

This study will use a multi-faceted concept of violence that is based on core characteristics: violation, intent, subjectivity. One observation that will guide the discussion is that only suffering absolute terror renders the violated completely mute. Most often, the affliction of physical, psychological or other forms of violence is temporary and its effect not total, meaning that the violated has the resources to recover his or her voice, to create a narrative through memory of what happened. This can be characterised as a process that is often embedded in vernacular healing practices. The body of literature on violence, especially that by historians, usually limits itself to the time of conflict or to its immediate aftermath. However, to reach an understanding of the experience of violence, its study needs to allow for its ambiguity and to take a long-term perspective.

MEMORY

Since the late 1980s, a rich body of literature has evolved on memory, the second theme of this study.[52] Maurice Halbwachs' early work in the 1920s established that memory is crafted by making sense of experience through social frame-works, shaped by the intersection of the individual and society. Halbwachs distinguishes between individual memory (*mémoire individuelle*) and collec-tive memory (*mémoire collective*), with the former located within the latter.[53] Following Halbwachs' distinction, here, however, different terms will be used, namely personal and social memory.[54] Thus the social condition of memory can be further stressed, as can memory's role in fostering or destabilising social cohesion.[55] Also, the use of personal memory emphasises its role vis-à-vis iden-tity and personhood rather than the notion of containment embedded in the term 'individual', a cross-culturally problematic concept.

Historians who work with oral testimony strive to grasp the meaning with which memories invest the past and to interpret it. In contrast to written source exegesis which positions the historian into a necessarily one-sided dialogue with text, oral history allows the researcher direct access to meaning through communication. However, the disentangling of event, experience, memory, and meaning is a complex process that greatly depends on the interviewee's col-laboration as well as the communicative environment. The historian's task is further complicated by the fact that memory is expressed not only in narra-tive, but also in practice – body language, rituals, and everyday spatial routines, for example – and represented by place and other mnemotopes such as photo-graphs and mementos.[56]

The way in which narratives of the past are shaped is thus already an expression of their meaning. This draws attention to a further characteristic of memory – its provisionality. Memory is an important means of placing one-self socially, of shaping identity in the present in relation to the past and in projecting the future. Memory nurtures personal and shared identities within the wider framework of collectives as moral arenas.[57] Peter Burke's understand-ing of history as social memory can therefore be reversed, as social memory is in fact 'making history'.[58] It is in this sense that memory is negotiated. The memory pool of a given community is not equally accessible. Access to the recounting of the past is privileged and closely linked to gender, age, and social status, as well as to the professionalisation of the memory trade.[59] An old man might attempt to establish his authority over things of the past by recount-ing an oral tradition which women and younger men would – or could – not recite. However, it would be wrong to assume that only the 'experts', such as elders, can provide historically relevant narratives, as their approach to memory is socially mediated and because such relevance always depends on the specific research interest. Malian Amadou Hampaté Bâ's famous dictum – 'In Africa, when an old man dies, it's a library burning' – needs to be expanded to include the death of any person of any gender or age.[60] Memory is not an open resource, but nor is it scarce either.[61] Rather than being a finite corpus, it has the potential of being infinitely expandable. Moreover, memory carries the potential of being subversive, even – and maybe especially – when hegemonic discourse, such as that of the state, attempts to control remembrance.[62]

In short, it has been argued that memory is social, provisional, and selective. The negotiation of social memory is in fact history in the making. This complex crafting of individual and social memory is complemented by silences – experi-ences forgotten, not given meaning in the first place, repressed, or simply not shared.[63] Hand in hand with these silences go absences, here thought of in the spatial rather than the metaphorical sense. Absence then refers to a place where a massacre took place that no one remembers, to an area considered to be traditionally taboo with no explanation given. In addition, as French philosopher Jacques Derrida first pointed out in the 1960s, presence and absence are not signifiers of a Manichean world. There can be a presence of absence,[64] such as a fruit tree that serves as a mnemotope because it signifies the absence of a homestead next to it, now destroyed, and the family massacred. Similarly, silence can indicate a voicelessness caused by a horrific, violent experience. In the aftermath of such incidents, memories of violence play a particularly important role in asserting personhood. At the same time, forgetting, silence, and absence can also be powerful signifiers.

Memories can cause strife, but they are also essential to healing individuals and communities, as seen with the testimony given to the Truth and Reconciliation Commission in South Africa in the 1990s during its investigation of the crimes committed during the phase of the armed struggle under white minority apartheid rule.[65] The role of memory in post-conflict situations is apparent in practices ranging from western style speech therapy to spiritual healing that requires a narrative of the past.[66] Violence aims at silencing the attacked and thus at producing a victim, someone robbed of agency and personhood.[67] Giving experiences of violence a voice through memory is an important approach to overcoming victimhood and to creating and stabilising social cohesion.

LANDSCAPE

The third theme of the book is landscape. Landscape is located at an intersection between ideology, practice, and aesthetics. It thus allows a whole range of disciplines, in fact all of the humanities and social sciences, to engage with the knowledge, imagination, and representation of the environment. Landscape is made and unmade in debate and thus can be seen as a complex process to which different realms of society contribute.[68] It can be understood as layers and layers of maps, which at times are overlapping, obscuring, complementary, or contesting. These layers map wider societal – and power – relations. It is in this sense that the concept is used here, with a focus on the processual character of landscape. Examining the Honde Valley through landscape allows for insight into vernacular discourses about identity and belonging.[69] Moreover, ideas about and imaginations of landscape also informed settler interest and state intervention into agricultural practices, both of which were important in mobilising opposition leading up to the Second Chimurenga and in shaping the course of the war. Hence, in contestations within the communities and between valley inhabitants and insurgents as well as the state, landscapes of violence emerged that mapped space regarding danger and safety, memory and forgetting, the vernacular and the universal. Spiritual landscapes became sites of contestation in the struggle over the frontier status of the valley and allowed for a recovery of a sense of belonging and social cohesion during and after conflict.

Writing Violence

'They shot the white girl first.'[70] Toni Morrison's opening sentence to her novel *Paradise* in its matter of fact simplicity, an everyday description of unfolding events, is one of the most powerful beginnings to a fictitious narrative of violence and the human condition. It leaves the audience shocked and repulsed to read this sentence given the book's title. At the same time, the merging of the mundane – it could have been 'they harvested the maize first' – with the prospect of the unimaginable and scandalous draws the reader to return to the sentence and to read beyond it. The novelist has the artistic freedom to mould the narrative to achieve any self-set goal. The historian is faced with a different challenge. In the first place, the task is to create a narrative that is academically sound – well-researched, relevant to current debate, and fulfilling the formal standards of the discipline. Moreover, the historian needs to engage the audience through a historical account that critically reflects on the sources and that can only be an approximation of the past. When some of these primary sources are research-generated interviews and the topic is violence, the task is formidable.

Morrison can choose to open her novel with this disturbing and intriguing sentence, rendering the first mentioned character to victimhood and typifying her as a 'white girl' with all the implications this carries for a reader. Apparently, withdrawing the agency from one of her characters and majestically telling a complex, interwoven story of race, gender, and age in the US past does not affect a girl who actually lived and was killed nor indeed impacts her loved ones. Historians, however, deal with the life-worlds of people who did inhabit the past, and who they might personally know. This raises questions about the ethics of creating academic narrative. In writing about violence, the author faces a triple challenge: sensationalism, voyeurism, and authority.

The prevalence of violence in popular culture, such as in images in the media, film, music, video games, and advertising, has been much debated. These representations tend to sensationalise violence by emphasising goriness, victimhood, and horror. In the popular media blood clearly leads, whereas academic and developmental writing tends to be more polarised. Here one finds on the one hand the blood-soaked narrative side-by-side with the empathy-seeking emphasis on victimhood, often portrayed by compromised children, and on the other hand almost sterile accounts where violence may be the topic, but suffering appears almost absent. All three representations are problematic, because they abuse the auctorial power. One example is Carolyn Elkins' study of the British counter-insurgency campaign against Kenya's Mau Mau in the 1950s. She briefly discusses the insurgent attack against the Ruck family that saw the parents and their six-year-old son killed. In her book, Elkins includes a photograph of the mutilated body of the child *in situ*, something that in no way enhances her argument but does provide a gory image.[71]

Voyeurism, or what Valentine Daniel calls the 'pornography of violence',[72] poses the second challenge. The author's task is to break the distance between the audience and the topic, to make the gaze falter and hence connect, similar to challenging the voyeurism of having dinner in front of a television programme that shows children dying of starvation. Engaging the gaze is important, because otherwise the violation is replicated in the consumption of its representation, in the act of reading – or seeing, as it were. In addition, the author faces the almost unattainable, to make real what is close to impossible to understand, namely, suffering. Roth and Salas point out that it 'is the responsibility of the intellectual in the face of crisis and its remembrance: to sort representations so as to provide a framework for reinterpreting the inaccessible'. They emphasise that 'Narrative is present from beginning to end, providing the framework through which experiences can be *had* – as well as come to terms with.'[73] Author Philip Gourevitch reflects brilliantly on the problem.

Gourevitch recreated from his earlier award-winning book a short text in which he raises the question of how one can comprehend horror, in his case the Rwandan genocide of 1994.[74] In his narrative, Gourevitch takes the reader with him on a disturbing journey to Rwanda that begins with his bewilderment at his own voyeurism, his inability to connect the remnants of violence he sees in the aftermath of the genocide with the suffering they represent. He portrays the distance in terms of aesthetics, with what he perceives as his grotesque fascination with the beauty and thus surreality of the human remains. In this way, he allows the reader to gaze with him, to be drawn towards looking more closely, all the while sharing his sense of horror at himself for what appears such callousness. Gourevitch also uses tactility as a means to create reality: his reader listens with as him a human skull crushes under a foot. Thus Gourevitch connects his reader with what he himself experienced and makes any distancing impossible; the reader of his text cannot become a voyeur or escape reflecting on voyeurism and the sensationalisation of violence.[75]

The third problem any author discussing violence faces is to write responsibly without endangering those studied or risking a sense of violation when personal memories are shared and later used for academic purposes. This is a particular concern when writing about recent or contemporary conflict. At the same time, it is possible that an interview or written source reveals unforeseen personal information. In the case of oral history, which insists on the interviewee's auctorial power over the spoken, recorded, and transcribed text, there is the question of whether the historian is bound by that code of conduct, even if the interview reveals the interviewee having committed war crimes in the past.

At this point, the author does not suggest a fully satisfying answer for the creation of academic historical narrative about the topic of violence and suffering. Certainly, in this study every attempt was made to avoid sensationalism and most of the interviewees and some of the locations of written sources were treated anonymously in order to protect those who generously made this research possible. Still, the question of voyeurism is more difficult to address. One approach is to deepen the dialogue of oral and written sources with narrative and argument through continuous critical examination of the primary material. In addition, sometimes quoting at length may reveal the grain and texture of the evidence as well as a broad range, and at times contradictory set, of perspectives. One technique applied sparingly is to switch to first person narrative when the personal experience of the author is of importance to the analysis.

The Honde Valley

The Honde Valley became the research site for this study for two reasons. One, spending a year abroad at the University of Zimbabwe, the author participated in a weekend outing to the Eastern Highlands organised by the students' union. The sightseeing included Honde View, a panoramic spot in Nyanga National Park where the escarpment drops vertically by almost a thousand metres and allows the visitor to gaze into the Honde Valley and beyond into Mozambique. It was a combination of the dramatic difference between the sub-tropical and settled valley in contrast to the fir-treed national park, together with an amazing scent – which later turned out to be coffee and tea blossoms – rising up with the hot breeze from the valley bottom to the cool crisp mountain air that right then and there made the author decide that she wanted to learn about that place. It was the passion for the place that laid the ground for this study.

More importantly, once the Honde Valley was identified as the potential research site, it became apparent that it was indeed an ideal location to research violence. The valley is an unusual and diverse area due to its remoteness from direct central state interference that lasted until the mid-1950s, its abundant environmental resources that make it, together with two other such small areas, unique to southern Africa, and due to its location on the border with Mozambique. Moreover, the area had never been studied. The first incidents of violence remembered are raids by Gaza warriors in the nineteenth century, followed by the first war that affected the valley, the Makombe war of 1917–1920. During the 1970s, four armies operated in the Honde Valley: the Rhodesian army, the Front for the Liberation of Mozambique (FRELIMO), the Zimbabwe African National Liberation Army (ZANLA), and Mozambique's National Resistance Movement (RENAMO), which used the area as an infiltration route into Mozambique. In 1984, RENAMO, by then based in Mozambique, returned, staging attacks in the valley, and moving through into Zimbabwe.

The area actually consists of two valleys divided by the Pungwe River: the more humid and warmer northern Pungwe Valley and the southern Honde Valley. The name Pungwe Valley is not usually applied in this area, hence the name Honde Valley is used throughout this study. The area was sparsely populated until a major influx began in 1948, the resettlement being part of the enforcement of land segregation legislation. By 1977 the estimated population was 60,000 and by the mid-1980s 80,000.[76] The local language is chiManyika, spoken on both sides of the border, a dialect of Zimbabwe's majority language Shona.

The valley is approximately sixty kilometres long, between seven and twenty kilometres wide, and covers an area of 722 square kilometres.[77] The altitude ranges from 650 metres above sea level to a maximum of 2,000 meters.[78] Topographically, the valley bottom is interspersed with hills and granite peaks. The climate is sub-tropical, with high annual rainfall that rises with the altitude and roughly from the south to the north. The mean maximum temperature in the northern part of the valley is about 28°C and the mean minimum is about 11°C.[79] The western slopes are heavily forested, whereas most of the lower lying areas are cultivated, interspersed with grass-, shrub-, and woodland.[80] Due to this specific climate a wide range of fruit is grown in the valley, in addition to food and plantation crops, such as tea, coffee, and cotton. By the mid-1980s less than twenty-five per cent of the households owned cattle.[81] This small number of livestock was due to the occurrence of tsetse fly, particularly in the northern part of the valley, and also to losses during the Second Chimurenga.

The Honde Valley consists of three communal lands (CLs), namely, Holdenby, Manga, and part of Mutasa North Communal Land, as well as three tea and coffee estates. In 1962, Manga, Umtasa North, and Holdenby Native Reserves became Tribal Trust Lands (TTLs), renamed CLs in 1980. In order to provide more land for African settlement, three so-called Special Native Areas (SNA) were created in the valley in 1950, namely SNA 'A' and 'B' (Umtali), which became part of Mutasa North TTL, and SNA 'A' (Inyanga) that became part of Holdenby TTL. The northern part of the valley was first called Holdenby, then SNA 'A' (Inyanga). All three plantations are adjacent to or in Holdenby: The Pungwe Valley estate, a parastatal, to which Katiyo estate (tea and coffee) and Rumbizi estate (tea) belong; the Eastern Highlands Tea Estates; and Aberfoyle Tea Plantations (tea and coffee). Eastern Highlands Tea Estates and Aberfoyle are part of Holdenby Block, an area reserved for European ownership under white minority rule. To the north, the valley borders onto Chief Tangwena's area, to the west onto the Rhodes Nyanga National Park – extended in the mid-1990s to incorporate part of the valley slopes, and to the southwest and south-east onto forestry estates. To the east lies Manica Province in Mozambique.[82]

When the British South Africa Company (BSAC) established administrative structures in Southern Rhodesia in the 1890s, the valley was arbitrarily divided between Umtali District and Inyanga District. This caused numerous problems and partly explains the lack of administrative control. One predicament was the area's accessibility. The southern part of the valley had its first road from 1931, but the north remained inaccessible from Inyanga District until the mid-1950s.[83] Part of the counter-insurgency campaign, the administrative boundaries were re-delineated in 1973 when Mutasa District was created. This covers roughly the area of the Mutasa area, including the entire Honde Valley.[84] The administrative borders have remained unchanged since independence. The Honde Valley is part of the Mutasa paramountcy. With the establishment of colonial administration at the beginning of the twentieth century, paramount chieftaincies were not acknowledged by the state, except for the Ndebele kingdom. Where such centralised political structures existed, such as in the Mutasa area, the principal ruler, here the *mambo* (king), was demoted to chief, the chiefs became sub-chiefs, and the lower officeholders were renamed 'kraalheads' (*masabhuku*). Restoration attempts after independence on the part of the Mutasa dynasty failed.

In the Honde Valley there are eight chieftaincies, namely, Chikomba, Zindi, Muparutsa, Mandeya II, Manga, Saumani, Samaringa, and Mpotedzi. There are four chieftaincies on the fringes, namely, Tangwena, Sherukuru, Nyamandwe, and Nyamaende. Mpotedzi and Sherukuru are chieftaincies reserved for female office holders, although due to land alienation in the 1940s, there has been no new appointment for the latter. Until 1973, the most northern part of the Honde Valley was under Chief Tangwena's jurisdiction but was then reassigned to Chief Chikomba.[85] The colonial state also created three 'tribal authorities'. With administrative problems arising from the *mamboship* being divided between two districts, Mambo Mutasa appointed a representative for Inyanga District, including Manga and Holdenby CLs, but with no land of his own. Thus, Chief Mpatsi ruled from 1950 to 1965 and Chief Mafi from 1968 to 1973, when the office was withdrawn and no successor appointed.[86]

Finally, a brief note on terminology. Dipesh Chakrabarty observed that using western rather than vernacular terms in historical writing reproduces the Eurocentric views of the past, with the west as 'a silent referent'.[87] Here, a compromise is made to retain the readability of the text without luring the reader into semantic assumptions. Where it appears appropriate, local terms are used, but at times in anglicised form such as mamboship (kingship). The colonial and post-colonial administrations refer to Mutasa as chief and chieftainship and the lower ranking political authorities as headmen. Local usage instead is king (*mambo*) and paramountcy or mamboship and chiefs (*ishe*) instead of headmen. With the exception of quotes, or when important to a specific argument, post-colonial place names and spellings will be used throughout. Hence Zimbabwe will be referred to as such for the Rhodesian period. Zimbabwe changed names several times under white minority rule: Rhodesia, Southern Rhodesia, and Zimbabwe Rhodesia. White Zimbabweans who considered – or today still consider – themselves to be Rhodesians will be referred to as such. This serves to denote a sense and the reality of citizenship under minority rule, rather than a racial category, even though the country was run under the banner of white supremacy during the liberation war.

Methods & Sources

Historian Reinhart Koselleck has argued that 'sources have the power of veto', though he concedes that sources 'never tell us what we should say'.[88] For oral historians, however, this suggests a false sense of security, because an interviewee might very well vociferously lay claim to his or her authoritative interpretation of the past. Wherever possible, then, it is of crucial importance to support interviews with written sources and vice versa in order to be able to craft a historical narrative that does justice to the full range of past experiences and events.[89] For that reason the research for this study includes a range of methods and a variety of sources beyond those more commonly found in a historian's toolbox. Discussing these in some detail might appear indulgent. However, studying political violence may require a research strategy that is particularly complex and not necessarily obvious. Moreover, examining past suffering invests the historian with particular responsibility, and it is important to make the research expertise and methods transparent so that the reader is curtailed in holding the author accountable for the analysis.

The written sources on which this study is based encompass government, mission, business, and private papers. The National Archives of Zimbabwe (NAZ) contain few direct references to the Honde Valley, largely due to its relative inaccessibility to the state until the mid-1950s. More evidence was available at the National Records Centre (NRC), where the more recent files are kept. Other government offices that were invaluable to this research include the Provincial Administrator's Office (PAO) and the Department of Rural Development (DERUDE) in Mutare, the District Administrator Mutasa's Office (DAO), the Ministry of Agriculture, the Central Statistical Office (now ZIMSTAT), and the Agricultural Development Authority Coffee and Fruit Project office in Hauna. Mission churches have barely any presence in the valley, but the archives of the United Methodist Episcopal Church at Old Mutare Mission (OMMA) nevertheless proved useful. The archives of the Catholic Commission of Justice and Peace (CCJP) contain invaluable materials on human rights abuses, and two newspaper archives were most useful, namely those of the *Herald* in Harare and the *Manica Post* in Mutare.

Perhaps the most significant written sources are those that were made available by individuals and businesses with interest in or relating to the Honde Valley. These include correspondence, reports, memoranda, photographs, and other illustrations. It had been assumed that most war-related government files had been destroyed during the transition period to independence, as the outgoing government had issued the official order to shred or burn any sensitive material.[90] However, in the course of this research it transpired that it was not unusual for government employees to retain some records. At times, practical problems intervened in accessing them, as was the case with a parastatal where the burning of files had been interrupted by the arrival of ZANU officials in spring 1980. There the author located security records relating to the Second Chimurenga that had been hastily hidden at that time and since been used as roof insulation. A rather unexpected aspect of research then involved organising a long ladder to retrieve the files. Also, Rhodesian soldiers, despite being under strict orders not to do so, took photographs of their exploits of war as trophies that still had their place in family photograph albums in the 1990s. Some of these photographs and other memorabilia have since been posted on Rhodesian webpages on the Internet.[91] Evidence in private possession, in particular the security memoranda regarding the Chimurenga and the RENAMO wars, provided invaluable sources for this study. A unique find among the privately held papers were those of the Ziwe Zano Society, an African initiated church established in 1932 that opened a mission in the southern part of the Honde Valley in 1938.

The owners of most of the privately held papers, both individuals and business managers, asked the author to treat the holdings anonymously and are listed in the bibliography with assigned acronyms. Anonymity was also promised to most of the interview and conversation partners. Pseudonyms will be used throughout, unless an exception was permitted or he or she is a particularly prominent person whose identity is apparent. The memory of the liberation war might be fading in the twenty-first century, but the political situation in Zimbabwe makes it pertinent to respect the oral research code of protecting the identity of those whose voices made this study possible.

The methods employed included broad canvassing for written sources relating to the valley's past, and then reading them critically against the oral testimony and through the lens of personal experience in the area. In addition, participant observation and oral history served to generate sources. The field research occurred over a long core period of eighteen months, from June 1991 to November 1992, with preliminary visits to the Honde Valley in 1988 and 1990 and follow-up stays in 1993 and 1996. Consequently, long-lasting relationships were built, crucial for generating the necessary basis of trust for valley inhabitants to share memories of past suffering. Also, importantly, the author saw the valley during different stages of the RENAMO insurgency and in its aftermath and thus could observe how both everyday life and the nature of interviews changed over time.

In all, the author conducted 177 formal, open-ended interviews, of which 73 were taped; this largely occurred in the Honde Valley, but also took place in other parts of Mutasa District and the country. The majority of the interviewees were male and female valley inhabitants, representing a range of biological and social age, educational qualifications, social status, and roles within the communities investigated; most had been civilians during the liberation war, some had been combatants and had fought elsewhere. There was a bias towards elders regarding the numbers of interviews, although this was to some extent balanced by closer aquaintance with some of the younger interviewees. Interviewees also included Rhodesian administrative staff, soldiers, and combatants who had been deployed in the valley before and after independence. The security situation at the time of research made it impossible to travel to the Mozambican side of the border. Nevertheless, many of the valley inhabitants have lived on both sides at different points of their lives, and thus the one-sitedness of the field research could be somewhat compensated through the translocal memories that emerged in interviews. Moreover, the valley does constitute a defined place of belonging, even though the political border is an artificial colonial creation.[92]

The author personally conducted all the interviews in English and chiManyika, the local Shona dialect; one archival interview transcript is specifically identified as such. The author's linguistic ability is best summarised by an elder who exclaimed: 'You don't speak Shona, but you speak it with a chiManyika accent.'[93] In other words, the author was never fully fluent in chiManyika, but over the course of time could follow well enough what was being said. Towards the end of the main research period, two co-wives in the Honde Valley proposed marriage on behalf of their husband. They were interested in gaining a young wife for the household. They approached the female head of the author's host household, the approximation of an aunt in the absence of blood-kin, and that afternoon, when all the women were down in the wetlands fetching water or working in the gardens, the author's command of chiManyika was good enough to jokingly – and very publicly – decline the offer. It turned out to be advantageous to bring local interpreters to interviews, since sometimes talking to the same interviewee in the company of a young woman, then of a middle-aged man or bringing along a research assistant who would help with introductions allowed for a more thorough understanding of the dynamic of each situation. As a result, certain patterns emerged.

The open questions about the area's past, and in particular about the Second Chimurenga, were met with gendered and age-specific answers. Male elders appeared to find it safe to tap into family and social memory by first relating their genealogy and then by talking about the nineteenth century. Only after a more trusting relationship was established did they relate more recent events. Women, on the other hand, initially responded that they were merely women and had nothing to tell, then shifted into accounts of personal memories, such as their arrival in the area as young brides. Women serve as enforcers of tradition as much as men. In exogamous societies, however, women by definition are newcomers. In this case, in a society where they have no land use rights other than through male guardianship, it was no surprise that women were reluctant to relate social memory of a community of which they are part, but only as structural outsiders. Male elders, on the other hand, when from the area, and especially newcomers who had been incorporated into the local moral ethnicity through their acceptance of the vernacular civic virtue, were more likely to establish their legitimacy as keepers of historical knowledge by referring to the more remote past, in this case the nineteenth century. Here, one key to moral ethnicity is this claim of a pre-colonial past which, due to the nature of the population mobility in this frontier area, is associated with heritage and community rather than ancestral claims to land and authority, as is common elsewhere in Zimbabwe.[94]

Young men who had been combatants felt free to share their personal memories of the liberation war. As youngsters with guns, they had challenged the elders' authority during the liberation war and thus had every reason to relate those memories freely, whether or not they did in fact fight for freedom. Their memory is one of a glorious past, a moment of escaping gerontocratic control, soon to be recaptured by the elders of the state and the community. Finally, young women related their war experiences of the Chimurenga almost exclusively through informal communication. Their virtue was compromised by the war, a period of lapsed parental control.

In short, any view of the past, be it personal or social memory, was informed by the interviewee's position in the community – mediated by gender, age, social status, and the role he or she played during the liberation war – and thus provided a social commentary on the war, identity, and community. This embeddedness of memory in social process and power relations, and its interwovenness with identity, poses challenges to the oral historian. In addition to the possibility of finding oneself talking about a period of time seemingly unrelated to the research topic, in fact a century apart, which at the time was deeply disconcerting to the graduate student researcher, there are also the very real risks of compromising the interviewee's standing in the community and possibly even endangering his or her life. Still, the opportunity of gaining insight into the making of identity during times of duress is invaluable.

The oral historian has both the advantage and the disadvantage of working with research-generated sources. The text is created in dialogue with an active voice and agency on the part of the interviewee, so much so that some historians have suggested referring to the interviewee as the oral historian, as it is he or she who crafts the historical narrative. The research situation is more complicated when method and interpretation involve listening for silences,[95] as all research must do, but in this case with the option of becoming proactive and breaking such silence as the interviewer may ask specific questions and directly address the interviewee's apparent omissions. This requires understanding the specific social norms and practices and the notion and reality of safety in the researched area. For example, in order to learn more about the ongoing RENAMO war, this researcher decided to find and live with a host family in Sagambe, an area of the valley which particularly suffered from cross-border incursions. Setting up research in this manner turned out to be impossible. After many polite but evasive conversations, the host family in the end decided that it was too dangerous for the researcher as much as for themselves, and even though nobody ever directly provided the reason, it turned out that on the day of the planned move, RENAMO transported a major shipment of drugs through this area.

In short, memory reflects positionality and its representation in historical narrative, and it is actively shaped both by the interviewee and the historian. In a well-researched project, the interviewee's agency is balanced by the historian through their communication being interlaced with other interviews, written sources, and, if applicable, participant observation. While the historian's analysis can only be volatile, oral history simultaneously allows for texture and voice that written sources cannot provide.[96]

The difference between the research situations when the Honde Valley was a combat zone compared to the period after the October 1992 ceasefire was striking. During the RENAMO war, both interviewer and interviewees avoided themes and events that could have endangered individuals and the welfare of the community, and there was also a pronounced absence of conversations about the role of youths during the liberation war of the 1970s. Absence and presence in relation to violence was also marked in women's daily conversations. Space and spatial practices are gendered in the rural areas. At a certain time of the day, the place where women fetch water from the river and bathe, the gardens, and the paths to and from the residences is communally considered female space. The homosocial discourse both finds expression and is marked by loud conversations between women, often shouted over long distances between gardens or along the paths, that remind males to stay away. Women clearly enjoy this freedom and often joke and tell stories that sexually mock men. Part of these exchanges was also the constant reminding of sites of violence. While resting in the shade, women recalled killings, torture, and abductions marked by mnemotopes such as trees and homesteads. Strikingly, while the RENAMO conflict was going on, these reminders referred exclusively to the 1970s. Soon after the October 1992 ceasefire in Mozambique, the discourse changed. Suddenly, stories of the recent atrocities surfaced. These accounts circulated in the community, at times leading to accusations of witchcraft, and these were also shared in the interviews.

So far, the emphasis has been on the active role interviewees play in shaping not just the immediate interview situation, but possibly also the research agenda.[97] When memories reach back to experiences of violence, this adds the dimension of possible psychological impact played out within the context of conflict or post-conflict situations. Cross-culturally, it is in times of crisis that individuals and groups of people reach for religious and spiritual explanations and comfort. The most striking example in this research that illustrates the intermingling of cosmology, gender normativity in the investigated society, the legacy of conflict, and the power of the interviewee, is that of a woman who was in her early thirties.

Nora (a pseudonym) first caught my attention because she was a well-known healer in one locality. When I indicated my intention of interviewing her, I learned from neighbours that during the liberation war she had been a sex worker in a makeshift brothel, serving African government soldiers at the settlement where she still lived. Any attempt to seek her collaboration failed. She frequently offered to treat my back injury from which I suffered, with much sexual innuendo, as did male healers, because a woman's back pain was commonly associated with being sexually active. But Nora always joked away any suggestion of sitting down to talk. One evening, after numerous such encounters, while I was staying with a female friend at that settlement and doing some knitting, there was an unexpected knock at the door. It was Nora. Again she joked that she could treat my back, and as we continued knitting baby blankets, she suddenly started to go into a trance.

The spirit who possessed her came out quickly. It was the spirit of a sex worker who had been employed at the brothel during the war. The spirit spoke through Nora and related how she and the other young women had collaborated with the local guerrilla unit to ambush their clients, an action that resulted in a fire fight and saw several policemen injured and killed. I had come across the attack in government documents, including the suspicion that sex workers had been involved, and had seen the bullet holes still in evidence. As the spirit spoke through Nora, she also had Nora masturbate in our presence while she related the story. My hostess carried on knitting, as if nothing out of the ordinary were happening, a sure sign that she assumed we should appease the spirit by listening calmly. When Nora came out of the trance, she covered herself and apparently remembered nothing. She left in good spirits.

This encounter adds another dimension to oral history and research-generated sources. While it is well established for historians to work on religion and spiritual phenomena, how does one treat a spirit's testimony as evidence? According to vernacular cosmology, the spirit of the sex worker broke the silence of the living and shared her knowledge of the war. The living and the spirits of the dead, if not inhabiting the same realm, do certainly together shape the sense of community and communal wellbeing. Can the historian deny this as a legitimate source? At the same time, how can the historian undertake an analysis and interpretation of a source that claims to be a voice of the deceased using the body of a living person as its vessel? The performative aspect of possession often complicates the ability to understand rather than to assign meaning. In this case of public masturbation, the actions were so far beyond acceptable behaviour that a conversation about what had happened in the mundane surroundings of friends knitting, rather than in a ritual setting, was impossible.

In short, the oral research-generated source is a text which represents a person's memory invested with meaning. This, however, is mediated through the interview situation: how the interviewee was chosen, the relationship between the two, and the actual act of communication. The oral historian in the pursuit of recovering the past is in a double bind. First, interviews are an act of communication that cannot be compared with, for example, reading a diary entry; they are invested with multiple layers of interest and positionality that alter the meaning created through memory. As is the case in all acts of communication, the meaning the interviewee wishes to communicate is not necessarily what the historian understands. Second, for the oral historian, listening for silences involves agency which goes beyond the options written text provides, even if that means not asking certain questions – or not writing about the answers.

Organisation of the Argument

This book is organised chronologically, with each substantive chapter focusing on a particular aspect of violence. Chapter two introduces the Honde Valley as a frontier area from the mid-nineteenth century onwards. While much of the literature on the frontier treats it as transitory, the chapter traces how a frontier ethnicity took shape which, as the rest of the book shows, came to stay for a long period of time. Chapter two examines how three developments transformed the local sense of belonging: first, the emerging role of the valley as a buffer zone against intrusions from the east during political centralisation of the Mutasa polity and second violent interaction with raiding warrior parties from the Gaza state made it into a frontier area. Third, early manifestations of the Rhodesian colonial state and the delineation of the border with Mozambique, turned the valley further into a borderland. The Honde Valley was a frontier area for the pre-colonial Mutasa polity and for the colonial states, all of which offered its inhabitants different but overlapping sets of life-chances. Danger and opportunity have been continuing themes shaping local identity and informing later appropriations of violent events. The narrative is based in part on oral interviews which add two perspectives to the written record. One angle is the powerful role social memory of the valley's past has played in twentieth-century conflict, which has allowed local residents to face young men with arms with authority as frontier people. Second, interviews with female chiefs fill the silences in colonial and mission records on hegemony in the Mutasa polity.

Chapter three changes the perspective by examining landscape imaginations of the area on the part of African and European pioneers from the 1930s to the 1950s. These had a profound impact on the incorporation of the area into the colonial economy and its encounters with Christianity, both highly gendered processes. While outside perceptions generally agree in portraying the valley as a dangerous and remote wilderness, European administrators and settlers asserted notions of power in a discourse which sexualised this landscape by emphasising that it needed to be penetrated, whereas African immigrants who saw themselves as pioneers perceived the valley as a dark wilderness and a challenge to their enlightened way of life as Christian modernisers. Juxtaposing African and European pioneers profoundly challenges the dichotomous view of coloniser and colonised and thus contributes to the new colonial history. The research for this chapter included work with two sets of privately held papers that provided unique insight, the original correspondence by the first white settlers establishing the tea plantations in the northern Honde Valley, and the papers of Ziwe Zano Society, which started its own mission station in the southern part of the area.

Chapter four maps initial guerrilla–civilian interactions in the 1970s against the backdrop of earlier rural grievances. From the 1950s, the Rhodesian settler state began to have a direct presence in the valley. As soon as the colonial administration began to intervene in land use practices, the frontier people felt that their way of life was threatened and women in particular resorted to non-cooperation and protest that was not necessarily nationalist, but shaped by a radically local agenda. The first young men with AK-47s who arrived and introduced themselves to valley inhabitants were FRELIMO fighters, members of Mozambique's liberation army, who hence unwittingly prepared the ground for ZANLA as they settled local grievances and became sons of the soil. This and the following chapter profited greatly from interviews with Honde Valley inhabitants who lived there during the war, fled across the border to Mozambique, or fought in the liberation war elsewhere, as well as combatants who were based in the area. In addition, privately held records document the everyday dealings of war.

Chapter five examines insurgency and counter-insurgency during the Second Chimurenga and how this war was experienced by and impacted on local communities. First, the chapter shows that the different models of mobilisation as developed in the Zimbabwean historiography by Kriger, Lan, and Ranger are not necessarily exclusive, nor even contradictory. The socio-political geography of an area and its strategic opportunities or limitations can at times be so small-scale that it is more useful to acknowledge complex constellations of politicisation and mobilisation rather than to develop all-encompassing meta-narratives of political violence and insurgency. One way of breaking down such persuasive narratives – important as they are as part of nationalist discourse and later post-colonial nation-building – is to take a radically local perspective. Examples of dating and naming will be examined to show the relativity and ambiguity of events through the lens of individual experience and memory.

A core element of the counter-insurgency campaign was the forced villagisation of the entire valley population from 1976. The argument here is that the liberation war afforded the settler state the opportunity – to paraphrase Prussian General Carl von Clausewitz – to continue the use of agricultural policies by other means, as enforced land use and labour measures became a central part of the counter-insurgency campaign. The chapter shows also that, however violent and dramatic forced resettlement was for those who experienced it, at least for some of the villagers their new circumstances provided them with a social or economic niche during a period of violent upheaval and coercion. With Caroline Elkins' controversial study of villagisation and detention camps during Mau Mau in Kenya, the debate about such measures as part of counter-insurgency has revived, and it appears important to contribute a detailed case study.[98] In addition to the sources laid out for chapter four, the author also interviewed former Rhodesian district employees and the technocrat who planned the villagisation exercise in the valley. For this and the following chapter it was invaluable to conduct research in the valley at different stages of the RENAMO conflict in order to gain a sense of daily life during war.

Chapter six provides an analysis of the years following Zimbabwean independence. In the Honde Valley, so-called dissidents violently challenged the new state. This was a period when tensions repressed during the war finally surfaced. At the same time, the task of transforming the war economy and socio-political structures of the Rhodesian state into a stable post-settler society involved the reconciliation of liberation ideology with material and planning needs on the ground. This led to the resurfacing of memories of violence. Most of the existing literature focuses on nationalism leading up to independence, the development effort of the post-colonial state, and then the sad decline of the state and political elite. The political developments of the immediate post-independence period are under-researched. For Zimbabwe, the southern dissident campaign that led to thousands of killings committed by the government in the 1980s has overshadowed the larger question of how a nationalist party or liberation movement can gain legitimacy as a ruling party. Here, this was not a question restricted to Matabeleland, but one that was to be answered throughout the country. This chapter argues that this is a universal problem, not only in the process of decolonisation in fact, but with any major regime change. The chapter examines also the RENAMO insurgency into Zimbabwe, in response to which the government re-introduced villagisation in the early 1990s.

What follows is a discussion of reconciliation and social healing. Spiritual healing can provide an understanding of unspeakable experiences and memories within known systems of knowledge. At the same time, communities under duress can seldom afford to voice, or even show, discord. Once security returns, however, multiple layers of memory and forgetting signifying identity, belonging, and past experience emerge. Space is invested with meaning, creating landscapes of violence that ingrain a sense of belonging and serve as mnemotope, being home for both spiritual security and danger. Company archives and privately held papers made it possible to trace the crisis of political legitimacy in the Honde Valley. Story-telling and gossip provided insight into the re-emerging frontier identity. The book concludes with an epilogue on an optimistic note. War may rage hot and cause suffering, but such disruptive experiences can be overcome. It appears to be time to look to Africa and to places such as the Honde Valley to learn more about social healing and reconciliation.

Notes

1. For a historian's treatment of Guernica, see Carlo Ginzburg, 'The Sword and the Lightbulb: A Reading of Guernica', *Disturbing Remains: Memory, History, and Crisis in the Twentieth Century*, Michael Roth and Charles Salas (eds) (Los Angeles, CA, 2001), pp. 111-77.
2. The connection between desire and spatiality is derived from the concept of desire lines, as discussed by Martin Hall, 'Afterword: Lines of Desire', *Desire Lines: Space, Memory and Identity in the Post-Apartheid City*, Noëleen Murray et al. (eds) (London, 2007), pp. 287-98.
3. Interview #80.
4. John Lonsdale, *Unhappy Valley: Conflict in Kenya and Africa*, in Bruce Berman and John Lonsdale (London, 1992), vol. 2, chapters 11 and 12.
5. Carolyn Nordstrom's study shares a similar understanding of danger and creativity, albeit with a stricter definition of the frontier as the frontline in conflict and from an anthropological perspective. See *A Different Kind of War Story* (Philadelphia, PA, 1997).
6. Allen Isaacman provides a comprehensive review of the older Africanist literature; 'Peasants and Rural Social Protest in Africa', *African Studies Review*, 33, no. 2 (1990), pp. 1-120. For a critical discussion of the Chimurenga historiography, see Terence Ranger, 'Nationalist Historiography, Patriotic History and the History of the Nation: The Struggle over the Past in Zimbabwe', *Journal of Southern African Studies*, 30, no. 2 (2004), pp. 215-34. Donald Moore provides a useful review of

the resistance literature in his article on the highland area bordering the Honde Valley, 'Subaltern Struggles and the Politics of Place: Remapping Resistance in Zimbabwe's Eastern Highlands', *Cultural Anthropology*, 13, no. 3 (1998), pp. 344-81. For a critical take on anthropology's focus on resistance, see Michael Brown, 'Resisting Resistance', *American Anthropologist*, 98, no. 4 (1996), pp. 729-35.

7 Terence Ranger, *Revolt in Southern Rhodesia 1896-7: A Study in African Resistance* (London, 1967).

8 Terence Ranger, 'Connections Between "Primary Resistance" Movements and Modern Mass Nationalism in East and Central Africa', Part 1, *Journal of African History*, 9, no. 3 (1968), pp. 437-53, Part 2, 9, no. 4 (1968), pp. 631-41.

9 Terence Ranger, *Peasant Consciousness and Guerrilla War in Zimbabwe: A Comparative Study* (London, 1985), pp. 206, 216. See also his more recent, post-nationalist, *Voices from the Rocks: Nature, Culture and History in the Matopos Hills of Zimbabwe* (Oxford, 1999). For a concise review of Ranger's lifework, see John Lonsdale, 'Agency in Tight Corners: Narrative and Initiative in African History', *Journal of African Cultural Studies*, 13, no. 1 (2000), pp. 5-16.

10 Allen and Barbara Isaacman, *Mozambique: From Colonialism to Revolution* (Boulder, CO, 1983), *Slavery and Beyond: The Making of Men and Chikunda Ethnic Identities in the Unstable World of South-Central Africa, 1750–1920* (Portsmouth, NH, 2004). See also Allen Isaacman, 'Social Banditry in Zimbabwe (Rhodesia) and Mozambique, 1894–1907: An Expression of Early Peasant Protest', *Journal of Southern African Studies*, 4, no. 1 (1977), pp. 1-30 and *Cotton is the Mother of Poverty: Peasants, Work and Rural Struggle in Colonial Mozambique, 1938–1961* (Portsmouth, NH, 1996).

11 See, for example, Philip Bonner and Noor Nieftagodien, *Alexandra: A History* (Johannesburg, 2009); Belinda Bozzoli, *Theatres of Struggle and the End of Apartheid* (Athens, OH, 2004); Adam Ashforth, *Witchcraft, Violence, and Democracy in South Africa* (Chicago, IL, 2005). In addition to scholarly treatments, South African historiography also includes autobiographical and other partisan literature, for example, Ronnie Kasrils, *Armed and Dangerous: My Undercover Struggle Against Apartheid* (Portsmouth, NH, 1993). Zimbabwean partisan history has produced some truly interesting work that has added important nuances to the debate: positionality, activism, and post-coloniality. See Jeremy Brickhill, a Zimbabwe African People's Union (ZAPU) ex-combatant, 'Daring to Storm the Heavens: The Military Strategy of ZAPU, 1976-79' and 'Making Peace with the Past: War Victims and the Work of the Mafela Trust', *Soldiers in Zimbabwe's Liberation War*, Ngwabi Bhebe and Terence Ranger (eds) (London, 1995), pp. 48-72, 163-73; also, more problematically, ex-combatants and later members of government such as Josiah Tungamirai, 'Recruitment to ZANLA: Building up a War Machine', *Soldiers in Zimbabwe's Liberation War*, pp. 36-47; Dumiso Dabengwa, 'ZIPRA in the Zimbabwe War of National Liberation', *Soldiers in Zimbabwe's Liberation War*, pp. 24-35; Fay Chung, 'Education and the Liberation Struggle', *Society in Zimbabwe's Liberation War*, Ngwabi Bhebe and Terence Ranger (eds) (Oxford, 1996), pp. 139-46 and *Re-Living the Second Chimurenga: Memories from Zimbabwe's Liberation Struggle* (Uppsala, 2006). Martin Rupiya served in the Zimbabwe National Army for seventeen years and wrote 'A Political and Military Review of Zimbabwe's Involvement in the Second Congo War', *The African Stakes of the Congo War*, John Clark (ed.) (New York, 2002), pp. 93-105. See also Terence Ranger's *Are We Not Also Men? The Samkange Family and African Politics in Zimbabwe 1920–64* (London, 1995). The sources used for this study include Ranger's own contemporary correspondence.

12 See, Jocelyn Alexander et al., *Violence and Memory: One Hundred Years in the 'Dark Forests' of Matabeleland* (Portsmouth, NH, 2000).

13 David Lan explained that when he conducted his anthropological fieldwork in Dande in the early 1980s, a female elder took the initiative of inserting herself into his research so that he had no choice but to write about her, while in his fictional writing as a playwright he could simply omit her. Zimbabwe Research Days, 'Zimbabwean Lives', St Antony's College, Oxford, 7-8 June 1997.

14 In his discussion of world history and narrative, Steve Feierman points out that a strictly regional historiography, although it has the advantage of a shared language, does not suffice. It falls short in creating meaning of the past specific to a locale if diversity, circulation, and concepts are not carefully placed within broader connections. 'Afrika in der Weltgeschichte: Regionale Konfigurationen des Sozialen', *Afrikanische Geschichte und Weltgeschichte: Regionale und universal Themen in Forschung und Lehre*, Axel Harneit-Sievers (ed.) (Berlin, 2000), pp. 9-22; also 'Africa in History: The End of the Universal Narrative', *After Colonialism: Imperialism and the Colonial Aftermath*, Gyan Prakash (ed.) (Princeton, NJ, 1995), pp. 40-65.

15 See also Ngwabi Bhebe, *The Zapu and Zanu Guerrilla Warfare and the Evangelical Lutheran Church in Zimbabwe* (Gweru, 1999).

16 David Lan, *Guns and Rain: Guerrillas and Spirit Mediums in Zimbabwe* (London, 1985).

17 Norma Kriger, 'The Zimbabwean War of Liberation: Struggles Within the Struggle', *Journal of*

Southern African Studies, 14, no. 2 (1988), pp. 304-22 and *Zimbabwe's Guerrilla War: Peasant Voices* (Cambridge, 1992).

[18] Kenneth Manungo, 'The Peasantry in Zimbabwe: A Vehicle for Change', *Cultural Struggle and Development in Southern Africa*, Preben Kaarsholm (ed.) (Harare, 1991), p. 123.

[19] The most significant shift in the historiography of the Second Chimurenga since the early 1990s has been on the theme of women and war, with several studies exploring the topic. The initial focus on one of the liberation armies, ZANLA, has also been somewhat balanced out by more recent studies of ZIPRA. Most treatments added case studies which at times expanded the timeframe to include the so-called dissident period in the south of the country or the political struggles of veterans in the context of Zimbabwe's 'Third Chimurenga' since 2000. See Josephine Nhongo-Simbanegavi, *For Better or Worse? Women and ZANLA in Zimbabwe's Liberation Struggle* (Harare, 2000); Tanya Lyons, *Guns and Guerrilla Girls: Women in the Zimbabwean National Liberation Struggle* (Trenton, NJ, 2004), Eleanor O'Gorman, *The Front Line Runs through Every Woman: Women and Local Resistance in the Zimbabwean Liberation War* (Woodbridge, 2011); Ranger, *Voices from the Rocks*, Alexander et al., *Violence and Memory*, Zvakanyorwa Sadomba, *War Veterans in Zimbabwe's Revolution: Challenging Neo-colonialism and Settler and International Capital* (Woodbridge, 2011).

[20] Ranger, 'Patriotic History'.

[21] Robert Mugabe, *The Third Chimurenga: Inside the Third Chimurenga* (Harare, 2001), p. 40.

[22] Frederick Cooper, 'Conflict and Connection: Rethinking Colonial African History', *American Historical Review*, 99, no. 5 (1994), pp. 1516-45; also Thomas Spear, 'Neo-Traditionalism and the Limits of Invention in British Colonial Africa', *Journal of African History*, 44, no. 1 (2003), pp. 3-27; Eric Allina-Pisano, 'Resistance and the Social History of Africa', *Journal of Social History*, 37, no. 1 (2003), pp. 187-98. Bethwell Ogot presents a criticism that departs from current debate in 'Rereading the History and Historiography of Epistemic Domination and Resistance in Africa', *African Affairs*, 52, no. 1 (2009), pp. 1-22.

[23] Ann Laura Stoler and Frederick Cooper, 'Between Metropole and Colony: Rethinking a Research Agenda', *Tensions of Empire: Colonial Cultures in a Bourgeois World*, Ann Laura Stoler and Frederick Cooper (eds) (Berkeley, CA, 1997), pp. 1-56.

[24] Examples for the new colonial history include Jean Allman and Victoria Tashjian, *I Will Not Eat Stone: A Women's History of Colonial Asante* (Portsmouth, NH, 2000), Luise White, *Speaking with Vampires: Rumor and History in Colonial Africa* (Berkeley, CA, 2000), Derek Peterson, *Creative Writing: Translation, Bookkeeping, and the Work of Imagination in Colonial Kenya* (Portsmouth, NH, 2004), James Giblin, *A History of the Excluded: Making Family a Refuge from State in Twentieth-Century Tanzania* (Oxford, 2006), and David Pratten, *The Man-Leopard Murders: History and Society in Colonial Nigeria* (Bloomington, IN, 2007). See also Steven Feierman's much earlier *Peasant Intellectuals: Anthropology and History in Tanzania* (Madison, WI, 1990), which had a major impact on the field.

[25] For a simplified approach to African agency, see chapters 1 and 3 of the otherwise useful study by Jeremy Prestholdt, *Domesticating the World: African Consumerism and the Genealogies of Globalization* (Berkeley, CA, 2008). In contrast stands Chuck Ambler's discussion of public consumption that carefully reads the multiple meanings of appropriation and enactment of western culture. Charles Ambler, 'Cowboy Modern: African Audiences, Hollywood Films, and Visions of the West', *Going to the Movies: Hollywood and the Social Experience of the Cinema*, Richard Maltby et al. (eds) (Exeter, 2008), pp. 348-63.

[26] Recent contributions still within the resistance paradigm include David Maxwell, *Christians and Chiefs in Zimbabwe* (Manchester, 1999) and Nhongo-Simbanegavi, *For Better or Worse?* For a rare attempt to write about conflict within the new colonial history paradigm, albeit by a sociologist, see Bozzoli, *Theatres of Struggle*. For post-colonial conflict, see Anthony Douglas, *Poison and Medicine: Ethnicity, Power, and Violence in a Nigerian City, 1966–1986* (Portsmouth, NH, 2002).

[27] Paul Collier et al., *Breaking the Conflict Trap: Civil War and Development Policy*, World Bank Policy Research Reports (Washington, 2003); Paul Collier, *The Bottom Billion: Why the Poorest Countries are Failing and What Can Be Done About It* (Oxford, 2007), chapter 2, and *Wars, Guns, and Votes: Democracy in Dangerous Places* (New York, 2009).

[28] Collier, *Bottom Billion*, pp. 3, 7.

[29] Ibid., p. 17.

[30] See the authoritative report by the Catholic Commission for Justice and Peace, *Gukurahundi in Zimbabwe: A Report on the Disturbances in Matabeleland and the Midlands 1980–1988* (New York, 2007).

[31] Collier, *Bottom Billion*, chapter 11.

[32] Ibid., p. 192; xi.

[33] Carolyn Nordstrom, *Shadows of War: Violence, Power, and International Profiteering in the Twenty-*

First Century (Berkeley, CA, 2004), pp. 106-7. Nordstrom's *Global Outlaws: Crime, Money, and Power in the Contemporary World* (Berkeley, CA, 2007) focuses on what she calls 'extra-legal networks' (p. xvii).

34 Nordstrom, *Shadows of War*, pp. 110, 129.

35 Paul Richards, *Fighting for the Rain Forest: War, Youth and Resources in Sierra Leone* (Portsmouth, NH, 1996), p. xxiv.

36 Robert Kaplan, 'The Coming Anarchy: How Scarcity, Crime, Overpopulation, Tribalism, and Disease are rapidly Destroying the Social Fabric of our Planet', *The Atlantic Monthly*, 273, no. 2 (Feb. 1994), pp. 44-76.

37 Samuel Huntington, 'The Clash of Civilizations?' *Foreign Affairs*, 72, no. 3 (1993), pp. 22-49 and *The Clash of Civilizations and the Remaking of World Order* (New York, 1997). For an excellent critique, see Edward Said, 'The Clash of Ignorance', *The Nation*, 273, no. 12 (2001), p. 11.

38 See Michael Barnett, *Eyewitness to a Genocide: The United Nations and Rwanda* (Ithaca, NY, 2003), Philip Gourevitch, *We Wish to Inform You that Tomorrow We Will Be Killed with Our Families: Stories from Rwanda* (New York, 1998).

39 Sharon Lamb critically questions the categories of victim and perpetrator but concludes that there is a clear dichotomy in *The Trouble with Blame: Victims, Perpetrators, and Responsibility* (Cambridge, MA, 1996). Useful studies on perpetrators include Lee Payne, *Unsettling Accounts: Neither Truth nor Reconciliation in Confessions of State Violence* (Durham, NC, 2nd ed. 1999); Allan Young, 'America's Transient Mental Illness: A Brief History of the Self-Traumatized Perpetrator', *Subjectivity: Ethnographic Investigations*, João Biehl et al. (eds) (Berkeley, CA, 2007), pp. 155-78.

40 Johan Degenaar, 'The Concept of Violence', *Political Violence and the Struggle in South Africa*, N. Manganyi et al. (eds) (Basingstoke, 1990), p. 72; also his earlier version, 'The Concept of Violence', *Politikon*, 7, no. 1 (1980), pp. 14-27.

41 Degenaar, 'The Concept of Violence', pp. 71-4, passim.

42 David Caute, *Under the Skin: The Death of White Rhodesia* (Harmondsworth, 1983), p. 34, passim.

43 *The Rhodesian Fighting Forces*, no. 2 (1977), n. p.

44 Nevertheless, the disorder can be traced back two hundred years to the beginnings of Enlightenment in western society. Michael Trimble, 'Post-Traumatic Stress Disorder: The History of a Concept', *Trauma and Its Wake. Vol. I The Study and Treatment of Post-Traumatic Stress Disorder*, Charles Figley (ed.) (New York, 1985), pp. 5-14; see also Allan Young, *The Harmony of Illusions: Inventing Post-Traumatic Stress Disorder* (Princeton, NJ, 1997). For the connection between PTSD and memory see Richard McNally, *Remembering Trauma* (Cambridge, MA, 2003). For the evolution of the psychological and psychiatric field of trauma studies, see Charles Figley (ed.) *Mapping Trauma and Its Wake: Autobiographic Essays by Pioneer Trauma Scholars* (New York, 2006).

45 The leading historian in this area, Dominick LaCapra, has published widely on Holocaust survivors' trauma and memory and the wider theoretical and epistemological repercussions of trauma studies. See his *Writing History, Writing Trauma* (Baltimore, MD, 2001), *History and Memory after Auschwitz* (Ithaca, NY, 1998), *History in Transit: Experience, Identity, Critical Theory* (Ithaca, NY, 2004), chapter 3, and *History and Its Limits: Human, Animal, Violence* (Ithaca, NY, 2009), chapter 3. Young provides a critical discussion of PTSD as the perpetrator's mental illness in *America's Transient Mental Illness*. See also Cathy Caruth (ed.), *Trauma: Explorations in Memory* (Baltimore, MD, 1995) and Daniel Schacter, *Searching for Memory: The Brain, the Mind, and the Past* (New York, 1996), chapter 9.

46 Matthew Friedman, 'Posttraumatic Stress Disorder: An Overview', United States Department of Veterans Affairs, National Centre for Posttraumatic Stress Disorder, http://www.ptsd.va.gov/professional/pages/ptsd-overview.asp.

47 See also the new concept of cultural trauma, albeit understood as memory routinisation and the creation of a 'master narrative of social suffering'; Jeffrey Alexander, 'Toward a Theory of Cultural Trauma', *Cultural Trauma and Collective Identity*, Jeffrey Alexander et al. (eds) (Berkeley, CA, 2004), p. 15.

48 Peter Ucko and Robert Layton, 'Introduction: Going on the Landscape and Encountering the Environment', *The Archaeology and Anthropology of Landscape: Shaping Your Landscape*, Peter Ucko and Robert Layton (eds) (London, 1999), p. 16. For the connection between memory and place, see Oren Baruch Stier and Shawn Landres (eds), *Religion, Violence, Memory, and Place* (Bloomington, IN, 2006).

49 Arthur Kleinman, 'The Violences of Everyday Life: The Multiple Forms and Dynamics of Violence', *Violence and Subjectivity*, Veena Das et al. (eds) (Berkeley, CA, 1997), pp. 226-41. For the complexity of the concept and the difficulty of studying violence, see David Riches, 'The Phenomenon of Violence', *The Anthropology of Violence*, David Riches (ed.) (Oxford, 1986), pp. 1-27. The field is further complicated by some of the literature. One example is Donald Donham's

discussion of the concept of violence where he claims that its study beyond 'warfare and evolutionary theories of aggression' only saw a turning point with Scarry's 1985 volume, disregarding such path-breaking work as that by Frantz Fanon of the 1950s and 1960s and that of Hannah Arendt. Donald Donham, 'Staring at Suffering: Violence as a Subject', *States of Violence: Politics, Youth, and Memory in Contemporary Africa*, Edna Bay and Donald Donham (eds) (Charlottesville, VA, 2006), p. 16; 16-33; Elaine Scarry, *The Body in Pain: The Making and Unmaking of the World* (New York, 1985); Frantz Fanon, *Black Skin, White Masks* (New York, 1963 [1952]) and *Wretched of the Earth* (New York, 2004 [1961]), Hannah Arendt, *On Violence* (New York, 1970).

50 Johan Galtung, 'Violence, Peace, and Peace Research', *Journal of Peace Research*, 6, no. 3 (1969), pp. 167-91; Kleinman, 'The Violences of Everyday Life', p. 239 and *What Really Matters: Living a Moral Life Amidst Uncertainty and Danger* (Oxford, 2006). Anthropologists have so far been leading in producing studies on existential experiences of violence. See, for example, Nancy Scheper-Hughes, *Death Without Weeping: The Violence of Everyday Life in Brazil* (Berkeley, CA, 1992) and Diane Nelson, *A Finger in the Wound: Body Politics in Quincentennial Guatemala* (Berkeley, CA, 1999).

51 Kleinman, 'Violences of Everyday Life', pp. 228-31.

52 In 1997, the *American Historical Review*, 102, no. 5, celebrated ten years of scholarship on memory by dedicating a forum to the topic. For an excellent discussion of the debate and the argument that memory operates within the realm of 'power, stratification, and contestation', see, Jeffrey Olick and Joyce Robbins, 'Social Memory Studies: From "Collective Memory" to the Historical Sociology of Mnemonic Practices', *Annual Review of Sociology*, 24 (1998), p. 122; also, Gavriel Rosenfeld, 'A Looming Crash or a Soft Landing? Forecasting the Future of the Memory "Industry"', *Journal of Modern History*, 81, no. 1 (2009), pp. 122-58, Jennifer Cole, 'Memory and Modernity', *A Companion to Psychological Anthropology: Modernity and Psychocultural Change*, Conerly Casey and Robert Edgerton (eds) (Malden, MA, 2005), pp. 103-20.

53 The classic and still tremendously useful study on memory is Maurice Halbwachs's *On Collective Memory* (Chicago, IL, 1992 [1941/52]). Recent books include Pierre Nora's volumes on commemorative sites, *Les lieux de mémoires*, vol. 1-3 (Paris, 1984–1992), Paul Ricoeur's *Memory, History, Forgetting* (Chicago, IL, 2004 [2000]) and Alison Winter's *Memory: Fragments of a Modern History* (Chicago, IL, 2012).

54 For social, as well as embodied, memory, see Paul Connerton, *How Societies Remember* (Cambridge, 1989), chapter 1. For a critical discussion of historians' uses of memory, see Wulf Kansteiner, 'Finding Meaning in Memory: A Methodological Critique of Collective Memory Studies', *History and Theory*, 41, no. 2 (2002), pp. 179-97.

55 For a brief discussion of the origins of the concept 'social memory' with Emile Durkheim in 1923, see Jan Assmann, 'Collective Memory and Cultural Identity', *New German Critique*, no. 65 (1995), pp. 125-33. For the concept of social cohesion, see Emile Durkheim, *The Elementary Forms of Religious Life* (Oxford, 2001 [1912]). For social cohesion, memory, and violence, see Heike Schmidt, 'Entangled Memories: Bindung and Identity', *Unraveling Ties: From Social Cohesion to New Practices of Connectedness*, Yehuda Elkana et al. (eds) (Frankfurt/Main, 2002), pp. 199-212. For the connection between memory and identity, see John Gillis, 'Introduction: Memory and Identity: The History of a Relationship', *Commemorations: The Politics of National Identity*, John Gillis (ed.) (Princeton, NJ, 1994), pp. 3-24; also Dena Eber and Arthur Neal, 'Introduction: Memory, Constructed Reality, and Artistic Truth', *Memory and Representation: Constructed Truths and Competing Realities*, Dena Eber and Arthur Neal (eds) (Bowling Green, OH, 2001), pp. 3-18.

56 For an attempt to reconstruct memories of the trans–Atlantic slave trade through an examination of ritual and other performative practices, see Rosalind Shaw, *Memories of the Slave Trade: Ritual and the Historical Imagination in Sierra Leone* (Chicago, IL, 2002). See also Paul Connerton's suggestion to locate memory not just in narrative but embedded in the body itself. *How Societies Remember*, chapter 3. On memory, trauma, and the body, see Aleida Assman, *Erinnerungsräume: Formen und Wandlungen des kulturellen Gedächtnisses* (Munich, 1999), chapter 4.

57 For the connection between memory, identity, and suffering, see Elizabeth Tonkin, *Narrating Our Pasts: The Social Construction of Oral History* (Cambridge, 1992), p. 112.

58 Peter Burke, 'Geschichte als soziales Gedächtnis', *Mnemosyne, Formen und Funktionen der kulturellen Erinnerung*, Aleida Assmann and Dietrich Harth (eds) (Frankfurt/Main, 1991), pp. 289-304.

59 In the area of this study there are no griots or professional story-tellers. However, some forms of knowledge of the past are restricted to ritual experts.

60 Amadou Hampaté Bâ, Unesco General Meeting, Paris, 14 December 1960.

61 Arjun Appadurai, 'The Past Is a Scarce Resource', *Man*, 16, no. 2 (1981), pp. 201-19.

62 In the late 1990s, Richard Werbner postulated a 'postcolonial memory crisis', with 'popular counter-memory' increasingly contesting 'state memorialism'. See Richard Werbner, 'Introduction: Beyond Oblivion. Confronting Memory Crisis', *Memory and the Postcolony: African Anthropology and the Critique of Power*, Richard Werbner (ed.) (London, 1998), p. 1. Such counter-hegemonic subversiveness had been practiced long before the 'postcolonial era'. See Johannes Fabian, *Memory Against Culture: Arguments and Reminders* (Durham, NC, 2007), chapter 7. See also Osumaka Likaka, *Naming Colonialism: History and Collective Memory in the Congo, 1870–1960* (Madison, WI, 2009), Jennifer Cole, *Forget Colonialism? Sacrifice and the Art of Memory in Madagascar* (Berkeley, CA, 2001).

63 On the complexity of memory, see Fabian, *Memory Against Culture*, chapters 8 and 9. For psychological studies on memory and forgetting, see Daniel Schacter, *The Seven Sins of Memory: How the Mind Forgets and Remembers* (Boston, MA, 2002), *Searching for Memory*, chapter 4; 'Memory Distortion: History and Current Status', *Memory Distortion: How Minds, Brains, and Societies Reconstruct the Past*, Daniel Schacter (ed.) (Boston, MA, 1995), pp. 1-43 and, in the same volume, John Krystal et al. 'Post Traumatic Stress Disorder: Psychobiological Mechanisms of Traumatic Remembrance', pp. 150-72.

64 Jacques Derrida, *Of Grammatology* (Baltimore, MD, 1974 [1967]).

65 For an insightful discussion of silence see Heidrun Friese, 'Silence – Voice – Representation', *Social Theory after the Holocaust*, Robert Fine and Charles Turner (eds) (Liverpool, 2000), pp. 159-78. For the controversy over the Truth and Reconciliation Commission's success, see François du Bois and Antje du Bois-Pedain (eds), *Justice and Reconciliation in Post-Apartheid South Africa* (Cambridge, 2008); and Audrey Chapman and Hugo van der Merwe (eds), *Truth and Reconciliation in South Africa: Did the TRC Deliver?* (Philadelphia, PA, 2008).

66 For healing in the aftermath of Zimbabwe's liberation war, see Pamela Reynolds, *Traditional Healers and Childhood in Zimbabwe* (Athens, OH, 1996); Heike Schmidt, 'Healing the Wounds of War: Memories of Violence and the Making of History in Zimbabwe's Most Recent Past', *Journal of Southern African Studies*, 23, no. 2 (1997), pp. 301-10.

67 Degenaar refers to this as the 'muteness of violence'. 'The Concept of Violence', pp. 84-5.

68 Thomas Mitchell changed the debate with his understanding of imperial landscape as process. 'Imperial Landscape', *Landscape and Power*, W.J. Thomas Mitchell (ed.) (Chicago, IL, 1994), pp. 5-34; also see Ute Luig and Achim von Oppen, 'Landscape in Africa: Process and Vision. An Introductory Essay', *Paideuma*, 43 (1997), pp. 7-45. Sally Falk Moore prefers 'the term "process" to "practice" precisely because process conveys an analytic emphasis on continuous production and construction without differentiating in that respect between repetition and innovation. A process approach does not proceed from the idea of a received order that is then changed. Process is simply a time-oriented perspective on both continuity and change'. See 'Explaining the Present: Theoretical Dilemmas in Processual Ethnography', *American Ethnologist*, 14, no. 4 (1987), p. 729.

69 Pathbreaking for the historical study of landscape was David William Cohen and E.S. Atieno Odhiambo's *Siaya: The Historical Anthropology of an African Landscape* (London, 1989); see also Simon Schama, *Landscape and Memory* (New York, 1995), Kate Darian-Smith et al., *Text, Theory, Space: Land, Literature and History in South Africa and Australia* (London, 1996), Barbara Bender and Margot Winder (eds), *Contested Landscapes: Movement, Exile and Place* (Oxford, 2001), Pamela Stewart and Andrew Strathern (eds), *Landscape, Memory and History: Anthropological Perspectives* (London, 2003); Samuel Truett, *Fugitive Landscapes: The Forgotten History of the U.S.–Mexico Borderlands* (New Haven, 2006); JoAnn McGregor, *Crossing the Zambezi: The Politics of Landscape on a Central African Frontier* (Woodbridge, 2009); Jan Bender Shetler, *A History of Landscape Memory in Tanzania from Earliest Times to the Present* (Athens, OH, 2007). For a broader discussion of historiography, see William Beinart, 'African History and Environmental History', *African Affairs*, 99, no. 395 (2000), pp. 269-302.

70 Toni Morrison, *Paradise* (New York, 1998).

71 Caroline Elkins, *Imperial Reckoning: The Untold Story of Britain's Gulag in Kenya* (New York, 2005), pp. 42-3. In contrast, see David Anderson's account of the Ruck killing, *Histories of the Hanged: The Dirty War in Kenya and the End of Empire* (New York, 2005), pp. 93-8, 102-7. Elkins and Anderson, both historians writing about the same conflict with the same focus – British counter-insurgency – published in the same year, both by trade publishers, could not be more different in crafting narratives of the past. Anderson interweaves the depiction of atrocities and suffering with historically structuring arguments, without sensationalising the events and experiences he describes. Another example from Elkins's writing, albeit in a popular genre, is her review of Helene Cooper's memoires of the her childhood in Liberia, which Elkins begins with the claim: 'The skeletal remains of Africa's numerous civil wars litter the continent' from the east to the west coast. Caroline Elkins, 'African Idyll', review of *The House at Sugar Beach: In Search of a Lost African Childhood*, *New York*

Times Book Review, 5 September 2008.

72 E. Valentine Daniel, *Charred Lullabies: Chapters in an Anthropography of Violence* (Princeton, NJ, 1996), p. 4. For a literary discussion of violence and narrative, see Nancy Armstrong and Leonard Tennenhouse (eds), *The Violence of Representation: Literature and the History of Violence* (London, 1989).

73 Michael Roth and Charles Salas, 'Introduction', *Disturbing Remains: Memory, History, and Crisis in the Twentieth Century*, Michael Roth and Charles Salas (eds) (Los Angeles, CA, 2001), p. 5.

74 Philip Gourevitch, 'Among the Dead', *Disturbing Remains: Memory, History, and Crisis in the Twentieth Century*, Michael Roth and Charles Salas (eds) (Los Angeles, CA, 2001), pp. 63-73; Gourevitch, *We Wish to Inform You*.

75 For a thorough discussion of trauma and narrative, see LaCapra, *Writing History*, chapter 1.

76 'Internal Affairs Men now Learn the Arts of War', *Sunday Mail*, 26 February 1978; 'Mutasa Constituency Seminar, Planned Development of the Mutasa District', n.d. [1986?], Establishment of Vidcos and Wadcos Committees, PAO. Estimates vary greatly and at times are much lower, such as the population census for 1969, which stated 35,050, and for 1982, which stated 56,929 as the total population for the three communal lands. Government of Zimbabwe, Central Statistical Office, *1982 Population Census: A Preliminary Assessment*, (Harare, 1984), p. 14.

77 Government of Zimbabwe, Honde–Pungwe Valley: Integrated Rural Development Plan, vol. 1, Project Environment (Rome: 1985), p. 5, DAO.

78 Ibid., p. 6.

79 Government of Zimbabwe, Ministry of Internal Affairs, Tilcor, *Pungwe Valley Project Report* (Salisbury, 1976), NAZ.

80 Government of Zimbabwe, *Honde-Pungwe Valley*, vol. 1, table 28, p. 28.

81 Ibid.

82 Donald Moore conducted an excellent study on the Tangwena area. See *Suffering for Territory: Race, Place, and Power in Zimbabwe* (Durham, NC, 2005). For relevant work on Mozambique's Manica Province, see Mark Chingono, *The State, Violence and Development: The Political Economy of War in Mozambique, 1975–1992* (Aldershot, 1996); Eric Allina-Pisano, 'Negotiating Colonialism: Africans, the State, and the Market in Manica District, Mozambique, 1835–1935', PhD thesis, Yale University, 2002. For the Mutasa area, see H.H.K. Bhila, *Trade and Politics in a Shona Kingdom: The Manyika and their Portuguese and African Neighbours 1575–1902* (Burnt Mill, 1982).

83 Annual Reports, Umtali District, 1931, S235/509, NAZ, Inyanga District, 1959, S2827/2/2/7, NAZ, Inyanga District, 1960, box number 62328, NRC.

84 DC Umtali to PC, 29 March 1972, PER5 Chief Mutasa, PC to Secretary for Internal Affairs, 4 September 1973, PER5 GEN, DAO.

85 Secretary for Internal Affairs to PC, 28 November 1973, DC Inyanga to PC, 18 February 1974, PER5 Chief Mutasa, DAO.

86 'Confidential Questionnaire: Tribal Land Authorities', n.d. [1965?], PER5 Chief Muparutsa, DAO, Secretary for Internal Affairs to PC, 14 December 1973, PER5 GEN, DAO, PNC to CNC, 5 November 1948, NC Inyanga to PNC, 22 August 1951, PER5 Chief Mutasa, PAO, PER5 Chief Mafi, PAO. The role of Chief Mponda as the 'tribal authority' for the Mutasa North Reserve was highly contested. Umtali District, Annual Report, 1966, box number 88459, NRC.

87 Dipesh Chakrabarty, *Provincializing Europe: Postcolonial Thought and Historical Difference* (Princeton, NJ, 2000), p. 27; chapters one and six.

88 Reinhart Koselleck, *Futures Past: On the Semantics of Historical Time* (New York, 2004), p. 151.

89 For a similar argument, see Lillian Hoddeson, 'The Conflict of Memories and Documents: Dilemmas and Pragmatics of Oral History', *The Historiography of Contemporary Science, Technology, and Medicine: Writing Recent Science*, Ron Doel and Thomas Söderquist (eds) (New York, 2006), pp. 187-200.

90 Julie Frederikse, *None But Ourselves: Masses vs. Media in the Making of Zimbabwe* (London, 1982), p. iv. The holdings of the Rhodesian army papers at the British Empire and Commonwealth Museum are incomplete and currently inaccessible.

91 For virtual Rhodesia, see, for example, Rhodesians Worldwide, http://www.rhodesia.com/.

92 Mozambicanist colleagues confirmed that the archives in Maputo would not have added in any substantial manner to this research. Still, it needs to be acknowledged that the author only has at most rudimentary reading knowledge of Portuguese.

93 Interview #12.

94 For the classic model of claims to ancestral land during the liberation war, see Lan, *Guns and Rain*; Marja Spierenburg later conducted an in-depth study in the same area, *Strangers, Spirits, and Land Reforms: Conflicts about Land in Dande, Northern Zimbabwe* (Leiden, 2004).

95 Michel-Rolph Trouillot, *Silencing the Past: Power and the Production of History* (Boston, MA,

1995); Donald Moore and Richard Roberts, 'Listening for Silences', *History in Africa*, 17 (1990), pp. 1-7.

96 For an excellent critical discussion of oral history, see Alessandro Portelli, *The Battle of Valle Giulia: Oral History and the Art of Dialogue* (Madison, WI, 1997). See also Karen Fields, 'What One Cannot Remember Mistakenly', *Memory and History: Essays on Recalling and Interpreting Experience*, Jaclyn Jeffrey and Glenace Edwall (eds) (Lanham, MD, 1994), pp. 89-106. For a critical evaluation of life histories, including the historian's power advantage and possible ethnocentricity undermining the research, see Kirk Hoppe, 'Whose Life Is It, Anyway? Issues of Representation in Life Narrative Texts of African Women', *International Journal of African Historical Studies*, 26, no. 3 (1993), pp. 623-36; Heidi Gengenbach, 'Truth-Telling and the Politics of Women's Life History Research in Africa: A Reply to Kirk Hoppe', *International Journal of African Historical Studies*, 27, no. 3 (1994), pp. 619-27; Kirk Hoppe, 'Context and Further Questions: Response and Thanks to Heidi Gengenbach', *International Journal of African Historical Studies*, 28, no. 2 (1995), pp. 359-62. See also Luise White et al. (eds) *African Words, African Voices: Critical Practices in Oral History*, (Bloomington, IN, 2001).

97 A prominent and much criticised example of the interviewee's power in shaping the research is Marjorie Shostak's *Nisa: The Life of a !Kung Woman* (Cambridge, MA, 1981). For a critical evaluation, see Hoppe, Whose Life, p. 625.

98 The comparative relevance of villagisation includes the counter-insurgency campaign against Mau Mau in Kenya, and also Mozambique, Malaya and civil efforts such as *ujamaa* in Tanzania and collectivisation in the former Soviet Union.

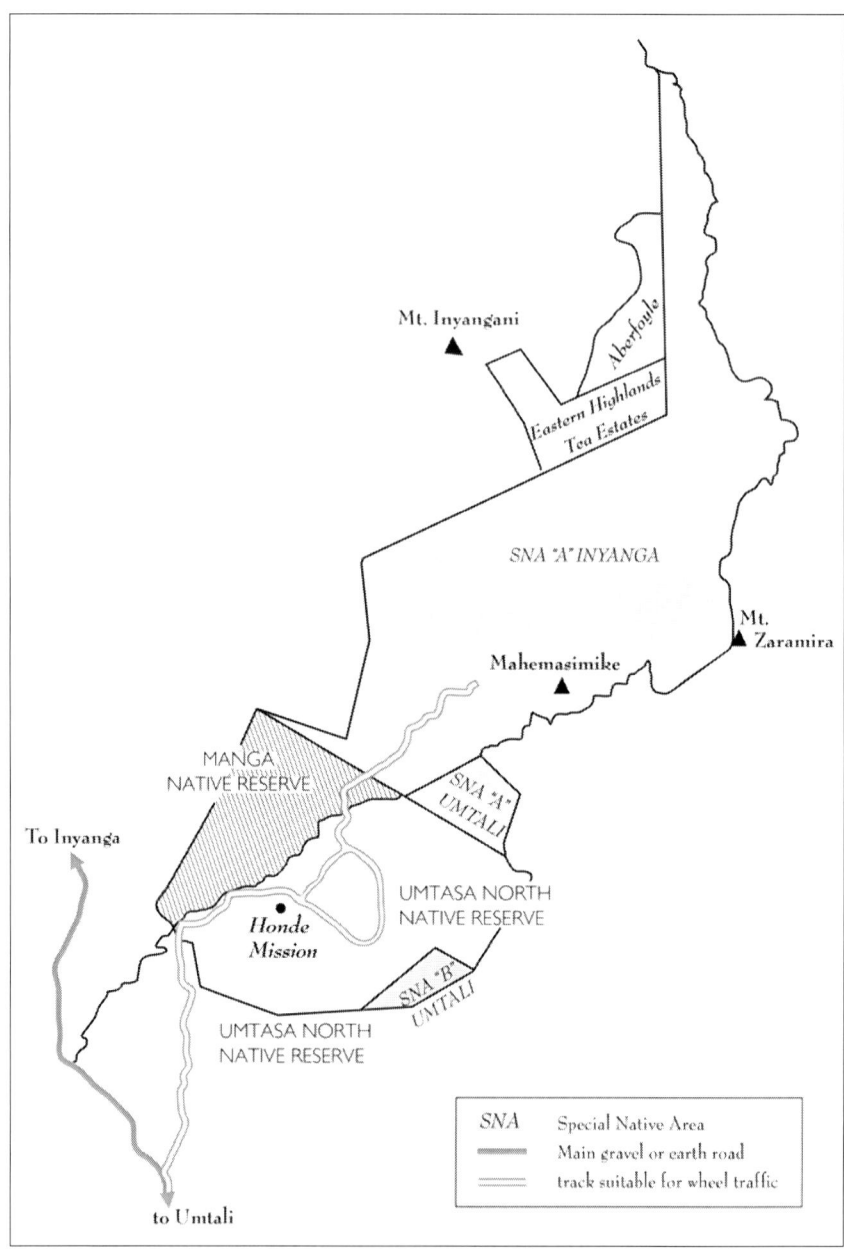

Map 2 Honde Valley, c. 1961

2
Living on the Frontier
Opportunity & Danger

An elder, when asked about the history of the Honde Valley, first related his genealogy and family history.[1] Then he went on to say that 'Long back, this country was a vast area, with no boundaries. Borders were set up after the arrival of the Portuguese and, er … and Cecil Rhodes. That was when they limited movement of people …. [Previously] people settled freely.'[2] The creation of the border between Rhodesia and Portuguese East Africa contributed significantly to the making of the valley as a frontier area. However, it did not impose as much of a rupture as the elder claims with his narrative of colonial alienation: the colonial border was not the first or only boundary in the area.[3] Before the advent of colonial partition, the valley and its inhabitants were already bounded in various ways: topographical and climatic separation as well as cultural and political demarcation. All these boundaries were continually re-delineated and thus their meaning locally made during ongoing negotiation processes that mediated a sense of belonging with outside threats. Hence, the frontier identity, located in a field of tension between opportunity and danger emerged.[4]

The valley has been prone to violence from the 1830s at the very least. In the nineteenth century, it took shape as a frontier area. Newcomers were usually attracted by the opportunities such an area offers, for example, ample land and remoteness from centralised political authority. At the same time, however, warfare and other forms of violence, in particular raiding and state interference, presented incentives to leave. When the colonial state began to establish its presence through attempts to rationalise space, including the mapping of 'tribal authorities', in order to create legible communities of colonial subjects, local responses to this violation included flight and temporary displacement. These strategies became ever more important during times of war. When talking about the Second Chimurenga and his choice to seek refuge in Mozambique, an elder contrasted the fate of 'those living in the interior' with 'those who live along the border':

> You know what happens? When war breaks out, those who live along the border bear the full brunt of it. Much suffering occurs to such people. Life is a bit better for those living in the interior. If the people try to live with war, they either get maimed or killed,

so they run away. We were running away from imminent death. There was no joy in this. We could not simply wait for death to strike. No![5]

He thus characterised the Honde Valley as a particularly dangerous place and contrasted it with the relative security of the interior.[6] The imposition of the colonial border transformed the frontier identity, shaping a distinct moral ethnicity whose social memory was disrupted by constant movement and at the same time informed by the assertion of cohesion through shared claims to the distant past before colonial intervention. Consequently, when asked about the liberation war of the 1970s, male elders often responded by talking about the nineteenth century. When the valley inhabitants experienced a period of prolonged insurgent violence between the 1970s and the 1990s, they drew on local frontier traditions, as will be shown in later chapters. The distinct frontier ethnicity in the area has clearly shaped the local experience and understanding of violence, and the social memory of past conflict has been an important part of this identity.

The considerable body of literature on the frontier ranges significantly in its interpretation of the search for a new sense of belonging beyond the realms of the familiar that characterises frontier people. These studies show that such groups usually imagine themselves as pioneers who leave the metropole and venture into an imagined no man's land. Beginning in 1893, with his presentation at the American Historical Association Meeting, Frederick Turner's seminal study of the North American frontier critically and systematically challenged the pioneer myth with its claim of expanding the boundaries of civilisation. He argued that the frontier was not so much a breaking ground for the existing civilization, but that the moving frontier was the site of an evolving creation of American identity.[7]

While Turner's work has been much criticised for its rather schematic explanation of tidal migration waves that are periodically followed by metropolitan society, it nevertheless firmly established frontier studies as a field of inquiry.[8] In some cases, as Igor Kopytoff paradigmatically states for Africa before colonialism, the frontier experience is one of cyclical fragmentation in which members of communities challenge the elders' authority and move beyond the boundaries of social and political structures in order to escape control and conflict. Once a new order is established, another break-off is then likely to occur, and thus the frontier mode of life is perpetuated.[9] In other cases, the out-migration aimed at re-establishing the authority that had been undermined in the metropole, as was the case with Afrikaner communities in South Africa and some of the Ngoni migrations in the context of the so-called 'mfecane'.[10]

The settling down of the newly arrived involves the negotiation of social cohesion within the group of newcomers and between them and those who are already settled at the frontier. To this day, the 'clash of civilisations' paradigm is prevalent in understanding this historical process.[11] This is highly problematic, because it presupposes discrete civilisations that meet confrontationally in a hierarchical manifestation of cultural and political achievements. Instead, while clashes frequently occur and tend to be legitimised with notions of difference, the experience of the unfamiliar is, more often than not, gradual and hybrid or cosmopolitan in character. The Honde Valley provides a case for this argument. Here, the frontier is understood not as provisional but as stable, albeit as ambiguous and as a social and cultural process, a theme that is further explored in chapter three.[12]

The Honde Valley has been an area of population movement for as long as historical memory reaches into the past. Its inhabitants understand the area to be part of the Mutasa mamboship, but at the same time political belonging is primarily expressed through allegiance to local chiefs. In the past, the valley communities were highly incorporative. This chapter shows that the ease of immigration was based on three main factors: the agricultural potential of the area, the remoteness from centralised political authority, and the ideal of civic virtue that, if accepted in its vernacular articulation by the newcomers, made them members of the community and gave them access to land and other resources. What emerged was a frontier ethnicity rooted in land use, knowledge of the past and of the sacred landscape that is ruled by prohibitions but is crucial for fruition, and allegiance to the chief, together making an identity which is not transitory, but there to stay.

The main reason why the area became a frontier is that it has been specifically prone to bouts of insurgent violence yet at the same time attracted immigrant groups. Since the end of the Cold War, warfare and civil disruption in post-colonial Africa have shaped the social experiences of increasing numbers of African men, women, and children. Hence, a consideration of alternative political identities beyond the acknowledged concepts of ethnic group, political tribalism, and nation seems in place. The Honde Valley presents a case study which allows these possibilities to be explored. The very frontier experience that has characterised the area since the mid-nineteenth century provides an insight into understanding African cosmopolitanism and the creativity of violence.

This chapter is concerned with the period between the 1830s and the 1920s. It examines important developments that transformed the sense of belonging in the valley: the centralisation of the Mutasa polity, the incursions by warrior parties from the Gaza state to the south-east, and the early manifestation of the colonial state. This is followed by a discussion of frontier ethnicity in the Honde Valley. It will be argued that, as part of the Mutasa kingdom, it served as a buffer zone between polities located east and west of it. By the turn of the century, a distinct sense of danger and opportunity prevailed and was further transformed by the delineation of the colonial border which bounds the valley, when the area became part of Rhodesian territory. The valley's frontier identity, shaped by violence, became crucial in the wars between the 1970s and the early 1990s, when valley inhabitants drew on local frontier traditions, as is shown in later chapters.

The Mamboship Frontier: The Valley as a Buffer Zone

During the nineteenth century, political centralisation processes led to the rise of three major polities west and east of what today is the international border: Mutasa in the area known as Manyika, possibly dating to the late seventeenth century; Makombe in Barwe, identified as Barué or Barue in colonial sources, a paramountcy that had already existed for centuries; and a new polity established in the 1820s further away to the south-east, the Gaza state. The increasing presence of Portuguese traders, entrepreneurs, and warlords,[13] and then, towards the end of the century, the competition between Portugal and the Mozambique Company on the one hand, and Cecil John Rhodes' British South Africa Company (BSAC) and British interests on the other, all focused on delineating colonial territory shaped the rule of *mambo* Tendai (1870–1902), who in turn made every effort to secure his sphere of influence.[14] The Honde Valley, topographically separated from Mutasa's mainland through the escarpment but opening onto and thus vulnerable to Mozambique, came to play a crucial role in this by becoming a buffer zone against intrusions from the east. Thus elders explain that it was Tendai who assigned the role of sentinel to distinguished warriors and royal women in the valley. A spirit medium and councillor from Chief Zindi's area explained his chieftainship's role:

> This was all a forest – a big forest. We were staying at Madzitire area, in the mountains …. We stayed there as sentinels long back…. When we saw fire burning, we sent people there to find out who they were. That was when there were not yet many people here.[15]

In 1982, *mambo* Abishai Chimbadzwa Mutasa (1982–1994) became ruler of the Mutasa area after a prolonged contentious succession debate. During the colonial period, if not before, every time a new *mambo* (king) had to be appointed there was a succession struggle, something that also held true for chieftaincies and sub-chieftaincies. In fact, the negotiated nature of appointments of 'traditional authorities', which contrasts greatly with the colonial notion that customs clearly regulate succession and who was to participate in decision-making, reflects more than the shortcomings of colonial knowledge;[16] it also illustrates local understanding and practices of political power. From a vernacular perspective, the traditional veneer of assigned status by birth, the sense of entitlement to political office by specific members of the royal lineage, and the assumption of a clearly stratified society was challenged when political alliances renegotiated civic virtue and custom on these occasions.[17] This was certainly the case with Abishai Mutasa's ascent to the mamboship that was pitched in the vein of a new beginning and a renewal of Mutasa's glory of the past. The *mambo* himself insisted on his royal claim: 'According to us I am not the chief, I am the King …. Today, chief – it has no meaning really.'[18] He further emphasised the fact that the legitimacy and practice of his rule were based on traditions derived from his pre-colonial predecessors, in particular from *mambo* Tendai.[19] The claims within the mamboship of the golden, pre-colonial age of the Mutasa kingdom – claims aimed against the government and local policies – became highly politicised in the late 1980s. At the time, RENAMO groups operating in the area promised such rule in order to garner support, as had been the case in the 1950s, in the context of nationalist mobilisation, when there had been talk of appointing the *mambo* as 'Paramount Chief of Manicaland'.[20]

A Zimbabwean newspaper article on the 1982 appointment celebrated the new *mambo* as continuing Tendai's legacy: 'a great-grandson of the most colourful and bravest Mutasa in the entire dynasty – Tendai'. The article further claimed his ancestor's importance to the nation: 'It could be said in part that the new Zimbabwe owes a section of its present history and geography to the shrewdness, cunning and astuteness of [Tendai].'[21] Such perceptions of his local and regional role might well be exaggerations, but during the transition period he did make significant contributions to re-shaping the mamboship from a sovereign polity to a chieftainship under colonial rule. Also, it was under Tendai's government that the Honde Valley took shape as part of the mamboship boundary, inhabited by frontier people.

MAKOMBE

During the nineteenth century, the mamboship's most powerful neighbours were the Makoni chieftainship in the west and the Makombe paramountcy in the east and north-east.[22] During the Mutasa succession wars of 1870 to 1875, Tendai fought adversaries who had taken refuge in Chief Makoni's area and who were backed by Chief Makombe.[23] Relations between Mutasa and Makombe appear to have been even more strained in the 1880s, when *mambo* Tendai developed a close relationship with the Portuguese *prazeiro* (crown land holder), warlord, and government representative Manuel Antonio de Souza (1835–1892). Over the course of four years de Souza attempted to conquer Makombe, which he succeeded in doing in 1883, having already established his headquarters in the 1850s at Gorongoza, visible from the Honde Valley on a clear day. Makombe, on the other hand, continued to resist de Souza's rule and finally succeeded in killing him in 1892.[24] Furthermore, according to oral traditions, Tendai married two of Makombe's daughters, who arrived with 'a great wealth of livestock', but suspecting them of plotting against him he, on the advice of his councillors, sent both of them back after some time.[25] In short, the Mutasa polity was bounded to the east by a political enemy.

After *mambo* Tendai broke off his association with de Souza in 1890, nevertheless relations between Mutasa and Makombe failed to improve, even though both resented the continuing Portuguese influence. In 1896, Tendai's son Chimbadzwa and his daughters Muredzwa and Chikanga fell out with their father after the death of their mother, Tendai's chief wife. They accused one of the junior wives of being responsible for their mother's death and when Tendai did not agree to punish the accused, the three siblings and five hundred of their followers sought refuge in Makombe's area. They returned in 1897.[26] Some evidence suggests that his children's self-chosen exile was one reason why Tendai did not participate in the First Chimurenga, the anti-colonial rising against BSAC rule during 1896–97.[27] It was significant that Muredzwa and Chikanga were chieftainesses, both of whom had been directly appointed by Tendai as part of his attempts to stabilise his realm.[28] Muredzwa became the most important *ishe* (chief) within the mamboship and *mhondoro* (senior spirit medium), and she was to become the most senior woman in the royal lineage, which gave her a singularly important role in succession decisions.[29] Moreover, Chimbadzwa as eldest son was the king-designate. Makombe, harbouring Tendai's three politically most important children, must have deepened the already existing rift between these centres of power.

So far it has been argued that the Makombe paramountcy presented a threat to *mambo* Tendai's rule by providing shelter for his opposition and, as is explained in more detail below, by supporting Mutasa's enemies during military conflict. Makombe's influence was most directly felt at the eastern fringes of the mamboship, with the exposed Honde Valley of great geopolitical importance. Separated from the rest of the mamboship by the dramatic drop in elevation, the southern fringes of the valley border the core area of the polity on the plateau with Honde views from Binga Guru, Mutasa's spiritual and political centre and royal burial ground. An elder explained the importance of the area as a buffer zone: 'Mutasa sent his sons here to prevent Makombe from coming to take over this land, after waging a war. So he sent Chikomba to this area, and Mandeya was tasked to look after that land and so on, right up to Mutare.'[30] Towards the end of Tendai's rule, the scramble for Manyikaland added another external threat that shaped his approach to power and the frontier character of the valley, not least because it brought about the formation of the colonial border.

THE SCRAMBLE FOR MANYIKALAND

Competition over gold mining rights was the primary impetus driving the BSAC, the African Portuguese Syndicate, which represented other South African businesses, and various Portuguese interests, whose local agents were the entrepreneur–adventurers de Souza, Andrada, and Rezende, to stake out their claims in Manyikaland. At first, *mambo* Tendai tried to play the various sides against each other. However, after he sided with the BSAC, with whom he signed a treaty on 14 September 1890, this became exceedingly difficult.[31] The scramble resulted in what H.H.K. Bhila calls the 'partition of Manyikaland'.[32] The mamboship lost only a small area which was directly ruled by its chiefs, but having already suffered recession in long-distance trade it now became effectively cut off from most of its sphere of economic influence which, through trade links, extended to the Zambezi River and east towards the Indian Ocean coast.[33] In 1890, *mambo* Tendai allegedly said, 'I have been pressed on all sides by the *assegai* [spear].'[34]

Tendai's attitude towards Portuguese interests, and de Souza in particular, was ambivalent. De Souza, a Goan who had attended a seminary,[35] had followed a political and military career in Portuguese East Africa. From 1863, he served as *capitão mór* (military governor) of Manica and Kiteve, which lie in central Mozambique between the Zambezi and Sabe rivers.[36] In November 1890, his fate changed radically when Tendai was instrumental in the infamous incident where several Portuguese men, including de Souza, Andrada, and Rezende, who were at that time trying to secure the Portuguese claim over Manyikaland, were captured by Captain Forbes and the British South Africa Police (BSAP) at the *mambo's* headquarters. Apparently, the Portuguese had lost the *mambo's* favour in 1889 by supplying weapons to chiefs Makoni and Katerere.[37] An elder related the incident as he remembered it to be told by his father, who had been one of Tendai's warriors. The BSAP interpreter played a crucial role in explaining that 'the people of Mutasa' should stand back and let the police take action in arresting Gouveia (de Souza's African name):

The white men then entered the room where Gouveia was and arrested him. After handcuffing him, they slapped him, threw him into the wagon and took him to Machipanda [a military post]. Gouveia never came again to quarrel with Mutasa, but he had already drawn this border.

H.S.: So the border had been drawn?

It had already been drawn, and they had wanted to draw it further inland to include Rusape.[38]

This account indicates that the border was already a local reality that was soon part of everyday life, even before Britain and Portugal formalised it in 1891. The elder emphasised de Souza's humiliation of being arrested, handcuffed, and 'slapped'. It is also remarkable that he named de Souza as the one who drew up the border, which might well reflect the reality of geopolitics: de Souza had been the 'big man' of the region for decades.

In the Honde Valley, de Souza is remembered as a powerful man and trader. Chief Mandeya's father, for example, told M. Reid, who had been District Commissioner (DC) Inyanga:

that he remembered Gouveia passing through his village on his way to Chief Mutasa to remonstrate with him for parleying with the English. He was a short, very stout man, said Mandeya, with a long black beard which he parted in the centre and tied behind his back. When he came through the bush in his *machila* [stretcher bed] he was always preceded by a drummer beating a drum to announce his approach.[39]

Bhila gave a similar account of de Souza's visits to Mutasa: 'On such occasions he was carried by his porters on a stretcher bed of poles and cloth. His wife, an African, walked beside the stretcher, and armed Sena people made up his escort.'[40] The account as related by Reid ends with a description of de Souza's death while fighting Makombe's army in 1892. Newitt points out that he had already faced political death following his arrest and deportation to Cape Town in 1890.[41]

De Souza is also remembered in family histories. So, for example, when an elder related his patrilineal descent, he explained that his paternal great-grandfather came from Bocha in Maranke district, where he was occupied with hunting elephants and trading ivory. He had a son, the elder's grandfather, who became a porter. As a young man, the grandfather met de Souza in Sena, on the Zambezi River. De Souza then 'asked him to accompany him inland' to his headquarters at Gorongoza, where he was employed to herd the cattle. The Portuguese presence east of Mutasa provided not only the chance to engage in lucrative activities, but also, more generally, increased opportunities of mobility and of new experiences.[42]

THE MAMBOSHIP FRONTIER

The Portuguese economic, military, and political presence that became more pronounced east of the Mutasa area in the second half of the nineteenth century, together with the threat that the Makombe paramountcy posed and the

Gaza warrior raids still to be discussed, had a profound impact on *mambo* Tendai's rule. Tendai introduced major innovations that temporarily stabilised the area politically and economically: he established new chieftaincies, solidified existing ones, and as part of this approach appointed royal women so that there were up to ten in office at the point of colonial occupation.[43] In the 1990s, emphasising Tendai's role in transforming the polity, *mambo* Abishai Mutasa argued that he had inherited structures of authority from his great-grandfather, such as the forty-two chieftaincies (*isheships*) within the mamboship. He maintained that *mambo* Tendai 'believed he can rule by his headmen' and continued to explain the particular role of the chiefs in the Honde Valley: 'Those who were there, they specifically had the job to look out for people who might penetrate into the interior.'[44] It is probably not coincidental that the *mambo*'s headquarters are located at Binga Guru, close to the southern edge of the valley and have a stunning view of the area.

According to oral traditions, at least six chiefs were based in the valley prior to Tendai's rule: Chikomba, Mandeya, Manga, Sakarombe, Saruchera, and Zindi.[45] Apparently, Tendai added one female chieftainship, Mpotedzi, whose first incumbent was one of his own daughters.[46] He further appointed two new warrior chiefs: Muparutsa, who was probably made chief after having assisted him in his succession dispute, and Sahumani, who was installed after proving himself in the Makoni wars.[47] What the written record leaves out is that Tendai assigned the warrior chiefs royal women who had spiritual authority and, at times, also controlled political power. Appointing deserving warriors could also provide military protection of the border.[48] At the same time, female chiefs, being close relatives and directly chosen by the *mambo*, were apparently thought of as less likely than male counterparts to wage war against him or to leave the mamboship with their followers. This notion was facilitated by the practice of sending these royal females to their chieftaincies as prepubescent girls.

Apparently, the *mambo* chose them not only for being close kin: in the case of his daughters Muredzwa and Chikanga with his senior wife, Tendai appointed them also because they were spirit mediums.[49] Being away from home, gaining political authority was something the girls then had to learn while growing up, being advised on local matters and decision-making from elders of the common lineages over whom they had to preside. The close bond to the *mambo* was retained in part through the rule that the biological fathers of a chieftainess' children were not to be known; the descendants, contrary to usual custom, inherited the royal totem (*mutupo*; signifier of clan membership), and were considered the *mambo*'s children. In addition, when a chieftainess died, only another female could replace her. Not being a hereditary office, each time the *mambo* chose the incumbent.[50]

In considering the reasons for Tendai's policy of appointing royal women to office balancing male power at first appears convincing, though the thought that women would be less prone to rebel is undermined by the occurrences in 1896/97, when Muredzwa and Chikanga left the mamboship in protest against their father's stance regarding their mother's death. In the late nineteenth century, with senior spirit mediums having been mostly, and possibly exclusively, women in the mamboship, it is more plausible that Tendai chose females for office because they could provide spiritual protection in addition to political allegiance. Accordingly, they were forces to be reckoned with, as the colonial state especially learned in its struggles with Muredzwa over her land.[51]

Tendai appointed a female political authority to Muparutsa, who inhabits the sacred landscape of the Mahemasimike granite formation in the middle part of the Honde Valley, and was still in office in the 1990s. As a *mhondoro* and a *muzvare* (daughter of a chief; here chieftainess), Muparutsa held court, distributed land, and was responsible for the spiritual well-being of the community, an important role she also performed after independence, while the male chief largely served as a figurehead throughout the colonial period.[52] In the late 1970s, *muzvare* Muparutsa's support for the liberation war in her role as *mhondoro* was significant in an area just a few miles from the main government military base in the valley. Already elderly, she crossed the border into Mozambique, where she cleansed the ZANLA fighters leaving for and returning from combat.[53] Born during the final warrior raids, this *muzvare*'s life spans the unfolding of the valley as a frontier area that culminated in modern guerrilla warfare from the 1970s to early 1990s and which initially crystallised in response to a different threat from the east, in this case raiding warrior parties from the Gaza state.[54]

Danger on the Frontier: The Valley as a Raiding Ground

The raiding warrior parties of the Gaza state, which emerged in southern Mozambique in the 1820s as a result of the Ngoni migrations, the so-called *mfecane*, and which was finally destroyed by the Portuguese in 1895, had a profound impact on the frontier character of the Honde Valley. The first attacks apparently occurred in the Muparutsa area in 1832, coinciding with a major drought that disrupted trade throughout the region. The incursions intensified after the Gaza ruler Umzila moved the capital to just east of the Chimanimani mountains, bringing it in much closer proximity to the valley and the mamboship, before coming to an end in 1888/89.[55] These raids reached as far north as the Zambezi River and as far west as the Great Zimbabwe ruins. Their main purpose was to obtain cattle, gold, women, and ivory. They also served to establish tribute payments through intimidation, as was the case with the Mutasa mamboship. Gaza made its claim to superiority clear in 1888, when *mambo* Tendai's proposal to marry the ruler's daughter was perceived as an insult. A raiding party was to take revenge, but apparently the conflict was solved peacefully.[56]

The literature usually refers to the Gaza warriors as Ngoni, Nguni, Shangaan or Gaza. Difficulty in labelling partly arises from the intricate assimilation process that was part of the establishment and expansion of the Gaza state.[57] For simplification, here the warriors will be referred to by their Honde Valley name, *madzviti*, a chiShona word used in four of its dialects, namely chiNdau, chiKaranga, chiManyika, and chiZezuru, that refers in general to raiders. The literal translations of *madzviti* are 'invaders' and 'large solitary grasshoppers (inedible).'[58] This supports the perception of *madzviti* as small and isolated groups of overpowering and ruthless young men for whom raiding was their livelihood, suddenly appearing, taking what they desire, and then disappearing. In the Honde Valley it is a name commonly applied to the Gaza warriors, without further ethnic reference, and thus the emphasis lies in their mode of interaction with the area, not their political or cultural origin. In fact, in the late twentieth century, valley inhabitants referred to RENAMO fighters as *madzviti* when they operated in a mode of nightly attacks and abducted children.[59]

The meaning of *madzviti* as young male insurgents is in common usage throughout the region, extending even to southern Tanzania, where Ngoni societies introduced their raiding-based livelihood. In kiSwahili, however, the broad meaning of warriordom is also present: *vita*, i.e., war, warrior; to raid, to invade.[60] Hence, one may argue that depending on the speaker and historical context, the term could connote military power and prowess as well as protection, or the outside threat of illegitimate young warrior violence. In the Honde Valley *madzviti* now signify the latter only. Referring to insurgents as *madzviti* may thus be one way of appropriating the historical memory of nineteenth-century illegitimate violence as much as it was a commentary on the RENAMO war more than a hundred years later. In accordance with this, oral traditions portray *madzviti* as young men living off people living on the frontier. This is reflected in an account given by an elder: 'If they had wanted land, they would have taken it because the Shangaans were fierce warriors. But they did not want the land.... The *madzviti* simply attacked, collected whatever they wanted, and went back. They acted just like hunters.'[61]

The frontier area is thus remembered as the hunting ground of the *madzviti*, as their resource. In contrast to other areas, the booty aimed at by the raiding parties was primarily women rather than livestock, the latter largely unavailable due to tsetse fly. Men and women will claim that Manyika women are unattractive, because all the beautiful ones were taken by the *madzviti*. An elder explained: 'The *madzviti* raided us here, and they used to come from their homeland. They fought against us – these *madzviti*. They also abducted women and went away with them. They came from their homeland.... They murdered people, and also made others pay tax.'[62] Social memory of the *madzviti* thus represents a profound sense of vulnerability of life at the frontier, in particular the failure of men to protect their communities, mostly the women of reproductive age as well as children. In contrast, oral traditions have preserved the memory of perseverance and of overcoming the invaders.

At least three of these traditions relate the activities of the invading warriors in the Honde Valley. Jason Machiwenyika recorded one of these narratives at the beginning of the twentieth century and two of them survived in the memories of elders in the 1990s. Machiwenyika recorded a tradition that relates the arrival of the *madzviti* in the Honde Valley during the rule of *mambo* Matida (c.1845–c.1865).[63] The warriors are said to have sought to settle peacefully in different chieftainships in the Honde Valley, such as Zindi, Samanga, Sakarombe, Saruchera, and Sanyamandwe, and to have married daughters of chiefs and councillors. After some time, however, they began to challenge the *mambo*'s authority and eventually plotted to kill all the men but spare the women and children. One of the warriors revealed this plan to his 'Honde Valley wife' when he was drunk and she in turn informed the elders. *Mambo* Matida then called his male and female chiefs and conspired with them to get the *madzviti* drunk in order that they could be overpowered and killed.[64] This was done, but four *madzviti* escaped and reported the massacre to their ruler, Gungunyana, who sent his warriors to the area to seek revenge. This is said to have established a tribute system, now with *mambo* Bvumbi in power (c.1865–1870).[65] In this oral tradition, the *madzviti* arrived as immigrants who came to settle, but in the end they did not forget their role as invaders, for which the valley inhabitants ultimately punished them with death.

A male elder related the second tradition, the events of which appear to have taken place in the Honde Valley during *mambo* Tendai's rule:

> That name Samanga derived from the *madzviti*. They used to come and raid here. They couldn't come, I mean, they couldn't penetrate the big place, the hiding place, Binga Guru [*mambo*'s headquarters]. So they would go along wherever they could get people. So Samanga was in a remote place … and he was an easy target to the enemy. He was too far in between other people. So the *madzviti* came there and they were doing their butchering. They were speaking … their language and my people would hear *mangamanga*, *mangamanga*, meaning you are lying. So then they were nicknamed Samanga and then that name became popular. Up to now it's Samanga.[66]

Manga is a chiManyika word with a range of diverse meanings, while *mangamanga* is derived from Ngoni, translates as 'deceitful fact or utterance', and thus tallies with the perception of the invaders.[67] Most importantly, the elder emphasised the vulnerability of the Honde Valley as a frontier area compared to the safety in the centre of the mamboship.

The third oral tradition relates how valley inhabitants killed the *madzviti* by deceit. They served the warriors manioc, pretending it was yam, which it closely resembles. Unlike yam, manioc has to be boiled more than once in order to rid it of the deathly cyanide it contains. This victory over the invaders is claimed by several chieftaincies, for example Samanga, Muparutsa, and Chikomba, thereby illustrating the importance of the account to political identity.[68] Chief Chikomba and his father explained:

> Father: The *svikiro* [spirit medium] told us the *madzviti* would be coming – these Shangaans you are referring to. We then prepared these *manzongo* [manioc] … When they came, they ate them, thinking that they were eating *madhumbe* [yam].
>
> Chief: The *svikiro* told the people to do all this. And when they invaded and saw the prepared food – *manzongo* – they ate it and died.[69]

They continued to say that the deceased returned as *shave* (alien spirits), who are revered in a possession cult. These spirits are said not to trust the valley inhabitants up to the present:

> Father: They do not eat *madhumbe*. If they see you with a *dhumbe*, the *shave* comes out.
>
> Chief: When these maNguni have their ceremony here, the *dzviti* ritual – if you go there with *madhumbe*, the real *madhumbe*, they chase you away.[70]

During my research in the valley, I was negotiating my own outsider position. When visiting a household for the first time, I was usually offered some exceptional food to honour me as a guest of status. On such occasions, I was seated like a man, sitting on a stool, while the women prepared tea or coffee, which could take a long time if firewood had to be collected and water fetched from the stream. When the women served me the beverage, they also offered me some special food. In prosperous households I was asked to pick a chicken and to slaughter it, though there was evident relief when I explained that I did not eat meat and thus the precious livestock could be saved. As word spread of my strange condition the cause was eventually interpreted not as vegetarianism but rather as related to my *mutopo* (totem), the signifier of clan membership that also prescribes a food prohibition. Instead, the most valuable cash crop, usually a large pink pineapple or avocado, sometimes a pawpaw, was offered, or, if available, slices of bread, which was a luxury because it had to be store-bought. The one exception occurred in Samanga. The women prepared the meal and I ate from communal bowls with the men. I was surprised to see yam, food that I had never been offered in the valley, but I helped myself heartily. I noticed a hush, embarrassed laughter, relief, and after a while one of the female elders explained that somehow the women had forgotten that they could not serve me manioc. She assumed I would understand, but I still did not grasp the significance of what had happened, other than that I was grateful that at a first visit I was not treated as a stranger – except for sitting with the men as an honorary male. Finally, the male head of household joked that I was clearly not one of the *madzviti*. It was then that it became clear to me how powerful the memory of those invaders still was. Serving manioc was seen as a local weapon that might be used to harm an intruder, unfamiliar with the local ways.

Accounts of the *madzviti* raids which valley inhabitants have contextualised and reinterpreted through their historical experience are part of today's discourse. They feature in oral traditions, storytelling, ritual practices, healing discourses, life and family histories, and daily conversations. The pervasiveness of *madzviti* in valley discourse and practices opens insight into its frontier identity, woven from memories of the past, experiences in the present, and imaginations of the future. The *madzviti* of the twentieth century, RENAMO, also brought violence and disruption. In August 1992, a local elder fended off an attack on his homestead by heavily armed RENAMO fighters using a bow and arrow; for days the account of that incident and stories about the Gaza warriors were told while household members sat around the fire, sharing their evening meal. Against this backdrop, the account of valley inhabitants who had tricked the most powerful warriors of their time generated a sense of empowerment that people drew on in these insecure times. The double-sided sword of the frontier's danger and opportunity proved to be powerful.

In the nineteenth century, the *madzviti* raids engendered a centralisation process, both of settlement patterns and political authority. In some areas, the attacks apparently caused temporary displacement: An elder from the Chikomba area related: 'When they invaded, people ran away to hide in caves, and if the *madzviti* left, people came back to their homes.'[71] In *ishe* Zindi's area in particular, and probably in others such as Manga and Nyamaende, settlement patterns changed more permanently. The chief explained:

We stayed up in the mountains. When we espied them [*madzviti*] coming, we rolled down boulders on them. Up in the mountains, we had boulders which we sent rolling down on these invaders. Some were killed and others would just be injured…. That is why we lived in the mountains.

Sabhuku Gogodi: We wanted to see them approaching.

Chief: Yes. [laughs][72]

Such accounts provide a clear notion that valley inhabitants sought refuge from the *madzviti*, abandoning the indefensible valley bottom and foothills, an adaptation that is supported by archaeological evidence. When Europeans surveyed Chief Zindi's area for the first time in 1952, they found remnants of recent as well as old settlements with 'meadow-like clearings' and terrace structures in the rainforest on the western slopes.[73] The sites discovered in the northern part of the valley appear to be similar to those examined close to the source of the Pungwe river that are part of the Nyanga complex, possibly the largest complex of ancient structures in Africa. One difference can be identified: the plateau sites include pit structures that probably functioned to hold livestock – a precaution that was unnecessary for valley inhabitants who usually lived in the lower areas infested by the tsetse fly.[74] The settlement sites are characterised by stone enclosures and sophisticated terracing to enable agricultural production while avoiding erosion.[75] Radiocarbon dating locates these settlements within a broad range, from 1300 to 1900, which would include the roughly sixty years of *madzviti* raids in the area.[76]

Robert Soper, the lead archaeologist of the most substantial excavations so far, dismisses the idea of defence settlements as an explanation for Nyanga, because some of the sites are located in low-lying areas and were thus indefensible.[77] Instead, he comes to the conclusion that agriculturalists sought the steep slopes despite the increased labour input because their soils were more fertile compared to the plateau or valleys, and further that the stone buildings were not created for protection but simply in the absence of wood.[78] Without drawing on archaeological expertise, it still appears that Soper's findings fall short in two aspects when applied to the Honde Valley: the advantages of sentinels and the spiritual protection provided even in lower-lying areas. Evidence suggests that during the succession dispute of the 1870s even *mambo* Tendai sought refuge with Chief Zindi at Mount Nyangani, a spiritual landscape that holds danger yet also offers protection.[79]

It is quite possible that the valley population and those of the Nyanga complex should be seen as separate historical formations, as Soper and other archaeologists, historians, and colonial administrators so far suggest, and that a transfer of knowledge from the plateau people to the valley inhabitants when the latter sought refuge on the mountain slopes did not occur. Still, the ability to negotiate different environments and demands on settlement structures was part of the vernacular knowledge, and the identification with the chief and chieftainship due to the formation of defence communities characterised the frontier identity of valley inhabitants from the mid-nineteenth century at the very least. In short, while the evidence is not conclusive on the extent of the occupation of higher lying areas, social memory and archaeological findings do point in that direction. The frontier character of the valley required a strategic reading and use of landscape.

The time of the *madzviti* raids is remembered as the period in which a specific kind of communality arose, necessitated by the need of common defence, and it is therefore not surprising that the end of the raids is remembered as an important turning point. This is true of *ishe* Zindi, who characterised the onset of the colonial period as the pacification of the area, and at the same time the beginning of land appropriation – even though the latter affected the northern part of the valley only from the 1950s. He said:

> The *madzviti* came to plunder and loot. They also murdered people. Yes. No wonder they were feared. Yes…. This was put to an end by the coming of the white people. All along our forefathers had been living in those mountains. They were staying there up to the time the white people came.[80]

This notion of a turning point can also be found in life stories. This was the case when *muzvare* Muparutsa was asked when she was born. The elders who were present interrupted, chuckling and commenting upon such an obviously useless question, but she said with great authority and pride: 'My mother was four months pregnant with me, the last time the *madzviti* raided this area!'[81]

In short, the heightened pressure from the east, from the Makombe paramountcy, from the Portuguese presence, in particular in the person of de Souza, and from the *madzviti* raids, contributed significantly to shaping the political structure of the Mutasa mamboship during the late nineteenth century. As part of this development, the Honde Valley gained new significance within the wider polity as a zone of ambivalence in which people lived on and off the border, as was the case with the raiders and the raided. The establishment of the Rhodesian state frontier further transformed the character of the Honde Valley.

The Colonial Frontier: The Valley Bound & Unbound

A former member of the district staff Mutasa explained that during the liberation war, in the 1970s, the Honde Valley was the 'hottest', that is, the most contested area in the entire country. Being easily accessible from Mozambique and its lush vegetation and rugged topography providing ample opportunities for cover, it was difficult for the Rhodesian state to defend the valley against incursions from the east. It was in this context that Mutasa said: 'The Honde Valley is a piece of Rhodesia in Mozambique. That was the problem.'[82] The decision to position the border east of the Honde Valley caused difficulties to the central state not only during the Chimurenga and the RENAMO war. The challenges of inaccessibility from the Zimbabwean plateau and the resulting lack of administrative control already prevailed from the time the border was agreed on in 1891. Hence, *mambo* Abishai Mutasa explained that state control of the border through police or the army could only fail, whereas Tendai's system of posting chiefs had been highly successful: 'You wouldn't pass the border unnoticed.'[83] The Honde Valley was not merely 'a part of Rhodesia in Mozambique', but was almost entirely beyond state control. However, while the state did not succeed in directly establishing its presence in the area before the mid-1950s, the imposition of colonial rule nevertheless impacted the valley frontier.

Border studies have been a vibrant field of investigation ever since the late 1980s. From a historical perspective, borderlands are an attractive topic because of their spatial ambiguity and processual character. This applies despite the apparent preciseness of boundaries, such as international borders. Spatially, a borderland would seem to be clearly defined by its proximity to a border. Although such a border creates such distinctions, it is inevitably never entirely successful in separating communities, networks, and so on. At the same time, however, the creation of a border triggers the rise of new connections, be they through the movement of people, goods, or knowledge. Temporally, the meanings and practices attached to a borderland undergo change, as the interplay between the state's concern over consolidating its power along its margins and vernacular interests unfolds.[84]

The contestation between the state and borderland inhabitants and transients – such as refugees, smugglers, and travellers – over power, meanings, and practices is both constant and ever-changing, embedded in political and economic circumstances and social life-worlds. The challenge when studying borders is to analyse the multiple angles of this unfolding power struggle and to map local and trans-local experiences in a long-term perspective.[85] This approach to border areas certainly challenges the nation state and colony as unit of study,[86] yet the view that (colonial) borders can be seen as a wedge or fracture dividing communities and polities and disrupting local identities[87] is still often put forward uncritically. Even though this might frequently be the case, this notion runs the risk of reproducing imperial fantasies of colonial power and of portraying African societies as merely responsive. Paul Nugent has emphasised that African boundary practices and ideologies of separation and exclusion during and after the period of colonialism may well be rooted in those that existed before the onset of colonial rule.[88] Achille Mbembe has pointed out that the notion of the colonial imposition of borders creating a reality of separation on the ground needs to be questioned and that locally 'the domestication of world time … takes place by dominating space and putting it to different uses' instead.[89]

Hans Medick observes that in Europe in a process of *longue durée* state and nation were made at the political border, but that the meaning of the border was shaped locally.[90] This unfolding process also applies to political boundaries imposed by a colonial government. Part of the production of meaning in the Honde Valley was the use of the border demarcation itself, the signifiers of scientific knowledge, copper and iron from the beacons, gained vernacular application as cooking pots and spears.[91] In addition, different types of boundaries – political, economic, military, cultural – change at their own pace, and not usually simultaneously.[92] They are negotiated in a variety of ways that can be distinct, overlapping, or competing. The multi-valence and meaning of the colonial border locally made and remade might well explain why it has been both ignored and utilised by valley inhabitants over time. Still, the delineation of political borders was part and parcel of European expansion. It was the first step of the colonial rationalisation of space and as such an inherently violent rupture.

The Honde Valley provides an example of a colonial border that could be ignored, consequently undermining colonial authority. When colonial rule caused suffering, people often chose to use the border for their own ends or to directly resist the state. In the Honde Valley, the imposition of the colonial border added an additional layer to the existing frontier identity, but it also was experienced as a turning point. Here, after a brief discussion of the early colonial impact on the area, it will be shown why and how the border was delimitated east of the Honde Valley and what effect it had on life there.

In what follows, emphasis will be given to the ambiguity and processual character of the Honde Valley as a borderland. First, enframing will be discussed as a colonial administrative practice, followed by three stages of borderland articulation in an interplay between the colonial state and vernacular practices and meanings: the establishment of the international border between Rhodesia and Portuguese East Africa, its demarcation, and the practices of its control and daily unraveling.[93] Hence, it will be shown that the making and unmaking of the colonial border created the Honde Valley as a borderland and at the same time transformed it as a frontier area.

ENFRAMING

After the turn of the twentieth century, once Britain and Portugal had agreed upon the borderline, both colonial governments tried to impose in the Mutasa area what historian Timothy Mitchell in his study of colonial Egypt called 'enframing'. Mitchell is mostly concerned with 'disciplinary mechanisms' derived from Michel Foucault's understanding of power, while here the focus is on the creation of colonial subjects and their legibility.[94] Mbembe has characterised such practice and ideology as colonial violence: colonisation is 'inscribed in the first place in a space they [the colonisers] endeavour to map, cultivate, and order' and the colony is then a place 'where violence is built into structures and institutions'.[95] Honde Valley inhabitants thus remember European influence before the 1950s as the introduction of tax, land rent, and administrative structures, as migrant labour opportunities, and as serving in 'Hitler's War'.[96] The colonial policies were the same as elsewhere in the territory, although their implementation proved to be particularly challenging along the border.

Every colonial power was concerned with making its colonised populations subject to law and establishing an economy that would at least finance the colonial project, preferably generating quick profit. Rhodesia was no exception to this, and identifying chiefs to hold responsible for providing the numbers of taxpayers and labour when needed, as well as enforcing tax collection, was one of the first steps the new administration took. In part of the colony, enframing included the demarcation of land use as early as the 1890s, but in the Honde Valley it was not fully introduced until the 1950s. Here, 'enframing' began with delineating 'traditional authorities'. This practice of tribalisation and the creation of colonial chiefs now answerable to the colonial administration served to conduct a population census, to establish local government, and to register all eligible hut tax-payers under the 'traditional authority' of the area in which they lived.[97] The policy prescribed the recording of existing political structures, with the clear purpose of creating standardised units of administration that facilitated tax collection and the control of population movement in particular. Where the implementation of these policies appeared to require more 'traditional' units, the administration increased the number of *masabhuku* (kraalheads), the lowest ranking political office. The chiShona word *sabhuku* (the prefix *sa-* expresses ownership, *bhuku* is a pidginised form of 'book'; *sabhuku*, therefore, is the owner of the book) reflects the office holder's task of collecting tax which was signed off at the office of the Native Commissioner (NC) who kept the 'books' (tax registers). An elder explained:

> The idea of *sabhuku* was brought about by the white people when they wanted us to pay taxes. They felt they had to set up *masahbuku* whose duty was to monitor who and who had not paid taxes. Because of this, many people were reluctant to be *masabhuku* since they looked down upon the role. Others, however, became *masabhuku*.[98]

Except for ritual duties, these *masabhuku* usually soon had the same responsibility as 'sub-chiefs' (*sadunhu*); they held court, had a council, and were answerable to the chief of the area. Moreover, the office became hereditary.[99]

Another aspect of enframing was the creation of administrative districts. The result was that the mamboship was split into three parts: most of the area was divided between Umtali district – including the seat of the *mambo*, its adjacent area, and the southern part of the Honde Valley – and Inyanga district, which comprised the valley's larger and less accessible northern section; finally, a small portion was lost to Portuguese territory.[100] When the latter occurred, members of the chieftaincies' lineages were installed on the Portuguese side of the border, as happened with Mandeya II.[101] Such arbitrary colonial administrative divisions caused grievances, although it should be noted that far more land was lost due to colonial land appropriation within Rhodesia compared to the impact of the formal border.[102] In 1928, in order to facilitate local government, the colonial state imposed the Mponda chieftaincy as paramount to Mutasa chiefs in Inyanga and their estimated three thousand followers in the southern part of the Honde Valley, with Mponda at the same time answerable to the *mambo*.[103] It appears, however, that this colonial chief did not gain authority in the eyes of valley inhabitants, despite his lineage's claim to be autochthonous, having predated the arrival of the first Mutasa.[104]

In addition to political and spatial delineation, early enframing also entailed the imposition of tax. Across the border, the Mozambique Company had introduced tax in 1892 and stipulated that from 1894 it could no longer be paid in produce in order to force African men into the cash economy.[105] It appears that the first attempt to collect hut tax in the Inyanga portion of the mamboship, however, was made only in 1900. Land rent was introduced in 1904, then extended in 1909 to include unalienated land. Expecting resistance against the land rent, the NCs Inyanga and Umtali, together with a small patrol of BSAP, assembled the political authorities – chiefs, sub-chiefs, and *masabhuku* – for a two-day meeting in March 1904. Chief Mandeya from the Honde Valley flatly refused to go unless ordered to do so by Mutasa, and while all others attended, with only the exception of Sakarombe, the attitude of the assembled 350 chiefs was apparently 'far from respectful'. The meeting quickly came to a deadlock when Tendai's daughter, chieftainess Muredzwa, addressed the colonial administrators as the spokesperson for all the office holders, stating clearly that while none of them had any intention of working for or paying tax to farmers, taxation by the government was a different matter. She added that resettlement was only acceptable if that meant staying close to the home area.[106] Earlier, in 1894, her sister Chikanga had also resisted the colonial regime, leading to the so-called 'Chikanga Affair' when she refused to provide labour for the BSAC.[107] Enforcing tax payments, whether hut tax or land rent, in the Honde Valley was particularly difficult because of its inaccessibility from the west, and as late as 1935 the occupants of the northern part still did not pay.[108]

Those most effectively targeted by the colonial state were migrant labourers, because African men were only allowed to leave the district and gain employment if they carried their pass. That in turn meant they had to be registered tax payers and it allowed their NC to keep track of them. In general, however, enforcing colonial policies proved to be a problem, and in 1907 much effort was made to disarm the African population in the Mutasa area and to undercut the weapons' trade to Makombe. Between May and July of that year, the BSAP recovered large numbers of muzzle-loaders and modern rifles.[109] Despite this apparent success, in January 1908 almost the only crimes reported for Umtali district were related to firearms, and *mambo* Mutasa was suspected to be involved in the arms thefts that led to another 400 weapons surrendered in the northern districts.[110] By the mid-1990s, many households in the Honde Valley owned muzzle-loaders, indicating that colonial weapon control never succeeded.

BORDER DELINEATION

The scramble for Manyikaland was a particularly contested one because of the area's gold deposits. Hence, both colonial powers, Britain and Portugal, politicised the boundaries of Tendai's rule in order to uphold and ultimately legitimise their geopolitical aspirations in the area. The Berlin Conference of 1884–1885 stipulated that colonial possessions could only be claimed if the colonial power imposed effective occupation and notified the other signatories.[111] The BSAC legitimised its claim over what was to become Southern Rhodesia through the Rudd Concession of 1888, a treaty with the Matabele ruler Lobengula. The assertion was based on the (wrong) supposition that the kingdom raided and therefore *de facto* ruled over all what later became Rhodesia.[112] Still, the crown granted the BSAC a royal charter in 1889, and the company established the colonial territory during the following year. A similar approach was taken in Manyikaland, although the BSAC did not concede the mamboship the special status of a kingdom. After signing a treaty with *mambo* Tendai on 14 September 1890, the BSAC's claims on land up to the Indian Ocean were based on the alleged boundaries of his dominion.[113]

The Portuguese, on the other hand, maintained they had 'ancient rights' because of their presence in the area since the sixteenth century. They further claimed that *mambo* Tendai had handed his country over to de Souza in 1875. At the time, Tendai was fighting for the mamboship and had asked de Souza for military support. The *mambo* sent him an elephant tusk filled with soil 'from the spirit medium's hut', which the latter interpreted as traditional practice indicating that Mutasa submitted to him, and Andrada claimed that the mambo subsequently paid tribute to de Souza. This was contested by Tendai.[114] Such submission is unlikely because, as Newitt points out, there is no evidence of de Souza's presence in the Mutasa heartland, while the claim that Mutasa had submitted to the Portuguese before the arrival of the BSAC was an important political argument during the scramble.[115] Andrada also maintained that effective occupation dated back to the creation of Manica Province in 1884, followed by his 1888/89 expedition to Manyikaland, and that it truly was effective given the Portuguese civilising mission on the ground.[116] Finally, reversing the BSAC approach, the Portuguese insisted that the mamboship belonged to the raiding and tribute areas of the Gaza state, which was under Portuguese rule, and that it thus belonged to Portuguese East Africa.[117] This claim reached as far west as the Makoni chieftainship, which had been part of the tribute-paying zone.[118] The geopolitical background to the 'scramble' largely explains why, after the border convention, it took twenty-one years to ratify the Barué Boundary of 1912.[119]

The delineation of political borders is an important precondition for a working colonial state after occupation, as in fact any nation state strives to eliminate 'rough edges'.[120] The success of implementing colonial authority in the Honde Valley depended in the first place on claiming it as Rhodesian territory. A close examination of how the Manica frontier of the Anglo-Portuguese border, from 1898 known as the Barué Boundary,[121] was demarcated is crucial for three reasons. First, social memory in the area identifies the introduction of the border as an important turning point in the making of the Honde Valley as a borderland and a frontier area. Second, border practices were subversive, not least because when the colonial powers were still operating with spheres of influence and later, while the boundary was delineated, the border had already gained local meaning and uses. Third, the boundary commissioners provide the only written eyewitness accounts of the valley at the turn of the century. In addition, the border itself challenges the still commonly held view that African borders were determined in the metropole and especially the ever-persisting myth that Africa was partitioned at the notorious Berlin conference.[122]

The initial border agreement was the Anglo-Portuguese Convention of 1891 which stipulated that the border between Rhodesia and Portuguese East Africa should run along 'longitude 33° east of Greenwich';[123] hence the Honde Valley became part of Rhodesia. The Convention specifically stated that the line should 'be deflected so as to leave Mutassa [sic] in the British sphere'.[124] It was thus a de facto acknowledgement by the BSAC that Mutasa's rule did not extend much further east than the 33° longitude, or roughly the current border. Despite this Convention as well as the Anglo-Portuguese Delimitation Commission of 1892, the exact course of the boundary remained contested diplomatically and unclear on the ground. In 1896, the NC Umtali complained that the Portuguese were collecting tax and exercising jurisdiction on BSAC territory.[125] It is mainly because of this administrative ambiguity that the Leverson Boundary Commission was appointed in 1898 to demarcate the 'Barué Boundary' that stretched from the 18°30' south latitude, where Mount Panga bounds the Honde Valley to the south-east, to Mount Karera near the Mazoe River to the north. Boundary commissioner Julian Leverson reported that:

> The officials connected with the Department of Native Affairs were the ones most anxious to have the delimitation continued. They pointed out that at present there is a large district in which the position of the boundary is still quite unknown, and that consequently they cannot undertake the proper control and protection of the natives living on the British side of it, nor collect the hut tax.[126]

Leverson spent two weeks in the Honde Valley.[127] According to the 1891 Convention, the boundary commissioners were held to follow, where possible, 'natural' border lines such as rivers and mountain ridges, although they were not allowed to deviate from the longitude by more than ten kilometres. Hence, the border does not follow the Kaerezi River the whole way to its junction with the Ruenya, although the Honde Valley is in part demarcated to the east by Mount Zaramira and Mount Panga.[128]

The delimitation of the Barué Boundary was based on one beacon, pillar one at Mount Zaramira, which proved, however, to have been imprecisely measured. Therefore, in 1903, the Under-Secretary of State of the Colonial Office complained to the BSAC that the border was located too far to the west, although he conceded that the total area 'lost' due to this error was probably not 'more than 100 square miles'.[129] Nevertheless, lengthy negotiation with the Portuguese government ensued, culminating in a new boundary commission whose task it was to rectify the course of the border and to beacon it.[130] In 1905/06, the Barué Boundary Commission, consisting of three members, set about their task. The BSAP appointed Henry Y. Sawerthal of the Survey Department and the Portuguese government assigned two naval officers, Captain Neuparth, a hydrographer, and Lieutenant Xavier Cordeiro.[131] They spent three-and-a-half months in the Honde Valley and the adjacent area, starting from a camp on the left bank of the Honde River, near Mount Zaramira, on 30 May 1906. They then moved to the River Ruera in the north of the valley, from where they proceeded further to the Kaerezi River, finishing their task with a final meeting on Portuguese territory, in Massekesse on 24 September 1906.[132] The Barué Boundary Agreement, which minimally changed the earlier findings, was finally ratified in 1912 after protracted negotiations.[133]

In 1909, in reference to his work as boundary commissioner of the Barué section, Sawerthal wrote:

> It took me several days to search through the voluminous correspondence; checking of compilation and the plotting and c. [sic] of the data – but the chief delay in transmitting the paper has been caused by my ineptitude as a typewriter [sic]. It has been literally a labour after my last attack of fever and nerves on edge.[134]

It is not clear whether two years later Sawerthal's psychological state, his 'nerves on edge', were due to his experiences in the Honde Valley. However, his dispatches during this time do, to a certain degree, show him to be undone by local circumstances. Sawerthal paints a picture of an extreme frontier area whose inhabitants almost defeated the commissioners in fulfilling their task of applying scientific knowledge to an African landscape.

In 1898, Commissioner Leverson decided to leave most of his porters behind at a base camp near the Pungwe Falls when he proceeded into the Honde Valley, rather than to be dependent on a large supply of labour. As a result, he could report that his Portuguese colleagues had great difficulty in keeping pace due to problems with carriers: 'Owing to the difficulty of obtaining and feeding porters, it [the Portuguese escort] had been provided with wagons, and was trying to make a practicable road as it advanced.'[135] In March 1906, NC Umtali Hulley had warned Sawerthal that the closest his stores could be transported to the border by ox wagon would be twenty miles, if they were acquired via Darwin district, in the north-west. He predicted that two hundred carriers could be recruited, but only with difficulties, and firmly stated that there could be no more than sixty loads of sixty-pound bags. He concluded his letter ominously: 'From Zaramira North [it] is out of my district and I am not sorry.'[136] Despite the precedence of the earlier boundary commission and this advice, Sawerthal insisted on his own approach.

Sawerthal's work as boundary commissioner began well, with meticulous planning regarding the stores, which included everything a gentleman needed on such an excursion, such as Swiss powdered milk, although the wine and port were provided by his Portuguese colleagues. He listed his requirements precisely, as in the case of the northern part of the boundary for which he requested 'four camels to go between the Rivers Mazoe and Gaeresi; each camel to carry two water casks, wooden or iron, to be attached to their saddles and of fair weight when full; three horses fully equipped who are accustomed to the smell and sight of camels.'[137] Once in the field, however, Sawerthal found the environment hostile and eventually faced grave organisational problems as almost all of his African porters had deserted by July. Already then, the commissioner was concerned for the success of his mission, and he embarked on feverish correspondence with the NC. But the NC Inyanga insisted that he could not provide labour: 'Short of being forced, boys will not go to Sawerthal. I regret to put it so plainly but every boy I ask expresses distinct aversion for this work.'[138] In September, the Portuguese delegation was leaving for the coast, and of the approximately three hundred carriers with whom he had started out, Sawerthal was left with only twenty-two whom he had recruited only for 'short service'. The exact reasons for the desertions are not known, but considering the difficulty the NC had in recruiting anyone to do the required work, it appears likely that the refusal was due to a combination of factors that included the availability of higher paid and more prestigious mine labour opportunities on both sides of the border and a refusal to leave the plateau for the highly malaria-affected lower-lying areas.[139] Desperate, Sawerthal turned to the Surveyor General, whom he asked to organise sufficient carriers to save him from abandoning a total of 267 loads and his personal effects at the end of the survey.[140] The stores were finally recovered when tax defaulters were sent from Umtali and Mtoko districts.

In addition to the labour problem, Sawerthal was also concerned about the beacons, which he saw as the only guarantee of a permanent border on the ground: 'Provided, of course, that the 586 beacons will be kept in periodical repair and that the line which has been cut at such great trouble and expense through the thorn bush and timber belts will be kept cleared up, the Barué Boundary cannot be mistaken.'[141] However, in addition to the problems of maintenance, he feared sabotage and pilfering, as was common elsewhere:

2. 1905/06 Boundary Commission: 'Counting carriers before setting out on march, camp at Mount Zaramira' (Source: National Archives of Zimbabwe)

3. 1905/06 Boundary Commission: 'Carriers quitting camp near Pungwe Falls'
(Source: National Archives of Zimbabwe)

> It may be added here that when I was near the North Eastern boundary last August I found those beacons that I saw robbed of the iron piping and tin plates. I should therefore not be surprised to hear of the rest of the iron piping etc. having been abstracted similarly for use by the native distilleries or being turned into *assegai* or blunderbusses.[142]

Clearly, the boundary commissioner did not appreciate the local usages of the sought-after metal that marked the top of the beacons. In short, the described components of Sawerthal's experiences as boundary commissioner were the 'nerves on edge' caused by his dependency on African cooperation and the threat of seeing his scientific work undermined. He was further hampered by his imagination of the African wilderness as almost impenetrable and chaotic, representative of an imperial view of African landscapes – an aspect that will be examined in more detail in chapter three.

Sawerthal struggled to survey the area and to map the border. He emphasised that the lack of fix points challenged his scientific approach:

> The few huts near the border are constantly being changed for new abodes and even headmen shift about ever and anon as scarcity of crops compels them frequently to do. Roads or other notable features do not exist. It is therefore not possible to furnish fuller descriptions of the beacons such as is suggested on the interesting sheet extracted from the proof of the Niger–Chad Boundary Commission.[143]

Fix points such as streams, fruit trees, boulders, and riverbank gardens appear to have been invisible to the European surveyor's eye, but the border, even before and while it was in the process of being delineated, was visible to Africans, a fact well appreciated by some colonial administrators. In 1902, the NC Mtoko reported that given that there were 'no beacons defining the border and no maps showing the kraals and physical features of the route taken by the commissioners, one has to rely entirely on information given by natives'.[144] The NC thus conceded that he was 'entirely' dependent on African interpretations of the boundary. In 1908, the NC Mazoe reported his frustration when he observed that there were a number of tax evaders settling in the undeclared no man's land, and that he had to await the official demarcation before he could act.[145] As soon as there was a notion that a political border had been established, it was immediately put to good use by African men and women. Once the border was agreed upon by the two colonial powers, both struggled to enforce it on the ground.

BORDER APPROPRIATION

Various uses of the border became well-established, even before it was beaconed and then ratified in 1912. As early as 1899, the NC Inyanga reported that the inhabitants of the northern part of the Honde Valley were 'anxious' to know the exact borderline.[146] Vernacular appropriations manifested themselves in a range of patterns such as displacement, labour migration – which often resembled displacement because men were both driven to and chose to seek employment elsewhere – the continual crossing of the border, and simply ignoring it. With the movement of people came flows of goods, ideas, and also diseases. The reasons for these border uses in the Honde Valley were partly the absence of state

authority and partly differences between British and Portuguese colonial policies and practices that provided incentives for people to make strategic choices
on specific issues in favour of one territory. Among the most common border
uses in the years immediately before and after its ratification were tax evasion
and labour recruitment – both as flight from and in search of employment – as
well as flight from land rent, impending prosecution, drought, and war.

As soon as the Rhodesian government made its presence known on the
ground, individuals, groups, and entire chieftaincies chose to cross into Portuguese territory, although such migration also occurred in reverse. Boundary
commissioner Leverson had reported that during the 1892 delineation the eastern side of the border from Massekesse to the Chimanimani mountains was
almost uninhabited. Even taking into account that in some areas people might
have hidden from the commissioners or were still displaced from the *madzviti* raids, the sheer volume of border-crossing only a few years later indicates
that its establishment attracted people to move into the borderland.[147] As early
as 1902, residents of Portuguese East Africa moved onto Rhodesian territory in
Umtali district, and Chief Tangwena, whose headquarters had for some time
been located east of the border just north of the Honde Valley, attempted to
negotiate his move onto Rhodesian territory. In 1899, the NC Inyanga reported
that 'The paramount Chief Tangwena is most eager to belong to this territory
and complains to me of Portuguese Officers worrying him', but by 1906 he
had already returned with his people to Mozambique in order to avoid land
rent.[148]

One of the earliest recorded cases of the displacement of a chieftaincy
occurred in the Honde Valley. Chief Chikomba and most of his followers
crossed the border into Mozambique in 1904, apparently in order to avoid land
rent. Four years later, during the ongoing negotiation process with the colonial
administration, the chief told the NC Inyanga that he would be prepared to
return if his followers were exempt from paying the tax.[149] That same year the
NC reported that patrolling the district he found that, 'There are great stretch-
es of ground lying idle … the former residents having crossed the border into
Portuguese Territory.'[150] As late as 1925 Chief Chikomba's son complained that
his people were crossing the border to avoid land rent and dog tax.[151] In 1906,
the NC Inyanga estimated that in his district alone 14,820 people – 9,505 adults
and 5,315 children – had crossed the border in order to avoid the hut tax.[152]

Chiefs Chikomba, Tangwena, and Katerere negotiated with the colonial
states on behalf of their followers, but most cross-border movement was not as
organised, although it was cyclical. By 1906, seasonal tax evasion had become
common practice. Sawerthal, whose own carriers, together with other men in
the area, 'cleared' into Portuguese territory in order to avoid forced recruitment
for the unpopular work as well as to evade tax collection,[153] observed:

> Further I have to report that the absence of well-defined paths in the past, and the
> entangled state of the approaches to this part of the district, choked as they are with
> dangerous … creepers and abounding in swamps, has given the natives a sense of their
> security from interference from without, so much so that no sooner had the Chief
> Military Commandant of the Barué District moved away from the border, than hordes
> of British natives telling [sic] themselves safe from interference crossed into Portuguese
> territory to evade the tax-collection and the native census taking. I have ascertained that

this is an annual recurrence, to be repeated later on by Portuguese natives crossing into British territory in their efforts to elude the tax.[154]

Three years later, the NC Inyanga observed 'the usual emigration to Portuguese Territory by border natives' due to the impending tax collection.[155] In Umtali district, the NC found that chiefs and headmen, when informed that the tax would come into force, expressed 'dissatisfaction, and in some cases they said they would rather leave the territory than pay the tax. There will probably be some little difficulty in collecting the tax at the start.'[156] For the Honde Valley this pattern lasted at least into the 1930s.[157] In addition to avoiding land rent and hut tax, labour contract evasion also drew people across the border, or at least to the Honde Valley, an area almost beyond the colonial state's reach. It was a rare exception that a BSAP trooper spent four and a half weeks in the southern part of the valley in 1908, giving him the opportunity to arrest five deserters, whom he took back to Umtali, the provincial capital.[158] It was twenty years before another colonial official, NC Umtali Bazeley, would patrol the valley.[159]

Similarly, when the dog tax was introduced in January 1913, Africans either killed or hid their dogs, while those living close to the border 'sent their dogs to friends in Portuguese Territory'.[160] Indeed, the NC Inyanga had been 'informed' by residents of his district that they did not intend to pay the tax and warned him that they would rather kill their dogs, which would in turn have serious consequences for their livestock. When the NC refused to budge, they put their threat into effect.[161] Away from the border, hiding dogs could get people into trouble. In his nationalist memoirs, published at a crucial phase of the liberation war in 1972, Lawrence Vambe provides an emotional account of colonial violence during his childhood in Chishawasha, not far from Harare, that illustrates both the determination to go through with concealing their dogs, and also the dangers of tax evasion. He recalls that after the introduction of dog tax, which his family had not paid, a white policeman came by his grandparents' homestead. Only his grandmother had her wits sufficiently about her to go and lock all the dogs in one of the huts, but when they barked, her scheme was discovered, and the policeman humiliated the entire family and arrested his grandfather.[162] Other frequently reported uses of the border were attempts to escape prosecution, for example, in a number of murder cases, where alleged culprits took flight to Portuguese East Africa,[163] or where defendants were from east of the border.[164] There was at least one instance of avoiding arrest for alleged witchcraft practices through this action.[165]

Other uses of the border included economic transactions. With people, goods such as alcohol and drugs also crossed the border, which became important for three reasons. The first was illegal trade and smuggling.[166] In 1903, for example, there were suspicions that 'a professional gun thief' had stolen weapons from the BSAP camp at Inyanga and sold them to Chief Makombe, who needed arms for his resistance against colonial rule.[167] Cotton seed – unsuitable for high altitude areas – found its way into Inyanga district in 1924, and by the 1940s the NC suspected that gold was being sold in Mozambique.[168] Second, some traders from Portuguese Massekesse tried to take advantage by doing business over the border without having acquired a hawker's license, much 'to the detriment of the resident merchants.'[169] Finally, market disparity, such as food shortages in one territory, triggered cross-border trading.[170]

The border was not only actively appropriated, but it was also simply ignored, possibly most often through the practice of labour migration.[171] By 1915, local men refused to sign labour agreements to do farm work in Inyanga district, preferring to work in mines, where the wages were higher.[172] Initially, it became more common for men to seek employment in Mozambique, at least until World War I. Part of the attraction was probably the stronger bargaining position for men from Zimbabwe, not least because such workers' breach of contract could not be easily prosecuted by the Portuguese authorities. Already by 1907, however, the Rezende mine in Penhalonga, the southern part of the mamboship, was in full production.[173] There, in addition to employment for men, Mutasa women also generated cash income: they supplied the mines with food and charcoal.[174] The Mutasa area quickly became one of the sources of labour for South Africa too, and the Honde Valley was traversed by one of the migration routes connecting men, possibly from as far away as southern Tanzania, with South African mines and urban industries.[175] By 1924, a number of taxpayers from the Honde Valley were working in Johannesburg.[176] Other examples of the border being ignored include famine displacement and residential arrangements. As late as 1959, the PNC Manicaland complained that in the Honde Valley people resided on one side of the border, but ploughed on the other, and in the 1990s, some tea estate employees crossed the border daily, even though it was heavily mined at the time.[177]

In short, people, goods, and ideas moved across the border in times of crisis, both seasonally and as part of everyday life, using it as a tool to subvert or directly challenge the colonial state, which was limited by its bounded jurisdiction and fragile hegemony, or having that effect by simply ignoring the border.[178] At times, displacement followed patterns that had existed before colonial occupation, such as the search for a frontier area, possibly with new patrons. In this sense, the border areas were the true frontier of the Rhodesian state. On the other hand, for those people living close to it, the border brought not only a new set of opportunities, but also dangers of incursion, crime, and violence. The Honde Valley was not unique as a borderland, although its exceptional topography and climate, together with its frontier identity that had existed before the colonial border was established, made for a distinct frontier ethnicity. This identity was further shaped by the Makombe war of 1917 to 1920, referred to as the Barue Rebellion by the colonial powers.

The First War, 1917–1920

Elders remember the Makombe War as 'the first war' in the Honde Valley.[179] This underlines the argument that the *madzviti* of the nineteenth century were not primarily seen as warriors but as invaders or raiders.[180] At the same time, the war's prominent position in social memory indicates just how big an impact the immigration of refugees to the area had, especially as no fighting occurred in the valley itself. Instead, those who took flight from the conflict brought with them stories of violence that further shaped the valley's frontier ethnicity.

The origins of the Makombe War go back to 1916.[181] In that year, Portugal, which up to then had remained neutral, decided to join the Allied Powers in World War I, and deployed troops on the border between Mozambique and what then was German East Africa, as British and Belgian troops approached from the west and north. The demand for porters was tremendous, with up to 90,000 pulled into military service; meanwhile, recruitment for carriers and the army began in the Barwe area. Wachimanyika, who collected oral histories in the Mutasa area at the time, included a fresh account of the grievances this caused: with young men being forcibly recruited, the *sepoi*, the colonial police, coerced the remaining men, boys, young girls and women into forced labour, to do the most unpopular work, such as road construction. In addition to the harsh labour regime, the spark to anti-colonial resistance was frequent instances of prepubescent girls being raped. When Barwe elders complained to Fereta, a Portuguese official, he then gave the order to his men to rape the girls in front of their fathers.[182] Sexual violence had been prevalent in the years leading up to the conflict, but the raping of and physical damage to young girls, including fistulas as a result of the injuries they sustained – the youngest, for example, were cut open to allow penetration – were unprecedented. The implications this had for the entire kin group caused the suffering that sparked the war.[183] Finally, there were also reports that once the counter-insurgency campaign started, the auxiliary troops took women and children captive which further aggravated the grievances. As one of the refugee women testified: 'the Ngoni auxiliaries took her daughters of ten and twelve years old and her four-year-old son to "make them slaves in our own land"'.[184] The sexual atrocities were so severe that the Rhodesian colonial government came to despise the Portuguese even more deeply, which might explain the relatively generous treatment of Barwe refugees.[185]

The war began in March 1917, a year after the northern frontier opened. According to Reid, Chiefs Tangwena and Makombe had struck a marriage alliance, and it was Makombe's son by Tangwena's daughter who rose against the Portuguese in 1917.[186] By May 1918, during the final phase of the war, the Barwe leader had in fact sought refuge with his family in the Tangwena area.[187] The sheer scale of the conflict, with up to 15,000 rebels, was due to the insurgents having formed a broad alliance between the contestants in the Barwe succession and with their followers, spirit mediums, and 'big men' who operated at the periphery of colonial society.[188] However, when the Portuguese recruited as many as 30,000 Ngoni men to suppress the uprising, the conflict was ended with the utmost brutality towards the end of 1917. It was, however, followed by another year of fighting on the northern border between Rhodesia and Mozambique, with skirmishes into the 1920s, as most of the rebels had retreated across the border and thus had a vantage point from which to continue with attacks.

Initially, the refugees appear to have moved in order to escape the violence and the danger of conscription; next, the punitive expeditions of 1917 sent many across the border; and finally, between April and September 1918, many fled the famine caused by drought and the scorched-earth tactics of the Portuguese colonial army.[189] From the end of 1919 onwards, refugee numbers rose again due to renewed repressive measures by the Portuguese.[190] In Inyanga district most of the able-bodied males registered with the NC and left the area in order to engage in migrant labour.[191] Despite the rapid absorption of many Mozambican men into the colonial economy, the refugees caused the administration logistical problems, as many of the women and children had to be issued with rations. As early as August 1917, the NC Inyanga reported:

> During the month a considerable number of Natives from Portuguese Territory took refuge in this district. They arrived without food or property of any kind. They stated that their kraals and crops had all been destroyed during the fighting, and they were anxious to settle in some part of this district which is not too cold. It was found necessary to issue them with rations at this station pending some arrangements for their disposal.[192]

Throughout the war, women and children found themselves caught between the danger of being captured by auxiliaries, 'the hostage system' as Portuguese officials called it, or by rebel groups.[193] In May 1917, a group of ten women and twenty-five men – apparently elders – and children who had fled the Makombe warriors arrived in Darwin district. One woman testified that they had become separated from the men because they could not run as fast when the rebels arrived. The women were all captured, taking the risk of being killed, as she had witnessed happen to others; they managed to flee after five days in captivity.[194] Indian store-owners suffered looting by the rebels and some also sought refuge on Rhodesian territory. One Indian refugee testified that he had been a captive for a while and saw a man and a woman with her small child brutally murdered after they tried to escape: 'They gave as their reasons for this that those who were not with them were against them and if [they] were allowed to travel through the country unmolested – they would inform against the rebels.'[195] Overall, refugee testimony paints a clear picture of the vulnerability of women and children who, when attacks occurred from either side, were usually abandoned by the men.[196]

The Makombe war is still remembered in the Honde Valley, and not only by descendants of refugees. This is partly due to the influx of people during the first distinct immigration wave, which imprinted itself in social memory. An estimated 100,000 people fled the war from Mozambique to neighbouring countries and many followed until the mid-1920s.[197] Of the 13,000 refugees in Zimbabwe, in Inyanga district alone there were estimated to be 4,000 by June 1918, with more still arriving.[198] The actual numbers in the district were probably much higher, as the refugees tended to settle in difficult terrain close to the border. In Chief Katerere's area, those displaced people who decided to stay after the war allegedly outnumbered the local population.[199] In mid-1918, the CNC suggested that the refugees should be permanently settled in Chikore Reserve in Makoni district or two areas along the border in Inyanga district, one in the northern part of the Honde Valley. He recognised the difficulty this would cause in terms of controlling this population and in helping them to seek work in the Penhalonga area because the valley was so remote.[200]

Throughout the border region, some refugees were displaced temporarily, others permanently. In the Honde Valley most chose to stay, and up to the 1950s chiBarwe, Makombe's language, was still commonly spoken there.[201] This wave of immigration reshaped power relations in the valley: some refugees even became *masabhuku*, although the majority of them strengthened the position of those already in power by becoming their followers.[202] It appears, however, that some refugee families remained in close contact with each other and retained a sense of their place of origin. Their descendants moved back into Mozambique during the Second Chimurenga but later returned.[203]

The Makombe war was particularly brutal and is remembered as such.[204] One of the refugee's sons contended that it was 'total war'.[205] The immigrants brought stories of violence with them that shaped local perceptions of such experiences, even though there was a clear notion that the war was fought elsewhere. An elder explained: 'We were not affected here, but it brought untold suffering in Mozambique.'[206] The displaced, however, found only relative safety in their refuge and this possibly also affected their new neighbours. Short-distance displacement proved dangerous, especially when refugees attempted to play both sides. For example, four women and their children who returned to Mozambique in 1917 in order to recover food they had left behind were captured by Portuguese troops.[207] Incursions aimed at punishing the refugee communities took place, such as in 1925, when Portuguese colonial troops raided a group of fifty families in the Honde Valley for their foodstuffs in retaliation for avoiding labour conscription.[208] These border uses illustrate the ambiguity of the frontier area that provides a livelihood between danger and opportunity. Still, if borderland residents are prone to experience violence, why then have people chosen to settle there? It appears that a great advantage of life in the valley has been the relative ease with which newcomers have been incorporated into local communities.

The Making of a Frontier Society

John Lonsdale's theorem of 'moral ethnicity' and 'political tribalism' as the inner and outer architecture of political identity provides a sophisticated framework through which to understand the Honde Valley's frontier identity. Political tribalism is situational; it usually arises from competition with other groups over resources.[209] This became important for male Honde Valley residents at the beginning of the twentieth century, when waged employment required them to hold an identity card that indicated their tribal affiliation. Soon it emerged that employers preferred Manyika men over most other 'tribes' for higher paid and more prestigious jobs, such as cooks and mine labour, because of their reputation within colonial society of reliability and relative cultural sophistication.[210] It is the inner architecture of identity, though, that truly made the frontier ethnicity in the valley, an ethnicity that was negotiated along the axes of gender, age, and knowledge.[211]

According to Lonsdale, moral ethnicity is universal and processual, in the sense of being debated over time, though often expressed in terms of tradition and custom. This ethnicity is articulated in a society's civic virtue and reflects 'the common human instinct to create out of the daily habits of intercourse and material labour a system of moral meaning and ethical reputation'.[212] Hence, what makes a member of a given group valuable is assessed in terms of practice and discourse.[213] This study examines the valley's frontier ethnicity through time in those terms, and to do so in particular during periods of stress arising from conflict and violence. This chapter has traced the historical genesis of this specific frontier ethnicity and its emergence as a borderland. What remains to be addressed is why people would move into such a potentially dangerous area and how the frontier identity remained stable as people moved in and out of the valley.

William Shack has pointed out that access to power is crucial in determining the structural position of strangers, 'power' being defined as the 'competition for and the exercise of control over political and economic resources'.[214] In agricultural societies, environmental resources are particularly important in this context. Usable land in the Honde Valley was available until the late 1970s and hence could be freely allocated by chiefs in order to strengthen their following without causing scarcity and thus competition with other inhabitants. Reciprocity could be achieved relatively easily given the constant demand for human labour to work the area's great agricultural potential. One option was, and is, for women to work on the chief's fields (*zunde*) in order to produce grain for rain rituals and for drought stocks for the community. The statistics on the Makombe War refugees are not conclusive, but it seems that the majority were women, and the gendered practice of labour contribution through working the *zunde* might well have facilitated the incorporation of women compared to men, with the former possibly seeking male patrons.[215]

Also, the unique agricultural potential and the abundance of fruit made it easy for refugees from war and drought to settle. In that sense an elder claimed: 'What caused an influx of people is the free way some settled here.'[216] He explained that his father, a Makombe refugee, had decided to stay rather than to return home or to move on.[217] At the same time, it was significant that before the forced resettlement of large numbers of households into the valley after 1948 the number of immigrants at any one time was relatively small, with the sole exception of the Makombe refugees. The smallness of scale in relation to the resources available was a factor in the successful absorption of newcomers.[218] In addition, the relative remoteness from centralised political authority, that is, the colonial state and the mamboship headquarters, allowed for relative local autonomy. A returning migrant labourer, for example, could become a 'big man',[219] and a war refugee could become a *sabhuku* due to lax administrative control and, paradoxically, the government's need for willing agents of centralised power. With so much fluidity regarding population movement, and the apparently ever-changing character of communities, the question arises as to what made for continuity and social cohesion in this frontier society.

Eric Allina-Pisano conducted his research on the history of the Manyika area and the emerging colonial economy on the Mozambican side of the border. He came to the conclusion that Manyika identity was rooted in place rather than through kinship, although he concedes that a sense of belonging to the community was also important.[220] Valley inhabitants answered in the same manner, but this study comes to almost the opposite conclusion: allegiance and belonging relate primarily to the chieftaincy, not to the land. In fact, when somebody from the valley says 'I come from Zindi' (or Chikomba, or Muparutsa), they are making a spatial reference to where, at that given point of time, the chieftaincy, whether the chief or his contestant and his or her followers, resided – something that, as has been shown above, changed frequently in the early colonial period, at least for people along the border. It is all too easily forgotten, as Eric Worby has pointed out,[221] that part of the colonial tribalisation effort was spatialising identity. It cannot be denied that colonial knowledge and its production affected people on the ground, but one would be mistaken, as the history of the colonial border clearly shows, to assume that such delineation reflected or directly shaped people's identities. The argument here is not to disregard the importance of place. On the contrary, vernacular knowledge of agricultural, spiritual, and historical landscape is a significant part of frontier ethnicity and the sense of belonging. The traditional claims to land for settlement as it unfolded during the colonial era, with the Tangwena chieftaincy possibly the best-known case in Zimbabwe,[222] provide useful examples. It is clear that these were political arguments, not much different from de Souza alleging that Mutasa's gift of an elephant tusk meant his submission, a theme that will be further explored in chapter three. Regarding moral ethnicity, however, such claims to unalienable land, and even ancestral graves, are contradicted by spatial practices in Africa before, during, and after colonialism.[223] The relationship between spiritual landscape and belonging is more complex and will also be discussed in later chapters.

Until the 1990s at the very least, any immigrant in the Honde Valley who was prepared to acquire the vernacular knowledge necessary to meet the expectations of civic virtue and thus to become a reputable and valuable member of the community was made welcome. This entailed following certain rules regarding ritual prohibitions and land use patterns, and showing allegiance to the local chief who allocates the land.[224] Men were expected also to acquire the area's social memory and gendered practices because, with few exceptions, chiefs allocated land use rights only to men, and the immigrants became intimately connected to the spiritual and social wellbeing of the entire community. Such a mode of incorporation is not static, even though it might be articulated in a discourse of tradition. In this frontier area, moreover, the potential for innovation and change appears to have been especially pronounced, as Martin Lewis and Kären Wigen more broadly suggest: 'Historical border zones in particular have acquired unexpected prominence as sites of cultural innovation.'[225]

The incorporation of newcomers was so successful that differences of origin and ethnic delineation quickly become irrelevant within the communities, remaining merely reference points for individual and family identity. As an elder explained:

I am muUngwe [from Makoni], but I am now referred to as Manyika. [laughter] Because my grandfathers were born here, where they lie buried.

H.S.: So you can change?

This was possible when the white people ran the country, and if you told them you do not want to be referred to as Manyika, they wrote down your tribe as muUngwe. The white people accepted this …. I am also educating my children that we are not Manyika, but MuUngwe. I also teach them of our history, and how we came to settle here.[226] [laughter]

H.S.: Why did people who come to settle in the Honde Valley refer to themselves as Manyika?

One reason is that if the person is from Mozambique and he continuously calls himself that, he is jeered at by the locals, who call him muBarwe or muSena. So, in order for him to see himself as their equal, he says he is Manyika …. It is not possible for one to boast that one and one's family are from Mozambique. You cannot stay in other people's land by continuously boasting in that way. It is impossible. You have got to find a name that makes you identical with the rest.[227]

This same elder described how easy it was to manipulate the colonial state and emphasised that immigrants had to adapt, to become 'identical with the rest', in order 'to live in peace.' Although they might change their cultural practices and assimilate, the elder insisted on the importance of retaining a core identity as an individual and family through one's totem and through passing the family history on to younger generations. Thus, the name changed but the totem remained the same. At times, this ethnic ambivalence of the frontier society resurfaced, such as when there was need for spiritual healing that would only be successful if the 'real' totem is known.[228]

The success of the valley's frontier ethnicity in retaining its attraction to immigrants over a long period of time, despite the strain that life on the frontier entailed, is astonishing. Political competition did arise in the nationalist period of the 1950s and 1960s among the valley population, but, as will be shown later, even during the Second Chimurenga and the RENAMO War, internal tensions rarely caused violence. Nonetheless, underneath the shared moral ethnicity and social memory lies family memory, as the elder pointed out. Identity and belonging must therefore be understood as layered and interwoven, though at times, particularly in the sphere of spiritual manifestations, practices and narratives, events, experiences, and symbolic displays may threaten to tear that social fabric.

Conclusion

The frontier identity in the Honde Valley today is shaped in part by the memory of its beginnings: the role of the area as a buffer zone for the mamboship and the first significant violence experienced during the intrusions by the warrior parties from the Gaza state. The valley evolved into a frontier area during the nineteenth century, and its local identity and way of life were significantly transformed under the rule of *mambo* Tendai that bridged the turning point between the late pre-colonial and early colonial periods, when the boundaries and significance of the mamboship were redefined. External influences shaped this process, especially the imposition of colonial rule, which initially showed its imprint with the delineation of 'traditional authorities', tax collection, and the demarcation of the colonial border. By the mid-1920s, the valley had become the settler state's frontier through its absorption of large refugee populations from Makombe and its continuing inaccessibility to, and thus lack of legibility and governance by, the Rhodesian side.

Throughout the twentieth century the Honde Valley provided an environment open to newcomers that allowed its inhabitants to negotiate their lives between dangers and opportunities specific to a frontier area, a zone located on the margins of central political power. The Honde Valley shows that despite the suffering such developments cause, fluidity, rupture, and dislocation can signify the strength of African societies, in this case a distinct frontier identity that requires a shared moral ethnicity rather than the multiplicity that population fluctuation might suggest. A complex historical process located between danger and opportunity that also included the introduction of the colonial border shaped this frontier ethnicity along the axes of gender, age, and knowledge. Young women's particular vulnerability during conflict and the pinnacle of female political and spiritual power under *mambo* Tendai's rule, young male power asserted through the roles of warriors, colonial soldiers, or migrant labourers, and the elders' gendered vernacular knowledge were all significant building blocks in the making of this identity. The following chapter examines what happened when African and European pioneers, seeking the frontier as atavistic wilderness beyond civilisation, moved into the valley in the early 1930s.

Notes

1 'Family' and 'household' are both imprecise terms that tend to imply a western lens; here they will nevertheless be used to loosely refer to household communities and kinship groups. There has been a significant anthropological debate about the concepts. For historical treatment, see Shula Marks and Richard Rathbone (eds), 'The History of the Family in Africa', special issue, *Journal of African History*, 24, no. 2 (1983); Megan Vaughan, 'Household Units and Historical Process in Southern Malawi', *Review of African Political Economy*, no. 34 (Dec. 1985), pp. 35-45.

2 Interview #84.

3 For the terminology of 'frontier', 'border', and 'boundary', see Michiel Baud and Willem van Schendel, 'Toward a Comparative History of Borderlands', *Journal of World History*, 8, no. 2 (1997), p. 213. See also Igor Kopytoff, 'The Internal African Frontier: The Making of African Political Culture', *The African Frontier: The Reproduction of Traditional African Societies*, Igor Kopytoff (ed.) (Bloomington, IN, 1987), p. 9; Anthony Cohen, 'Boundaries of Consciousness, Consciousness of Boundaries: Critical Questions for Anthropology,' *The Anthropology of Ethnicity: Beyond 'Ethnic Groups and Boundaries'*, Hans Vermeulen and Cora Govers (eds) (Amsterdam, 1994), pp. 59-79.

4 The notion of the frontier as a process dates back to the 1960s. See Ray Billington, 'The American Frontier', *Beyond the Frontier: Social Process and Cultural Change*, Paul Blog and Fred Bohannan (eds) (Garden City, NY, 1967), p. 7, passim; also Robert Berkhofer, 'The North American Frontier as Process and Context', *The Frontier in History: North America and Southern Africa Compared*, Howard Lamar and Leonard Thompson (eds) (New Haven, CT, 1981), pp. 43-75; David Cherry, *Frontier and Society in Roman North Africa* (Oxford, 1998). Hal Langfur examines indigenous meaning and practice of the colonial frontier in eighteenth-century Brazil, albeit without a border, in *The Forbidden Lands: Colonial Identity, Frontier Violence, and the Persistence of Brazil's Eastern Indians, 1750–1830* (Stanford, CA, 2006).

5 Interview #85.

6 See interview #133.

7 Frederick Turner, 'The Significance of the Frontier in American History (1893)', *History, Frontier, and Section: Three Essays by Frederick Jackson Turner* (Albuquerque, NM, 1993), pp. 59-91 and *The Frontier in American History* (New York, 1920).

8 Kopytoff provides an Africanist critique of Turner's frontier thesis; 'The Internal African Frontier,' pp. 12-16. For a comparative volume on African and American frontiers, see, Howard Lamar and Leonard Thompson (eds), *The Frontier in History: North America and Southern Africa Compared* (New Haven, CT, 1981).

9 Kopytoff, 'The Internal African Frontier,' pp. 3-84.

10 Hermann Giliomee, *The Afrikaners: The Biography of a People* (Charlottesville, VA, 2003), Carolyn Hamilton, *The Mfecane Aftermath: Reconstructive Debates in Southern African History* (Johannesburg, 1995); see also Jeremy Foster, *Washed with Sun: Landscape and the Making of White South Africa* (Pittsburgh, PA, 2008), Laura Mitchell, *Belongings: Property, Family and Identity in Colonial South Africa (An Exploration of Frontiers, 1725-c. 1830)* (New York, 2009).

11 Samuel Huntington, 'The Clash of Civilizations?' *Foreign Affairs*, 72, no. 3 (1993), pp. 22-49.

[12] For other Zimbabwean frontier societies, see David McDermott Hughes, *From Enslavement to Environmentalism: Politics on a Southern African Frontier* (Seattle, WA, 2006), Pius Nyambara, 'Ethnic Identities and the Culture of Modernity in a Frontier Region: The Gokwe District of Northwestern Zimbabwe, 1963-79', *Movements, Borders, and Identities in Africa*, Toyin Falola and Aribidesi Usman (eds) (Rochester, NY, 2009), pp. 200-25. A substantial study on violence on the border and frontier in the US in the eighteenth and nineteenth centuries is James Brooks, *Captives & Cousins: Slavery, Kinship, and Community in the Southwest Borderlands* (Chapel Hill, NC, 2002). For the US-Mexican border and current debate, see Samuel Truett and Elliott Young, 'Making Transnational History: Nations, Regions, and Borderlands', *Continental Crossroads: Remapping U.S.-Mexico Borderlands History*, Samuel Truett and Elliott Young (eds) (Durham, NC, 2004), pp. 1-32, Kathleen Staudt, *Violence and Activism at the Border: Gender, Fear and Everyday Life in Ciudad Juárez* (Austin, TX, 2008).

[13] 'Warlord' is here understood as an entrepreneur who uses violence as a means to economic ends in areas beyond state control. Ironically, these Portuguese men were at the same time representatives of the Portuguese government and some, such as de Souza, became Africanized. Georg Elwert, 'Markets of Violence', 'Dynamics of Violence: Processes of Escalation and De-Escalation in Violent Group Conflicts', Georg Elwert et al. (eds) *Sociologus* suppl. no. 1 (1999), pp. 85-102; Malyn Newitt, *Portuguese Settlement on the Zambezi* (London, 1973), p. 313, Allen Isaacman with Barbara Isaacman, *The Tradition of Resistance in Mozambique* (Berkeley, CA, 1976), pp. 28-30, 49, Allen Isaacman, *Mozambique: The Africanization of a European Institution, The Zambezi Prazos 1750–1902* (Madison, WI, 1972), Malyn Newitt, 'The Portuguese on the Zambezi: An Historical Interpretation of the Prazo System', *Journal of African History*, 10, no. 1 (1969), pp. 67-85.

[14] For the early Portuguese presence in Mozambique, see Newitt, *Portuguese Settlement on the Zambezi*.

[15] Interview #111.

[16] For a classic study on colonial knowledge, see Bernard Cohn, *Colonialism and Its Forms of Knowledge: The British in India* (Princeton, NJ, 1996). For missionary knowledge in the wider region, see Patrick Harries, *Butterflies and Barbarians: Swiss Missionaries and Systems of Knowledge in South-East Africa* (Oxford, 2007).

[17] The Mutasa succession disputes somewhat resemble Edna Bay's portrayal of political power in Dahomey in the eighteenth century. Edna Bay, *Wives of the Leopard: Gender, Politics, and Culture in the Kingdom of Dahomey* (Charlottesville, VA, 1998), p. 7.

[18] Interview #6. For an account of the *mambo* insisting on being addressed as king, see interviews #42 and 148, conducted with a senior civil servant.

[19] Interview #6.

[20] NC Inyanga to PNC, 20 February 1956, boxnumber 103986, NRC.

[21] The article states that it is based on information from Chimbadzwa elders. 'Thousands Prepare to Fete Their New Chief', *Sunday Mail*, 18 April 1982. For a brief account of how Abishai Mutasa staked his claim, see Anita Jacobson-Widding, *Chapungu: The Bird That Never Drops A Feather, Male and Female Identities in an African Society* (Uppsala, 2002), pp. 57-9.

[22] There is some evidence that the Makombe paramountcy had already shaped the political and economic situation from the late fifteenth century. H.H.K. Bhila, *Trade and Politics in a Shona Kingdom: The Manyika and their Portuguese and African Neighbours 1575–1902* (Burnt Mill, 1982), pp. 4, 12-13, 124-8; Stan Mudenge, *A Political History of Munhumutapa c.1400–1902* (Harare, 1988), p. 49. There is, however, no reference to these earlier relations in the Machiwenyika manuscript. Jason Machiwenyika, 'The History and Customs of the Manyika People and Manyika', MA/14/1/2, NAZ. Not much is known about Machiwenyika. A convert to Christianity, he worked at the Mission Press at Old Umtali, the first Methodist Episcopal mission station in Zimbabwe and located in Mutasa's area. He recorded Manyika oral traditions and historical knowledge in chiManyika between the 1900s and 1920s until his death in 1922. His work was translated into English in 1943. The original manuscript was destroyed, but the transcripts were deposited in the NAZ in 1945.

[23] Lessons 24 and 111, Machiwenyika.

[24] Bhila, *Trade and Politics*, pp. 199, 222-7; Isaacman with Isaacman, *The Tradition of Resistance*, pp. 49-57; Newitt, *Portuguese Settlement*, p. 314. David Beach disagreed on de Souza's hegemony, see *The Origins of Moçambique and Zimbabwe: Paiva de Andrada, the Companhia de Moçambique and African Diplomacy 1881-91*, History Seminar Paper, 89 (Harare: University of Zimbabwe, 1992), p. 11. For de Souza's biography, see Newitt, *Portuguese Settlement*, pp. 312-4 and *A History of Mozambique* (Bloomington, IN, 1995), pp. 288-90; Bhila, *Trade and Politics*, pp. 216-30. For the period between de Souza's arrest and his death, see Leroy Vail and Landeg White, *Capitalism and Colonialism in Mozambique: A Study of Quelimane District* (London, 1980), pp. 108-12.

[25] Lesson 109, Machiwenyika.

26 Bhila, *Trade and Politics*, pp. 223-7, 244-6.

27 Ibid., pp. 239-42; also David Beach, *War and Politics in Zimbabwe 1840–1900* (Gweru, 1986), pp. 132, 148. For a different interpretation, see Terence Ranger, *Revolt in Southern Rhodesia 1896-7: A Study in African Resistance* (London, 1967), p. 197.

28 For more detail on chieftainesses, see Heike Schmidt, *Muredzwa Superwoman: Mapping Areas of Female Power in the Mutasa Mamboship, Eastern Zimbabwe*, Institute of Commonwealth Studies Collected Seminar Papers (London 1993). Jacobson-Widding, in her study of gender in the mamboship, *Chapungu*, misses the important political roles women have and continue to play.

29 Inyanga District, Monthly Reports, March 1904, N9/4/18, NAZ, Shepherd Machuma, 'Treatment of Women and Their Role in the Society', ca. 1970, boxfile 275, shelf d, north wall, OMMA. For more detail, see Schmidt, *Muredzwa*.

30 Interview #80.

31 Bhila, *Trade and Politics*, pp. 244; 225-7, 232; Beach, *The Origins*, pp. 45-51.

32 Bhila, *Trade and Politics*, pp. 232-44. For a detailed account of the partition, mostly from British sources, see Philip Warhurst, *Anglo-Portuguese Relations in South-Central Africa 1890–1900* (London, 1962), chapter one. For the complementary perspective by one of the participants in the scramble, see Joaquim Paiva de Andrada, *Report and Protest of the Affairs Occurred at Manica* (Cape Town, 1891), *Manica: Being a Report Addressed to the Minister of the Marine and the Colonies of Portugal* (London, 1891); also Eric Axelson, *Portugal and the Scramble for Africa, 1875–1891* (Johannesburg, 1967), pp. 232-42.

33 For a conservative estimate of Mutasa's area and the trade connections, see Eric Allina-Pisano, 'Negotiating Colonialism: Africans, the State, and the Market in Manica District, Mozambique, 1835-1935' (PhD thesis, Yale University, 2002), pp. 33-5, 42.

34 Bhila, *Trade and Politics*, p. 234.

35 BSAC Administrator, Manica Reports, A1/6/1-2, NAZ.

36 Newitt, *Portuguese Settlement*, p. 314.

37 Beach, *The Origins*, p. 43.

38 Interview #80.

39 'Mutasa and Gouveia', n.d., RP.

40 Bhila, *Trade and Politics*, p. 226. De Souza was married according to customary law to at least one of Chief Makombe's daughters. BSAC Administrator, Manica Reports, A1/6/1-2, NAZ. Even during a visit as important as the one in 1890 that led to his arrest, de Souza was accompanied by a woman, this time apparently Goanese and also carried in a *machila*. Andrada, *Manica*, 14.

41 Newitt, *Portuguese Settlement*, p. 330-1.

42 Interview #84. Allina-Pisano emphasises the connection the mamboship had via the Zambezi with the Indian Ocean trading system through the export of gold. 'Negotiating Colonialism', pp. 33-5.

43 Bhila, *Trade and Politics*, pp. 22-3; PER5 Chief Mutasa, PAO and DAO; Appointment of Chief Mutasa of the Manyika Tribe, box number 57577, NRC; Machuma, 'Treatment of Women'.

44 Interview #6.

45 Chiefs Mponda, Nyamaende, Sanyanga, and Sanyamandwe occupied the fringes of the Honde Valley. Lessons 89, 91, and 110, Machiwenyika; 'Sanyanga', 5 August 1977 and 'The vaManyika', RP; also Bhila, *Trade and Politics*, pp. 176, 185.

46 Lesson 112, Machiwenyika; Selwyn Bazeley, 'Manyika Headwomen', *NADA*, 7 (1940), pp. 3-5; Rose Blennerhassett and Lucy Sleeman, *Adventures in Mashonaland* (London, 1893), pp. 131-4; Bhila, *Trade and Politics*, pp. 16, 23.

47 Lesson 111, Machiwenyika. Missionary Sells claimed that Muparutsa was Tendai's older brother. Reverend E. Sells, 'The History of Manicaland Rhodesia 1832–1897,' 1969, box file 44, north wall, shelf a, OMMA. For a different view, see Michael Gelfand, *The Spiritual Beliefs of the Shona: A Study Based on Field Work among the East-Central Shona* (Gwelo, 1977), pp. 14-15; also 'The vaManyika', RP.

48 Bhila, *Trade and Politics*, p. 23, J. G. Storry, 'The Settlement and Territorial Expansion of the Mutasa Dynasty', *Rhodesian History* 7 (1976), pp. 26-7.

49 Bhila, *Trade and Politics*, p. 16.

50 Interviews #10, #11, #31, #6; also Shepherd Machuma, 'Persons: Life History of Joshua Muredzwa', file 262, shelf d, north wall, OMMA.

51 Andrada, *Manica*, p. 14; interviews #132 and #43, with a forester.

52 Interviews #10, #19. During the late colonial period, the state's understanding was that *muzvare* Muparutsa had a *dunhu* (chieftaincy area) at Mahemasimike with five to eight 'kraals'. Family Tree Muparutsa, 11 December 1965, PER5 Chiefs and Headmen, DAO.

53 Interview #136 with a female Muparutsa elder.

54 Interview #10.

55 Bhila dates the first incursion to 1832, albeit only based on one group interview. Bhila, *Trade and Politics*, p. 176. Liesegang dates raids in the area to the early 1830s, but proposes that those were likely to be Ngoni groups on their way further north and not warrior parties sent from the Gaza state. Gerhard Liesegang, 'Nguni Migrations Between Delagoa Bay and the Zambezi, 1821–1839', *African Historical Studies*, 3, no. 2 (1970), p. 321; also Newitt, *A History of Mozambique*, p. 296. Sells identifies the end of the raiding as 1888., 'The History of Manyikaland,' p. 4.Andrada claimed he had observed that raids had ceased in 1881, see 'Captain Paiva de Andrada's Zambesi Expedition, 1881', *Proceedings of the Royal Geographical Society and Monthly Record of Geography*, New Monthly Series, 4, no. 6 (1882), p. 374; also Malyn Newitt, 'Drought in Mozambique 1823–1831', *Journal of Southern African Studies*, 15, no. 1 (1988), pp. 15-35.

56 Bhila, *Trade and Politics*, p. 188; also pp. 169-91, 216-30; Newitt, *A History of Mozambique*, pp. 256-62, 290-7, 348-52, 357; Douglas Wheeler, 'Gungunyane the Negotiator: A Study in African Diplomacy', *Journal of African History*, 9, no. 4 (1968), pp. 586-7; John Rennie, 'Christianity, Colonialism and the Origins of Nationalism among the Ndau of Southern Rhodesia 1890–1935' (PhD thesis, Northwestern University, 1973), pp. 135-64; Allen and Barbara Isaacman, *Mozambique: From Colonialism to Revolution* (Boulder, CO, 1983), pp. 18, 23-4. For an older but still useful study of the Gaza state, see Gerhard Liesegang, 'Beiträge zur Geschichte des Reiches der Gaza Nguni im Südlichen Moçambique 1820–1895' (PhD thesis, University of Köln), 1968.

57 Gerhard Liesegang, 'Notes on the Internal Structure of the Gaza Kingdom of Southern Mozambique, 1840–1895', *Before and after Shaka: Papers in Nguni History*, Jeffrey Peires (ed.) (Grahamstown, 1981), pp. 178-209; Rennie, *Christianity, Colonialism*, pp. 144-52.

58 M. Hannan, *Standard Shona Dictionary* (1959; repr. Harare, 1987). The term *madzviti* was used in areas raided by Ngoni groups, albeit recorded in a range of spellings. Newitt talks of *Maviti* or *Machiti* for the Manica area; 'Drought in Mozambique', p. 25. MacGonagle encountered the terms *madzviti* and *mabziti* in interviews in the chiNdau-speaking border region of Zimbabwe, see Elizabeth MacGonagle, *Crafting Identity in Zimbabwe and Mozambique* (Rochester, NY, 2007), pp. 96, 102. Karl Weule used the terms *Maviti* and *Mazitu* in his early twentieth-century account of southern Tanzania, *Negerleben in Ostafrika: Ergebnisse einer ethnologischen Forschungsreise* (Leipzig, 1908), p. 150.

59 In the context of nineteenth-century raiding, sources use the ethnic labels 'Shangaan' and 'Ndebele' frequently and interchangeably, although the mamboship was never raided by the Ndebele state. Lesson 20, Machiwenyika; interviews #6, #125; also interview #111, Bhila, *Trade and Politics*, pp. 93-115.

60 *A Standard Swahili–English Dictionary* (1939; repr. Oxford: Oxford University Press, 1990).

61 Interview #80. This view differs significantly from Bhila, who claimed that 'Manyika–Nguni relations were, by and large, cordial'. Bhila, *Trade and Politics*, p. 191. For Ngoni raids in the Mutasa area see also Liesegang, 'Nguni Migrations', pp. 321, 329.

62 Interview #125. Another elder explained that the *mambo* often succeeded in appeasing the *madzviti* by paying tribute in cattle, but that they also took women whom 'they wanted to have as their wives'. Interview #80; see also NC Umtali, 'History of the Natives in the Umtali District', 19 January 1904, N3/33/8, NAZ.

63 Lesson 20, Machiwenyika.

64 Ibid.

65 Lesson 21, Machiwenyika.

66 Interview #39.

67 Hannan, *Standard Shona Dictionary*; also lesson 21, Machiwenyika and 'How the Shangaans Came to Manicaland', n.d., RP.

68 According to Bhila, in response to the first *madzviti* raid, 'the Manyika people' devised a warning system and a 'poisoning strategy' in Chief Sanyatwe's and Chief Sakarombe's areas. Bhila, *Trade and Politics*, p. 176.

69 Interview #3. For a different version of the same oral tradition, see, 'The vaManyika', RP.

70 Ibid.

71 Interview #80. According to Bhila, people hid in the hills throughout the mamboship. *Trade and Politics*, pp. 175, 185.

72 Interview #4.

73 George Williamson and Co. Nairobi, Report on Inyanga Block, Eastern District, Southern Rhodesia, 1952; H.O. Thomas, 'Report on the Tea-Growing Possibilities of the Inyanga Block', Nairobi, 23 October 1952, PPC.

74 For the function of pit structures, see Robert Soper, *Nyanga: Ancient Fields, Settlements and Agricultural History in Zimbabwe* (London, 2002), p. 91. For earlier treatments of the archaeological findings, see John Sutton, 'Irrigation and Soil-Conservation in African Agricultural History: With

a Reconsideration of the Inyanga Terracing (Zimbabwe) and Engaruka Irrigation Works (Tanzania)', *Journal of African History*, 25, no. 1 (1984), pp. 25-41; David Beach, *Archaeology and History in Nyanga, Zimbabwe*, History Seminar Paper, 97 (Harare: University of Zimbabwe, 1995).

75 Soper, *Nyanga*.

76 Ibid., p. 2.

77 Robert Soper, *The Terrace Builders of Nyanga* (Harare, 2006), pp. 1; 1-4.

78 Soper, *Nyanga*, p. 132.

79 Andrada, *Manica*, p. 8. The role of the Zindi chieftaincy and spiritual landscape in relation to violence is discussed in detail in chapter six.

80 Interview #5.

81 This dates *muzvare* Muparutsa's birth to 1888 or 1889. Interview #6; also Sells, 'The History of Manyikaland', p. 4.

82 The interviewee further implied that the valley population's political allegiance was particularly ambivalent. Interview #59.

83 Interview #6.

84 Baud and van Schendel suggest a model of five stages of borderland evolution, which, as the authors themselves concede, is too static. 'Towards a Comparative History', p. 224.

85 For the importance of border studies, see Thomas Wilson and Hastings Donnan, 'Nations, State and Identity at International Borders,' *Border Identities: Nation and State at International Frontiers*, Thomas Wilson and Hastings Donnan (eds) (Cambridge, 1998), p. 25. For an ethnography of border communities, see Harri Englund, *From War to Peace on the Mozambique–Malawi Borderland* (Edinburgh, 2002). A classic volume on the history of borders in Africa is A.I. Asiwaju and Paul Nugent (eds), *African Boundaries: Barriers, Conduits and Opportunities*, (London, 1996). For an update on the debate, see Toyin Falola and Aribidesi Usman (eds), *Movements, Borders, and Identities in Africa* (Rochester, NY, 2009).

86 A pathbreaking study which demonstrated forcefully the problematic of the nation state as unit of study is Peter Sahlins, *Boundaries: The Making of France and Spain in the Pyrenees* (Berkeley, CA, 1989). For a most useful review of the current debate, see Truett and Young, 'Making Transnational History'. Allen Howard and Richard Shain observe that the consideration of space in African history dates back only to the 1990s, see 'Introduction: African History and Social Space in Africa,' *The Spatial Factor in African History: The Relationship of the Social, Material, and Perceptual*, Allen Howard and Richard Shain (eds) (Leiden, 2006), p. 1.

87 A. Kambudzi, 'Zimbabwe–Mozambique Border,' *Zimbabwe's International Borders: A Study in International and Regional Development in Southern Africa*, vol. 1; *Zimbabwe, Mozambique, Namibia, and South Africa*, Solomon Nkiwane (ed.) (Harare, 1997), pp. 25-41.

88 See Paul Nugent, 'Arbitrary Lines and the People's Minds: A Dissenting View on Colonial Boundaries in West Africa', *African Boundaries: Barriers, Conduits and Opportunities*, Anthony Asiwaju and Paul Nugent (eds) (London, 1996), p. 60.

89 Achille Mbembe, 'At the Edge of the World: Boundaries, Territoriality, and Sovereignty in Africa', *Public Culture*, 12, no. 1 (2000), pp. 260-1.

90 Hans Medick, 'Zur politischen Sozialgeschichte der Grenzen in der Neuzeit Europas', *SOWI*, 20, no. 3 (1991), p. 163; also Sahlins, *Boundaries*. Samuel Truett refers to the opaqueness of the border region as 'fugitive landscapes'. *Fugitive Landscapes: The Forgotten History of the U.S.-Mexico Borderlands* (New Haven, CT, 2006).

91 Sawerthal, Memorandum on Semi-official letter, 12 January 1905, L2/2/6/7, NAZ.

92 Alf Lüdtke and Hans Medick, 'Einleitung', *SOWI*, 20, no. 3 (1991), p. 155.

93 Such three stages are also suggested by Baud and van Schendel, 'Towards a Comparative History', p. 215.

94 Timothy Mitchell, *Colonising Egypt* (Cambridge, 1988), p. 35, passim. For the modern state's desire for legibility of its citizens in order to maintain the rule of law, see James Scott, *Seeing Like a State: How Certain Schemes to Improve the Human Condition Have Failed* (New Haven, CT, 1998).

95 Achille Mbembe, *On the Postcolony* (Berkeley, CA, 2001), p. 174. Students of the colony frequently draw on the comparative context of the nation state, while the reverse is rarely the case. An exception is Gyanendra Pandey's concept of routine violence in the nation state that parallels Mbembe's argument about the creation of colonial subjects. See Pandey, *Routine Violence: Nations, Fragments, Histories* (Stanford, CA, 2006). Kären Wigen discusses multiple meanings of maps and state power in her study of Japan, *A Malleable Map: Geographies of Restauration in Central Japan, 1600–1912* (Berkeley, CA, 2010).

96 A group of migrant labourers from the Honde Valley joined a battalion in South Africa and participated in World War II. One elder remembered distinctly how, in May 1945 he had marched into the ruins of Berlin with the 'victorious troops of the British Empire', where he encountered German

children begging him for food (Interview #83). For a contemporary example of enframing from the perspective of forests and environmental management in South Africa, see Jacob Tropp, *Natures of Colonial Change: Environmental Relations in the Making of the Transkei* (Athens, OH, 2006).

97 See Eric Worby, 'Maps, Names, and Ethnic Games: The Epistemology and Iconography of Colonial Power in Northwestern Zimbabwe', *Journal of Southern African Studies*, 20, no. 3 (1994), pp. 371-92; Thomas Spear, 'Neo-Traditionalism and the Limits of Invention in British Colonial Africa', *Journal of African History*, 44, no. 1 (2003), pp. 3-27; Terence Ranger, *The Invention of Tribalism in Zimbabwe* (Gweru, 1985) and 'The Invention of Tradition Revisited: The Case of Colonial Africa', *Legitimacy and the State in Twentieth-Century Africa: Essays in Honour of A.H.M. Kirk-Greene*, Terence Ranger and Olufemi Vaughan (eds) (Houndmills, 1993), pp. 62-111. For the role of missionaries in the creation of tribes, see Herbert Chimhundu, 'Early Missionaries and the Ethnolinguistic Factor During the "Invention of Tribalism" in Zimbabwe', *Journal of African History*, 33, no. 1 (1992), pp. 87-109. By 1900, the local administration still had only a rough idea of the chieftainship structure, even in the mamboship's southern area that was easily accessible from the provincial capital. Umtali District, Annual Reports, April 1900, N9/1/6, NAZ.

98 Interview #84.

99 See interviews #53 and #111. Both interviewees were *masabhuku* and related the genealogy of their office. This view of *sabhuku* as *sadunhu* did not apparently apply everywhere. See Donald Moore, *Suffering for Territory: Race, Place, and Power in Zimbabwe* (Durham, NC, 2005), pp. 171-4, 228.

100 It is not clear how many chieftainships the colonial partition allocated to Portuguese territory. An elder claimed six of 'Mutasa's sons' were cut off by the border (Interview #80). Other evidence suggests not more than three chiefs were affected. See 'Tribes of the Eastern and South Eastern Border', n.d., RP. The Chikomba, Mandeya II, and Nyamaende and probably also the Mponda, Muchena, and Nyakukwanika chieftaincies lost part of their land.

101 'The vaManyika of the Honde Valley', 17 September 1976, RP.

102 Umtali District, Annual Reports, 1898, N9/1/4, NAZ; Robin Palmer, *Land and Racial Domination in Rhodesia* (London, 1977), pp. 68, 266-7.

103 Chiefs and Headmen 1915–1936, S1561/10, NAZ.

104 Lesson 45, Wachimanyika.

105 Mozambique Company, *Handbook of the Mozambique Company: Province of Manica–Sofala* (London, 1893), p. 82.

106 Umtali District, Quarterly Reports, December 1900, N9/3/3; Inyanga District, Monthly Reports, March 1904, N9/4/18; CNC Mashonaland, Annual Reports 1908, N9/1/11, NAZ.

107 Bhila, *Trade and Politics*, pp. 241-4.

108 P.H. van Niekerk to NC Inyanga, March 14, 1935, S603 NC Inyanga, NAZ.

109 Umtali District, Monthly Reports, May 1901, N9/4/8, June and July 1907, N9/4/20, NAZ.

110 Umtali District, Annual Reports, 1907, N9/1/10, NAZ.

111 For brief critical discussions of the concept and practice of effective occupation, see Geoffrey de Courcel, 'The Berlin Act of 26 February 1885', pp. 254-7, 258-9 and Immanuel Geiss, 'Free Trade, Internationalization of the Congo Basin, and the Principle of Effective Occupation', pp. 263-80, both in *Bismarck, Europe, and Africa: The Berlin Africa Conference 1884-1885 and the Onset of Partition*, Stig Förster et al. (Oxford, 1988). For a critical evaluation of the conference, see Simon Katzenellenbogen, 'It Didn't Happen at Berlin: Politics, Economics and Ignorance in the Setting of Africa's Colonial Boundaries', *African Boundaries: Barriers, Conduits and Opportunities*, Anthony Asiwaju and Paul Nugent (eds) (London, 1996), pp. 21-34.

112 See Ian Phimister, *An Economic and Social History of Zimbabwe 1890–1948: Capital Accumulation and Class Struggle* (London, 1988), p. 6.

113 Bhila, *Trade and Politics*, p. 237. For the BSAC's view of the scramble, see BSAC Administrator: Manica Reports, A1/6/3-4, NAZ.

114 Bhila, *Trade and Politics*, p. 223. Lesson 71, Machiwenyika; Shepherd Machuma, box file 248, shelf d, north wall, OMMA; Interview #80.

115 Andrada, *Manica*, pp. 8-9. For this point, see also Newitt, *Portuguese Settlement*, p. 315. Bhila follows Andrada, see Bhila, *Trade and Politics*, p. 225.

116 Andrada, *Report and Protest*, p. 5; also Beach, *The Origins*.

117 Bhila, *Trade and Politics*, pp. 188-90.

118 NC Makoni, 'Re History of Makoni Natives,' December 2, 1903, N3/33/8, NAZ. Beach referred to these aspirations as 'Andrada's greater Mozambique', which would have included about half of what became Zimbabwe. See Beach, *The Origins*, attached map.

119 Sir Edward Grey, Foreign Office, to Gaisford BSAC, London, 16 October 1911, A3/4/1/1. The adjacent boundary section to the south was similarly disputed. See Correspondence, Boundaries, Umtali-Melsetter, A3/4/8, NAZ. Unfortunately, McDermott Hughes does not discuss the aspect of

the border delineation in his case study of the frontier at the southern section of the Anglo-Portuguese border; *From Enslavement to Environmentalism*. For the entire border, see Ian Brownlie, *African Boundaries: A Legal and Diplomatic Encyclopaedia* (London, 1979), pp. 1219-37. Philip Warhurst presents a discussion of the adjacent boundary section to the north-west in 'A Troubled Frontier: North-Eastern Mashonaland, 1898–1906', *African Affairs*, 77, no. 307 (1978), pp. 214-29.

120 Baud and van Schendel, 'Towards a Comparative History', p. 214. For the border as a factor in the stability of the nation state, see Ricardo Larémont (ed.), *Borders, Nationalism, and the African State* (Boulder, CO, 2005).

121 Barué Delimitation Commission, Minutes of a Meeting Held at Mount Zaramira, 28 June 1898, L2/2/6/6, NAZ.

122 See, for example, the programmatic title of Katzenellenbogen's chapter, 'It Didn't Happen at Berlin' and the subtitle of the volume *Bismarck, Europe, and Africa: The Berlin Africa Conference 1884–1885 and the Onset of Partition*, Stig Förster et.al.

123 Africa No. 5 (1891). Papers relating to the Anglo-Portuguese Convention, signed in Lisbon on 11 June 1891, presented to both Houses of Parliament by Command of Her Majesty, June 1891, A/1/1/3, NAZ.

124 Ibid. For the view that the border was drawn in an entirely arbitrary manner, see Kambudzi, 'Zimbabwe–Mozambique Border'.

125 NC Umtali to Secretary BSAC, March 5, 1896, A1/1/3. For reverse allegations, see Portuguese Territory: Reported Incursions into, 13 December 1896-26 February 1897, A1/10/1, NAZ.

126 Copy of dispatch number 3, Leverson to Marquess of Salisbury, 12 December 1898, L2/2/6/6. Unfortunately, Leverson's dispatches focus entirely on delimitation matters and contain nothing on his impressions of the valley. Leverson had also been the BSAC commissioner in 1892. See Julian Leverson, 'Geographical Results of the Anglo-Portuguese Delimitation Commission in South-East Africa, 1892', *The Geographical Journal*, 2, no. 6 (1893), pp. 505-18.

127 Leverson met with the Portuguese commissioners near Mount Zaramira on 24 July 1898. From there he proceeded along the Ruera Valley (2 July) until he reached the watershed on 8 July. Copy of minutes from Leverson to Marquess of Salisbury, 31 December 1898, L2/2/6/6, NAZ.

128 Copy of dispatch number 1, Leverson to Marquess of Salisbury, 10 August 1898, L2/2/6/6, NAZ.

129 Under-Secretary of the Colonial Office, Bertram Cox, to Secretary BSAC, London, 14 June 1905, L2/2/6/7, NAZ.

130 L2/2/6/6, NAZ.

131 Memorandum by Chief Secretary BSAC, 23 December 1904, L2/2/6/6, Sawerthal, Boundary Commissioner, Department of Lands, 'Process-verbal No.10-14,' 2 November 1906, L2/2/6/8, NAZ.

132 Sawerthal, 'Process-verbal No. 10-14'. The colonial presence of the boundary commission was a unique event in the Honde Valley and the seemingly endless line of four hundred carriers moving through the area must have been impressive – and demanded significant supplies; even so the boundary commission is not part of social memory (See photo no. 3). This is probably the case because the commissioners were not perceived as violent intruders, nor did their work introduce a rupture; rather, the boundary commission was merely one episode in a long, drawn-out process.

133 Treaty Series 1912 No. 21: Agreement between the United Kingdom and Portugal Respecting Boundaries in East Africa (Barué Section – from the Mazoe River to Latitude 18°E 30' South), Lisbon 22 July-09 August 1912, presented to both Houses of Parliament by Command of His Majesty, December 1912, A3/4/1/1, NAZ.

134 Sawerthal to Private Secretary, 2 April 1909, ibid.

135 Copy of despatch number 1, Leverson to Marquess of Salisbury, 10 August 1898, L2/2/6/6, NAZ.

136 NC Umtali Hulley to Sawerthal, Umtali, 6 March 1905, ibid.

137 Chief Secretary BSAC to Ordinance Officer, 28 March 1905, L2/2/6/7, NAZ.

138 Telegram from Scouts Inyanga to Native Department, 13 September 1906, L2/2/6/8, NAZ.

139 Inyanga District, Monthly Reports, February 1915, N9/4/28, NAZ.

140 Telegram from Sawerthal to Surveyor General, 10 September 1906, L2/2/6/8, NAZ.

141 Sawerthal to Surveyor General, 2 April 1909, A3/4/1/1, NAZ.

142 Sawerthal, 'Memorandum on Semi-official letter dated 6 January 1905 from Major R.P. O'Shea to Sir William Milton', 12 January 1905, L2/2/6/7, NAZ.

143 Sawerthal to Surveyor General, 2 April 1909, A3/4/1/1, NAZ.

144 Mtoko District, Monthly Reports, August 1902, N9/4/12, NAZ.

145 Mazoe North District, Monthly Reports, May 1908, N9/4/21; also Inyanga District, Annual Reports, 1899, N9/1/5 and Darwin District, Monthly Reports, January 1910, N9/4/23, NAZ.

146 Inyanga District, Monthly Reports, January 1899, N9/4/2, NAZ.

147 Leverson, 'Geographic Results', p. 515.

148 Inyanga District, Monthly Reports, January 1899, N9/4/2; Umtali District, Monthly Reports, May

1902, N9/4/12. By 1900, Chief Tangwena still resided on the eastern side of the border. Inyanga District, Annual Reports, 1900, N9/1/6, NAZ; Moore, *Suffering for Territory*, p. 132.

149 Apparently Chief Chikomba also had a personal reason to leave, as he was in conflict with *mambo* Mutasa over a child pledging case. NC Inyanga to Acting CNC, 16 November 1904; NC Inyanga to Acting CNC, 31 January 1906, NUC2/3/1; NC Inyanga to SON, 5 May 1908, NUC1/4/1, NAZ.

150 Inyanga District, Monthly Reports, April 1908, N9/4/21, NAZ. The SON predicted that 'many' residents of Inyanga, Umtali, and Melsetter Districts would move across the border in order to avoid paying land rent. SON Division 3, Half-Yearly Reports, 31 December 1908, N9/2/3, NAZ.

151 Meeting of the Minister of Native Affairs, CNC, Chiefs, and Headmen, Inyanga District, January 23, 1925, S1561/10, NAZ.

152 Inyanga District, Annual Reports, 1906, N9/1/9, NAZ.

153 Telegram from NC Inyanga to CNC, 30 July 1906, L2/2/6/8, NAZ.

154 Sawerthal to Surveyor General, 20 August 1906, ibid.; also Inyanga District, Monthly Reports, September 1907, N9/4/20, NAZ. Eric Allina-Pisano, 'Borderlands, Boundaries, and the Contours of Colonial Rule: African Labor in Manica District, Mozambique, c. 1904-1908', *International Journal of African Historical Studies*, 36, no. 1 (2003), pp. 59-82.

155 Inyanga District, Monthly Reports, October 1909, N9/4/22; also Umtali District, Monthly Reports, January 1906, N9/4/19, NAZ.

156 Umtali District, Monthly Reports, October 1912, N9/4/25.

157 Inyanga District, Annual Reports, 1932, S235/510, NAZ.

158 BSAP Snelling to Coffin, October 22, 1908, box file: Coffin Correspondence, north wall, OMMA.

159 NC Umtali Bazeley to CNC Salisbury, 3 May 1928, S1561/10, NAZ. Andrada had visited the Honde Valley. See 'Captain Paiva de Andrada's Zambesi Expedition', p. 373.

160 Inyanga District, Monthly Reports, January and March 1913, N9/4/26 and December 1912, N9/4/25; Umtali District, Monthly Reports, October 1912, N9/4/25, NAZ.

161 Inyanga District, Monthly Reports, December 1912, N9/4/25 and January 1913, N9/4/26, NAZ.

162 Lawrence Vambe, *An Ill-Fated People: Zimbabwe Before and after Rhodes* (London, 1972), pp. 14-20.

163 Inyanga District, Monthly Reports, August 1907, N9/4/20, February 1917, N9/4/32, May 1918, N9/4/34, Annual Reports, 1932, S235/511; Darwin District, Monthly Reports, October 1911, N9/4/24, NAZ.

164 Umtali District, Monthly Reports, January 1903, N9/4/14; also Intendant of Barwe to NC Inyanga, Vila Gouveia, 2 July 1926, S603 NC Inyanga, NAZ.

165 NC Melsetter to SON Umtali District, 21 December 1918, S1561/10; also Assistant Magistrate Bazeley to the Magistrate Umtali, Inyanga, 3 July 1925, S603, NAZ.

166 Umtali District, Monthly Reports, January 1899, N9/4/2, NAZ.

167 Ibid., May 1901, N9/4/8 and May 1903, N9/4/15, NAZ.

168 BSAP Lodge to NC Inyanga, Inyanga, 11 October 1924, S603 and NC Inyanga, Acting NC Inyanga Nesbitt, Evidence Written, vol. 1, Native Production and Trade Commission 1944, ZBJ1/2/2, NAZ.

169 Civil Commissioner and Magistrate Umtali to Kennedy, BSAC, 23 October 1891, T2/17/1, NAZ.

170 Melsetter District, Monthly Reports, March 1912, N9/4/25, NAZ.

171 In 1920, NC Hulley reported that ignoring the border was common practice in Manyikaland. NC Hulley to SON Salisbury, Mtoko, 29 December 1920, S1542/T7, NAZ.

172 Inyanga District, Monthly Reports, February 1915, N9/4/28, NAZ.

173 Cecil Hulley, *Memories of Manicaland* (Umtali, 1980), p. 72.

174 Umtali District, Annual Reports, 1907, N9/1/10, NAZ. Andrada reported that Mutasa men were already working in Mozambican mines from 1888. Andrada, *Manica*, p. 10. For the opportunities the colonial economy opened up for African women until the gendered backlash that began in the 1920s, see the path-breaking work by Elizabeth Schmidt, 'Farmers, Hunters, and Gold-Washers: A Re-evaluation of Women's Roles in Precolonial and Colonial Zimbabwe', *African Economic History*, 17 (1988), pp. 45-80 and 'Patriarchy, Capitalism, and the Colonial State in Zimbabwe', *Signs* 16, no. 4 (1991), pp. 732-56.

175 Umtali District, Annual Reports, 1938, S235/516. Certainly by the 1940s Ngoni men from southern Tanzania were working in Mafeking and Johannesburg and had married Tswana and Zulu women. Memory of their ancestors' immigration from South Africa in the 1830s might have led some to seek a similar route that led through the Mutasa area. ACC 155/M5/6, Tanzania National Archives.

176 Dick Rewesanyi to NC Inyanga, Johannesburg, received 8 February 1924; Dick Musapatika to NC Inyanga, Johannesburg, 26 June 1924; Dick Maramba to NC Inyanga, Johannesburg, 28 June 1924; Rewesayi Rafael Charamba to NC Inyanga, Johannesburg, received 1 September 1924; Balthasar Muretwa to NC Inyanga, 10 September 1924, Johannesburg, S603 NC Inyanga, NAZ. Note the use of "Dick" at a time when African men and women who were not Christianised did not yet use western style first names and patronyms, as required by the practice of enframing.

177 Mtoko District, Monthly Reports, October 1910, N9/4/23, Melsetter District, Monthly Reports, October 1912, N9/4/25; Umtali District, Annual Reports, 1933, S235/511; PNC to Administrator Vila de Manica Portuguese East Africa, Umtali, May 11, 1959, box number 62328, NRC; also Inyanga District, Annual Reports, 1928, S235/506, Acting NC Darwin to CNC Salisbury, May 30, 1923, S1542/T7, NAZ.

178 For the argument of colonialism as a fragile project, see Heike Schmidt, 'Colonial Intimacy: The Rechenberg Scandal, Homosexuality and Sexual Crime in German East Africa', *Journal of the History of Sexuality*, 17, no. 1 (2008), pp. 25-59, 'Who is Master in the Colony? Propriety, Honor, and Manliness in German East Africa', *German Cultures of Colonialism: Race, Nation, and Globalization, 1884-1945*, Geoff Eley and Bradley Naranch (eds) (Durham, NC: Duke University Press, forthcoming).

179 Interview #78. The female elder who identified the Makombe rising as the first war in the valley did so against her personal experiences of conflict and suffering; during the same interview she complained bitterly about her forced removal from one of the tea plantations, about the horrors of the liberation war, and how she and her husband were left in abject poverty without their children.

180 MacGonagle translates *madzviti* simply as warriors in her glossary and also provides this as the main meaning in her discussion. See *Crafting Identity*, pp. 102, 163.

181 The following account is largely based on Newitt, *A History of Mozambique*, pp. 415-20.

182 Fereta later took flight through the Honde Valley. Lesson 79, Wachimanyika; also testimony by Kugayisa of Masanga District, Mtoko District, 24 April 1917, A3/18/38/1, NAZ. Ranger refers to the sexual violence as 'girls were seduced by the *sepoys*'. However, he also identifies sexual violence as the main grievance that led to the war. See 'Revolt in Portuguese East Africa: The Makombe Rising of 1917', in *African Affairs*, 2, St Antony's Papers, 15 (London, 1963), p. 64.

183 One of the witnesses was a *sepoy*, and even he testified to the effect that the rape of young girls was a major cause of the war, though he claimed that he had taken no part in it. Major Spain, Several Statements Taken from Portuguese Refugees, Including those from Secretary to Administrator, Masanga, and Master of Posts and Telegraphs, Massanga, Makaha, 4 April 1917, A3/18/38/1, NAZ; also Elioth Makambe, 'The Nyasaland African Labour "Ulendos" to Southern Rhodesia and the Problem of the African "Highwaymen", 1903–1923: A Study in the Limitations of Early Independent Labour Migration,' *African Affairs*, 79, no. 317 (1980), p. 552.

184 Assistant Magistrate Feira to DC Broken Hill, Northern Rhodesia, 17 October 1917, A3/18/38/3. Many aspects of the Makombe conflict, including the enslaving of war captives by auxiliaries, is strikingly similar to the Maji Maji war. See Heike Schmidt, 'The Maji Maji War and Its Aftermath: Gender, Age, and Power in South-Western Tanzania, c. 1905–1916', *International Journal of African Historical Studies*, 43, no. 1 (2010), pp. 27-62 and '"A Deadly Silence Predominated in the District": The Maji Maji War in Ungoni', *Maji Maji: Lifting the Fog of War*, James Giblin and Jamie Monson (eds) (Leiden, 2010), pp. 183-219.

185 Ranger, 'Revolt in Portuguese East Africa', pp. 72-4.

186 'The Samembere Headmanship: Inyanga District', 10 June 1975, RP. For a different account that emphasises that the initiative was taken by a spirit medium who succeeded in creating the political alliance, see Allen and Barbara Isaacman, *The Tradition of Resistance*, p. 162.

187 NC Inyanga Bazeley, Border Report Inyanga District, 27 May 1918, N3/26/4, NAZ.

188 Newitt, *A History of Mozambique*, p. 419.

189 Inyanga District, Annual Reports, 1917, N9/1/20; Monthly Reports, April to June 1918, N9/4/34 and July to September 1918, N9/4/35, NAZ.

190 Inyanga District, Monthly Reports, December 1919, N9/4/37, NAZ.

191 Ibid., May 1919, N9/4/36, NAZ.

192 Ibid., August 1919, N9/4/33, NAZ.

193 Assistant Magistrate Feira to DC Broken Hill/Northern Rhodesia, 19 October 1917, A3/18/38/3, NAZ.

194 Testimony by Chizuza, Mount Darwin, 14 May 1917, also testimony by Jobe Sula, Mount Darwin, 8 May 1917, A3/18/38/1, NAZ. The hostility against Makombe in Darwin District went so far that people in one area asked for permission to join the Portuguese forces to defeat the rebels. Statement by Chief Mpuka, Assistant Magistrate to the Secretary in Livingstone, Feira, Northern Rhodesia, 7 October 1917, A3/18/38/3, NAZ.

195 Testimony by Assham Rostrum, Mount Darwin, 8 May 1917, A3/18/38/1, NAZ. The file contains a number of eyewitness accounts of such killings.

196 This strikingly resembles Marcia Wright's accounts of female vulnerability and slave raiding areas in the wider region. *Strategies of Slaves and Women: Life-Stories from East/Central Africa* (New York, 1993).

197 Ranger, 'Revolt in Portuguese East Africa', p. 57.

198 Administrator BSAC Chaplin Drummond to High Commissioner for South Africa, August 15, 1918, A3/18/38/4; Inyanga District, Monthly Reports, June 1918, N9/4/34, NAZ. For a slightly different estimate, see René Pélissier, *Naissance du Mozambique: Résistance et Révoltes Anticoloniales (1854–1918)* (Orgeval, 1984), Vol. 2, p. 678.
199 NC Inyanga to CNC, 12 October 1923, NUC2/3/3, NAZ.
200 CNC to Director of Land Settlement, 15 July 1918, N3/26/4, NAZ.
201 Interviews #85, #80, NC Inyanga to CNC, January 30, 1929, S604, NAZ. For more detail, see, chapter three.
202 Acting NC Darwin to CNC, 22 May 1928, S138/4. At times, entire homesteads, in this case with more than forty adults, crossed the border. Melsetter District, Monthly Reports, January 1910, N9/4/23, NAZ.
203 Interview #84.
204 See David Beach, 'The Uses of the Colonial Military History of Mozambique', *Cahiers d'Etudes Africaines*, 26, no. 4 (1986), p. 712.
205 Interview #84.
206 Interview #83.
207 Border Patrol to NC Inyanga, 8 September 1917, N3/26/4, NAZ.
208 NC Inyanga to CNC, 3 July 1925, S138/4, NAZ.
209 John Lonsdale, *Unhappy Valley: Conflict in Kenya and Africa* by Bruce Berman and John Lonsdale (London, 1992), vol. 2, chapters eleven and twelve.
210 Inyanga District, Annual Reports, 1903, N9/1/8 and 1927, S235/505, NAZ; interview #32; also Terence Ranger, 'Missionaries, Migrants and the Manyika: The Invention of Ethnicity in Zimbabwe', *The Creation of Tribalism in Southern Africa*, Leroy Vail (ed.) (London, 1989), p. 140, passim.
211 For the current discussion of frontier identity, see Peter Geschiere (ed.), *The Perils of Belonging: Autochthony, Citizenship, and Exclusion in Africa and Europe* (Chicago, IL, 2009), Charles Maier, '"Being There": Place, Territory, and Identity', *Identities, Affiliations, and Allegiances*, Syla Benhabib et al. (eds) (Cambridge, 2007), pp. 67–84; Anthony Cohen (ed.), *Signifying Identities: Anthropological Perspectives on Boundaries and Contested Values* (London, 2000).
212 John Lonsdale, 'Moral Ethnicity and Political Tribalism', *Inventions and Boundaries: Historical and Anthropological Approaches to the Study of Ethnicity and Nationalism*, Preben Kaarsholm and Jan Hultin (eds) (Roskilde, 1994), p. 132.
213 See also Steven Feierman, *Peasant Intellectuals: Anthropology and History in Tanzania* (Madison, WI, 1990), p. 27; for Feierman's conceptual discussion of practice and discourse, see pp. 27–45.
214 William Shack, 'Introduction', *Strangers in African Societies*, William Shack and Elliot Skinner (eds) (Berkeley, CA, 1979), p. 12.
215 For women working on the *zunde* to lay the ground for their household's immigration, see BSAP Trooper Alney border patrol to NC Darwin, 17 March 1918, enclosed in CNC to Secretary BSAC, 4 April 1918, A3/18/38/3, NAZ. Marcia Wright argues that, despite women's extreme vulnerability, in contexts of negotiating marginality, compared to men it tended to be easier for some women to be incorporated into dominant groups. Wright, *Strategies*, pp. 42–3.
216 Interview #84. In contrast, Robert Gordon argues that it was the lack and not the abundance of resources which, together with remoteness, made the frontier in Namibia. See *The Bushman Myth: The Making of a Namibian Underclass* (Boulder, CO, 1992), pp. 209–10.
217 Interview #84.
218 Shack, 'Introduction', p. 10. For the impact of demographic changes during the 1950s, see chapter three.
219 Interview #148.
220 Allina-Pisano, 'Negotiating Colonialism,' pp. 38–9.
221 Worby, 'Maps, Names, and Ethnic Games'.
222 Moore, *Suffering for Territory*.
223 The Isaacmans' study of Chikunda identity provides a tremendously sophisticated analysis of the making and remaking of ethnic identity, including the creation of an ancestral shrine. Their work demonstrates the importance of historical depth in the interpretation of identities. Allen and Barbara Isaacman, *Slavery and Beyond: The Making of Men and Chikunda Ethnic Identities in the Unstable World of South-Central Africa, 1750–1920* (Portsmouth, NH, 2004).
224 Interviews #113, #55, #56.
225 Martin Lewis and Kären Wigen, *The Myth of Continents: A Critique of Metageography* (Berkeley, CA, 1997), p. 192.
226 Interview #80.
227 Ibid.
228 Interview #20; also Kopytoff, 'The Internal African Frontier,' p. 7.

3
Pioneers & Modernisers
Landscapes of Violence

The Honde Valley has served to newcomers as a canvas upon which they project their notions of wilderness and alterity. This chapter is concerned with immigrants whose imaginations of landscape and self-perceived roles as pioneers and modernisers significantly shaped their lives in the valley and through their interactions those of the valley inhabitants. In her study of the eighteenth-century Caribbean, Jill Casid examined a period when imperial landscape imaginations and notions of alterity prevailed, even though the projects of modernity and modernisation had not yet shaped land-use practices as they did later in colonial Africa. Still, her findings are pertinent. Following W.J.T. Mitchell in discussing landscape as a multi-layered process embedded in power contestations, Casid succeeds in providing an analysis that moves beyond a simplifying resistance paradigm or metropole-centred approach by insisting on landscaping as 'a mutable and unstable practice'.[1] She observes that 'The tools and dreamwork, the phobias and desires fuelling empire and its resistance converge in the field of imperial landscaping and its foundational displacements'.[2] Hence she identifies the connection between empire and power with landscape imagination and land use practice. It is this concept of landscape that underlies the following discussion of both African and European self-proclaimed pioneers. It will be shown that the pioneer identity is violent in nature because its landscape appropriation, be it ideological or practical, is an act of asserting power over people and land.

Outside observers of the Honde Valley were united in perceiving it as a wilderness, remote and unexplored, still caught in darkness, lacking the light of Christian civilisation and modern development. Unusually for southern Africa, these imaginations lasted into the second half of the twentieth century. In 1951, the Native Commissioner (NC) Inyanga was instructed to explore Holdenby SNA (Special Native Area) in the northern part of the valley. He described the area as follows:

> For the greater portion it is mountainous and has rivers flowing across it which pass through huge and grotesque gorges. It has been entered to a distance of six miles by road and it now remains to penetrate to the central parts and along the long narrow strip of the recently added Crown land adjacent to the Portuguese border.[3]

In the late nineteenth century the colonial government had decided to leave narrow strips along the border reserved as Crown land in order to create a no man's land that would prevent uncontrolled border crossings. That aim, however, had turned out to be futile and the failure was finally acknowledged in 1920.[4] The area was beyond reach of the colonial state and considered as 'practically unknown' by 1956.[5] It was as late as 1958 that the administration urged the NC Inyanga to explore the northern part of the valley:

> Lack of a road of any sort in the North East section of Holdenby is a handicap to the development of that area. This part of Holdenby is a wilderness of hills, streams and swamps, and a road will be difficult to construct there, but if funds are available next year an exploratory track will be cut into the area for a start to enable us to get in there.[6]

This man on the spot was arguing that basic exploration, let alone the imposition of effective colonial rule, depended on the construction of roads, even with plantations already functioning and regardless of African mobility in the area. A curious image emerges: an NC ordering a road gang of local people who know the area well to build a road which he can follow in order to explore its surroundings. Little had changed from the days of boundary commissioner Henry Sawerthal, who, in 1906, had struggled to demarcate the colonial border while he observed Africans using it, and who was affected by what he perceived as impenetrable vegetation.

However, in contrast to colonial perceptions of remoteness that required penetration, the Honde Valley was well connected with the wider world as migrant labourers had generated a market for consumer goods. As early as 1927, the NC Inyanga had observed that local African women acted very differently from those elsewhere in the colony. While usually women wanted their men to stay at home, he found that:

> the Manyika woman on the contrary, demands that she shall be decently dressed and fed, and urges upon her husband that it is his duty to go and earn the required sum of money for that purpose. Where he becomes obdurate and refuses, she will often threaten to leave him and go to the mines as a prostitute.[7]

For Honde Valley residents, the proximity of salaried labour opportunities at mines on the Portuguese side of the border and just south of the valley in Penhalonga probably meant that consumerism arrived early in the area. Elioth Makambe, in his work on Malawian migrant labourers in Zimbabwe, argued that in response to the Makombe War of 1917–1920, many of the workers avoided colonial interventions, organising larger groups to travel together instead, hence seeking strength in numbers while traversing the conflict area. One assembly point was the Pungwe River, and in 1938 a food depot for migrant workers was present in the Honde Valley.[8] Certainly, local purchasing power and taste for imported goods emerges from evidence given at a court case in the early 1950s, when a man was charged with doing business as a general dealer without a license in Holdenby.

In October 1952, a European corporal of the British South African Police (BSAP) patrolled the area and found 'a typical pole and dagga hut' from where the wife of the accused was selling goods. It is not known how the merchandise was brought into Holdenby, but it is likely that it was smuggled across the border.

In his testimony, the corporal appeared particularly incensed that the goods were imported.[9] The accused, who held a hawkers' license, attempted to defend himself by arguing that 'When I go out selling goods I leave my wife at this hut – so that she can sell such things as paraffin and other heavy articles which I cannot carry on a bridle.'[10] The policeman discovered a great number of such 'heavy articles'. These included twenty-two rolls of cloth, three blankets, one suitcase, and seven tablecloths displayed outside the store and paraffin, Vaseline, Sunlight soap, combs, knives, a kettle, minerals, candles, mirrors, Minora blades, Dunlop rubber solution, cups, pots, pens, pencils, plough shares, 'trinkets', spanners, and tinned fish inside the hut.[11] Thus it appears that items such as pencils and rubber solution had a market even before there were schools or roads in the area. The man was fined £25 or 60 days imprisonment with hard labour.

This chapter explores the initial encounters and further interactions between those immigrants who perceived the valley as a wilderness and the valley inhabitants with their frontier identity, which by the 1930s was well embedded within the changes brought about by the imposition of colonial rule and the rise of colonial markets. Dane Kennedy, in his classic comparative study on settler societies, argues that in Southern Rhodesia the 'frontier era' came to an end in 1897 with the British South Africa Company (BSAC) victory in the First Chimurenga, which effectively ended large-scale military resistance against colonial rule. What followed was, according to Kennedy, the manifestation of hegemony through 'institutional authority'.[12] This study follows Kennedy's periodisation of colonisation and the imposition of colonial rule on the ground, but contests the notion of a temporary frontier era. The previous chapter introduced the Honde Valley as an area that remained the Rhodesian frontier after 1890, and in fact until independence in 1980. In addition, colonialism was not a monolithic project, not even in a single colony; thought, practice, and identity that were non-contemporary, recurrent, and cyclical were as much present as were continuity and change. This chapter illustrates this by examining three waves of newcomers between the 1930s and 1950s. Their arrival further transformed the colonial manifestation of the frontier ethnicity in the Honde Valley, which was firmly in place by the late 1920s and defined by the tension between opportunity and danger, fluidity, openness to immigration, and various uses of the colonial border.

African pioneers of the Ziwe Zano Society founded the first mission station in the valley in 1938; European pioneers arrived in 1952 and swiftly established two tea plantations; and from 1948 the colonial government began the forced resettlement of chiManyika-speakers into the valley from land reserved for European occupation on the highveld. All three groups shared a self-perception as modernisers, and all saw the valley as backward and as a remote wilderness, but each group approached its engagement with the frontier people differently. Another outside impact on the valley was the sudden expansion of missionary activities that transformed the religious landscape in a manner that had repercussions until the liberation war of the 1970s. Ultimately, the ideologies and practices of newcomers to the Honde Valley from the 1930s to the mid-1950s saw them excluded or assimilated in various ways, a process that further shaped the valley's frontier identity. The chapter examines these groups of modernisers in turn.

African Pioneers: Bringing Light into the Wilderness

The Ziwe Zano Society was an African self-help organisation created by African Methodists in the Mutasa area, and from 1958 also an African initiated church. In the spirit of a pioneer, a female church elder emphasised that 'we started the Honde Valley'.[13] Ziwe Zano's founding myth as pioneers whose mission it was to bring light into the wilderness of the Honde Valley is recorded in the 1959 history of the society:

> Early in 1938 a group of simple, honest Christian men left their employments and friends. They embarked upon a wageless, sacrificial missionary career in the Honde Valley…. These men wound down the roadless Honde Valley, then undeveloped and inhabited sparsely by people of a very low culture; strongly controlled by superstitious trust in ancestral spirits.[14]

These Christian pioneers hence imagined the valley as a place of primitive people, sacrifice, and suffering. What this depiction of the task ahead does not mention is the significant role of the female pioneers, the fact that four small mission schools were already established in the area, even if they were barely active,[15] and that the southern part of the 'roadless Honde Valley' was in fact accessible by road, next to which the founders established their mission. This road had been built with paid labour provided by the Anglican St Augustine's mission in Penhalonga and had opened to wheel traffic in 1931. When Ziwe Zano members went to settle in the valley in 1938 after three months of surveying and construction, D.M. Katsidzira and S.M. Kanyenze and their families arrived on ox-wagons, assisted by Colonel Valentine, a supporter of the society, who lent them his 'chauffeur-driven motorcar'.[16] Such apparent inconsistencies emphasise the significance of society members' self-perception as pioneers and modernisers and hence their project of alterity, which shaped their relations with the valley inhabitants.

On 20 January 1932, at the constitutive meeting of the society, which had twenty-two members, Davidson Murashwa Katsidzira, its founder, said a prayer in which he declared that Africans should come together in order to improve their lives:[17] 'Now is the time for calling of Africans to unite and have abundant life like other nations.' Everyone at the meeting cried for the nation of Africa. After praying, the aims and laws or rules to be followed were made.[18] Thus, the foundations of Ziwe Zano (Lift Yourself Up!)[19] were laid. The idea of self-help and an African way of life were crucial to the members, informing their thinking and practices, and were part of their self-representation in their writings. In 1944, the government-appointed Godlonton Commission invited the society to give testimony as part of their fact-finding mission regarding African modernisation, with a focus on the economic sphere:

> 'As you make progress, do you intend to teach students to live as Europeans do, or are you just going to leave them as they are?' – 'We want to teach these people to live nicely at their kraals, and also to help their own people; to teach them cleanliness, and to be industrious and help their own people; but we have no intention of teaching them to imitate Europeans.[20]

The founders of the Ziwe Zano Society thus clearly understood themselves as modernisers who did not wish to emulate western civilisation.[21] Their goal was to live a Christian life according to their own understanding and to teach young people how to do so at their industrial school in the Honde Valley, beyond the colonial frontier.

Members of Ziwe Zano lived in 'the realm of the word'.[22] Several of the men kept what they understood to be books – histories of the society, biographies and autobiographies, copies of incoming and outgoing correspondence recorded in exercise books and ledgers.[23] Together with oral and archival sources, these papers provide an unusually rich record that give insight into these pioneers' theology, self-perception, and experiences and reveal unique African voices on belonging, community, and landscape in the Honde Valley.

ZIWE ZANO SOCIETY

Ziwe Zano's founders were brought together by a set of shared experiences. They had witnessed the arrival of the white settlers and missionaries, and they belonged to the first generation of Africans in Manyikaland to convert to Christianity, receive mission education, and be trained as teachers and lay preachers.[24] These men knew each other well. Although they were posted across northern Manyikaland, they met regularly at prayer meetings and theological courses. They all had a strong concept of self-advancement and belief in industrial skills, as propagated by the American Methodist Episcopal Church, through which they had received their baptism. Terence Ranger, writing about peasantisation in Makoni District in the early colonial period, argued that 'the American Methodist Episcopal Church preached the gospel of the plough and aimed to turn out modern agricultural entrepreneurs'.[25] This ethic is reflected in the words of a female elder in the society: 'We desired to work for the Lord. … you can even tell from the name – Ziwe Zano … which stands for a black person must strive to have an idea that God…. the Lord appreciates those who work for him.'[26] Even so, many of the young men barely made a living as mission teachers at outlying schools or as lay preachers.

Katsidzira constantly complained about the relatively low pay, and throughout his nephew's three-volume manuscript the problem of raising money for *lobola* (bride-price) is a recurrent theme. Men were usually forced to interrupt work for the Methodist Church, and later the Ziwe Zano Society, and to become migrant labourers in order to generate these sums of money.[27] In customary marriages the groom's kin group paid *lobola* to that of the bride in the acknowledgement that the latter were giving up a daughter and her productive and reproductive capabilities and also to forge a reciprocal relationship between the two groups. Mission converts, however, were bound to marry in church and to honour the monogamous union. This usually meant the young men could not or did not wish to rely on their family to provide the *lobola*. In their generation, often only part of a family converted, which caused rifts or moral concerns. These young men of John Iliffe's 'age of improvement'[28] had elevated themselves as early converts and through working for the mission church, but they could not compete with the manliness of mineworkers nor get married easily without the help of their kin. From the 1920s, they also became much concerned with the moral debate between the missionaries, African elders, and the colonial state over African women's mobility and sexuality.[29]

Two important factors convinced the twenty-two founding members of the Ziwe Zano Society to pursue their goals independently in 1932: the Great Revival of 1918 and the Great Depression. The Great Revival that started at Mount Chiremba, next to Old Mutare Mission, the colony's founding American Methodist Episcopal station, located in the Mutasa area, was an important turning point in mission Christianity in Manyikaland, because now the African preachers spread the gospel in their own right, not as emissaries of the mission church. Small groups of believers went to the villages to convert people and to share their experiences of possession by the Holy Spirit.[30] The new theology became rapidly attractive as the colonial state began to make itself more strongly felt on the ground through the enforcement of land and population control and when the Great Depression added economic frustrations to the sense of crisis in the early 1930s.

Terence Ranger argued that in Makoni, one of the districts in which Ziwe Zano members resided, the overall crisis of the 1930s led to 'an upheaval of consciousness which found its expression mostly in new religious ideas'.[31] Such initiatives included the founding of African initiated churches: two of the best known and most widely accepted were the Gospel of God Church, established by Johane Masowe from Makoni district in 1932, and the African Apostolic Church, started by Johane Marange from Maranke district, southwest of Mutare, in the same year. Both founders were former Methodists and both churches became known as Vapostori.[32] It is against this backdrop that the Ziwe Zano Society was initiated in 1932, also with a clear sense that the original members had been given their mandate by the Holy Spirit and not by the mission church or the colonial state, albeit still under the umbrella of the Methodist mother church.[33] Four years later, the society formulated their goals to establish a mission which was to become their headquarters and a school which aimed at helping male and female African school drop-outs and other females to acquire industrial skills. Their main concern was that colonial modernisation was undoing the moral ways of old, affecting young women in particular by providing them with the mobility to seek employment and patrons in towns and mines.[34] In 1938, these modernisers became pioneers who moved beyond the frontier, into the Honde Valley.

HONDE MISSION AND INDUSTRIAL SCHOOL

The mission's location in the southern part of the Honde Valley, close to Chiwawadzira mountain, had not been Ziwe Zano's initial choice.[35] But after a two-year search, in 1938, Katsidzira asked for permission to look for a site he had heard of in Umtasa North Reserve. He went to see Maison Mvere, who told him: 'Yes there is land where there are very few people, in the valley of Honde River.'[36] Katsidzira might have recognized the frontier mode of life that the newcomers encountered from his childhood. Born circa 1890 in the Mutambara area, a borderland in the Chimanimani district, he was fifth and youngest child of a chiBarwe-speaking family. An older sister, after whom he was named, had been abducted by warriors from the Gaza state, and he spent most of his childhood on Portuguese territory, where his family lived until their return in 1918.[37] Nevertheless, it was under his leadership that the pioneers sought exclusion.

The mission founders arrived with a perception of the valley as remote, unpopulated, and wild. Compared to other reserves in the colony, the area was indeed isolated. Despite communication lines with the south and east, Umtasa North Reserve, located in the southern part of the Honde Valley and 'created' in 1917 by the Native Reserves Commission,[38] remained largely inaccessible from the west and the north and was thus removed from state control, as emerges in a complaint by the NC Inyanga from 1933 reporting on his patrol in Manga Reserve:

> This is an extremely difficult district to patrol owing to the mountainous nature of the country and the length of the boundary adjoining the Portuguese Territory. [T]his reserve had not had a thorough patrol for four years and the natives had become rather lax in complying with the various laws.[39]

Comparable to boundary commissioner Sawerthal's view of the valley, who observed 'the absence of well-defined paths in the past, and the entangled state of the approaches to this part of the district, choked as they are with dangerous … creepers and abounding in swamps', in the first years of the twentieth century[40] the pioneers saw it in much the same way. This is how one of Ziwe Zano's female elders remembered her initial impression of the valley:

> When we first arrived here, a lot of lions roamed about…. There were no people here…. It was a forest, a woodland. It was all forest! … Lions used to roam around here…. We were not attacked due to the grace of the Lord…. It was just plain, with only mud. The only rivers that had water were the Honde and Botsokari. All these other small rivers had nothing. There was nothing, it was all plain.[41]

The Ziwe Zano history of 1959 similarly characterised early life at Honde Mission: wandering wild animals made nights restless and life desperately insecure.[42] Although these descriptions of its wildness are probably exaggerated, at the time the NC Inyanga also claimed that the north-eastern part of the valley abounded with lions, leopards, and wild dogs, and the Land Development Officer (LDO) observed in 1947 that leopards were plentiful in the Mahemasimike area. Living conditions were undoubtedly difficult, with its hot climate and tropical vegetation to which most of the newcomers were not accustomed. At the same time, however, environmental resources such as trees facilitated the construction of the mission and became crucial for the early success of the undertaking.[43] Nor was the most southern part of the Honde Valley as 'wild' or as isolated from the rest of the colony as Ziwe Zano members made out, and the area was certainly not uninhabited. Their perception of the valley caused problems with the local population from the very beginning, even though it did not stop their early successes.

NC Bazeley had advised the pioneers to ask the local chief for permission to settle as soon as they arrived.[44] Katsidzira and Reverend Murashwa found Chief Samaringa at a beer-drinking party at his homestead.[45] Beer parties were one manifestation of John Lonsdale's arenas of moral debate. They were important because they were occasions for re-enacting the gender division of labour, social status differentiation, and a reassertion of social cohesion and communal wellbeing. Such communal drinking is usually done to celebrate a good harvest, to reciprocate for work parties of neighbours who help each other in labour-intensive times in the agricultural cycle, on ritual occasions, or funerals and weddings. The production of beer by women and its consumption with the gendered and age-specific seating arrangements – the men sitting on stools and the women and children on the ground, females serving the beer, approaching the men on their knees – manifest social cohesion as well as hierarchies of status. However, as much as such opportunities served to re-assert male elder authority, they could also be a time of challenge. The NC Inyanga observed the impact of wage labour as early as 1927 when he found that young men and even women not only joined with the elders in the drinking, but that they demanded to partake in consuming the more prestigious strong beer (*musungwa*) previously reserved for 'privileged persons only'.[46]

When Katsidzira and Reverend Murashwa happened upon the chief and his party, the beer was passed to the visitors, as hospitality requires, but they declined. The men asked the Ziwe Zano elders about their denomination and Katsidzira explained that the Methodist Church does not allow the consumption of alcohol. Upon hearing this 'They asked him another question saying, "Do you want to establish your church in our area so that you will forbid us from having our nice drink?"' Chief Samaringa then angrily shouted: 'Do you think that this man will move around in your houses forbidding you from drinking beer?'[47] This account of the initial encounter between Ziwe Zano and the valley population from the Katsizira books is significant, for it provides inside into their mode of interaction for some time.

From a valley perspective, two aspects emerge. Specific aspects of mission Christianity, such as differences in prohibitions and rules between denominations, were already known in the Honde Valley by the late 1930s, at a time when mission stations had not yet been established in the area. This most likely is due to the migrant labour experience. Such knowledge was crucial in negotiating competing systems of belief and power. More importantly, the valley inhabitants' response shows just how precarious the initial encounter was for the negotiation of inclusion or exclusion against the backdrop of power and authority. Ziwe Zano elders' refusal to participate in the communal consumption of beer must have appeared to those present as a brusque refusal to adopt local ways and to thereby become part of the community. Their conduct was immediately interpreted as a potential threat to the local way of life and the chief's outbreak shows that he saw his authority challenged. A stance of suspicion and caution remained typical in these interactions for time to come.

Despite the conflictual turn of events, Chief Samaringa referred Katsidzira back to the NC and instructed him to consult Chief Mponda on the matter, who in turn gave his permission. *Mambo* Mutasa challenged Mponda's authority to allocate land to Ziwe Zano and was subsequently presented with 'gifts' of some money and articles produced at the mission.[48] In the end, the meeting with headman Samaringa and his elders in 1938 was crucial in establishing Ziwe Zano in the area. However, Honde Mission and Industrial School found little local support. Another elder, Musumba, wrote: 'The people around [Honde

4. Honde Mission, 1992: Old maternity ward, with Mount Chiwawadzira in the background (Source: Heike I. Schmidt)

Mission] were hostile.'[49] Nevertheless, its remoteness had made the valley an ideal site for these self-help men and women who did not wish 'to imitate Europeans'.[50] They sought the frontier in order to move beyond Rhodesian state control and without the intention of finding a population to convert, as would usually be the case with missionaries. Initially, then, Ziwe Zano members did not direct their efforts towards the valley population: 'Their chief aims and objects were to teach industry to older boys and girls from all over.'[51] This they did through the Methodist networks the founders of Ziwe Zano maintained with their peers.

In 1939, more members of the society joined life at the mission, and Ziwe Zano opened the Honde Industrial School. From the beginning it was agreed that those members living at the mission should teach without pay and keep neither personal possessions nor money, apart from the bare necessities.[52] By the end of that year the founders had erected mud huts which served as dormitories and started cotton fields. From 1940, the cotton yield provided sufficient supplies for girls' spinning courses, and by 1944 the maize harvest averaged 300 to 400 bags in a 'good year'.[53] Soon an abundant curriculum was introduced. Word spread throughout the region that Ziwe Zano was offering industrial training for free, even subsidising students.[54] This proved mainly successful in attracting girls from Manyikaland. By the beginning of 1941 the industrial school had thirty-nine students,[55] increasing to 113 four years later. The majority of the students continued to be girls and young women (85), most baptised Methodists or Anglicans. Their ages ranged from thirteen to twenty-six, but most of them (49) were seventeen or eighteen years old.[56] It is clear that keeping daughters out of harm's way, free tuition, and the fact that the school was the only one of its kind in the country at the time made it a success.[57]

Environmental resources, of crucial importance for enabling the society to provide free tuition and the materials needed for the industrial courses, were abundant until the early 1950s.[58] It was typical for the incorporation of newcomers in the valley at the time that, during the initial encounter at the beer-drinking party, neither the chief or the other men appeared to have raised concerns over resource allocation, such as land.[59] In addition to land, timber and water were also important. In 1941, great effort was made under the supervision of L.K. Kasambira to dig irrigation trenches to feed from a river nearby. A hammer mill to enable grinding and sawing was installed, which led to important breakthroughs: larger amounts of maize could be pounded and timber could be easily cut. The Location Superintendent Umtali, W.J. Brown, had sold the mill and saw to the society. He was so impressed with their commitment that he recommended the Godlonton Commission of 1944 to visit Honde Mission, and he himself praised the modernisers when giving evidence:

> I notice in my travels about this country that hardly any European town is a credit to us. We do not take advantage of the facilities for water power. When you go to the Hondi [sic] Gorge you will see that the Natives have adapted the water to serve their purposes, in domestic, industrial and a number of other ways.[60]

From their earliest days, then, Ziwe Zano had support from European sympathisers regarding the idea of African self-help, even though interaction with the valley inhabitants remained minimal during the first few years of their presence.

Dealings between the Ziwe Zano members and students with the valley inhabitants focused on the innovations the society brought to the area: consumer goods, medical services, and academic education. Due to the valley's relative remoteness from markets, local people showed a marked interest in the goods produced at the mission: chiefly cloth, sandals, furniture, and also maize.[61] Moreover, once the clinic opened in 1945, it drew many patients, mostly maternity cases, including people from Portuguese territory.[62] Society members used the opportunity to attempt conversion. In the words of the Methodist Church: 'out-patients under Kanyenze's care have an opportunity of hearing the Word of God, before they were given medicines'.[63] From the early 1940s, Ziwe Zano also made efforts to establish two primary schools in the valley, but faced administrative obstacles. It was during the struggle with the government and the Methodist mother church over the opening of the schools that the members' perception of the valley changed radically – they redefined their outsider status and claimed the valley as their spiritual landscape.

THE FIRE OF MOSES: PIONEERS MEET FRONTIER PEOPLE

Early in 1943, when Ziwe Zano failed to obtain permission from the government for opening schools, Katsidzira felt that Honde Mission itself was threatened. He decided to fast and to pray. Night prayers commenced:

During the Easter of 1943 prayers continued and children were divided into groups each group with its leader. After evening prayers, the people would go to their secret places for prayer. This was practiced mostly by girls.

One night Lord God visited one of the girls groups which had remained at prayer. He appeared to them in form of fire. The girls first saw the sparkling fire in a bush and the flame became bigger and spread over a considerable part of the forest. The leaves and grass seemed to be burning but there was no smell nor smoke…. The fire was just unnatural. The girls shouted, 'Come and see the fire of Moses.' People flocked to the place…. All the souls already saved, received the Holy Spirit. The sinners repented. Some of them were bumped against the ground and moved like snakes. Those who had evil spirits were [cleansed].[64]

Ziwe Zano members compared this experience of the Pentecost with the Great Revival of 1918.[65] In their perception, 'This [fire] showed the presence of Lord God's power in Ziwe Zano Society work.'[66] The Honde revival radically altered society members' understanding of and approach to the valley. The wilderness inhabited by roaming lions and the forest that could be utilised in the name of modernisation now was illuminated by the light of Moses' fire. Nightly prayers for the members and students in the hills became customary and, for the next ten years, until 1953, Ziwe Zano began to organise camp meetings at which fire, now interpreted as manifestations of the Holy Spirit, was seen in the vicinity of the mission and other parts of the valley, as well as in the neighbouring Nyamukwarara Valley. At these meetings Ziwe Zano sought converts and established outstations.[67]

It is striking that mainly women were attracted to prayer meetings,[68] these being an opportunity to challenge societal restrictions on their public expression and mobility. Notwithstanding the prominent roles of a few royal women, such as *muzvare* Muparutsa, whose Mahemasimike granite range is visible from Honde Mission, both according to frontier ethnicity and in Methodist understanding, females were expected to be subservient and restricted in gendered spatial practices. Heteronormativity in a rural context prescribed that women of reproductive age were to move only between the homestead, the fields, the river garden, the river, and the source of firewood. The latter two, defined as women's workplaces, were to be approached on paths that at certain times of the day were reserved for women, and from dusk to dawn females were not to leave the homestead. Accepted exceptions were ritual and religious occasions and emergencies or communal activities such as beer parties.

The view that mobility endangered African women's morality was shared by the colonial state, which criminalised such women and ostracised them by deeming them insane. Elizabeth Schmidt has convincingly shown that the triple alliance between the colonial state, missionaries, and African male elders often clashed with capital interest and that missionaries and elders competed over the control of African women's sexuality. Consequently, the colonial state tended to side with the elders on issues such as polygyny and with African men in general on restricting women's mobility in order to retain colonial hegemony.[69] The prayer meetings, however, provided a justification even for young, unmarried women to spend all night outdoors unsupervised. What probably also appealed to these women is that possession by the Holy Spirit was neither mediated by men nor other religious authorities and that it was a communal experience.[70]

Such behaviour contested male gerontocratic control.[71] Still, despite the temporary attraction Ziwe Zano provided to females, few joined the church. One of those young women who did was Dinah Nyamunokora.

Dinah Nyamunokora was a young girl from the Honde Valley who first had spiritual visions in 1950 which informed her that, 'she had been sent to spread the gospel of Jesus Christ among man'.[72] In contrast to the more complex process of bringing out a spirit, as is discussed in chapter six, speaking in tongues, trance, public confession, and repentance are usually sufficient to validate legitimacy and authority on Christian religious matters, as was the case with Nyamunokora. Over the next two years, she addressed meetings, first in the Honde Valley and then also in other districts, to which she had been invited by resident Ziwe Zano members.[73] One of her greater accomplishments must have been converting a Methodist cleric, Reverend Chitombo of Mutambara, in 1951, a year before a vision brought her career of prophesy to an end.[74]

Among the recorded incidents at Ziwe Zano camp meetings are that of a woman who was exorcised of an evil spirit which had made her kill her infant children and one occasion during which an epileptic man was healed.[75] Katsidzira claimed that 'the whole of Honde Valley had a great revival of their souls and a big number of people were saved'.[76] However, by 1946, only two full members had been brought into the fold and the society's activities were still met with hostility.[77] With the arrival of thousands of African households evicted from the highveld beginning in 1948, camp meetings held some appeal to the many already proselytised newcomers,[78] but this did not last long as mission churches rapidly established a presence and Honde Mission became ever more thoroughly marginalised.

In short, the Ziwe Zano Society which established Honde Mission with its Industrial School in the valley in 1938/39 provides an example of African pioneers who sought a niche away from colonial interference, enabling them to pursue their modernising mission to provide industrial skills and a Christian lifestyle to young African women and men, far away from temptations, so that they could face the new world into which they had been born. The frontier status of the valley made it possible that agricultural production at Honde Mission flourished within a short period of time, and this success, together with the manufactured products and thriving marketing, stood in direct contrast to their founding myth of the valley as a remote wilderness. Moreover, through Moses' fire and the Honde Revival of 1943 that brought light into the uncivilised wilderness, the modernisers re-imagined the valley, now laying claim to it as their spiritual landscape, while also attempting to convert the frontier people, albeit without much success. The 1943 revival was a key experience for Ziwe Zano members and their students, even if the impact in the valley appears to have been marginal. By the 1990s only society members or people who lived in the immediate vicinity of the mission remembered the revival or knew of Ziwe Zano at all, despite its ongoing existence. The society's failure to become part of local communities placed its members in a fragile position upon the arrival of the liberation fighters in the 1970s; the church elders' disconnect from information regarding guerrilla presence and ZANLA's concerted effort at mobilising the school youths turned the mission into a hot spot of the conflict in the area. What nobody could foresee was that Chiwawadzira mountain would be the site of the biggest firefight of the entire liberation war in 1977, as is discussed in chapter five.

European Pioneers: Penetrating Wilderness

European pioneers first arrived in the Honde Valley as late as the 1950s, bringing with them their imaginations of an African wilderness that needed to be penetrated, tamed, explored, and controlled. Mapping and stabilising the frontier were integral parts of the expansion of European domination, of colonial control, and the modernisation project this entailed.[79] These were ways in which claims to and legitimacy of domination over an area were expressed as well as achieved. European expansion itself was characterised by a frontier approach to domination. Colonial exploration of the valley was late compared to other parts of the colony. In 1928, NC Umtali Bazeley inspected the southern part of the Honde Valley, that is, Manga and part of Umtasa North Reserve, for the first time.[80] The northern part, Holdenby, remained unexplored until the early 1950s. William Igoe acquired a large part of Holdenby Block in 1952, but 1956 the NC Inyanga had only this to report about the adjacent area reserved for African occupation: 'Holdenby, north of the Pungwe, is roadless, hilly, covered with tropical vegetation, and practically unknown.'[81]

Despite the geographic obstacles and lack of information about the area, Igoe started operations at his tea plantation, Aberfoyle, in 1952 and founded a second estate within six years, as well as running a forestry plantation on the plateau.[82] Igoe and the Europeans who worked for him saw themselves as pioneers at the settler frontier and imagined the valley as a wilderness that needed to be penetrated in order to be controlled. The discourse of these newcomers echoes Achille Mbembe's 'phallic gesture', the sexualised colonial violence that becomes a cultural practice imprinted on the colonised in practice, thought, and innermost being.[83] However, in contrast to Mbembe, who portrays such colonial violence as overpowering and successful in its objectification of the colonial subjects, the argument here is that it is crucial to gain a subtle, layered understanding of such violence, and in turn to allow for a range of interactions on part of the colonised. In the Honde Valley, the handful of Europeans who established tea plantations did cause suffering, not least through land alienation, but in the 1950s and '60s they were also ignored in the main by the local population. At times their presence was even interpreted as an additional layer of frontier opportunities, as long as they remained outsiders and did not interfere with the frontier way of life in the valley.

TAMING THE LANDSCAPE

Igoe appears to have commenced looking into land acquisition in Zimbabwe in earnest only in November 1951 and quickly set his sights on Holdenby Block, located in the northern part of the valley. He bought a portion of this largely unexplored land, approximately 48,000 acres, for £30,000, registered in his wife Karen Elizabeth's name, with himself as one of the three directors.[84] In 1954, he opened operations at Aberfoyle Plantations in *ishe* Zindi's area and in 1958 expanded the tea-growing further north into the Chikomba chieftaincy. At that point, the first plantation was renamed Eastern Highlands Tea Estates (EHTE) and the second became Aberfoyle, named after his father-in-law's rubber plantation in Asia. In 1948, the NC Inyanga emphasised the remoteness and isolation of the valley in the context of the planned resettlement of the African population from the highveld: 'owing to the broken nature of the country and the thick tropical vegetation the settlement of natives into this area will take some years because the country will have to be "tamed" as it were'.[85] Taming the landscape was exactly the intention that Igoe and his men had in mind.

The European pioneers' encounter with their wilderness underwent three initial stages: land acquisition, land exploration, and land cultivation. The colonial government reserved the north-western slopes of the Honde Valley leading up into Chief Tangwena's Kaerezi area as Inyanga Block, for white occupation. The BSAC granted the first title deed to the block, which initially consisted of roughly 154,400 acres (62,000 hectares), to the Anglo-French Matabeleland Company in 1895, issuing it in 1897. This was part of the BSAC's attempts to draw capital into the developing colonial economy.[86] At the time, the main impetus was to bring about a 'second Rand', that is, a gold rush as had happened in South Africa from 1886 at the Witwatersrand, which, together with the discovery of diamonds in 1867, had set into motion the mineral revolution in that country. But the second Rand never happened. In 1928, the Anglo-French Matabeleland Company went into liquidation, and in 1930 the property was split. The London Rhodesia Company (Lonrho) bought the southern part, the Holdenby Block, and the Hanmer brothers acquired the northern portion, which was approximately 90,000 acres in size.[87] In 1948, Lonrho sold their part to the Rhodesian Government,[88] which in turn sold it to a group of Rhodesian businessmen. The latter finally entered the agreement with Igoe in 1952.[89]

Igoe found that the agricultural potential of Holdenby Block had not even been established, and once his interest was drawn to the property, together with a crew, he went to investigate. Wightwick, Igoe's first local agent who had recommmended the land, emphasised with good reason the exceptional investment opportunity Holdenby Block offered:

> I think that this bit of country is quite unique and I doubt whether the opportunity to acquire land suitable for the planting of crops requiring a heavy rainfall is likely to occur anywhere else in Rhodesia. This is in fact the last large block of undeveloped land in the heavy rainfall area in the Colony.[90]

Igoe showed himself surprised that this prime land, including the more accessible parts at higher elevation, had remained uncharted:

> it is still incomprehensible to me that the top plateau has never been completely explored and, except for a reconnaissance made 25 years ago by an old inhabitant, no Europeans have penetrated into the interior of this extremely large block.[91]

Wightwick, in turn, explained why such a substantial piece of land was not only undeveloped, but still not even explored by the early 1950s. He emphasised the widespread practice of absentee landlordism and speculation:

> You must understand that in the early days large grants of land were made principally to mining companies. For instance the Inyanga Block originally belonged to the Anglo French Corporation who of course took it off the map and never saw it until they sold it.[92]

Wightwick provided examples of other companies which for decades had owned thousands of acres without even investigating their commercial potential. Although the myth of the partition of Africa during the Berlin Conference has been debunked, it is hard to overemphasise the element of land speculation in the early colonial period that had a two-sided effect on the local African population: on the one hand, in parts of the colony, the impact of the imposition of colonial rule was minimal, on the other hand, land appropriation was entirely arbitrary. Here, the first European owner, the Anglo-French Matabeleland Company had applied to the Administrator of Rhodesia, Jameson, for land in Matabeleland in 1894. Instead, they were granted Inyanga Block on the condition that they would spend '£60,000 in mining or farming operations' during the following years.[93] They did no such thing and in 1928 the company could not provide any detailed information to potential buyers, even though they had employed a European resident of the district, Major van Niekerk, as their agent from at least the previous year, a role that the major also fulfilled for other absentee landlords in the area.[94] His main task was to collect rent from African tenants and mission outstations and to represent the owners' interests towards local government representatives.[95] Still, he never inspected the land, nor did the NC Inyanga, and for Holdenby Block the situation only began to change with the 1952 exploration of the area.

Wightwick explained that 'In the early days you only developed places where you could get an ox-wagon in, and places where you could grow maize successfully.' He continued 'until roads penetrated into these districts ... the large holdings did not become broken up.'[96] Wightwick evoked the image of settler pioneers, prepared to take on the hard-ship to explore remote areas for development, here through the medium of ox-wagons which Peter Anderson referred to as 'the vehicles of frontier, the agents of encounter'.[97] Wightwick, however, contrasted the early settlers and the absentee landlords with the true pioneers of the frontier, entrepreneurs on the spot such as Igoe. Settlers – supported by the racial land policies in the young colony that made the best and most accessible land available to Europeans – might define the boundary between the known and the unknown, between settlement and no-man's land, yet pioneers move beyond that and create the frontier. Igoe was a wealthy company owner, but not a man usually found at the boardroom table. He and his wife Karen participated in investigating their property even in the very first stages which required them to climb the escarpment and to put up with tented camps.[98] Not surprisingly, the Zimbabwean *Farming Gazette Supplement* celebrated the World War II veteran as 'a London Irish businessman, fighter pilot and international rugby triallist' in 1985.[99]

Land acquisition was quickly followed by thorough land exploration. It was only in 1951, the year Igoe first learned about the area, that Holdenby SNA was to be inspected for the first time by the local NC.[100] Exploration of the commercial land certainly remained entirely in private hands. Initially, Igoe's plan had been 'to be entirely elastic' and to accommodate as many as ten plantations under the umbrella of Inyangani (Inyanga) Estates Ltd, each on a 999-year land lease.[101] That, however, did not transpire. Igoe set his mind on tea and timber, making contact with the Kericho Tea Research Institute in Kenya by the end of 1951, and by January 1952, he had an exploratory group on the block that started planting a tea nursery.[102] In April, Igoe hired George Williamson and Co., a Kenyan tea company and tea seed provider, to send experts, accompanied by local technocrats, to explore further Holdenby Block.[103] During a two-day visit, they found the slopes of the escarpment at a certain altitude suitable for tea growing, but they worried about the lack of roads. From the initial exploration to the mechanics of establishing working plantations, the effort required would be tremendous due to the district administration having yet to show a direct presence in the area as well as the challenges of topography, climate, and the lack of infrastructure.

Until 1960, Holdenby was connected with the southern part of the valley only by means of a dugout canoe ferry across the Honde River. According to a European observer from the 1920s, the 'swift and treacherous Hondi, [was] famous – or infamous – for crocodiles'.[104] Thus all materials had to be transported from the west, down the steep slopes from the Nyanga highveld where there was frost in winter, through the rainforest, to the sub-tropical foothills where the Eastern Highlands headquarters and the first nursery were established.[105] Starting in January 1952, the exploratory group quickly constructed a 17.5-mile pilot track that connected the area with Inyanga town, but work proved to be tedious: 'Our working parties inside the Block have faced considerable difficulties in maintaining supplies during the rainy season. For days on end, they were cut off and provisions were brought in by donkey.'[106] As a result, European staff were forced to live in tents and to depend on local food supplies. They hardly ever had the opportunity to leave the valley, the journey to the closest city for a weekend visit being too cumbersome. This impaired the well-being of staff, and one of the early managers was forced to resign, as he failed to cope with the situation.[107] What remained was the challenge of transport out of the valley. Igoe observed:

> It may appear astonishing in London that the owners of such a property were not interested in exploring it but the valley is a geographical oddity, its natural entrance being from Portuguese territory. To the west and south-west, mountain barriers, with nothing but native paths, bar entry and give little indication of the luxuriant vegetation that exists inside.[108]

The difficult western approach to the Honde Valley posed the same problem from the Portuguese perspective. From Mozambique, it was easy to enter the valley, but the steep slopes of the escarpment still had to be overcome if one wanted to travel further west. Hence, in 1890 the entrepreneur Andrada came to the conclusion that building a railway line to the Manica goldfields through the valley would not be feasible, because of the 'formidable barrier of mountains'.[109] Still, in March 1952, Igoe's local agent, Wightwick, predicted that road construction, estimated at a cost of £500-£800 per mile, would not be too difficult, because labour was available. He did concede, however, that the difficult terrain had clearly prevented this task from being done before.[110] Seven months later, when Hugh Thomas, a George Williamson man, inspected progress on the plantation, he found little change:

> The whole area is very inaccessible and it is only within the last few months that a start has been made towards driving an inlet into the property; very slow progress is, however, being made, mainly owing to the nature of the country to be traversed coupled with the fact that very little labour is at the moment available, and the road-head has not yet penetrated sufficiently far to be of any great practical use; the only means of access at the moment is therefore a very rough and mountainous jeep-track … some three miles into the property from the northern boundary. From there on any investigation must be carried out on foot, and a thorough traverse of the block would entail several weeks in camp and much heavy walking.[111]

Thomas's conclusion was that by October 1952 it was still impossible to even assess the area, let alone successfully establish commercial agriculture there. Igoe eventually proved him wrong, but transportation problems continued to challenge progress.[112] Taming the wilderness would remain important to the success of the plantations for the next few years, as would taming the frontier people.[113]

Mbembe observed that colonisation is 'an arbitrary, contingent, stark fact', an argument illustrated by the practice of naming, which is an important part of exploration.[114] Even before the imposition of colonial rule, Karl Mauch, probably the first western observer who travelled through the northern part of Inyanga Block in 1872, ventured to name two mountains Moltke and Bismarck and an area of supposed gold deposits the Kaiser Wilhelm Goldfield, names that remained in usage into the early twentieth century.[115] This clearly constituted mapping of a landscape as part of imperialist appropriation, albeit before Africa's partition, whereas Igoe's practice appears to have been entirely arbitrary and military style:

> In order to prevent confusion arising with so many rivers in the area prefixed 'Nyam' we have renamed the principal ones as follows: the first river on the way in from the north entrance is the Honey, the next the Butterfly, and the third, the Buffalo.[116]

Naming is part of enframing and a violent practice in its disregard for vernacular knowledge and cosmology. However, few of the colonial names appear to have left an imprint in the valley, including those of the rivers which today are known by their original names with their 'Nyam' prefix.

For pioneers like Igoe, penetrating and taming the land entailed more than establishing economically viable commercial agriculture, just as it did for settlers who limited their aspirations to the parts of the frontier that could be reached by ox-wagon. Igoe made it his project to create landscape, to transform the impenetrable wilderness into a place of familiarity. This practice of imperial landscaping found an expression in the sexualisation of African landscape in European narrative.[117] Colonial administrators, settlers, missionaries, explorers, technocrats, and entrepreneurs on the spot – such as Igoe – imagined African landscape as primordial virgin land that needed to be penetrated. This inher-

5. *Aberfoyle Tea Plantations, 1992: View towards Mount Tangwena and Sagambe*
(Source: Heike I. Schmidt)

ently violent stance both legitimised colonial land alienation and at the same
time invested such space with imperial meaning. The Comaroffs observed that
European colonialism as a cultural project involved 'practices that would dis-
place indigenous forms, recreating them in Europe's image'.[118] Such practices
included landscaping, naming, and creating acreage.[119]

The aesthetics of tea plantations are stunning in themselves. At Aberfoyle,
tea bushes are planted at exactly equal intervals on steep slopes, in clearly
delineated rows that follow the outline of each hill, with the fields bordered
by poinsettia and each tea bush kept pruned: the landscaping displays sheer
geometric mastery equalling the control exhibited at formal gardens such as
Versailles. An early element of the creation of this cultured and cultivated landscape was surveying, which made it possible to turn wilderness into acreage
and land for production. But there are still to this day patches of rainforest that
merge in the higher areas into pine forest plantations and Nyanga National Park.
In the mid-twentieth century, parts of Inyanga district had already enchanted
Europeans by their appearance as a Scotland in Africa, and Holdenby Block
contributed to this appropriation. Father Lewis, outspoken pro-settler and the
resident Anglican priest in the Honde Valley in the 1960s, wrote in his autobi-
ography about the highlands:

> The Downs themselves, with their settled European population and their holiday
> cottages, were largely the work of a handful of pioneers who arrived in the nineteen-
> thirties. Major McIlwaine and the Hanmer brothers found bare wind-swept hills,
> planted trees (especially pines which spread like wildfire) and ended up with another
> Scotland, complete with man-made lakes and waterfalls and trout-streams. The steep
> and winding lanes were often shrouded in a Scotch mist.[120]

In 1952, Igoe himself boasted that 'South of the Equator, there is no part of Africa that possesses a climate as healthy as this area', and that the appearance of the block was reminiscent of Scotland, albeit with a significantly better top-soil.[121] The resemblance to Scotland was further underlined by nearby highland tourist resorts that attracted the business community and the well-to-do, not least through the trout-fishing resources.

The absence of malaria and other tropical maladies in the Eastern Highlands, where the general elevation is around 6,000 feet, peaking at 8,504 feet on Mount Nyangani, Zimbabwe's highest mountain, made the area sought after by Europeans from their earliest presence until today. Cecil Rhodes himself first visited Nyanga in 1891, when he claimed 96,000 acres for his Rhodes Nyanga Estate, part of which he bequeathed to the state on his death in 1902 to establish Nyanga National Park, and he even thought about choosing the area as his burial site.[122] Henry Schlichter, an explorer and archaeologist, who spent time in the area examining its stone structures in the 1890s, declared that 'Inyanga is decidedly the pearl of Mashonaland'.[123] Accordingly, in addition to the sexualisation of African landscape that signified taking possession of it through penetration, the taming that followed allowed the human hand to create Scotch mist in Africa.[124] It is significant that the success in establishing commercial agricultural acreage is not prominent in this discourse. These pioneers saw modernisation efforts through capitalist enterprise as a given, while the challenges of the African wilderness throughout the colonial period, and here as late as the 1950s, crystallised in terms of power and control. Despite all difficulties, the taming of the land made rapid progress, but taming the frontier people proved to be a bigger obstacle.

TAMING THE PEOPLE

Colonial economies in Africa, during different periods of time, tended to suffer from labour shortages. The concern over labour certainly quickly became a central issue once planting commenced at the tea plantations in the Honde Valley. Decades later it escalated into a conflict over competing claims of belonging and ownership of landscape in the Zindi area, and land use remained at best of secondary concern until the liberation war when the guerrilla fighters promised to divide the plantations into family plots. Two episodes from Chief Zindi's area illustrate this argument: one the initial conflict over labour recruitment in 1954 and the second a dispute over the ancestral graves in 1992.

During the initial exploration of Holdenby Block early in 1952 most of the labour was recruited from areas adjacent to the valley, and the European pioneers were confident that the increased labour demand would be easily met with tenant labour once planting began.[125] Wightwick found that 600 potential workers lived on the property itself, with up to 3,000 close by available for recruitment.[126] In his report about the January 1952 exploration, Igoe compared the labour situation with that in Kenya and trusted that workers would be available:

provided we proceed carefully, even the women and piccaninnies [children] can be employed on the tea plantations if they are not treated badly at this stage and, later on,

6. *Chief Zindi at his homestead, 1992: Eastern Highlands Tea Estates in the background* (Source: Heike I. Schmidt)

> encouraged by generous wages to make their lives centre around the factory .... There are Native Reserves on almost all sides, which should keep us free from labour troubles provided an enlightened policy is pursued. Although the race in the district (Manicas) is not very energetic, this fate is compensated for by their extreme docility.[127]

Igoe added that building a school would further attract child labour, and he observed that 'being squatters, the natives are forced to work for us under pain of eviction'.[128] In 1954, when planting commenced at Aberfoyle, in 1958 renamed EHTE, Igoe set high hopes on the new road which would facilitate enforcement of tenant labour:

> Male labour is still a little shy and difficult to coerce because of the scattered and remote positions of their rondavels. Better results will be obtained when the road is completed and it is made possible for us to use native policemen to round up absentees. The fact that the Native Commissioners can come into the Block by car (some are well beyond middle age) will make a great difference. As far as I know, no Native Commissioner has been right through our Block, although they are assumed to have intimate knowledge of the areas they control.[129]

Despite all the predictions, few men from the Honde Valley worked on the plantations until the late 1970s, although women, juveniles and children could be employed for seasonal work.[130] From the very beginning, management was well aware of the advantages of the border proximity and migrant labour routes for labour supplies and soon began to rely on migrant labour, with the majority of workers coming from Malawi and Mozambique.

Since the 1930 Land Apportionment Act (LAA), labour agreements had been enforced throughout the colony in order to create a stable workforce for commercial agricultural production. Families were allowed to stay on the estate and cultivate limited areas of land, if, in return, the male adult members of the household worked at least 150 days per year for the company.[131] With commencement of operations in 1954, *ishe* Zindi refused to enter such a labour agreement.[132] Instead, he decided to move with his people across the estate boundary. In office since 1951, he recalled the incident, in the early 1990s:

> When they [Aberfoyle] came here, we assumed they wanted to plough only a small portion of land …. And we let them be …. I was not moved from there, no. They had told me that I was free to settle there, but then they would give me work to do. But I felt this was not beneficial – I could not stay on a farm when I was ruler of the land. That is why I did not take long to leave that place. When they marked their boundary, I found myself living within their tea plantation. I was within the tea plantation. So I decided to move. I then shifted and came to stay here.[133]

His new home was a mere 250 yards from the boundary with the plantation.[134] This move infuriated the estate manager, who complained to the NC Inyanga about it:

> We know you had already told all the Headmen and most of the natives in the area, that they could not move into the reserve, and that they are flagrantly disregarding your orders in doing so now. We have also been advised that Zindi has told all the boys not to carry their situpas [identity cards] when moving in our area, and that he is responsible for advising his followers to disobey your instructions. He is an extremely undesirable character to hold the position he has, and, if the above allegations against him are proved, I would suggest that you remove him from the district and demote him to shovelling coal at Wankie.[135]

Chief Zindi was never condemned to become a coal miner, but he did acquire the reputation of being rebellious. During the war of liberation he was sent into detention because he supported guerrillas operating in his area,[136] and in the 1990s, by then an elderly man, he still stood his ground against the plantation management.

The manager could do nothing to prevent this move by Zindi and so appealed to the NC for help, drawing on the racial land legislation in the settler colony. The Native Land Husbandry Act of 1951 determined that during the period of African land use evaluation no African was allowed to move onto land reserved for African occupation, and only those African men who were already resident in a reserve at that time were permitted to apply for land use rights. Therefore, the manager argued, Zindi's move was illegal according to the new legislation:[137]

> We would be extremely grateful for your assistance in squaring the move before it really gets out of hand. We rely on these natives and their wives to assist us in the development of the Estate, and as we are potential food growers and therefore an asset to the country, we feel that we should have the support of all concerned in stopping the present movement of our labour force which is detrimental to our producing the crops we intend producing, and therefore detrimental to the country.[138]

However, when the NC looked into the question, he found that while Zindi had indeed not been permitted to move, at the same time, the 1950 amendment of the LAA stipulated that Africans should be evicted from European land, Crown land, and Native Purchase Areas and that they were to be resettled into reserves within five years.[139] The NC referred the matter to the Provincial Native Commissioner (PNC), who came to the same conclusion:

> I very much doubt if you can force them to return to Aberfoyle Plantations, because by doing so you would be forcing them to commit a statutory offence i.e. illegally entering a European area …. However, I realize that the natives should be encouraged to enter into a labour agreement and I suggest you do what you can to bring this about.[140]

Hence, for a few years, the new legislation left the government in a limbo: on one hand, Africans were supposed to be evicted from European land unless they entered a labour agreement, but on the other, an uncontrolled move into one of the reserves was not allowable. So, according to law, Chief Zindi and his people could neither be forced to return to Aberfoyle, nor be allowed to stay in Holdenby Reserve. Zindi and his people refused to return to the plantation and the local labour supply remained a problem. Even so, in 1958 planting commenced at the new tea estate, now named Aberfoyle, in part in Chief Chikomba's area. Neither chief, Zindi or Chikomba, nor their followers entered a labour agreement, nor did they fight for their land; instead, they moved onto Holdenby Reserve.[141]

In the case of Chief Zindi, the dispute clearly represents a working misunderstanding with the plantation management that assumed an African 'traditional authority' would never voluntarily give up his land, while Zindi and his followers negotiated the ever-changing frontier landscape of the valley in practical terms, without a notable sense of suffering due to the move. In the absence of an outside threat, such as the nineteenth century *madzviti* raids, the slopes of the escarpment were not seen as prime agricultural land, which instead is located on the valley bottom and in the foothills, and previous chiefs Zindi and their followers had already resided at the boundary, but off Holdenby Block in 1925 and 1947.[142] When *ishe* Zinde declared of the mountain areas, his birth place, that 'I was not born here [in the foothills], but in those mountains. Yes. We stayed there generation after generation',[143] this was primarily a strategic and political claim. The strong sense of spatial boundaries as a resource, as had been the case at the turn of the century, in the days when border crossing was the order of every tax season, certainly underlay Chief Zindi's move barely across the estate line. This was clearly a provocation, and when opportune he would claim his ancestral lands wherever it would benefit his chieftaincy most.

Another major conflict arose between Chief Zindi, still in office, and the EHTE management in the early 1990s. Both Chiefs Chikomba and Zindi lay claim over spiritual landscape that is located on the tea plantations, access to which enables them to successfully negotiate the preservation of the ancestral graves on estate land. This is particularly pertinent for ritual purposes, because it is at the graves that the annual rain rituals are performed and thus the well-being of the entire community is ensured.[144] When one plantation broke the arrangement, competing claims to the meaning and practice of landscape came afore.

In 1991, the EHTE management decided to deforest the top of one of the hills in order to construct a helicopter landing place to give high level management easy access to the estate. The trees were felled, despite the fact that there is a landing strip for light aircraft nearby at Ruda, which can be reached comfortably from the estate offices in less than thirty minutes by car on a tarred road.[145] The patch of forest that was destroyed was home to the ancestral graves of the royal Zindi lineage, and was thus part of the area's spiritual landscape. At the time, the valley was experiencing the worst drought in living memory. In September 1992, on the verge of the next rainy season, when the elders started preparing for the rain ritual, management denied them access to the grave site. The urgently awaited rains failed to break. This caused heated debate in the surrounding homesteads as well as in the labour compounds on the estates.

The drought was attributed to the tree-felling and the ensuing desecration of the graves. In an interview with *ishe* Zindi in early October 1992, he and his *sabhuku* Gogodi brought the issue up repeatedly. Zindi emphasised his ritual responsibilities: 'My duties include performing rituals for the area …. Yes, and also to maintain order in the area, by performing rain-rituals'. Gogodi added that even the estate manager used to consult the chief in matters of rainfall: 'The white man who was there used to visit here and tell us that the tea was getting dry due to lack of rain, so we had to do something.' He went on to explain the current conflict:

> The changamire [chief] went to them and told them not to desecrate the graveyard, if they did not want to disturb rainfall. They refused to listen to him, saying that they had bought the land…. And that whoever had died would not resurrect, so they refused to compensate for the graves …. We were no longer allowed to visit the dense foliage and perform our rituals.[146]

The management refused to negotiate and the drought persisted. EHTE had to reduce their work capacity and lay off labour, and for one month Aberfoyle was forced to close down completely. Finally, the management was prepared to make a concession and began negotiations with Chief Zindi. In the end, both sides settled on a payment of compensation that included a nominal amount of money and some bags of millet for the brewing of beer for the ritual. The following day, 10 November 1992, the weather changed drastically with the onset of torrential rains. The rainfall was limited exactly to *ishe* Zindi's *dunhu* (territory).

Chief Zindi and the plantation management's contest over land and labour illustrates two arguments along the axes of tradition and resistance. Tradition could be a successful, if not powerful, tool used by African elders vis-à-vis colonial interests. One example for such strategic use of tradition and custom in the context of nationalism occurred in 1975, during the liberation war. Four men were charged with having called a meeting at Ruda with more than twelve Africans without permission from the government. During the court case, one of the accused defended himself calling upon custom:

> This is custom as Africans [sic] that when a child is born we say congratulations.
>
> By the court: You are now saying that this was a birthday celebration or something like

that?-----Yes. Our children had come from detention and were saying congratulations, and we had to have a feast.[147]

The defendant thus argued that release from detention was a rebirth, and that this was not a political act, but a traditional obligation to attend the celebration to welcome their children. In the discourse of power, such allegedly authentic claims as Chief Zindi's over ancestral lands worked within the system of colonial understanding that saw African societies as primitive tribes with one redeeming feature: unchanging in essence, and hence upholding authentic customs and traditions, albeit increasingly threatened by the modernising influences introduced by colonial capitalism.[148] Oddly, the historiography on land and belonging often still reproduces such notions of authenticity, although historically it has been shown for a long time that African societies have been characterised more often than not by mobility and change.[149]

At the same time, while tradition may be a successful tool, the agenda might at any given point be radically partisan rather than nationalist or one of resistance. In fact, the tension between a discourse of tradition and continuity and a discourse of change – caused by opportunity, desire, or necessity – is a key element both of moral ethnicity and political tribalism within and beyond this frontier society and lies at the core of chiefly and elder authority. Jim Scott developed the dual concept of the public and hidden transcript in order to grasp the majority's subordination. According to Scott, the public transcript is one of deference towards the dominant minority, while the hidden one is a divergent counter-discourse. The concept applies here, but not necessarily in the same manner. Instead, turning Scott on his head, one way of understanding Zindi's and other elders' claims over their ancestral lands – whether in negotiation with European settlers, the colonial state, or neighbours – can be seen as a public transcript that is strategic, but not of deference.[150] Thinking of tradition as a political tool is not to undermine any real sense of suffering when, in this case, land is appropriated or spiritual landscape is desecrated. What this approach does is to challenge the notion of the authentic vernacular, avoiding a return of scholarship into the realm of colonial knowledge or the resistance paradigm.

In short, in 1952, after sixty years of absentee landlordism and the violation of vernacular cosmology, land practices, and belonging by capitalising Inyanga Block through land speculation, European pioneers arrived who imagined the valley as a wilderness that needed to be penetrated and tamed. The valley residents ignored or undermined these attempts when men withheld their labour, while women and children began to work on the newly established plantations. Their strategic response resembles the border practices of the previous decades, but the land and landscape appropriations by European tea planters led to varying outcomes. In the Zindi area, the move from Holdenby Block barely left any imprint until the introduction of forced labour on the plantations as part of the counter-insurgency campaign during the liberation war, when they became major grievances. At the same time, displacement caused bitter resentment in the Chikomba area from the late 1950s onwards. This contributed to the single most deadly attack of the entire liberation war, the Aberfoyle massacre in 1976, with evidence pointing to an attack by ZANLA.[151]

Manyika Modernisers: Innovation & Integration

In the late 1940s, the Native Department began to resettle thousands of African households, typically into lower lying reserves in Manyikaland, as most of the best land, in part defined by high rainfall and a more accommodating disease environment, had been reserved for white occupation. This was part of a nationwide campaign to enforce the 1950 Amendment of the 1930 Land Apportionment Act, which meant the eviction of 'illegal occupants' of privately owned land, Native Purchase Areas, and Crown land within five years.[152] In the Honde Valley the consequences of the policy's implementation differed between the north and the south. Some evictees were allocated land in the southern part that belonged to Umtali district and consisted of Manga Native Reserve, Umtasa North Native Reserve and a small territory, SNA 'B' Umtali. Here, with road access and Honde Mission, infrastructure and marketing facilities were available. Others found themselves relocated to the significantly more remote northern part of the valley that belonged to Inyanga district, consisting of the two tea plantations and SNA 'A' Inyanga. The SNA consisted of two parts of the valley bottom, one directly adjacent to, and both east of Holdenby Block. This territory was only explored by the colonial administration in 1951 and renamed Holdenby Native Reserve.[153] Having an effective administration on the ground was partly hampered by the artificial split of the area between two districts, something that was only rectified in 1973 with the creation of Mutasa district. Despite regional variations, overall, the move to the Honde Valley proved to be dramatic for the newcomers as well as the valley inhabitants: the immigration waves caused rapid demographic and environmental change, quickly followed by adaptation. This time, however, the newcomers were not simply introduced to the local social protocol, for a process of mutual assimilation unfolded.

FORCED RESETTLEMENT

The relocation exercise into the Honde Valley began when the government moved two hundred families from Tsonzo in July 1948, after it had been designated as a Native Purchase Area. 'High veldt Manyika' is the term predominantly used in government correspondence in reference to Africans from Inyanga and Umtali districts who lived in high-altitude areas.[154] The NC Umtali had warned that this could lead to severe environmental degradation and that the movement had to be closely supervised.[155] However, lack of staff made this impossible. During the following two years the valley saw a major influx of newcomers who were threatened by evictions in Umtasa South Reserve and other areas in Umtali and Inyanga districts.[156] Umtasa North Reserve and Holdenby were soon declared to be 'fully populated'.[157] The valley had become a major resettlement area, even though the administration was clearly aware of its unsuitability.

Upon their arrival in the Honde Valley, many of the immigrants found themselves facing two major obstacles: unfamiliar disease and agricultural environments. In 1938, when Mvere, a Ziwe Zano supporter whose own family was relocated from Tsonzo to Holdenby ten years later, suggested the Honde Valley as a suitable site for Honde Mission, he pointed out: 'But there is a disadvantage with this place, there is a disease.'[158] The disease was malaria, which was – and still is – highly prevalent in the valley. Robin Palmer, in his classic study on colonial land policies, found 'a marked degree of cynicism' and 'magnanim-ity' in the Land Settlement Department when officials proposed the Umtasa North Reserve in 1914, as the land was deemed totally unsuitable for European occupation in the face of the heat, malaria, and other disadvantages.[159] In fact, in the early 1920s 'high veldt Manyikas' refused to move into lower-lying areas, which they considered to be 'too hot and too far away'.[160] Likewise, NC Inyanga Bazeley emphasised his doubts about the suitability of low-lying areas such as the Honde Valley for occupation by 'high veldt natives'. He argued in 1922:

> The ordinary high veldt Manyika native is almost, if not quite, as susceptible to malaria as a European and feels extreme heat almost as much. His huts are perched high up and are kept well ventilated, in places which the ordinary European would deem far too exposed to bitter winds.[161]

Along the same lines as Bazeley's advice in the 1920s, in 1949 the Health Department strongly urged against resettling Africans from the plateau into the valley, for a high mortality rate was expected, mainly due to immune defi-ciency.[162] Today, Manyika immigrants still remember that many of the first and second generation, especially children, died of malaria and of 'heat'.[163] Ironi-cally, in 1950, when there were plans for the Governor to visit Honde Mission, he was advised not to do so, 'as it lies low in the Honde Valley which is very malarious, and is served by an appallingly bad road'.[164]

The swift Manyika immigration had a dramatic demographic impact, and the sudden increase in population density, together with the unfamiliar cli-mate and soils, caused rapid environmental degradation. In preparation for the first immigration wave, the LDO Inyanga had inspected the area around the Mahemasimike mountain range, near Ruda. He found the vegetation thick and tropical and the land heavily wooded, with trees seven to ten meters high, and grass two to three. He emphasised that despite cultivation mainly taking place on very steep slopes, there was no erosion and crops were generally excellent.[165] This changed drastically with the rainy season of 1951/52. The newly arrived immigrants doubled the population at Ruda, cut down trees to clear land for cultivation, and, being accustomed to different ecological environments, were not familiar with local practices of soil conservation.[166] This sudden and large-scale impact was aggravated by that year's heavy rains which set into motion severe erosion from which the land never recovered. Two women who lived at Honde Mission at the time remembered this as a disastrous event. One said:

> Elder: It was either in 1951 or 1952 when there were heavy rains. I slept on top of the table, and I took the children's bedding and put them inside the house. Do you hear?

> Younger woman: Uh.

> Elder: We walked in much water which had flooded the house. There was all water inside.

Younger woman: Uh.

Elder: Yes. Much rain poured, and the stretch of treeless grassland appeared as if a caterpillar had worked the ground. It was an astonishing event.

Younger woman: There was lots of erosion taking place that time …. It's the erosion of that area she is talking about, because it was swampy then. When the trees were cut I think then they started … erosion …. When the people [highveld immigrants] came … they started cutting down trees.[167]

The significance of these environmental changes in the southern part of the Honde Valley becomes apparent in the problems which scarcity of resources brought about at Honde Mission. Whereas the mission had previously been self-sufficient, from 1954, provisions for students became a major problem. For the following two years, food was bought with savings and from the sale of all their cattle. In 1956, after these measures had failed to significantly improve the situation, it was decided to revise school and boarding fees and to reduce the intake of new students. In addition, society members donated money.[168] The environmental changes also had a direct impact on the curriculum, as the scarcity of timber affected carpentry courses. The sale of furniture in the valley and other areas had by then become an important source of income for the industrial school.[169] The situation at the mission was further aggravated when land was newly allocated in Umtasa North Reserve according to government directives which led to a reduction of Ziwe Zano's agricultural production area.[170] Elders of the society remembered that they just ploughed 'where they wanted' until the late 1950s, after which some of their land was taken, leaving them with only twenty-two acres. Consequently, there was not enough land for cotton cultivation, and the yarn for weaving courses had to be bought, although the reserve would become one of the major cotton-producing areas in the country by the early 1970s.[171] These developments contributed to financial problems at Honde Mission, which came to a head in the 1960s.

ASSIMILATION AND INTEGRATION

An elderly woman recalled that moving into the Honde Valley was generally referred to as going into the forest (*dondo*). 'High veldt Manyika' who moved into the area in the 1950s recall that the inhabitants whom they encountered were 'different', they were 'forest people', and initially the newcomers set themselves apart.[172] Their self-image as modernisers was shared by the colonial administrators, because many of them belonged to the first Africans in the colony to have embraced Christianity, literacy, and the peasant option. According to NC Inyanga, in 1922 they were 'generally regarded as in many ways the most useful and intelligent of the Mashona'.[173] But their residency in the valley was initially challenged by sickness, high death rates, and failure in agricultural production. Pitched as agricultural modernisers, elsewhere they had used the plough and grew cash crops.[174] In Holdenby, however, the tsetse fly interfered with animal husbandry, and the rough territory, with fields often located on slopes, made the use of ploughs largely impossible and required specific agricultural techniques in order to avoid erosion.[175] It thus became crucial for these newcomers to change their self-perception as pioneers and to assimilate to the frontier way of life instead.

When they arrived in the valley, most of the evictees differed from the residents in language, religious beliefs, agricultural knowledge, and marriage arrangements. The immigrants spoke chiManyika, were mostly Christians, and usually paid *lobola* (bride-price), whereas in Holdenby, chiBarwe, ancestral worship, and bride-service were prevalent.[176] *Lobola* refers to the transfer of goods, including livestock, and, with the onset of colonialism, also money from the groom's to the bride's kin group. Bride-service, on the other hand, denotes the practice of the groom living with and working for his in-laws' family. As explained above, the purpose is to establish a reciprocal relationship between the kin groups, and the ideal is that neither exchange is ever fully completed. In the case of *lobola* this means that a small part of the payment is withheld in order to emphasise the negotiability of social relations, and the change from serving groom to independent husband in the case of bride-service is not at all clear-cut either. Two significant differences emerge. In the case of bride-service, the relationship begins as a matrilocal arrangement with the usually young man working towards earning his first marriage. This differs significantly from a young woman who, after the wedding ceremony, finds herself socially isolated in her in-laws' household. Also, the increasing monetarisation of *lobola* during the colonial period allowed some young men, especially migrant workers, to rapidly gain relative independence from the control of male elders in matters of marriage. One male elder remembered: 'Long back, one home had only one wife. Some had four wives or more, that was accepted.' He pointed out that only access to cash income, which allowed men to pay bride-price, rather than to do bride-service or to draw on their father's cattle, made this development possible. 'That time, our fathers were so poor, and they suffered, so much that if, say, one wanted to marry, one had to make sure one's sister had been married so as to realise *lobola* to give to one's in-laws.'[177]

In the Honde Valley, as a direct result of the demographic shift and experiences of migrant labour among the male valley population, chiManyika gradually became the primary language, bride-price replaced bride-service marriage arrangements, and Christianity became popular. This process is reflected in *ishe* Mandeya's response to a delineation questionnaire in 1965, when he stated that his 'tribe' was 'Manyika and Barwe' and his language 'chiManyika'.[178] By the 1970s, District Commissioner (DC) Reid only found 'traces of Barwe influence' in Chief Chikomba's area and that 'many of their women seem to be of Barwe origin, but they are essentially Vamanyika'.[179] Reid's observation could well be wrong, for it is important to consider that men more easily adopted languages since most of them left the valley as migrant labourers. It was to their advantage to present themselves as 'Manyika' to gain access to preferred jobs.[180] Thus the use of Shona dialects appears to have become increasingly gendered, while at the same time in polygynous households it was no longer uncommon for one wife to stem from Matabeleland or South Africa, the place of male migrant work. Large polygynous households only became commonplace in the valley in the 1950s with the arrival of churches that supported brethren having as many wives as possible, often without *lobola*, and such church membership grew in popularity during the Second Chimurenga.[181]

The frontier ethnicity was transformed but it successfully accommodated the Manyika modernisers, or, to use John Lonsdale's phrase, it socialised 'human inequalities in local ways'. Today, when pressed for their ethnic identity, people in the valley will indeed claim to be Manyika.[182] Even though the evictees' immigration was sudden, massive, and state-enforced, what emerged was neither a simple dichotomy, nor a mere local 'imitation' of expressions of Manyika identity.[183] Instead, immigrants assimilated and integrated in a complicated and multi-layered social, cultural, political, and economic process and together with the valley residents reshaped the frontier ethnicity.

Mission Christianity: Blitz on the Souls

In 1946, the circuit inspector Nduna reported to the Rhodesian Annual Methodist Conference that the Honde Mission 'is just like a speck of light shining in a vast dark area'.[184] Two years later the situation started to change, as the first two hundred evicted families arrived and Nduna urged that 'These hordes of coming people need the Church and school badly.'[185] Most of the newcomers were already baptised as members of the Anglican, Methodist or Roman Catholic Churches and those in its proximity initially turned to Honde Mission. One of the society's founders recalled that 'the mission became popular when a lot of people came to stay here'.[186] Most people attending services or sending their children to Ziwe Zano's primary schools were therefore recent immigrants. But the missionaries swiftly followed their brethren.[187] In the Honde Valley, activities by all three major mission churches in the area led to intense competition over 'souls' and resources, over church members, schools, and mission sites.[188] In 1956, the NC Inyanga vividly described this competition which he had observed in the northern part of the district: 'The blitz on the souls … has been stepped up.'[189]

The NC Inyanga himself played no small role in this 'blitz'. In 1949, he convened a meeting with all interested mission representatives at Honde View. According to Father Anselm Corbett, one of the two Carmelite priests present, for the purpose of this gathering this vantage point conveniently provides 'a panoramic view of the place, spread out like a map'.[190] The intention was to partition the valley between the mission societies. The NC had also invited members of the European community and brought his own family along to the picnic. Corbett describes that he and Father Frank Markall 'dined out of our flasks of tea and packets of sandwiches while the rest had their servants prepare a huge barbecue. The allotment of sites was concluded quickly and without argument.'[191] Half a century into the colonial project, this casual enactment of the imperialist drawing board was another layer of the enframing of African societies and land, without any input from the population that was to benefit from the civilising mission.

Before the meeting, the Carmelites had already begun holding mass in the valley and located a site for a school close to Honde Mission, which they found to be 'rather primitive', though the valley appeared to be 'indeed a little Eden', with a view of the Mtarazi Falls and water free-falling for 2,400 feet in the distance. They were enchanted by the view, as had missionary Shropshire been in the 1920s, when he described the falls as 'magnificent'.[192] The Carmelites' first teacher was Enoch Sanehwe, a Manyika evictee who had appealed to them to commence service in the valley, a known alcoholic with barely any academic education from the St Barbara Mission area on the high veldt.[193] In 1951 the Catholic missionaries founded St Anna's, a mission close to the border, later renamed St Columba's, and in 1969 moved to Hauna.[194] The Church of England opened St Peter's Mission in Mandeya in 1958.[195] The American Methodist Episcopal Church contented itself with Honde Mission but opened a number of schools. As a result of these undertakings, by the late 1960s there were eighteen primary schools in Holdenby Tribal Trust Land (TTL): three Methodist, ten Anglican, and five Catholic. There were also four primary schools in Manga TTL and one each at the two plantations, Aberfoyle and EHTE, run by the churches.[196]

Competition between the denominations was so acute that complaints to the district administration were frequent, with missionaries from one church reporting others who were allegedly building schools and churches without authorisation. One such conflict occurred in the early 1960s between the Catholic and Methodist churches over a site at Pacije in Holdenby TTL.[197] Methodist minister Ntuli had already opened an unauthorised school nearby at Aberfoyle in 1957. When his congregation was evicted, he followed them and re-established the school at Pacije. In 1963, Father Kenny, the priest-in-charge at St Columba's Mission, sought to enforce the school's closure. [198] The DC complied and subsequently observed: 'I am in sympathy with the people as they need a school but it does seem to me that this 'fait accompli' technique should be stopped. Build first and ask afterwards is fast becoming the best way to obtain a school.'[199] Such rivalry between the mission churches brought tension also into local communities and during the era of nationalism religious affiliation became politicised. *Sabhuku* Pacije had favoured the Catholic endeavour to open a school, and some of his followers therefore accused him of being a ZAPU supporter.[200]

The 'blitz on the souls' also had an impact on Ziwe Zano. Acknowledging the failure of camp meetings as a means of gaining local support, and under the pressure of competition by the mission churches, the society's members came to realise that success in converting valley inhabitants depended on participating in the blitz, which meant the provision of academic education. In a drastic departure from their original agenda, in 1957 Kasambira propagated a three-year plan[201] for schools at four preaching centres which had been opened in 1944 and which he feared 'we are likely to lose because of having no academic schools'.[202] In the early 1960s, Honde Mission was forced to abandon the centres due to lack of local support.[203] Instead, the church elders returned to their original approach and expanded their work in industrial education, supported by allies outside the valley.

Since the 1930s, Kanyenze, one of the founding members of the society, had attempted to project their image as modernisers to potential sponsors and supporters. He won Colonel Valentine as a long-standing mentor, as well as the then NC Umtali Bazeley and other prominent Europeans and Asians of the Umtali community.[204] Kanyenze's efforts came to a peak in 1953, when the Ziwe Zano Society was invited to have a stall at the Rhodes Centenary Exhibition. This was a great success because the occasion spread their fame as a unique self-help organisation for school drop-outs throughout the Federation of Central Africa. They received correspondence from Europeans in Zambia and South Africa, and were financially supported for a while by the Rhodesian Lotteries. Kanyenze even met the Queen Mother on her visit to the Umtali area in the same year.[205] To the outside world the members of the society portrayed themselves as modernisers attempting to develop the valley,[206] but as far as Honde Industrial School itself was concerned the majority of students continued to come from areas outside the valley.[207] The society maintained its policy of industrial education, establishing two new industrial missions, albeit with little success: Rukwenjere Industrial School in Mtoko only briefly functioned in 1955 and Bakorenhema Industrial School in Maranke was only open from 1969 to 1970.[208]

From the very beginning, academic education had never been Ziwe Zano's mainstay and their insistence on self-reliance became the chief obstacle to partaking in the blitz.[209] In 1943, after the government had refused the society permission to open primary schools, the Ziwe Zano elders decided to approach their mother church for help and to lay out their programme.[210] The bishop eventually agreed and Honde District was created as part of the Methodist diocese, with Honde Mission as the only church.[211] This then allowed Ziwe Zano to open Honde River and Gatsi primary schools in 1948.[212] In the late 1950s they even developed a plan to turn Gatsi into a secondary school with boarding facilities.[213] However, the obstacles to gaining permission to run schools remained the same, with a stubborn assertion by the society's elders, Katsidzira in particular, that they would remain self-reliant, while the Methodist mother church insisted on supervision.

This ongoing tension, which dated back to the days of the Great Revival in 1918, was aggravated by the supervision question. The Katsidzira manuscript includes several accounts of deeply felt humiliation.[214] In 1944, Ziwe Zano members expressed their distrust of the European missionaries' ulterior motives to the Godlonton Commission:

> Is it not correct that you object to Mission supervision?

> We never objected to the principle of Missions. The trouble is that the money given to the Society is entirely for the African people and we do not know what help the Europeans shall give us, because the Europeans may grab the money and go away, for all we know; and yet, this money that we have saved, because it belongs to the African people and we do not want it to be wasted.[215]

Moreover, Katsidzira felt personally insulted by the Rhodesian Methodist Conference of 1947. He expressed his feelings in a letter to Bishop Booth, explaining that he had been refused the right to vote as minister of the church. He complained that this meant 'degradation of my full Minister's position in the Conference', and further that this treatment 'is only to drive me out from the Methodist Church Conference of Southern Rhodesia'. In the same letter he asked the Bishop: 'How can I work in life with a group that degraded my Minister position while I know I am in God's field in full?'[216]

Finally, supervision problems came to a head. After lengthy discussions between government departments, the issue was referred to parliament in 1956.

The Secretary for Native Affairs strongly advised against Ziwe Zano's self-administration of its schools:

> In spite of the success of the Ziwe Zano Society with its limited European supervision it is considered that in view of the trouble experienced in Kenya, which it is understood was to a great extent fostered in the schools under purely Native control, and from information known to the Prime Minister, it would appear to be highly undesirable that at the present time Natives should be permitted to operate Mission Schools without European supervision, and this aspect receives the constant attention of the Department.[217]

In the context of mass nationalism, Ziwe Zano's wish was declined, as the colonial government was much aware of the Mau Mau war in Kenya, which had just entered its final phase and was rooted, in part, in an independent school movement and a political theology that challenged mission Christianity and elders' authority. Katsidzira suspected that the Methodist Church wanted to take over Ziwe Zano's schools, and the society subsequently declared its independence from the 'mother church' in 1958.[218] When two of the church elders related the event, they asserted: 'We have always been independent!'[219] The Ziwe Zano Society thus became an African initiated church and in 1968 registered as a welfare society under the name of Ziwe Zano New Church Society.[220] The rather laconic response by the Methodist circuit superintendent in his annual report for 1960 was: 'We are very sorry but we shall pray for them.'[221]

By the late 1950s, Ziwe Zano had lost out in the religious 'blitz' in the Honde Valley and been weakened by an internal, generational split. Moreover, the society also lost full control over its academic schools when their administration was localised on demand by parents and the Education Department.[222] In 1960, the DC Umtali reported that the situation at Honde Mission was bleak: 'The Ziwe Zano Trade School in the Umtasa North Reserve appears now to be more or less moribund, and the attendance of pupils negligible.'[223] The Ziwe Zano pioneers had missed the opportunity of securing their position by converting the valley inhabitants or by winning over the new immigrants; the other 'high veldt-Manyika', however, did succeed in becoming local. Integration or exclusion would eventually draw a line dividing those who became vulnerable to violence during the liberation war in the 1970s and those who aligned themselves with the young men with guns.

Conclusion

Three distinct groups of pioneers and self-perceived modernisers arrived in the Honde Valley between 1938 and the 1950s. The Ziwe Zano Society members provide an example of African pioneers whose imagination interpreted the valley's landscape and inhabitants in terms of primitive alterity and who initially insisted on their own separateness. This challenges the dichotomous view of coloniser and colonised. Ziwe Zano missed the opportunity to become part of the frontier society. This self-chosen exclusion led to disaster when the freedom fighters arrived in the 1970s, because, cut off from a local economy of trust, the mission members were vulnerable to both sides of the conflict. The Europeans, by contrast, succeeded as pioneers by creating islands of white settlement that were largely independent from the valley population and were supported by their privileges protected by the colonial state. Only the Manyika immigrants gave up their view of an atavistic wilderness into which the state had thrown them, and in a mutual process introduced their markers of modernity – mission Christianity, literacy, and the peasant option – while embracing the frontier identity. All in all, beginning with nationalist mobilisation and culminating during the liberation war in the 1970s, those pioneers who remained isolated from the valley population became vulnerable to insurgent violence.

Notes

1   Jill Casid, *Sowing Empire: Landscape and Colonization* (Minneapolis, MN, 2005), p. 241.
2   Ibid.
3   Inyanga District, Annual Report, 1951, S2827/2/2/1, NAZ.
4   CNC to the Secretary, Administrator, 1 June 1920, A3/18/39/16, NAZ; also chapter two.
5   Inyanga District, Annual Report, 1957, p. 8, S2827/2/2/5, NAZ.
6   Inyanga District, Annual Report, 1958, S2827/2/2/6, NAZ.
7   Typical of the time, the NC interpreted African women's mobility as prostitution. Inyanga District, Annual Report, 1927, S235/505, NAZ.
8   Elioth Makambe, 'The Nyasaland African Labour "Ulendos" to Southern Rhodesia and the Problem of the African "Highwaymen", 1903–1923: A Study in the Limitations of Early Independent Labour Migration', *African Affairs*, 79, no. 317 (1980), p. 556; Umtali District, Annual Report, 1938, S235/516, NAZ. See also Peter Scott, 'Migrant Labor in Southern Rhodesia', *Geographical Review*, 44, no. 1 (1954), pp. 35, 40.
9   Rex vs Marume alias Masiwa X5016 Inyanga, case no. 132 of 1952, S2221/1, NAZ.
10 Ibid.
11 'Exhibit "A": list of articles seen at store on 22.8.1952', ibid.
12 Dane Kennedy, *Islands of White: Settler Society and Culture in Kenya and Southern Rhodesia, 1890–1939* (Durham, NC, 1987), p. 32.
13 Interview #65.
14 I.C. Musumba, 'A Short History for the Beginning of Honde Mission, Honde River School and Gatsi School', August 1959, box number 103986, NRC.
15 Ibid.; Correspondence Concerning Leases 1916-20 (Umtassa Reserve), box file 31, shelf a, north wall, OMMA; NC Umtali to CNC, 1 September 1941, S2791/4, NAZ; interviews #31, #138.
16 Umtali District, Annual Report, 1931, S235/509; Priest-in-charge, St Augustine's Mission to NC Inyanga, 24 August 1931, S603/1931; Inspector to Director Native Development Department Umtali, 1 October 1943, S2791/4, NAZ; M'buya, *A Little Leaven* (Salisbury, 1975), p. 57; John Pafiwa Katsidzira, no title [history of Ziwe Zano Society], vol. 1 (n.p. [Honde Mission], ms, n.d. [1976]), chapter 22. This manuscript which consists of three volumes provides a detailed history of Ziwe Zano Society in seventy-nine chapters and three handwritten volumes. They were dictated by D.M. Katsidzira's foster son in May 1976. The manuscript is in private possession.
17 'The Constitution of Bantu Zive [sic] Zano Society and Rules', 20 January 1932, S2791/4, NAZ. Accounts of the founding year differ. Ziwe Zano Society, Oral Evidence, Native Production and Trade Commission 1944, p. 1193, ZBJ1/1/2, NAZ, states 1933.
18 Katsidzira, vol. 1, chapter 13 and vol. 3, chapter 67, PPA.
19 A male elder who attended meetings at Honde Mission in the 1950s and 1960s remembered the motto as: 'No nation can lift another nation, but you yourself, you must help yourself!' Interview #32.
20 Ziwe Zano Society, p. 1199, ZBJ1/1/2, NAZ. Although this response might well have been shaped by giving testimony to a government commission, the same sentiment was frequently expressed in written accounts. For a similar observation on an African initiatedchurch, see David Pratten, *The Man–Leopard Murders: History and Society in Colonial Nigeria* (Bloomington, IN, 2007), p. 112.
21 When the author first presented the idea of Ziwe Zano as African modernisers in the early 1990s, the response among Zimbabweanists was critical, because the literature to that point had almost exclusively focused on the small African elite of academically educated men, usually government employees, and the recruiting ground for nationalist leadership after World War II. Since then, a few

publications along the lines of this argument have followed. David Maxwell, *Christians and Chiefs in Zimbabwe: A Social History of the Hwesa People* (Edinburgh, 1999), chapter two; Jocelyn Alexander et al., *Violence and Memory: One Hundred Years in the 'Dark Forests' of Matabeleland* (Portsmouth, NH, 2000), chapters one and two.

22 For the purpose of this study, the role of the books in making and expressing Ziwe Zano identity and cosmology will not be examined. An early monograph on the topic for a different community is Paul Landau's *The Realm of the Word: Language, Gender and Christianity in a Southern African Kingdom* (Portsmouth, NH, 1995); for a broader discussion of the written word, colonialism, and power, see Isabel Hofmeyr, *We Spend Our Years As a Tale That Is Told: Oral Historical Narrative in a South African Chiefdom* (Portsmouth, NH, 1994), especially chapter 3; Derek Peterson, *Creative Writing: Translation, Bookkeeping, and the Work of Imagination in Colonial Kenya* (Portsmouth, NH, 2004). The extensive debate about the Comaroffs' first volume *Of Revelation and Revolution*, which in part focused on their arguments about narrative, provides insight into the question. For the Comaroffs' detailed response, see, Jean and John L. Comaroff, *Of Revelation and Revolution*, vol. 2, *The Dialectics on a South African Frontier* (Chicago, IL, 1997), pp. 35-53.

23 Katsidzira, vol. 3, chapter 67; also Musumba, 'A Short History'; Sandy Mbodzekwa Kanyenze, no title [history of Ziwe Zano Society and copies of correspondence], 2 vols. (n.p. [Honde Mission], ms, n.d.), PPA; William Menzies, *An African Samuel Smiles* (n.p., n.d. [1956]).

24 Katsidzira, vol. 1, chapters 3 and 5, vol. 2, chapter 41; 'Teachers and Workers A-N up to 1928, Methodist Episcopal Church Rhodesia', box file 3, shelf d, south wall, OMMA; also Terence Ranger, 'Protestant Missions in Africa: The Dialectic of Conversion in the American Methodist Episcopal Church in Eastern Zimbabwe, 1900–1950', *Religion in Africa: Experience and Expression*, Thomas Blakely, et al. (London, 1994), pp. 301-5.

25 Terence Ranger, *Peasant Consciousness and Guerrilla War in Zimbabwe: A Comparative Study* (London, 1985), p. 43; 'Protestant Missions', pp. 287-8.

26 Interview #65.

27 Katsidzira, vol. 1, chapters 9, 15, 16, 25; vol. 2, chapter 41.

28 John Iliffe, 'The Age of Improvement and Differentiation (1907–1945)', *A History of Tanzania*, I.N. Kimambo and A.J. Temu (eds) (Nairobi, 1969), pp. 123-60.

29 Elizabeth Schmidt, 'Negotiated Spaces and Contested Terrain: Men, Women, and the Law in Colonial Zimbabwe, 1890–1939', *Journal of Southern African Studies*, 16, no. 4 (1990), pp. 622-48 and 'Patriarchy, Capitalism, and the Colonial State in Zimbabwe', *Signs* 16, no. 4 (1991), pp. 732-56; also Diana Jeater, *Marriage, Perversion, and Power: The Construction of Moral Discourse in Southern Rhodesia 1894–1930* (Oxford, 1993).

30 Shepherd Machuma, files 212, 264, and 271, shelf d, north wall, OMMA. For a detailed treatment of the revival movement and the role of the Methodist Church see, Ranger, 'Protestant Missions,' pp. 290-1, 304-9.

31 Ranger, *Peasant Consciousness*, p. 88. For the crisis of peasant society, see, ibid., chapter 2; Wolfgang Döpcke, *Das koloniale Zimbabwe in der Krise: Eine Wirtschafts- und Sozialgeschichte 1929–1939* (Hamburg, 1992).

32 For a religious history of the Masowe Apostles, see Isabel Mukonyora, *Wandering a Gendered Wilderness: Suffering and Healing in an African Initiated Church* (New York, 2007).

33 Katsidzira claimed that 'by the end of 1931 they [Katsidzira's and other Methodist African pastor-preachers] were in charge of the sects'. Katsidzira, vol. 1, chapter 13.

34 Kanyenze, vol. 2; copy of S. Kanyenze to NC Umtali, 12 January 1936, PPA. See also S2791/4, NAZ; Katsidzira, vol. 1, chapter 21. Around the same time Kanyenze had a vision of African girls going to hell for being 'evil doers'. Katsidzira, vol. 1, chapter 20.

35 Katsidzira, chapters 16, 17, 19.

36 Ibid., chapter 21.

37 Ibid., chapter 2; 'Founder of Honde Mission is Dead But Work Continues', *Umbowo*, 48, no. 10 (1965), p. 5.

38 NC Umtali Bazeley to CNC, 3 May 1928, S1561/10, NAZ.

39 Inyanga District, Annual Report, 1933, S235/511, NAZ.

40 Sawerthal to Surveyor General, 20 August 1906, L2/2/6/8.

41 Interview #65.

42 Musumba, 'A Short History'; also NC Inyanga to CNC, 18 February 1931, S603, NAZ; 'Report on Holdenby', 1947, box number 66721, NRC. It is common also for migrant labourers to provide dramatic accounts of the dangers their travels into foreign lands entailed; often those include encounters with lions. See interview #32. For European and African imaginations of the forest, see Albert Wirz, 'Die Erfindung des Urwalds oder ein weiterer Versuch im Fährtenlesen', *Penplus*, 4 (1994), pp. 15-36.

43 Interview #21 with two Ziwe Zano elders.

44 Katsidzira, vol. 1, chapter 21.

45 Ibid.

46 NC Inyanga to CNC, 27 January 1927, S603, NAZ. The most comprehensive study of rural African alcohol production and consumption is Justin Willis, *Potent Brews: A Social History of Alcohol in East Africa, 1850–1999* (Columbus, OH, 2002).

47 Katsidzira, vol. 1, chapter 21.

48 Ibid., chapters 21, 30.

49 Musumba, 'A Short History'.

50 Ziwe Zano Society, p. 1199, ZBJ1/1/2, NAZ.

51 Musumba, 'A Short History'.

52 Ibid.; also interview #136.

53 Ziwe Zano Society, p. 1200, ZBJ1/1/2, NAZ.

54 Katsidzira, vol. 1, chapters 23, 25, 34.

55 NC Umtali to CNC, 1 September 1941, S2791/4, NAZ.

56 Acting Director Native Education to Secretary for Native Affairs, 5 January 1945, S2791/4, NAZ.

57 Interview #21; Divisional Inspector Education, South Eastern Division, to PNC, 15 November 1948, S2791/4, NAZ.

58 Katsidzira, vol. 1, chapter 24.

59 Ibid., chapter 21.

60 W.J. Brown, Umtali Native Welfare Society, p. 1412, ZBJ1/1/2 and Written Evidence, ZBJ1/2/3, NAZ; also Katsidzira, vol. 1, chapters 24, 27, 33.

61 Katsidzira, vol. 1, chapter 30; Hwerekwere to CNC, 17 April 1946, S2791/4, NAZ.

62 Interview #21. Except for the subsequently established plantation facilities, the clinic served the entire valley population until the late 1970s, which by 1948 was estimated at 10,000. Director for Medical Services to Secretary for Native Affairs, 26 October 1955; Divisional Inspector South Eastern Division to PNC, 15 November 1948, S2791/4, NAZ.

63 *Journal for the Rhodesia Annual Conference: The Methodist Church* (1947), p. 366.

64 Katsidzira, vol. 1, chapter 31.

65 Ibid.

66 'Moses fire' was not exclusive to the Honde Valley. In 1954, the fire was seen at Ziwe Zano's industrial school in Mtoko and in 1964 at Battery Spruit, Penhalonga area, where the society had commenced building another school. Ibid., vol. 3, chapter 55.

67 Ibid., vol. 2, chapter 37. Titus Presler, who has provided the only other full academic study of the Honde Valley, wrote his theological dissertation on nightly religious meetings. He overlooked that Ziwe Zano started the Christian practice in the valley, nor does he take note of related work, such as Bella Mukonyora's excellent study on gender and nightly prayer meetings among the Vapostori, one of the churches he researched. In part, the limits of his research as much as his achievements might be explained by his positionality as an Anglican missionary and that he centred his endeavor at EHTE. Titus Presler, *Transfigured Night: Mission and Culture in Zimbabwe's Vigil Movement* (Pretoria, 1999); Mukonyora, *Wandering a Gendered Wilderness*.

68 Katsidzira, vol. 1, chapters 15, 23.

69 Elizabeth Schmidt, '"Patriarchy, Capitalism" and "Negotiated Spaces"'; Teresa Barnes, 'The Fight for Control of African Women's Mobility in Colonial Zimbabwe, 1900–1939', *Signs*, 17, no. 3 (1992), pp. 586-608; Lynette Jackson, *Surfacing Up: Psychiatry and Social Order in Colonial Zimbabwe, 1908–1968* (Ithaca, NY, 2005), chapter 4; also Derek Peterson, 'Morality Plays: Marriage, Church Courts, and Colonial Agency in Central Tanganyika, ca. 1876–1928', *The American Historical Review*, 111, no. 4 (2006), pp. 983-1010; Brett Shadle, *'Girl Cases': Marriage and Colonialism in Gusiiland, Kenya, 1890–1970* (Portsmouth, NH, 2006).

70 Interview #105. For spirit affliction and possession, see chapter six.

71 Two young women related their liberating experiences of attending Vapostori night meetings. Ibid. This also appears to have been true, albeit probably to a lesser extent, for women's organisations of mission churches and women's clubs. In 1970, the women's club instructor for Nyamukwarara Valley said of a netball match that it was a unique experience to play and to forget women's duties for a few hours: 'This was one of the best days I had ever experienced in life.' Women's Club Supervisor, Forestry Commission: Development Unit Organisation Manual, 19 September 1970, PPB; also Tumani Mutasa Nyajeka, *The Unwritten Text: The Indigenous African Christian Women's Movement in Zimbabwe* (Mutare, 2006); Gurli Hansson, *The Rise of Vashandiri: The Ruwadzano Movement in the Lutheran Church in Zimbabwe* (Uppsala, 1991), Sita Ranchod-Nilsson, 'Gender Politics and National Liberation: Women's Participation in the Liberation of Zimbabwe', (PhD thesis, Northwestern University, 1992), chapter 3, pp. 88-121.

72 At Easter 1950, a major revival took place at Honde Mission, when believers saw the church covered in

a white cloth. Katsidzira, vol. 1, chapter 31.

73   Ibid.

74   Ibid.

75   Ibid., vol. 2, chapter 40.

76   Ibid., vol. 1, chapter 31.

77   Circuit Inspector Nduna to Bishop Booth, 6 September 1946, file: Correspondence Bishop Booth, filing cabinet, west wall, OMMA.

78   Interviews #65, #32 and Musumba, 'A Short History'.

79   See Lindsay Proudfoot and Michael Roche (eds), *(Dis)Placing Empire: Renegotiating British Colonial Geographies* (Aldershot, 2005), W.J.T. Mitchell, 'Imperial Landscape', *Landscape and Power*, W.J.T. Mitchell (ed.) (Chicago, IL, 1994), pp. 5-34.

80   NC Umtali Bazeley to CNC Salisbury, 3 May 1928, S1561/10, NAZ.

81   Inyanga District, Annual Report, 1957, 8, S2827/2/2/5, NAZ.

82   B. Barry, 'Aberfoyle: Report on Visit to the Estate by Mr. B. Barry 21 February to 18 March 1960', PPC.

83   Achille Mbembe, *On the Postcolony* (Berkeley, CA, 2001), pp. 174-5. For an earlier discussion of the sexualised discourse of landscape appropriation, see Heike Schmidt, '"Penetrating" Foreign Lands: Contestations Over African Landscapes, A Case Study from Eastern Zimbabwe', *Environment and History*, 1, no. 3 (1995), pp. 351-76.

84   Copy of Agreement of Sale, 1952, PPC; NC Inyanga to SON Umtali, 12 February 1926, NC Inyanga to CNC, 20 July 1926 and 29 December 1930, S 604, NAZ; Local secretary of Lonrho to NC Inyanga, 13 January 1930, S603, NAZ; CNC to NC Inyanga, 6 September 1943, box number 150768, NRC; CNC to Under Secretary, Department of Lands, 27 February 1948, box number 62328, NRC; and Wightwick to Igoe, 21 November 1951, PPC.

85   NC Inyanga to PNC, 12 April 1948, S2588/1977, NAZ. A few months later also the land inspector characterised Holdenby as 'still untamed'. Land Inspector, Native Agriculture Department Umtali, to PNC, 'Report on South-Western Portion of Holdenby', 2 July 1948, box number 62328, NRC.

86   Surveyor General's Office to the General Manager, Anglo-French Matabeleland Co. Ltd, Belingwe, 4 August 1905, L2/1/6/1, NAZ. In 1926, Inyanga Block changed hands several times in quick succession. NC Inyanga to SON, 12 February 1926, NC Inyanga to CNC, 20 July 1926, S604, NAZ.

87   Local secretary of Lonrho Salisbury to NC Inyanga, 13 January 1930; NC Inyanga to CNC, 29 December 1930, S603, NAZ. For an excellent detailed study of the northern part of the block see Donald Moore, *Suffering for Territory: Race, Place, and Power in Zimbabwe* (Durham, NC, 2005), pp. 130-7, passim.

88   The government had been interested in Holdenby Block for 'native settlement' from as early as 1943 and bought the land, roughly 77,000 acres, at 6/- per acre in 1948. An area around the Mtarazi Falls, some 2,400 acres, was excluded from this transaction. CNC to NC Inyanga, 6 September 1943, box number 150768, CNC to Under Secretary, Department of Lands, 27 February 1948, box number 62328, NRC.

89   H. Wightwick to W. Igoe, Incomati Sugar Estates, Lourenço Marques, Portuguese East Africa, Umtali, 21 November 1951, PPC.

90   Ibid.

91   W. Igoe, Inyangani (Inyanga) Estates Ltd, 'Report', 9 July 1952, PPC.

92   H. Wightwick to W. Igoe (London), 19 March 1952, PPC.

93   Copy of letter from Little, Managing Director, Anglo-French Matabeleland Company, to the Manager of the BSAC, 19 October 1900, L2/1/6/1, NAZ.

94   CNC to NC Inyanga, 4 October 1927. Van Niekerk had moved to Rhodesia with his wife in 1892 and settled in Inyanga district in 1897. Major van Niekerk to Misses de Groot, 29 November 1950, Pioneer Reminiscences, Hist. Mss. WO 5/9/1, NAZ. Manager of the Standard Bank Umtali to NC Inyanga, 13 and 26 July 1928; NC Inyanga to the Manager, Standard Bank Umtali, 18 July 1928, S603, NAZ.

95   One of Niekerk's responsibilities was to collect rent for a Methodist mission site on Holdenby Block; by 1935 he was still failing to enforce the land rent. P.H. van Niekerk to NC Inyanga, 14 March 1935, S 603, NAZ; Correspondence Concerning Leases 1916-20 (Umtassa Reserve), box file 31, shelf a, north wall, OMMA.

96   Wightwick to Igoe, 19 March 1952.

97   Peter Anderson, 'The Human Clay: An Essay in the Spatial History of the Cape Eastern Frontier, 1811–1835' (MLitt. thesis, University of Oxford, 1993), p. 23; 147.

98   Personal correspondence with Brian Igoe, 15 July 2007.

99   'Aberfoyle: The Story of a Tea Estate', *The Farming Gazette Supplement*, 3 May 1985.

100 Inyanga District, Annual Report, 1951, S2827/2/2/1, NAZ.

101 Igoe, 'Report', 9 July 1952.

102 Danziger and Lardner Burke, solicitors to Messrs Scanlen and Holdenness, 'Inyangani Estates Ltd: H.D. Wightwick', 6 October 1952; Wightwick to Igoe, 21 November 1951; Evelyn Farreth, Tea

Research Institute of East Africa, Kericho to W. Igoe, 27 February 1952, PPC.

103 Williamson, 'Report on Inyanga Block', 1952.

104 Denis Shropshire, 'A Journey in Mashonaland', *African Affairs*, 51, no. 202 (1952), pp. 52–3.

105 George Williamson and Co., Nairobi, 'Report on Inyanga Block, Eastern District, Southern Rhodesia', 1952, PPC; Inyanga District, Annual Report, 1959, S2827/2/2/7, NAZ; Inyanga District, Annual Report, 1960, boxnumber 62328, NRC.

106 Igoe, 'Report', 9 July 1952.

107 Kirkwood and Peter Ring lived with their wives in tents for more than fifteen months, and Paddy O'Shea, Aberfoyle's manager from 1954, was unable to take any leave for four years. W. Igoe, 'Aberfoyle, Tea Report – 1954', 8 April 1954; 'Report to the Board of Directors of Aberfoyle Plantations Ltd on My Visit to the Company's Rhodesian Property – September/November 1958', November 1958, PPC. Ring worked for and lived at Aberfoyle from its beginning, in 1952, until his death in 1994. At the time, he was much talked about by employees of the estate, but he is rarely mentioned in the documentation.

108 Igoe, 'Report', 9 July 1952.

109 In 1890, on his way to *mambo* Mutasa's headquarters with de Souza, Andrada discovered the easiest way for travelling along the escarpment was to use a southern route that followed the Revue River upstream, through Penhalonga. Joaquim Paiva de Andrada, *Manica: Being a Report Addressed to the Minister of the Marine and the Colonies of Portugal* (London, 1891), p. 29; 38–9.

110 Wightwick to Igoe, 19 March 1952.

111 H. Thomas, 'Report on the Tea-Growing Possibilities of the Inyanga Block', Nairobi, 23 October 1952; Igoe, 'Report', 9 July 1952, PPC.

112 Thomas, 'Report'.

113 For a recent study in US history that examines 'Yankee' pioneers taming landscape, Native Americans, and white settlers whom they considered to be primitive, see James Schwartz, *Conflict on the Michigan Frontier: Yankee and Borderland Cultures, 1815–1840* (DeKalb, IL, 2009).

114 Mbembe, *On the Postcolony*, p. 174.

115 Karl Mauch, *The Journals of Carl Mauch: His Travels in the Transvaal and Rhodesia, 1869–1872*, E. Burke (ed.) (Salisbury, 1969), pp. 221–41.

116 Igoe, 'Report to the Board of Directors', November 1958.

117 Casid, *Sowing Empire*, p. 241, passim; Jean and John L. Comaroff, 'Through the Looking-glass: Colonial Encounters of the First Kind', *Journal of Historical Sociology*, 1, no. 1 (1988), p. 6. Here, the Comaroffs follow Terence Ranger's argument in 'Taking Hold of the Land: Holy Places and Pilgrimages in Twentieth-Century Zimbabwe', *Past and Present*, 117, no. 1(1987), p. 159.

118 Jean and John L. Comaroff, 'Through the Looking-glass', pp. 7–8.

119 For the Australian counterpart to settler imaginations and making of landscape, see Paul Carter, *The Road to Botany Bay: An Exploration of Landscape and History* (New York, 1988). Thomas Dunlap provides a concise critique of imperial land use and imagination in 'Creation and Destruction in Landscapes of Empire', *City, Country, Empire: Landscapes in Environmental History*, Jeffry Diefendorf and Kurk Dorsey (eds) (Pittsburgh, PA, 2005), pp. 207–25. Dunlap critiques what he identifies as the three settler dreams: the colony as the land of possibility, the universality and superiority of scientific knowledge, and the claim of being the true owners of the land. For the argument of mapping, naming, and agricultural practices as articulation of power, see Eric Worby, 'Maps, Names, and Ethnic Games: The Epistemology and Iconography of Colonial Power in Northwestern Zimbabwe', *Journal of Southern African Studies*, 20, no. 3 (1994), pp. 371–92.

120 Arthur Lewis, *Too Bright the Vision? African Adventures of an Anglican Rebel* (London, 1992), p. 184.

121 Igoe, 'Report', 9 July 1952.

122 Cecil John Rhodes to J.G. McDonald, 1896, in James Gordon, *Rhodes: A Life* (London, 1927), p. 217; Moore, *Suffering for Territory*, p. 131.

123 Henry Schlichter, 'Travels and Researches in Rhodesia', *The Geographical Journal*, 13, no. 4 (1899), p. 378.

124 See Helen Callaway, 'Purity and Exotica in Legitimating the Empire: Cultural Constructions of Gender, Sexuality and Race', *Legitimacy and the State in Twentieth-Century Africa*, Terence Ranger and Olufemi Vaughan (eds) (London, 1993), pp. 37–8; Joanna de Groot, '"Sex" and "Race": The Construction of Language and Image in the Nineteenth Century', *Sexuality and Subordination*, Susan Mendus and Jane Rendall (eds) (London, 1989), pp. 110–11. Anthony Chennels examined the Rhodesian self-image as 'civilisers of wilderness' in 'Cultural Violence During the Pax Rhodesiana: The Evidence from Rhodesian Fiction', a paper presented at the *Journal of Southern African Studies* Conference on 'Political Violence', Oxford, 25-27 June 1991. For a summary of the paper, see Terence Ranger, 'Afterword: War, Violence, and Healing in Zimbabwe', *Journal of Southern African Studies*, 8, no. 3 (1992), pp. 703–5.

125 At the time, Charles Hanmer, the owner of the northern part of Inyanga Block, similarly faced the problem of a local labour shortage. Moore, *Suffering for Territory*, pp. 140-6.

126 Wightwick to Igoe, 19 March 1952.

127 Director Aberfoyle Plantations Igoe to the Directors of Aberfoyle Plantations Ltd, London, n.d. [January 1952], PPC. For the early labour policies on the Mozambique side of the border, see Eric Allina-Pisano, 'Borderlands, Boundaries, and the Contours of Colonial Rule: African Labor in Manica District, Mozambique, c. 1904–1908', *International Journal of African Historical Studies*, 36, no. 1 (2003), pp. 59-82. Allina-Pisano argues that Manica chiefs and the colonial administration negotiated a modus vivendi in the early twentieth century that had local communities provide labour for such unpopular projects as road improvement and construction, and in turn those who participated were exempted from contract labour.

128 Director Aberfoyle Plantations Ltd Igoe to Directors of Aberfoyle Plantations Ltd, 'Inyanga', n.d. [1952], PPC.

129 Igoe, 'Aberfoyle, Tea Report – 1954'.

130 Ibid.

131 In an adjacent area, the Forestry Commission imposed a labour agreement that forced male tenants living in the Nyamukwarara Valley that became part of Stapleford Forestry Estate to work a minimum of 180 days annually for the estate. K.W. Groves, 'Report on the Tenant Area; Stapleford Forest Reserve', October 1956, p. 15, PPB.

132 Angus Cameron, 'Report on Mr. A. Cameron's Visit to Luleche, October 1957', 10 October 1957; Wightwick to Igoe, 19 March 1952, PPC; also Inyanga District, Monthly Report, February 1915, N9/4/28, NAZ.

133 Interview #4; M. Hagelthorn to PNC, 'Appointment of H/M Zindi', 11 June 1951, PER 5 Headmen, DAO.

134 NC Inyanga to PNC, 'Headman Zindi: Application for Removal by Aberfoyle Plantations Ltd', 21 September 1954, box number 93786, NRC.

135 Manager Aberfoyle Plantations Ltd Kirkwood to NC Inyanga, 14 June 1954, box number 93786, NRC.

136 Interview #4; also H. Gomes for DC Mutasa to the Secretary for Internal Affairs, 23 June 1977, PER 5 Headmen, DAO; DC Mutasa District A.J. Bundock to PC Manicaland, 17 July 1978, PER 5 Headman Zindi, PAO.

137 See various correspondences in box number 93785, NRC.

138 Kirkwood to NC Inyanga, 14 June 1954.

139 Land Apportionment Act, S2807/4, S2807/7; Natives Occupying Crown Land, S1194/190/27/6/1, NAZ; also Henry Moyana, *The Political Economy of Land in Zimbabwe* (Gweru, 1984), p. 129. The same conflict emerged on the northern part of the block, where the manager Charles Hanmer complained in 1951 that in England, before World War II, a tenant could be evicted and would have to fend for himself, but that apparently was not possible in Rhodesia. Charles Hanmer to CNC Mashonaland, Inyanga Downs, 22 March 1951, S2588/1977, NAZ.

140 PNC to NC Inyanga, 30 September 1954, box number 93786, NRC.

141 The Native Department acquired the land in 1951. Wightwick to Igoe, 19 March 1952. Most of Chikomba's displaced followers settled in Sagambe and Chavhanga areas, directly adjacent to the plantation. Interview #79.

142 PNC to CNC, 'Holdenby Farm', 26 February 1947, box number 62328, NRC; NC Inyanga to the District Veterinary Umtali, 13 November 1925, S604, NAZ. By contrast, Chief Muparutsa apparently asked for land on the plateau in the Scotsdale area when he and his people were informed of the Holdenby Block boundary in 1908. Inyanga District, Monthly Report, February 1908, N9/4/21, NAZ.

143 Interview #4.

144 Interviews #119, #53, #144; Headman Chikomba to the Manager Katiyo, 'Request for Transport for the Annual Rain Ceremony to and from Aberfoyle 27.10.1990', 22 October 1990, PPD.

145 The helicopter landing place gained much interest in the local press, for example, in the Mutare-based *Manica Post*.

146 Interview #4.

147 Another of the accused argued that 'it was not a meeting, it was a get togetherness, greetings to our brothers who have been in detention for ten years.' DC Mutasa to PC, October 17, 1975, attached: Umtali: The State vs. Rev. X, Moses Paradzayi, Y and Z, PER5 Headman Muparutsa, DAO.

148 Possibly the best known and most representative example for the British colonial view of colonial Africa and 'traditional' society is Frederick Lugard, *The Dual Mandate in British Tropical Africa* (London, 1922), pp. 69-72, 217, passim.

149 Maybe the most innovative approach to understanding what the authors refer to as 'Afromodernity' is the introduction to Jean and John L. Comaroff, *Theory from the South: Or, How Euro-America is Evolving Toward Africa* (Chicago, IL, 2012), pp. 7-49.

150 James Scott, *Domination and the Arts of Resistance: The Hidden Transcript of Subordinate Groups* (New Haven, CT, 1990); 'Domination, Acting, and Fantasy', *The Paths to Domination, Resistance, and Terror*, Carolyn Nordstrom and JoAnn Martin (eds) (Berkeley, CA, 1992), pp. 55-84; also *Weapons of the Weak: Everyday Forms of Peasant Resistance* (New Haven, CT, 1985). Tradition as political tool used in particular by male elders has been mostly discussed in the context of the negotiation of gender normativity and the creation of customary law. See, for example, Thomas Spear, 'Neo-Traditionalism and the Limits of Invention in British Colonial Africa', *Journal of African History*, 44, no. 1 (2003), pp. 3-27.

151 The incident is discussed in some detail in chapter five.

152 Moyana, *The Political Economy of Land*, p. 129. For the debate leading to the amendment, see LAA, S2807/4, S2807/7; Natives Occupying Crown Land, S1194/190/27/6/1, NAZ.

153 Inyanga District, Annual Report, 1951, S2827/2/2/1, NAZ.

154 NC Inyanga to SON Umtali, 27 May 1924, S138/196, NAZ.

155 NC Umtali to PNC, 23 June 1948, box number 62328, NRC.

156 Interviews #31, #130; also box number 93785, NRC.

157 Director of Native Agriculture, 'Carrying Capacity of Reserves and Special Native Areas', 20 October 1950, S2807/7; PNC to CNC, 24 January 1949, S2588/1977, NAZ.

158 Katsidzira, vol. 1, chapters 21, 26; Land Inspector Umtali to PNC, 26 August 1948, box number 62328, NRC.

159 Robin Palmer, *Land and Racial Domination in Rhodesia* (London, 1977), p. 117; Acting Director of Land Settlement to SON, 15 May 1914, L2/2/119, NAZ.

160 NC Inyanga to CNC, 31 August 1922, A3/18/39/16, NAZ.

161 Ibid.

162 Government Health Inspector Umtali to PNC, 10 May 1949, box number 62328, NRC.

163 Interview #32; also #130.

164 Secretary for Internal Affairs to Comptroller, Salisbury, 7 March 1950, S2810/2371, NAZ.

165 LDO Inyanga, 'Report on Holdenby', 1947, box number 66721, NRC; NC Inyanga to PNC, 12 April 1948, S2588/1977, NAZ.

166 Government Health Inspector Umtali to PNC, 10 May 1949; PNC to CNC, 30 May 1949; [NC Umtali?], handwritten memorandum, n.d. [1949], box number 62328, NRC.

167 Interview #66; also District Forest Officer G. Guy, 'Annual Report on Native Reserves Eastern Districts 1949', p. 4, box number 62328, NRC.

168 Katsidzira, vol. 2, chapter 45.

169 Ibid., chapter 54.

170 Reverend Kenyon to Bishop Dodge, 30 June 1958, box file 103, shelf b, west wall, OMMA. There is no data on the acreage available prior to 1958. See also LAA S2807/4; LAA S2807/7, NAZ.

171 Interview #21; also Umtali District, Annual Report, 1962, box number 62328 and 1967, box number 88399, NRC; interviews #60 and #61 with a former LDO.

172 Interview #70; also #65.

173 NC Inyanga Bazeley to CNC, 31 August 1922, A3/18/39/16, NAZ.

174 For the role of 'the Manyika' as modernisers, see Terence Ranger, 'Missionaries, Migrants and the Manyika: The Invention of Ethnicity in Zimbabwe', *The Creation of Tribalism in Southern Africa*, Leroy Vail (ed.) (London, 1989), pp. 118-50 and *Peasant Consciousness*, passim.

175 An official in the Department of Rural Development explained that, much to his surprise, he found that people in the Honde Valley used conservation measures that allowed cultivation on very steep slopes without causing erosion and which were more efficient than those enforced by the government. Interview #27.

176 Interviews #112, #127.

177 Interview #85; also #119.

178 Delineation Report, Inyanga District, 1965, p. 38, S2929/1/3, NAZ.

179 Some ritual words, such as terms for drum signals, prevailed until the 1970s. 'Drum Signals Used in Headman Chikomba's Country: Mutasa District', 14 May 1974, RP.

180 Interviews #112, #110. Ranger shows the link between language and ethnic identity in the context of migrant labour; 'Missionaries, Migrants and the Manyika'.

181 Interviews #67, #127.

182 John Lonsdale, 'Moral and Political Argument in Kenya', *Ethnicity and Democracy in Africa*, Bruce Berman et al. (eds) (Oxford, 2004), p. 77.

183 David Maxwell suggests the Cinderella model, *Christians and Chiefs*, pp. 114-16, chapter 2; also Alexander, *Violence and Memory*, chapter 2.

184 *Journal for the Rhodesia Annual Conference: The Methodist Church* (1946), p. 216.

185 Ibid., (1948), p. 49.

186 Interviews #65, #32; Musumba, 'A Short History'.

187 Musumba, 'A Short History'; NC Inyanga to PNC, 28 February 1957, box number 93785, NRC.

188 Other churches which established preaching centres in the 1950s include the Church of the Province of Central Africa, the Seventh Day Adventists, and Guta raJehova. Under-Secretary Administration to Secretary Native Reserves Trust, 29 June 1956, S2810/4203; PNC to Assistant Secretary Administration, 26 November 1953, S2810/2371, NAZ; interview #58.

189 NC Inyanga to PNC, 20 October 1956, S2810/4203, NAZ.

190 Anselm Corbett, 'African Encounter 1948–1951', *Celts Among the Shona: Early Experiences of Carmelite Missionaries to Zimbabwe*, Michael Hender (ed.) (Dublin, 2002), p. 71.

191 Ibid., p. 72.

192 Shropshire, 'A Journey in Mashonaland', p. 53.

193 Corbett, 'African Encounter', p. 71.

194 'History of St Columba's Mission', (St Columba's Mission: ms, 31 December 1987); DC Inyanga to Provincial Education Officer, 2 August 1969, box number 150768, NRC.

195 Fr Arthur Lewis, St Peter's Mission, Mandeya, 'Newsletter', August 1968, box number 150768, NRC.

196 DC Inyanga, 'Manicaland Province, African Primary Schools: Inyanga District, March 1965' and 'List of Primary and Secondary Schools: Inyanga District', n.d. [1966–69], box number 103986, NRC.

197 CNC to NC Inyanga, 13 March 1957, S2810/4203, NAZ; Circuit Inspector Manicaland North to DC Inyanga, 6 November 1963; DC Inyanga to Circuit Inspector, 26 February 1964, DC Inyanga to PC, 21 June 1965: Circuit Inspector to School Manager, St. Columba's Mission, 23 August 1965, box number 103986, NRC.

198 DC Inyanga to Reverend Ntuli, 13 September 1963, box number 103986, NRC.

199 DC Inyanga to Circuit Inspector, 7 January 1964, box number 103986, NRC.

200 'Evidence Pachije', 21 December 1964, box number 103986, NRC.

201 L. Kasambira to NC Inyanga, 25 March 1957, box number 103986, NRC.

202 L. Kasambira to Goodloe, Old Umtali Mission, 25 March 1957, box number 103986, NRC.

203 Katsidzira, vol. 2, chapters 41, 55.

204 Copy of Assistant Director of Native Education to Minister, 26 September 1958, PPA.

205 Katsidzira, vol. 2, chapter 41. For a short biography of Kanyenze, see M'buya, *A Little Leaven*, which is based on transcripts of interviews with Kanyenze. Interview #125 with the author.

206 Ziwe Zano Society, pp. 1193, 1195-6, ZBJ1/1/2; Kanyenze to NC Umtali, n.d. [received 6 June 1947], S2791/4, NAZ.

207 Deputy Provincial Education Officer Manicaland to Manager, 25 November 1974; Cruickshank to Deputy Provincial Education Officer, 22 July 1974, PPA.

208 Katsidzira, vol. 2, chapters 40, 41, 43, 46-57; vol. 3, chapters 58-73; Minutes of 'Honde Industrial Mission: Meeting of Creditors', 6 May 1971; Cruickshank to all creditors, 8 April 1971, PPA.

209 Katsidzira, vol. 1, chapter 29.

210 Ibid., chapter 32.

211 Ibid. Nyamukwarara Valley is situated south-east of and adjacent to the Honde Valley.

212 G.M. Huggins to Prime Minister, 27 January 1944, S482/70/43, NAZ. Honde was the only American Methodist district which had an African superintendent at the time. *Journal for the Rhodesia Annual Conference: The Methodist Church* (1943).

213 Musumba, 'A Short History'.

214 Katsidzira, vol. 1, chapter 32; Ziwe Zano Society, pp. 1197-8, ZBJ1/1/2, NAZ.

215 Ziwe Zano Society, p. 1197, ZBJ1/1/2, NAZ; also L.H. DeWolf, 'A Do-it-yourself Mission in Rhodesia', *The African Christian Advocate* (July to Sept. 1964), p. 7.

216 M. Katsidzira to Bishop Booth, 9 January 1950, file: Correspondence Bishop Booth, filing cabinet, west wall, OMMA.

217 Secretary for Native Affairs to Acting Secretary to the Cabinet, 24 January 1956, S2791/4, NAZ.

218 Katsidzira, vol. 2, chapters 45, 47. For the independent school movement and the political theology of Mau Mau, see John Lonsdale, 'Kikuyu Christianities', *Journal of Religion in Africa*, 29, 2 (1999), pp. 206-29 and 'Jomo Kenyatta, God & the Modern World', *African Modernities: Entangled Meanings in Current Debate*, Jan-Georg Deutsch et al. (eds) (Portsmouth, NH, 2000), pp. 31-66.

219 Interview #21.

220 Phillips to Walsh, for the Registrar of Welfare Organisation Salisbury, 22 July 1968, PPA.

221 *Journal for the Rhodesia Annual Conference: The Methodist Church* (1960), p. 56.

222 Musumba, 'A Short History'; Inyanga District, Annual Report, 1958, S2827/2/2/6, NAZ.

223 Umtali District, Annual Report, 1960, box number 62328, NRC.

4

The Frontier Society under Threat
Politicisation & Militancy

Rural grievances resulting from colonial policies and interventions have been a major theme in African Studies for some time and are well-documented in the case of Zimbabwe. Still, an approach that differentiates which state actions were tolerated from those that caused suffering, and for whom, and how such experiences affected the politisation of the rural population is pertinent. The previous chapter showed that colonial land alienation caused great suffering among the so-called 'highveld Manyika', while Chief Zindi and his followers endured the establishment of the tea plantations. This chapter traces politicisation from the mid-1950s, when the settler state began to fully show its presence in the Honde Valley, until 1974 and the arrival of young men with AK-47s, in this case Mozambique's liberation army FRELIMO, soon followed by Zimbabwe's ZANLA. What transpires is that no single model can explain the range of responses to state intervention, from accommodation to resistance, by the valley's inhabitants. In part, what applies is the observation Flame, a young female combatant in the Second Chimurenga and the main character of the film with the same title, makes: 'You always have a choice!'[1] Still, three elements clearly emerge: Women and chiefs were at the forefront of protest; civic virtue was much debated in the 1950s and 1960s; and the presence of guerrilla fighters facilitated radicalisation.

This chapter, which concerns itself with the period of mass nationalism, and chapter five, which examines the liberation war of the 1970s, show that three aspects played an important role for politicisation and mobilisation in the Honde Valley: state intervention, internal struggles, and appeals.[2] The latter two concepts are derived from Kriger's work on the Second Chimurenga, which made a significant contribution to the understanding of insurgencies. She argues that politicisation was driven by grievances largely caused by internal African power and status imbalances, rather than directly by the interventions of the colonial state or by guerrilla appeals, and that the latter often were replaced by coercion due to the unpredictable security situation and heavy reliance on local collaboration, especially with youths.[3] The first part of Kriger's argument emerges clearly in the discussion about peasant tea production.

In the Honde Valley, after land alienation and beginning with the implementation of agricultural policies, the colonial state threatened the frontier way of life and set into motion a gradation of suffering. While a few perceived the state presence as a new set of opportunities to draw on, most valley inhabitants were resentful. The politicisation process unfolded against a background of nationalist party presence, and when suffering reached an unbearable level for some, they turned to militancy. With chronological and diachronic sections, this chapter shows the development from responses against state intervention in agricultural practices, with the specific example of a tea outgrower scheme, to the shift to militancy in the 1970s. In the final part of the chapter the story of one family's border-crossing provides further insight into one of the main frontier strategies – displacement.

Protest & Non-cooperation in the 1950s & 1960s

The 1950s and 1960s were a period in Zimbabwe's past when urban mass nationalism and the implementation of harsh agricultural policies in the rural areas coincided and became the dual pivots for individual and communal experiences and actions. Throughout this period, the colonial administration tended to explain any obstacle to the implementation of their policies as stemming from nationalist agitation. However, true to the frontier identity, nationalist policies remained on the margins of political discourse in the valley, although they were certainly present.

What the colonial administration did observe was a process of politicisation and 'a new sense of African solidarity'. In 1955, the Native Commissioner (NC) Umtali complained about 'a continual change in the relationship between the Africans and the Administration'. He further maintained that, as NC, he was made responsible for 'unpopular innovations such as destocking [and] land limitation'. He concluded: 'There is nothing really tangible; just a feeling, an undercurrent, a new sense of African solidarity which may go further.'[4] In the Honde Valley, land husbandry measures, the introduction of tea as a cash crop, and land alienation for the establishment of a third tea plantation caused grievances that resulted in this sense of African solidarity, which largely expressed itself through protests, non-cooperation and occasional active resistance until the early 1970s. Often, women took the action: it was they who were most directly affected by state intervention, with migrant workers and party operatives introducing nationalist ideas at the same time.[5]

State intervention into African agriculture primarily consisted of land segregation and appropriation and the Native Land Husbandry Act (NLHA) of 1951. From the late 1940s, once the enforcement of segregated areas was under way, it quickly became clear that the state had to respond to overcrowding and land erosion if the settler regime wanted to uphold its privilege, initially put into law with the Land Apportionment Act of 1930, which reserved 51 per cent of the colony's territory for European occupation only, even though the European proportion of the population ranged from a mere 2 per cent to 5 per cent at most. Only 22 per cent of the land was allocated to reserves for the African majority population, with an additional 7.8 per cent that, with the 1941 amendment, became Native Purchase Areas and was enlarged to 8.2 per cent.[6] Reserve land was often inferior in terms of rainfall, fertility, and access to infrastructure.

As part of the modernisation efforts that characterised much of the colonial thinking at the time, as exemplified by the second colonial occupation in Kenya,[7] the NLHA of 1951 was intended to transform African agricultural practices that most technocrats, settlers, and politicians perceived to be atavistic and destructive.[8] The programme prescribed a population and livestock census and a detailed land evaluation of the African reserves. Subsequently, all this land was to be allocated according to the government's directives of land use, as set out in the NLHA, followed by the instruction of African cultivators in what the technocrats perceived to be appropriate agricultural techniques. Apart from the political implications of this racialised, white minority rule policy, the implementation of the Act had practical shortcomings from the outset. The African reserves provided uneven and mostly difficult livelihoods, and the only relief – the allocation of more and better land – was out of the question. In addition, the technocrats who implemented the NLHA believed in the universality of their scientific approach that went hand in hand with their disregard of vernacular knowledge. Moreover, whether European planners or African extension workers, they focused almost exclusively on male producers. Meanwhile women were most directly affected by state intervention in agricultural practices, because of the gender division of labour and because of the large number of female-headed households, while the men were absent through migrant labour.[9] This, together with understaffing and the general under-allocation of resources, meant that in many areas problems arose from the very beginning.

In 1954, the implementation of the NLHA began in the southern, most easily accessible part of the Honde Valley. The 'kraal appreciation' exercise – the population census and land survey which caused the reduction of Honde Mission's arable area – was never fully completed in Mutasa North Reserve, however.[10] From there, things progressed even more slowly in Manga and Holdenby Reserves. The Act was supposed to be fully applied by 1958,[11] but the reallocation of land in combination with managing the forced resettlement into the valley and having to deal with the resulting environmental deterioration led to land shortages, which further aggravated the situation.[12] Hence, the redelineation of land, marked by pegging, and the introduction of conservation measures such as contour ridging and the prohibition of streambank cultivation, in most cases followed even later, from 1966 onwards. Protests and non-cooperation appear to have accompanied the government actions every step of the way.

District staff frequently attributed any resistance they encountered to nationalist politicisation. In 1960, on the occasion of the first large-scale women's protest, the District Commissioner (DC) blamed their active resistance to and resentment against the NLHA to 'agitation' by the National Democratic Party (NDP), which he thought had spread south from Holdenby into Mutasa North Reserve.[13] The NC Inyanga had discovered the presence of the party in Holdenby in 1956: 'My information was to the effect that funds were being collected to solicit legal aid in combating measures taken by us to prevent streambank and shifting cultivation, tree cutting etc. There was also some chatter about having Mutassa [sic] appointed Paramount Chief of Manicaland.'[14] The matter was taken so seriously that the entry was removed from the district files and subsequently investigated by the CID. The NC claimed that for this 'fighting fund' a sum of approximately £119 was raised from all the chiefs in the Holdenby area, that is, Muparutsa, Zindi, Mandeya, and Chikomba. The money was collected by 'Towedzayi alias Mugarbi alias Dobson' at a meeting he had called. The NC further maintained that part of the money was set aside for delegates' expenses for a meeting of the Rhodesian African Association in Harare.[15] In 1955, the NC Inyanga had warned that Mugarbi was heading the 'Manyika Association', which was a political pressure group of migrant labourers, petitioning him about their grievances. He predicted that the Association would 'cause trouble some day'.[16]

In 1960, Chief Samanga opposed the land evaluation exercise, allegedly under the influence of 'NDP agitators', and in Chief Mandeya's area, where the party had held meetings, the DC Inyanga found the chief 'un-cooperative' and the people refusing to dip their cattle.[17] Three years later, not only had nationalist politics entered the valley, but the recent split by the Zimbabwe African People's Union (ZAPU) from the Zimbabwe African National Union (ZANU) had become highly politicised. This was evident in one of the mission school conflicts when *sabhuku* (village headman; pl. *masabhuku*) Pacije from Holdenby explained to the DC Inyanga that the *masabhuku* who had recently come to live in his area had approached him about opening a Methodist church: 'I refused because my people were Roman Catholics. They became angry and said it was a ZAPU church and that it was to be built at my kraal. They threatened to kill me.'[18] Between 1955 and independence in 1980, all major nationalist parties rallied for support in the Honde Valley: the Southern Rhodesian African Association was followed by the Southern Rhodesian African National Congress (1953–1963) and its successor, the NDP (1960–1961), replaced by ZAPU (1961–1987) and ZANU (1963–).[19] Clearly, the parties used the grievances caused by the colonial state to politicise valley inhabitants.

Many chiefs and their followers were prepared to resist the enforcement of conservation measures, so much so that in 1961 attempts to implement the NLHA came to a halt due to 'considerable hostility'. The DC Inyanga reported: 'At one stage in Holdenby and Manga the [agricultural] demonstrators were almost too afraid to move out of their houses, and all work and progress was virtually at a standstill.'[20] After the banning of the NDP in December 1961, the situation quietened temporarily.[21] With the successor parties ZANU and ZAPU forced underground in 1964, soon after they were founded, party politics in the region appear to have been mostly limited to towns, urban centres, and news carried by migrant labourers, with the exception of the Tangwena area. The lull in protests was temporary, though, a clear indicator that the grievances were expressed in vernacular mode, not in nationalist discourse. Those who were the living guardians of their people on behalf of their ancestors, the chiefs and sub-chiefs, emerged as leaders, and women, the most harshly affected by government agricultural policies, voiced their discontent loudly.

Observed or suspected non-compliance is a constant theme in the government files on the Honde Valley. But it was in 1960, when land allocation was still unresolved, even in the southern part of the area, five years after the exercise began, that the suffering became unbearable and women started to take matters into their own hands. In that year, a delegation of one hundred women went to see the DC Umtali (now renamed from NC). They complained of 'land shortages and hunger' and demanded more land.[22] This was truly a drastic step to take, considering that a woman could not claim land use rights in her own capacity – only in relation to a male guardian as daughter, wife, sister, or mother, unless she was widowed and thus became the chief's client.[23] In fact, when women resisted implementing land use measures, their male guardians were held responsible, such as *ishe* Zindi for his wives in 1967.[24]

Women's politicisation and activism were a direct reaction to state intervention having brought suffering into their lives. The impact of colonial agricultural policies was gendered, with men usually responsible for the digging of contour ridges and women typically affected by legislation prohibiting streambank cultivation, because vegetable gardening was and is largely seen as a woman's task. Moreover, in the 1960 confrontation, the women presented themselves as female household heads, with their husbands currently away in migrant labour. They explained that they belonged to the first waves of resettled people from the plateau. Hence, so they argued, they had a right to larger parcels of land in comparison to more recent immigrants. The Land Development Officer (LDO) and his staff investigated the claim and found food to be plentiful, but came across numerous contraventions of the conservation act. The DC subsequently reported:

> Inspections of lands to secure evidence for prosecutions resulted in further disturbances with the Land Development Officer and his African Staff virtually besieged in the rest house. 21 prosecutions for infringements of the Act are pending, as well as at least one case of stick throwing and one of assaulting a pegger. Inspections in the area have not been completed, and these will have to be pursued if all Land Husbandry measures in this area are not to be flouted. However, intimidation in the reserve is rife, and makes this distasteful task an unpopular one.[25]

The DC did not report how the women 'besieged' the Land Department's staff. Women roughing up men, as happened here, is a rare occurrence, but women occasionally would resort to a gendered measure of protest. They would strip, baring their breasts or even down to covering their genitals only, exposing themselves as most vulnerable in their female corporeality, thus strongly claiming the right to be heard. In the valley, such protest is remembered to have occurred, but it is not identified with any specific event.[26]

The sheer scale of women's activism is astonishing. In 1970, *mambo* Pafiwa Mutasa reported that three hundred women came to see him, 'complaining that they don't accept the chief's peggers or any agricultural staff members to peg their gardens'.[27] Women's prominent role in opposing the NLHA is reflected also in their numerous prosecutions. In 1956, twenty-one women and one man were charged with contravening Public Stream Bank Protection Regulations at Selbourne Estate, just outside the valley. Most women plainly stated at the court case: 'We were hungry.'[28] In 1961, the DC Umtali reported on Mutasa North Reserve: 'Irregularities which took the form of extending lands into the garden areas, ploughing over grass strips and demolishing beacons were politically inspired. In all 100 prosecutions ensued, mainly of women who were responsible for the offenses in the absence of their husbands in employment.'[29] Unsurprisingly, after these trials which held the women responsible for sabotage and non-compliance, the political situation in the area calmed down for some time, given that these women were heads of households and must have feared for the wellbeing of their children.[30]

In many parts of the country, chiefs were split in their allegiance, but in the Honde Valley most office-holders led their people into protest. In 1966, *ishe* Zindi, the same man who had asserted himself over the tea plantation management in the 1950s and later in the early 1990s, sent a group of thirty to forty people to meet the LDO's team in order to prevent them from pegging. He and his followers further resisted the digging of demarcation banks, and as a result the government threatened Zindi with prosecution.[31] Even so, the conflict further heightened in 1967 as Zindi continued to refuse to cooperate.[32] The government eventually made attempts to win the chiefs over, aware that the implementation of the NLHA could only succeed with their support. Digging, for example, could only commence if the chiefs provided labour and pegs. But these conciliatory efforts met with limited success, and in 1966 the DC Inyanga concluded that the chiefs, even if they were willing to cooperate, faced problems themselves: 'In fairness to them I think they have a very difficult time trying to convince their followers.'[33] Indeed, in the few areas where chiefs did collaborate with the settler government, their authority was challenged. In 1970, the government found *ishe* Chikomba cooperating, while his *masabhuku* were 'completely opposed to the implementation of a soil conservation programme'.[34]

On the eve of the liberation war, the settler government found itself in a significant bind. The early stages of implementing the NLHA had caused considerable hardship due to lack of resources, policy failure, and planning mistakes. In fact, in 1961, Provincial Agricultural Officer Plowes, who knew the area well, having served as LDO in the valley, blamed 'much of the political upset which has recently arisen in the Honde Valley' on the delay in tackling the land problem.[35] The grievances were aggravated when the technocrats tried to implement conservation measures, while the protests and non-cooperation they faced further hampered the completion of the exercise. Consequently, when the first guerrilla fighters arrived in 1974, valley inhabitants immediately pointed out those who had collaborated with the colonial administration, namely *ishe* Chikomba and the extension workers, as targets in order to regain their social and political equilibrium. By then, the government had taken another initiative, one related to the NLHA. This introduction of tea, as an outgrower scheme and in the shape of a third tea plantation, truly started what Norma Kriger named 'struggles within the struggle'.[36]

Tea: The Great Divider

One day in 1992, while walking in the Mapokana Hills in the Chikomba area, I noticed pre-teen boys parading their wire cars on a path that ran alongside a substantial tea field. Wire toys are common in many parts of Africa, including Zimbabwe, but I had never seen any in the Honde Valley before, as most boys rather carried slingshots to try to kill birds and small mammals. After admiring the vehicles which the boys proudly displayed, I asked the women I was with about this oddity. They loudly slapped their hands, rocked back and forth laughing, clicked their tongues, and explained that the day before the owner had put up a wire fence around his tea field. During the night, local youths had taken the fence down, and the boys, laying their hands on some of it, spent their time mocking the owner, who could not prove that they had made the cars from his wire. In the early evening, when fetching water and vegetables from the gardens, the women in the area enjoyed retelling the story over and over, and that continued during the evening meal among household members. In the former reserves, since independence Communal Lands (CLs), the prevalent understanding is that no living being can claim true ownership of the land. Most Zimbabweans believe that ownership lies with the ancestors, and, depending on one's political position, is administered in trusteeship from those who are deceased, be it by their direct descendants, chiefs, or the state. In the absence of title deeds, certainly in the Honde Valley, by the 1990s the vast majority of the population understood land use rights as a matter of communal responsibility, embedded in moral ethnicity, and the post-colonial local government in most parts of the area barely played a role in this regard, as is discussed in chapter six.

The intervention of the colonial state from the mid-twentieth century and the increasing population pressure did eventually undercut shifting cultivation practices, but even where a family might have held land use rights over specific plots of land for generations, the understanding is that these are alienable. If the male household head loses his standing in the community, which can have many causes, such as agricultural practices that lead to the deterioration of the land or to the anger of ancestors who may then punish the community with drought, he may subsequently lose his land use rights, at least over part of his land. Accordingly, the demarcation of agriculturally used land by a fence breaks the basic rules of civic virtue. In the case of the tea farmer whose fence was sabotaged by his neighbours' sons, this was taken seriously enough for the boys' actions to be condoned and for the events to become a told and retold story. By the 1990s, even though wire and enclosures had regained a truly sinister meaning, with the counter-insurgency measure of villagisation during the 1970s being remembered as 'living behind the fence', the incident was taken lightly enough to be joked about. In the years of mass nationalism and the liberation war, however, the introduction of tea as a cash crop grown by African cultivators in the Honde Valley became a major dividing factor, at times with violent consequences for those who accepted the innovation. When the frontier society was under threat from state intervention, social cohesion and moral ethnicity became ever more important.

So far it has been shown that the response to the NLHA, including the conservation measures, was overwhelmingly negative. Three factors contributed to making the Honde Valley one of the most important areas of agricultural experimentation and implementation in the country. The government continued its efforts to modernise African agriculture in the valley as part of its broader rural policies and especially after the Unilateral Declaration of Independence (UDI) on 11 November 1965, which was followed the next year by the first mandatory economic sanctions the United Nations declared, the importance of African cash crop production for the settler economy increased. Lastly, the unusual sub-tropical climate allowed an agricultural potential not found in any other area of that size reserved for African occupation in the region.

The first exploratory planting on Aberfoyle in 1952 included experimental cash crop plots for commercial agriculture, even though William Igoe appeared to have been set on growing tea in the valley and trees on the plateau from the very beginning. Coinciding with the NLHA, as early as 1952, the government attempted to introduce various cash crops in the reserves, and that same year, sixty-four farmers were apparently keen to join a rice scheme in Holdenby while others started to grow pineapples as a cash crop in Manga Reserve. Four years later, with the NLHA 'kraal appreciation' under way, the land department took the next step and established an experimental plot in Holdenby for identifying suitable crops by planting exotic fruit, 'Congo coffee', and spices from as far afield as Singapore.[37] As part of this exercise, the agricultural officers realised that some exotic plants such as lemons and granadillas were already growing in the wild, and that in at least one garden turmeric was being cultivated, before the imposition of colonial rule.[38] In all likelihood brought in by returning migrant labourers and immigrants from the east, a region with a Portuguese presence dating back to the fifteenth century, these exotic plants are certainly another trace of the valley's connectedness to the wider world, despite its relative isolation from the west. In what follows, the introduction of tea as an outgrower crop, with all its significant political implications for the affected communities will be examined, before the focus shifts to the establishment of Katiyo Tea and Coffee Estate, the third plantation in the valley.

TEA IS NOT EDIBLE

Today, in addition to its tea and coffee, the Honde Valley is well known for producing outstanding pineapples, avocados, mangos and other fruit and vegetables. This development dates back to the initial explorations in the 1950s. In 1958, triggered by the success of Aberfoyle, the government appointed an LDO whose specific task it was to establish the suitability of tea and coffee in order to focus local efforts on those crops.[39] Under his supervision, growing commenced with the first six 'family units' in *ishe* Zindi's area.[40] That same year, a 'Special Purpose Crops in the Eastern Districts Committee' was established and tabled its report in 1959. During this period, the implementation of the NLHA was interrupted in order to await the findings of this report, which was expected to endorse the allocation of land to cash crops. Once it was presented, however, the introduction of tea was then in turn hampered by the delay in allocating land according to the terms of the NLHA.[41] The report recommended tea and coffee as the main crops for the Holdenby and Manga areas,[42] and as a result the efforts to introduce a tea outgrower scheme were accelerated but soon faced difficulties. Tea was a cash crop that generated much opposition, because it is 'not edible',[43] rather it is a commodity produced exclusively for marketing and not for local consumption or redistribution.

In 1960, the government established tea and coffee nurseries in *ishe* Zindi's area,[44] but by 1962 only six growers had joined the scheme, and the NC reported that an 'antipathy to special crops' still existed.[45] The tremendous effort the government put into the tea scheme finally resulted in forty growers by 1966, twelve of whom had formed a co-operative society, but overall the crop remained unpopular.[46] In the following year, the DC Inyanga reported that the introduction of tea was still 'an uphill battle' and that the production had so far been very small.[47] The scheme faltered, even though outgrowers were provided with free seedlings, helped with planting, and supported by extension staff.[48] To some degree, the DC and the agricultural technocrats did grasp the reasons for this 'antipathy', but they failed to recognise that generating the outgrower scheme in the first place had had the perilous effect of further politicising the valley population by creating divisions.

One elder remembered that there was reluctance to grow tea simply because it was a new crop: 'When it was made known that people could now grow tea, a lot of people were reluctant – you know, if something is not familiar, you do not show enthusiasm towards it. That being the case, a lot of people refused to grow tea.'[49] This traditionalist argument was a common theme in interviews, conversations, stories, and gossip about tea outgrowers. Still, attributing tea's unpopularity to its novelty is an insufficient argument, because other exotic crops such as coffee were adopted.

The two main reasons why tea cultivation in the CLs and its outgrowers were resented by their neighbours were fear of land alienation and the notion that they were in breach of the most basic understanding of civic virtue. Although chapter three showed that the establishment of Aberfoyle Tea Plantation caused little grievance for *ishe* Zindi and his followers at the time, because the slopes of the escarpment were considered a place of refuge in times of danger and a spiritual landscape, and it was access to but not occupation of it that was important. The outgrower scheme was a different matter altogether, because the nursery and delineated cash crop lands were allocated in the foothills and on the valley floor. Thus, in 1966, when the expansion of the scheme came to a standstill, the DC Inyanga conceded that resistance was understandable:

> There is a certain amount of opposition to the growing of tea from some of the tribesmen – they consider that if tea is seen to grow well in an African area, the Europeans will take away the land to grow tea for themselves. As this district has been involved in the removal of persons from one area to another for many years, perhaps they have cause to be rather perturbed.[50]

Even in the early 1990s, the inhabitants of the valley still remembered these evictions. People, for example, who had lived in Chieftainess Muredzwa's or in the Bonda Mission area and who had refused to enter labour agreements as tenant workers, had been forcibly removed by the Wattle Company in the late 1940s.[51] A number of these families moved into the Honde Valley and their story became part of local discourse. First, they had been encouraged to grow wattle on their plots. Once the trees proved to be suitable to the area, however, they were evicted, capital moved in and established plantations. An elder recalled: 'They then thought this was the same plan all over again – this time with tea.'[52] Apparently, nationalists used this argument to rally people, so in 1956, when Mugarbi, a member of the Rhodesian African Association allegedly spread the word that Aberfoyle plantation was taking over the whole of Holdenby and that the resident population would then be displaced.[53]

The second main reason for resistance against tea was that the crop violated the notion of civic virtue. Three factors were crucial in this regard. First, as the wire toy anecdote illustrates, tea fields posit a claim to land that violates the vernacular understanding of community, entitlement, and responsibility. Once a sapling takes root and grows into a tea bush, it is a somewhat permanent plant. Even if neglected over long periods, it is persistent if grown in an appropriate climate, and when bushes are planted very close to each other, it is impossible to cut through a tea field; one can only walk between the rows. Tea, therefore, is a plant that marks space in a semi-permanent manner that even transcends the notion of fruit trees as signifiers of belonging. Moreover, tea bushes pose an almost impassable obstruction, whether fenced or not, and therefore express in a very concrete way a claim of ownership connected to the land on which they grow that was resented by most neighbours.

The practicalities of peasant tea-growing furthered the local sense of aliena-tion from the outgrowers. In contrast to coffee trees, which require pesticides and labour-intensive weeding unless the fields are planted with shade creep-ers, tea is a crop whose dependency on extension services exceeds that of most other cash crops, binding the peasant producer directly to a nearby tea planta-tion. Once a tea field is established it can last for many decades, but initially, seed, or in the case of the Honde Valley, saplings, have to be provided. More importantly, though, a crop such as coffee can, if necessary, be harvested, pre-processed and stored for periods of time without special technical requirements or knowledge. Tea leaves, on the other hand, start to oxidise the moment they are harvested. Consequently, the weight by which the producer is paid literally evaporates, and rapidly, within the first few hours and, just as importantly, the quality also deteriorates. For these two reasons, outgrowers depend on reliable truck pick-up from their fields, swift grading, and on sophisticated process-ing in a tea factory. As soon as valley inhabitants became outgrowers, their collaboration with the tea plantations and extension services meant that they contravened the general attitude of non-compliance and resistance. Moreover, given the government assistance provided to the first tea-growers, it appears that they did not have to depend on local working parties to establish their tea fields and thus the anticipated amount of sharing and redistribution of wealth in the community did not occur.

Finally, and possibly most importantly, tea cannot directly benefit the com-munity through consumption and the exchange of gifts. An elderly woman who had begun growing tea in the 1980s remarked that, 'We can now drink tea'.[54] What she meant was that she had a small cash income from her field which allowed her to buy tea leaves at a local store. [55] Generating a cash income, however, is not the same as producing something that can be used for commu-nal consumption, such as sorghum for beer-brewing or pineapples and other fruit for gifts to visitors or local marketing. Also, the full development of a profitable tea field takes years, thus the immediate economic benefit is not evi-dent.[56] When an area is productive, the household itself still cannot produce tea leaves for personal consumption, in contrast to coffee outgrowers, who would always roast some beans for their own use.[57] The first person to grow tea in the

Chikomba area was Chacha Mubhede. He was beaten up for so doing and, as a neighbour remembered, much hated:

> They hated Chacha for growing this crop which they said was not edible and also could not be used for the brewing of beer. That being the case, they argued, how did he know that there was any profit in it? They went further and accused him of trying to create problems for them. That was why they hated him.[58]

To summarise, in contrast to other cash crops, tea cultivation conveys a heightened sense of belonging, claim to landownership, and dissociation from moral economies in favour of a dependency on market relations – and it has one purpose only: to generate cash income.

Acts of sabotage, ostracising, and possibly envy by their neighbours were all reactions that the tea outgrowers had to accommodate. One young man recalled that his father, who had helped establish the nursery near Sagambe, was the second outgrower in the Chikomba area. As an African Development Fund (ADF) employee, he was not only encouraged to grow tea, but also informed about the benefits, namely additional cash household income.[59] Joseph Mtisi, in a paper on the tea outgrower scheme in Holdenby, argued that the first four tea-growers were all members of the Watchtower church and, he maintained, having already been marginalised, were thus ready to defy any hostilities by their neighbours.[60] Although this might be the case, the next two families to grow tea in Chikomba area were, at least by the early 1990s, Vapostori. As members of an African initiated church that, until recently, encouraged polygyny, Vapostori men who had many wives were singularly well-positioned to become tea outgrowers.[61]

A male household head is allocated land according to the size of his household, it being his responsibility to be able to take care of his dependents. A young Vapostori man explained that while his church encouraged him to have many wives, the only way to sustain such large families – in one case more than seventy children were born to one father – is through tea production, as each wife could earn money from her section of the tea field and thus look after her own children.[62] An elderly woman claimed that only Vapostori could profit as outgrowers, because they could draw substantially on family labour and because wives could cooperate in the management of their tea fields.[63] Arguably, both features characterise the 'big families' in the valley, as access to unpaid family labour proved to be vital to establishing a variety of economic activities.[64] The largest household I came across in Zimbabwe was a Vapostori church member in the valley who had twenty-three wives. To the chagrin of their neighbours, they effectively ran a tea plantation together. The co-wives pooled their and their children's labour, making business decisions as they saw fit, their husband being a migrant worker and thus away most of the time and represented by his widowed mother presiding over the household. In contrast to the successful adoption of tea after 1980, from the beginning of the scheme in 1958 until the early 1970s, outgrowers were frequently victims of intimidation and sabotage by neighbours: tea bushes were uprooted or cut during the night.[65] This internal strife escalated once the young men with guns arrived in 1974.

7. *Rumbizi Project Manager Geoff Baxter, Prime Minister Ian Smith, and Provincial Agricultural Officer Derryl Plowes, Tea Scheme, 1970* (Source: National Archives of Zimbabwe)

A TWIST TO THE OUTGROWER SCHEME

The stated goal of state intervention in Holdenby TTL regarding the introduction of tea had, from the very beginning, been to foster an outgrower scheme and not plantation production. But this was not to last. By 1966, after eight years of effort, there were only forty tea outgrowers – a meagre outcome. It was during this same year that *ishe* Zindi sent his men to stop the peggers from implementing the delineation according to the NLHA and when local resistance against both the Act, and the introduction of tea in particular, was at its height. In the following year, the Provincial Agricultural Officer took the initiative to hire a young man whom he trusted would have the knowledge and drive to turn things around in the Honde Valley.[66] Geoff Baxter grew up in Kenya and had been instrumental in establishing the Kenya Tea Development Authority, the first tea outgrower scheme. He re-assessed the tea-growing potential of Holdenby and in 1968 tabled the first of a series of reports in which he proposed an outgrower scheme largely modelled on the Kenyan experience.[67] Baxter suggested establishing the main block of tea at Rumbizi, under *ishe* Zindi, with a nursery in *sabhuku* Katiyo's area, under *ishe* Chikomba.[68] At the time, it was still a revolutionary idea that tea, seen by the British as a sophisticated crop requiring expert knowledge, could be grown by peasants, and in particular by

127

African producers, who were still commonly viewed as primitive and, at best, only just coming to grips with modernisation. Baxter, however, was convinced that if he micro-managed the project and gained an understanding of the valley population beyond its mere production potential, he could succeed. Unfortunately, that same year, 1968, the newly formed Tribal Trust Land Development Corporation (TILCOR) took over the nursery and changed the scheme completely: the outgrowers, perceived to be unprofitable, were to be managed by the ADF, whereas a 'nucleus estate' was to be established in the area of *sabhuku* Katiyo, adjacent to the border with Mozambique.[69]

Officially, TILCOR claimed the estate was 'to produce tea in marketable form in accordance with sound commercial practice and management'.[70] At the same time, the opportunity of 'gainful employment' and a 'ripple effect' would benefit the local people. Shifting cultivation was supposed to be replaced with 'sound agronomic and conservation techniques on a permanent basis'. The overall goal was stated as follows: 'Within the terms of the Act under which Tilcor was established the objectives may be simply stated as being aimed at providing a means whereby the inhabitants of the TTLs can benefit through the development and use of the local natural resources.'[71] In other words, TILCOR was a response to some of the problems that had arisen during the attempts to implement the NLHA. For the valley, the idea was that once the tea fields were fully developed, plantation-style, they were then to be handed over to 'selected plot holders'.[72] This never happened; Katiyo is still a plantation under TILCOR's successor, the Agricultural Rural Development Authority (ARDA), another parastatal. The initial plan of involving local farmers, or even putting them in charge, finally came to an end in September 2009. The plantation had been dysfunctional due to the Zimbabwean crisis for some time, and, solicited by the Zimbabwean government, Eastern Highlands Tea Estates came to an agreement with ARDA to enter a joint venture with Katiyo, investing US$2 million over the course of the first two years to rehabilitate the estate.[73] Then, in a shift of events, in December 2010 ARDA entered another joint venture with a private company owned by the Zimbabwean businessman Shingai Mutasa to return Katiyo to production.[74]

In August 1969, the clearing of tea fields and work on labour compounds commenced.[75] Under the heading 'sociological', TILCOR's 1971 report explains:

> To achieve the economic objectives of the scheme it is essential that due attention must be paid to the human element, both individual and communal.
>
> The infrastructure of the organisation provides for the establishment of such facilities as shops, clinics, beer-halls, schools and related services in concert with the expansion of the community. These facilities will be provided with an eye to causing as little disruption of tribal traditions and customs as possible, without jeopardising the economy and growth of the project.[76]

However, in September 1970, when all the tea fields were defined on the ground and some new lands bulldozed, 'the human element' felt sufficiently disrupted to leave their lands:

> The villagers within the nearest proximity of activities have abandoned their huts and moved elsewhere, some across into P.E.A. [Portuguese East Africa], others outside the

leased area, and some to areas within the leased area where no tea blocks have been marked. The total number of villages involved so far is eight. Rumours have it that almost all the inhabitants, now surrounded by the marked areas, will eventually move. No valid explanation is given, other than they do not want to get involved in tea growing. There are no signs of discontent and many of the males involved continue to work for the Estate. This is purely a voluntary move.

From a management point of view of the Estate, this is very acceptable. However, sociologically, a general exodus out of the leased area is not really a healthy sign, and is not one of TILCOR's principles.[77]

At this stage, the feared 'general exodus' did not occur, as only a minority of the resident population of approximately one thousand people, who lived in one hundred and forty compounds and belonged to six sabhukuships, appears to have left the area.[78] However, while the TILCOR officials were glad to be saved from enacting evictions, the 'sociological' aspect would prove crucial during the liberation war. The first trickle of border crossings was the beginning of a major movement, once life became unbearable for many, and with the arrival of guerrilla fighters, disputes with chiefs and tea-growers could be settled in more radical ways. The frontier people became militant.

FRELIMO & the Shift to Militancy

What had started as 'nothing really tangible; just a feeling, an undercurrent, a new sense of African solidarity which may go further' in 1955[79] took a leap into militancy with the arrival of young men with AK-47s in 1974. As early as 1967, Terence Ranger, who at times has shown tremendous historical insight into contemporary events, emphasised the significance of 1964 as the turning point towards militancy in Zimbabwe: 'In 1963 it was easy enough to assume that the whole of African political history in Rhodesia was leading to the emergence of the mass nationalist parties and that they were the final, triumphant form of organization. This has not proven to be so.'[80] In 1964, the year ZANU and ZAPU were banned, ZANLA, ZANU's armed wing, sent its first insurgent group – the Crocodile Gang – across the border to fight guerrilla-style hit-and-run attacks.[81] With the two parties forced underground, their leadership in detention or exile, and UDI met by Britain with a mere lukewarm response that focused on negotiation rather than intervention, it was clear that the time of hope for a radical improvement of African livelihoods through protest had ended. Hence, the phase of armed struggle began: the mass nationalist parties became liberation movements that formed armed wings.

Writing in the resistance paradigm and believing, as well as purposefully propagating, a master narrative of unity and purpose, Ranger missed a vital point. Not surprisingly, considering the early publication date, he overlooked the fact that actions undermining the settler regime were not necessarily informed by the larger nationalist cause. Consequently, 1964 was a crucial year for the country, but not for every Zimbabwean. So far it has been shown that from the 1950s onwards, once the frontier society in the Honde Valley perceived itself to be under threat from the state through the implementation of agricultural measures, chiefs and their followers, communities, and individuals resisted such intervention. Radicalisation commenced in the 1970s with the arrival of armed fighters whose presence served to broaden the measures of resistance taken, from flight to abductions, attacks on homesteads, and executions. In what follows, this process is examined through the case of *ishe* Chikomba and then through the political shift produced by the arrival of Front for the Liberation of Mozambique (FRELIMO) fighters.[82]

TAKING SIDES: CHIEF CHIKOMBA

From the late 1960s, a position of political non-commitment became increasingly untenable in the valley. The situation was probably most difficult for chiefs, who found themselves under pressure from both the government and their own followers to take sides as leaders. As shown above, most chiefs in the valley became what the government perceived to be 'politically minded',[83] such as Chiefs Zindi and Muparutsa. Zindi had already proved in 1954 that he was prepared to take a strong stance in his actions towards the tea estates. Muparutsa, however, provides an example of the gradual process of politicisation. In 1967, the Extension Officer Inyanga described Chief Moses Paradzayi Muparutsa as 'without a doubt the best type of headman we have ever had in Holdenby'.[84] But ten years later, the DC Mutasa, the district newly created in 1973 and encompassing the entire valley, wrote that the chief had been 'a thorn in the side of the Administration for a number of years'. He recommended Muparutsa's suspension and further complained: 'During my five months at Mutasa I have found Headman Muparutsa to be cunningly evasive and obviously unwilling to carry out his responsibilities to his people or to the Government.'[85]

Initially, Chief Muparutsa's appointment had been greatly resented by people in his area, because, being a Methodist minister, he refused to partake in any non-Christian ceremonies, including his own 'traditional' installation, to 'drink to the spirits', and also to acknowledge the political and spiritual authority of the *muzvare*, the chieftainess and senior spirit medium in the area.[86] Being seen as a government puppet at the height of resistance against agricultural measures, the chief complained to the DC Inyanga:

> I am working too much with the Government, they say. I have allowed demonstrators to supervise and advise people on good agriculture which is the main thing they have founded themselves on. They say we live in an African TTL and they claim the Government mustn't interfere with their way of living. They say the demonstrators have been sent by the Government to exploit African interests. They say these [agricultural] demonstrators are paving way for European settlement in African Tribal Land because they pretend to advise people to grow cash crops so that if they find out that crops like tea and coffee are prospering then Africans will be forced to leave the fields in which they will be growing the crops so that their land will be reserves only for Europeans.[87]

But things changed quickly; from being perceived as too loyal to the government by his followers in 1967, three years later chief Muparutsa was prosecuted for failing to enforce conservation measures.[88] In 1974, the DC Inyanga reported that: 'Headman Muparutsa attends my usual monthly meetings and frequently asks questions, sometimes embarrassing ones (e.g. Government's immigration policy) and I am of the opinion that he is fully aware of the political situation and needs watching. However, at the moment, I have nothing against him.[89]

The extent of the chief's political engagement finally came to light when he was prosecuted along with three other men for addressing an illegal political meeting of four to five hundred people at Gatsi Business Centre in Chief Samanga's area in January 1975. According to a BSAP constable, Muparutsa had proclaimed: 'When others will be saying "Forward Rhodesia", we should say "'Forward Zimbabwe"'.[90] The PC raised the question of his suspension, but the DC Inyanga defended the chief:

> Headman Muparutsa is known to be politically minded and whilst the present case is serious in certain respects, I personally would not recommend the cancellation of his appointment. He could well do more harm to the Government as a 'commoner' than as a rather unreliable Headman. I recommend that he be severely reprimanded and cautioned. This appears to be his first conviction.[91]

The chief remained in office until, finally, he was suspended in 1977, when he resisted forced resettlement.[92] It is not clear how Muparutsa's politicisation came about; nevertheless, this change was symptomatic of political processes in the Honde Valley at the time, when chiefs in particular had to declare their allegiance to one side or the other. In this regard, what happened in the Chikomba area, where the chief sided with the government, is worthy of examination.

Chiefly succession is always a prolonged and much-debated process. In Chikomba, after two years of discussions following *ishe* Naka's death in 1967, acting chief Tambudzayi Chikomba was installed against strong opposition from the contestant houses, possibly under pressure from the government.[93] Typical for the valley, Naka had been regarded as uncooperative by the district administration, while Tambudzayi, himself a tea outgrower, was considered to be loyal. Thus, the DC Inyanga argued: 'Headman Chikomba has assured me that he, together with his Tribal Land Authority, will enforce discipline and control in his area.'[94]

From the outset of Tambudzayi Chikomba's rule there were complaints against his conduct, accusations that he was corrupt, and that he exercised his chiefly authority arbitrarily. In 1970, during the time of radicalisation, four men, representing several of Chikomba's *masabhuku*, approached a Salisbury attorney for assistance in deposing the chief. The attorney wrote to the DC Inyanga on behalf of his clients: 'These gentlemen complain that the Chief is acting in a high-handed and despotic fashion which in their view makes him unfit to continue in that capacity.'[95] The DC responded saying that the claims would be investigated, but that in his view they were entirely unjustified. Rather than the chief having shown any shortcoming, he contended, the *masabhuku* were in fact 'completely opposed' to the soil conservation programme which the new chief had promised to enforce. He also stated that the plaintiffs in one of the cases were likely to be Mozambicans. He closed by emphasising the importance of 'tribal authority', that is local African government, and argued that 'the tribesmen in this particular area have, in the past, virtually done whatever they please to the detriment of the country and tribal cohesion'.[96]

The *masabhuku* did not, however, withdraw their charges. A few months later, the attorney explained that his clients had Rhodesian registration certificates, that they were fully prepared to assist in implementing the conservation programme, and that they did not pose vague accusations but presented concrete and detailed allegations.[97] Nevertheless, the DC insisted on his view: 'I wish to repeat my statement that Tribesmen in that area are doing their utmost to undermine the authority of the Tribal Leaders. This, you will agree, if successful, will lead to the complete break-down of authority in the area.'[98] He further responded to the points raised as follows:

> 1) It is not disputed that your clients were born in Rhodesia and have Rhodesian Registration Certificates. It is, however, common practice in the area in question for the tribesmen to have dual citizenship in Rhodesia and Moçambique when the authorities are pursuing their lawful business in Rhodesia and it is also common practice for the same tribesmen to move to Rhodesia when the Moçambican authorities are proceeding about their business in the area.

> 2) … In the area in question the majority of the Kraalheads are still attempting to undermine the Tribal Authorities, and have not, as they so glibly assured you, co-operated in the conservation programme.[99]

The response reflects the frailty of the political situation, and somewhat surprisingly the DC acknowledged that, eighty years into the colonial period, the government still had no control over African population movement across the border in the valley, and that neither local government nor agricultural policies had yet been successful.[100] In fact, in the same area, one of the tea outgrowers even found a new use for the border now that cash crops had been introduced. In 1975, he abandoned his tea gardens to work for Katiyo without repaying his debts to the ADF. The tea officer was not amused:

> He has a half hectare of tea within the Katiyo Tea Estates situated right up against the border with Moçambique. In fact he claims now to be a Moçambiquen [sic] and not a Rhodesian and apparently feels he is under no obligation to tend his tea or meet his loan repayment obligations.[101]

Ishe Chikomba's reply to the allegations is also relevant because it further illuminates just how tense things had become by 1970. The plaintiffs presented four instances of alleged injustice. First, the chief was accused of fining people for 'having a band play music without the chief's permission', a *'ngoma* [drum] party'.[102] The chief, in response, explained that he had forbidden holding such parties after dusk, stating that 'he [had] done this so as to exercise greater control and also because he adjoins the P.E.A. border and thus must know who is in the area', hence implying that what were probably spirit possession and healing meetings attracted participants from both sides of the border.[103] The second case accused the chief of imposing unjust fines for assault.[104] The other two charges focused on the chief's treatment of women, which was not surprising when one considers women's political outspokenness against perceived injustices during the 1950s and 1960s. The charges stated that Chikomba had caused resentment by imposing a levy of one shilling for every widow in his area and by compelling all married women, ten at a time, to work in his private fields without any compensation.[105]

Ishe Chikomba, in his reply, argued that the levy had to be paid by each widow when coming to *hombera* him, which in this context meant bringing gifts to pay tribute and to ask for land. A widow was expected to marry her deceased husband's brother or a close male relative, a practice that allowed her to regain a male guardian, but there were also alternatives open to her. If she declined to remarry, a widow could appeal to the local chief, who would then allocate land directly to her. According to Chikomba, it was his 'desire to register all widows in his area in regard to future land allocations [under the NLHA].' The chief claimed that the two plaintiffs, both widows, had not paid their respects and rather 'went to the Tea Estates as prostitutes',[106] a common accusation used against women who made independent choices. In other words, they had declined him as their patron and were seeking salaried employment instead. Finally, the chief denied having women working in his private fields. He attributed this misapprehension to a 'custom' in his area, according to which each *sabhuku* had to provide ten people every year in order to work on lands, called *zunde*, under the guardianship of the chief and set aside for the production of food to be used at official functions, such as court sessions and rain ceremonies, or in times of crisis, such as famine.[107] In the end, the chief personally attacked most of the plaintiffs.

The DC finally closed the case by reminding the chief of his duties: 'I have warned Chikomba to keep within the framework of the tribal laws, fees and penalties as laid down by the Chief [Mutasa] and his advisors. I have also warned him about taking any action against Mr Peck's clients and the other complainants mentioned in the attached correspondence.'[108] The verdict is another indication that, from the administration's point of view, having a loyal ally in a politically difficult area was more important than settling a dispute which clearly implicated the chief in some wrongdoing. That policy backfired badly during the Chimurenga, when chiefs became a prime target of guerrilla assassinations. From the plaintiffs' perspective, the outcome demonstrated that appealing to the government to execute justice in their trusteeship over 'tribal lands' led nowhere. As the leaders of the nationalist parties had to recognise in 1964, in 1970 Holdenby residents came to the inevitable conclusion that reform within the system was not possible. The nationalist parties formed armed wings and the frontier people soon found freedom fighters to assist them in settling their scores.

The resentment against *ishe* Chikomba finally came to a head in 1974. Further land appropriation for Katiyo estate contributed to this development,[109] as did the administration's increasing reliance on chiefs to enforce the tea scheme.[110] Chikomba apparently realised that he had chosen the wrong side, but it proved to be too late. In March 1974, the DC observed that *ishe* Chikomba would not approve any further land development on the tea estate unless the original idea of finding 'settlers' for tea blocks was implemented. The chief also demanded more details on future development, 'so that he could put something more specific to his people'. At the same time, though, the agreement to resettle one of his *sabhuku*, Chiwanza, and his followers was finalised, and in April *mambo* Mutasa received Rh$30 and *ishe* Chikomba Rh$330 as compensation.[111] In June, the surveyor's assistant allegedly spread a rumour that the land was to be divided into European farms, which contributed to a sense of insecurity among people living at Katiyo. This is reflected in their refusal to implement soil conservation measures, giving 'as excuse the fact that they did not know when they would be required to move'.[112] *Ishe* Chikomba was at least partially blamed for the situation and deeply resented for once again siding with the government. But the widespread dissatisfaction with the chief's conduct only turned into militancy when FRELIMO started operating in the area. In response to appeals, during the night of 29 July 1974, the fighters abducted the chief and took him across the border into Mozambique. By September, he was reported to be 'still alive but … being held by the FRELIMO for trial'.[113] Not long afterwards FRELIMO executed him.

FRELIMO: THE FIRST GUERRILLA ARMY ARRIVES

During the Chimurenga, many chiefs were killed throughout the country: thirty out of a total of two hundred and fifty-seven chiefs and fifty-four out of four hundred and fifty-four headmen. Six chiefs and sixteen headmen were killed in Manyikaland alone, which, together with Midlands, was the most affected province.[114] The abduction and execution of *ishe* Chikomba was therefore typical of the war.[115] Still, the incident was unique because the chief was tried and executed by FRELIMO, effectively a foreign power. In 1974, FRELIMO, fighting their war of liberation against the Portuguese, were operating in Manica Province in Mozambique, including the area adjacent to the Honde Valley. It appears that the main reason for local FRELIMO units to get involved with valley politics was to establish support structures.[116]

The Honde Valley, with its abundant agricultural potential, the intense exchange between people living on both sides of the border, and, by the beginning of 1974, a still negligible military government presence, made it an ideal place for guerrilla operations. FRELIMO fighters approached homesteads to ask for food and to recruit young men into their army. Some valley inhabitants joined up, and over the months FRELIMO soldiers became well-known to the women who fed them. In the early 1990s, women remembered these encounters: 'When those from there [FRELIMO] came here, they asked for *sadza* [meal-ie-meal porridge]. This was the same thing with the local boys [ZANLA].'[117] Women recalled their role as providers of food and other supplies as a matter of fact, as having merely fulfilled the duties expected of any female towards visitors, especially males. In conversations about such provisions, women did not appear to differentiate between FRELIMO or ZANLA fighters, and the fact that the former were fighting a liberation war for the neighbouring country, whereas the latter were *vana vevhu* (children of the soil), left no imprint in this particular context.[118] However, such support did not merely reflect notions of hospitality and gender normativity, but was also nurtured by local appropriations of guerrilla violence.

Kriger demonstrated that during the Second Chimurenga it was vital for guerrillas to establish and sustain support through 'appeals', and that with abstract notions of national liberation not always sufficiently tangible and the dependency of the fighters on the rural population being inevitable, frequently the young men (and occasionally young women)[119] with guns used their power to settle local conflicts violently. The fact that in the Honde Valley, both FRE-LIMO and ZANLA followed this tactic supports Kriger's argument that local agendas informed guerrilla actions,[120] though it would be too far-reaching to argue that such objectives shaped civilian–guerrilla relations in their entirety. Still, FRELIMO did become involved in the intimidation and killing of chiefs and government employees in the valley.

In the Chikomba area, different groups took their grievances to the FRE-LIMO fighters. Local inhabitants could now ask the guerrillas to intervene on their behalf in their continuing struggle against the government over land use issues, and also to act against the unpopular *ishe* Chikomba. His fate was partly sealed due to complaints by displaced people from east of the border. In 1973, the Mozambican liberation war heated up, and in response groups had crossed into the Honde Valley to seek safety.[121] They became concentrated in the Chikomba area, because apparently other chiefs and *masabhuku* would not accept these war refugees. Chikomba allocated land to them, but charged a fee for so doing, and on their return to Mozambique in 1974, once FRELIMO had liberated the area, they aired complaints about the chief's 'avaricious habits'.[122] In addition, from 1968, valley inhabitants had crossed the border to evade hard-ships and now, living under FRELIMO control, they had an opportunity to settle old scores.[123] In short, FRELIMO's involvement in local politics in the Honde Valley can largely be attributed to their dependency on a local con-stituency. Their involvement on both sides of the border further reflects that the frontier mentality prevalent in local communities informed FRELIMO's strategies.

From 1974, FRELIMO's presence in the valley and the area across the border widened the frontier people's range of options in order to safeguard their livelihoods. These included FRELIMO imposing punitive measures on alleged government collaborators, with local men carrying out such actions under the guise of being FRELIMO, and finally FRELIMO encouraging women to move to Mozambique. A male elder from the valley recalled the soldiers' political involvement:

> The FRELIMO came in '74, and they abducted *madhumeni* [extension officers], chiefs and others, including policemen ….
>
> H.S.: Why did FRELIMO kill these people?
>
> They said these people were nasty.[124]

That same year, a government report on the security situation stated that acts of violence were being committed by 'pseudo-FRELIMO'. These were alleged to be men from the Honde Valley who had crossed into Mozambique between 1968 and 1970, mostly in protest against the tea outgrower scheme and the establishment of Katiyo estate. This view is supported by a number of cases where these men intimidated government staff whom they accused of com-mitting adultery with local women. Furthermore, it was alleged that some of them were directly involved in FRELIMO activities, for example, the abduc-tion and execution of two agricultural extension officers.[125] The claim to control the sexuality of women who lived in the valley reinforces the notion that some of the physical violence and intimidation carried out was not aimed towards the larger cause of national liberation, but to safeguard civic virtue, now in the presence of a liberation army.

In 1975, the DC received an anonymous letter that accused *mambo* Mutasa of illicitly collecting money from his headmen:

> Sir, the District Commissioner,
>
> … Do you think that's right? Should we consult Salisbury about this matter? We also tried to find out about this from our ZEZURU Chiefs and they told us that it's chief Mutasa who demands these payments from the headmen.
>
> We let you know that we can kill him. We did not get this information from the headmen. We are children of the soil. Let us fight. Watch out you and chief Mutasa. But you are innocent whereas with chief Mutasa we do shoot.[126]

Without additional evidence, it is not possible to establish clearly whether 'pseudo-FRELIMO', FRELIMO, or ZANLA guerrillas wrote this letter.[127] One might regard it as a contradiction that the authors claimed to be freedom fighters but still appealed to the DC's authority over chiefly conduct. However, this underlines what the local agendas indicate, that the Second Chimurenga was a struggle for justice, with both liberation movements emphasising that it was a war for independence, not a racial conflict. Again, this supports Kriger's argument that intra-communal conflict needs to be considered to understand mobilisation and support structures of insurgencies.

After *ishe* Chikomba's abduction in July 1974, FRELIMO encouraged women whose husbands were away, working as migrant labourers, to cross the border and live close to the local FRELIMO camp. A group of women in the Katiyo area followed this advice.[128] Towards the end of the year, FRELIMO closed the border and displaced people or visitors from the valley were not allowed to return. An elder explained that FRELIMO was concerned about its own operations and wanted to avoid having any information passed on to Rhodesian officials.[129] A government security report claims that FRELIMO was worried about pseudo-FRELIMO activities that might lead to further security force deployment in the valley.[130] Moreover, FRELIMO was 'cross and wary about the police/army/I.A. [Internal Affairs] activity on this side', which was part of the follow-up operation after *ishe* Chikomba's disappearance.[131] It was, in fact, in response to the chief's abduction that the counter-insurgency effort in the valley began, though the government only fully stepped it up in 1976, when ZANLA's presence made the area the country's most contested war zone.

Frontier People on the Move: Displacement

The local ramifications of the transformation of the settler state under Rhodesian Front rule made life increasingly unbearable, and between 1968 and 1977 many Honde Valley inhabitants left. The arrival of the FRELIMO fighters in 1974 marked a turning point towards militancy, and this time of crisis, as the

8. Katiyo Tea and Coffee Estates, 1990: Tea fields, with Mount Zaramira and Mount Panga in the background (Source: Heike I. Schmidt)

liberation war entered the area, left these frontier people with three options: to stay and take sides in the conflict; to cross the border to find a new patron, to join the liberation struggle, or to seek a new frontier; or to move towards the centre of the settler state, away from the border, to relative physical safety. The latter option was usually preferred by government employees such as agricultural extension workers and Manyika immigrants who were business-owners or teachers and hence targeted by political violence. These valley inhabitants tended to chose internal displacement by moving onto the plateau, often to the so-called 'new area', in the vicinity of the Mutasa district office. This population movement involved only a few households and occurred mostly from 1974, when increasing militancy in the valley began to threaten their safety.

In Holdenby, a diverse group of households crossed into Mozambique between 1968 and 1970. Their reasons for so doing included loss of their land through the establishment of Katiyo estate or frustration with *ishe* Chikomba's arbitrary rule, while some were tea outgrowers who wanted to escape their harassment by their neighbours.[132] It is not surprising that the abduction and execution of *ishe* Chikomba intimidated other chiefs. One *sabhuku* moved after he was tipped off by some of his followers who had witnessed *ishe* Chikomba's trial and told him that he was next on the hit list because he was closely associated with the chief.[133] Thereafter, a wave of emigration ensued which consisted of the women urged by FRELIMO to resettle, and as soon as ZANLA began operating in the valley from 1975, young people left home to join the liberation war. A major shift occurred from late 1976 and throughout the following year, when most valley inhabitants tried to escape forced villagisation, a counter-insurgency measure. Young, unmarried girls and women were often sent into the cities or to areas away from the border and thus less affected by the Chimurenga, while the other household members went to Mozambique. The rallying point for most was Mount Zaramira, located on the border, ca. 3,630 feet high, and visible from most locations in the valley. The mountain had been the starting point from which the Barué boundary was delineated, and hence was a marker for imperial mapping and for resistance against it. Mount Zaramira was already part of the spiritual and political landscape of the area, and over the course of the 1970s gained multi-layered meanings of refuge, safety, vulnerability, and untold suffering, as will be discussed in some detail in chapter five.

In what follows, the experiences of one woman, *mbuya* Moyo, who crossed into Mozambique in 1974, will be examined. The purpose here is to gain insight into how valley inhabitants negotiated their lives through displacement once the young men with guns arrived. At the same time the goal is also to examine insurgency tactics. *Mbuya* is the polite way of addressing an elderly woman in Shona, with *sekuru* being the equivalent for a man. Moyo, as well as other names mentioned in her story, are pseudonyms. *Mbuya* Moyo's account is based on two formal interviews and other conversations with her and her next junior co-wife over the course of nine months in 1992 in Holdenby. The first interview was conducted between the author, *mbuya*, and her husband, with the second and third wife present for short intervals after a two-month period of acquaintance, and with the assistance of a male neighbour in his thirties who knew the family well. The second interview took place three months later, this time with *mbuya* Moyo alone, except for brief interruptions when neighbours and her co-wife passed by. On this occasion a close female friend of *mbuya* Moyo's stepped in towards the end of the interview and helped with translation. Whenever possible, this method of allowing interviewees to get to know the author and then to follow up with formal, taped interviews, preferably with different research assistants distinguished by gender, age, or other aspects of social status, such as their totem, was used to gain a deeper and multi-layered reading of the conversation.

Dissonances between *mbuya* Moyo's narrative and that of her husband are inevitable, and they do allow for a fuller understanding of both the gendered nature of the occurrences and also of the range of ways in which experiences of the same or similar events may differ. The excerpts of the interview transcripts given below are backed up with details that emerged in a number of informal conversations with *mbuya* Moyo. To be clear, this is no attempt at a full social biography, and the critique of life-stories, including the danger of claiming an emic, authentic and representative voice, is well taken.

Mbuya Moyo was born in Matabeleland in the late 1920s and is the senior of three wives. When a young woman, she married a man from the Katiyo area who was a few years her senior and who was working in a hotel in Bulawayo at that time. While still in Matabeleland, her husband took a second wife, more than ten years *mbuya*'s junior, and in 1990, when he retired from his work, he married a young woman in her early twenties. He proudly recalled that he had never depended on his father for raising *lobola* (brideprice), but that each time he got married he had accumulated enough money by himself. After 1980, the Moyos became members of a Vapostori church.

Mbuya and her co-wife lived with their husband for some time in Bulawayo. When *sekuru* Moyo decided to return to Manyikaland in the late 1950s, his two wives accompanied him. *Mbuya* remembered her arrival at her in-laws' homestead in the valley as being difficult, because life and people there were very different to Bulawayo, the second largest city in Zimbabwe:

> There is a vast difference …. Here, I use my hands to plough, like this. [demonstrates] In my home area, I yoke oxen and plough.… The way of life in Bulawayo is good, only the place becomes nasty if they do not get good rains. One good thing about this place is, you get good yields, and plenty of food, if you plough …. Oh, I walked all the way to this place. That is the major problem that I faced.… There was no transport.

Mbuya is one of the many women who came to the Honde Valley through marriage to a migrant labourer. Another woman, from urban South Africa, and also the senior wife, explained why she had come to the valley:

> If you know that love is blind! [laughter] Love brought me here.… Because my husband – tell her this! – [addressed to female research assistant] my husband stayed there. He spent sixty years in South Africa. After he had married me, he decided to come back home. I could not remain behind with the children, so I decided to come together with him.[134]

When presented with a *Zambia* (a piece of cloth) *mbuya* Moyo was overjoyed. She responded, switching to siNdebele, her mother tongue, that she would tie the cloth the 'real' way, the way she used to do it as an unmarried woman in Matabeleland. She performed this transformation by removing her headscarf (in the rural areas, married and older women cover their heads), wearing the cloth and doing a little dance, thus embodying a young girl. As was evident with other migrant labourers' wives, this situational code-switching is an indication of just how close to the surface, yet at the same time deeply embedded in her personhood, her earlier lifeworld still was even though she had lived in Manyikaland for thirty-five years or so. The nostalgia expressed in such encounters related a sense of belonging to her place of origin or a period of urban life, rather than a woman's longing for her youth.

After some time, *mbuya* Moyo got used to the new environment and to living with her mother-in-law in the Katiyo area. Her husband, who from then on worked in Mutare, the provincial capital, about forty-five miles away, stayed with his wives for a month three times each year and would visit for rare weekends, when possible. Her situation changed dramatically in the 1970s. *Sekuru* Moyo explained that migrant labourers were unaware of how the Chimurenga was evolving in their home areas, so much so that he learned only that war had arrived when a relative came to see him in Mutare in 1974 to tell him that his wives had left for Mozambique. *Mbuya* interjected dismissively: 'They [male migrant labourers] did not know of it.' Initially, when asked whether she had seen FRELIMO fighters 'with her own eyes' before the abduction of *ishe*

Chikomba in July 1974, her husband answered on her behalf: 'Oh, no!' and *mbuya* added: 'We did not see them, since they moved at night.' Later, and alone, she explained that she was visited by both FRELIMO and ZANLA and that she cooked for members of both armies.

Mbuya Moyo, like other women in the area, had been encouraged by FRE-LIMO to move to Mozambique, and the soldiers even provided transport for their possessions. *Sekuru* explained: 'They told us to take refuge, so that they would face *mabhunu* [Europeans; Boers] here.' *Mbuya* was prompted to cross the border when her homestead was searched by the Security Forces in April or May 1975, while her husband was away:

> *Mbuya*: We crossed over after they arrived at our homestead …
>
> Interpreter: The comrades?
>
> *Mbuya*: Yes.
>
> Interpreter: From Mozambique?
>
> *Mbuya*: No, those from here.
>
> Interpreter: The soldiers?
>
> *Mbuya*: Yes, they came to our homestead and entered first my room and then *mainini's* [the junior wife's]. And they vowed to shoot those who were around. They locked us indoors and held their guns and asked us to produce our identity cards, all of us, to find who had no identity card and whether we were harbouring *magandanga* [guerrillas].
>
> Interpreter: After they left, you decided to cross over?
>
> *Mbuya*: We felt things were becoming nasty for us, and that we might die. [laughter] We could not wait for that.

Sekuru Moyo added that the security forces were particularly suspicious of his homestead because of the goods he had bought with his salary. The patrol had taken his clothes as evidence that his wives were supporting guerrillas. Insurgents avoided carrying extra clothing because it gave them away easily, and thus a ready supply of such items was important to them. *Sekuru* remembered: 'These [indicates his wives] were saved by my clothes, which the soldiers found had my name written on them. [In the city] We sent our clothes for laundry, so we wrote our names on them.' Thus it was proved that the clothes belonged to one man and when *mbuya* told the soldiers where her husband worked in town, they verified her statement. Still, this incident brought things to a head.

Sekuru Moyo explained the move across the border:

> *Sekuru*: I went with my two wives.
>
> Interpreter: The two of you … with your family …
>
> *Sekuru*: My two wives only. I later left Mutare, but my wives had already gone to Mozambique.
>
> Interpreter [very surprised]: They were already there!?
>
> *Sekuru*: Yes.
>
> *Mbuya*: We fled by ourselves! [embarrassed laughter] …. He was informed of our

crossover by some people, who told him that there was no longer anybody at his homestead.

She further remembered the crossing:

> We were ferried by a car to …
>
> *Sekuru*: [cuts in] To have their goods ferried to the border.
>
> *Mbuya*: To [a store at the border], where our goods were off-loaded. We were then welcomed by the FRELIMO.
>
> *Sekuru*: Is that so?
>
> *Mbuya*: Yes, they helped us to cross into Mozambique.
>
> *Sekuru*: That was when my wardrobe got damaged; the mirror broke. This was my first wardrobe.
>
> H.S.: Then the FRELIMO told you where to settle?
>
> *Mbuya*: Yes. They welcomed people and arranged how they had to live. They also looked after the people that time.

Mbuya Moyo initially settled close, not more than five hundred metres from the border. She was allocated land for her huts 'in lines' along a road, close to a FRELIMO training camp. The degree to which the resettlement exercise was organised demonstrates how far FRELIMO had already transformed from a liberation movement in charge of a liberated area to putting a local administration into place, weeks before Mozambique gained political independence in June 1975. Later, the Moyo homestead was repeatedly moved, although the fields remained the same. *Mbuya* Moyo explained: 'After staying there for some time, I sneaked away in that direction. [Indicates] I went to see SaMoyo in Mutare. I had to inform him that nobody was at home since we had run away from war.' Asked how she had travelled to Mutare, *mbuya* Moyo gave her account of the difficult journey. It reveals much about the security situation on both sides of the border, how many risks she was prepared to take by carrying the responsibility as senior wife, as well as her close relationship with her *mainini*, her junior co-wife, while her husband appeared marginal in her war experiences:

> I left the place there at night went to … that man who helped people cross [the border] by canoe. From there, I went to [Mandeya] area, where I boarded a bus. If you travelled by bus, you were always asked for a *chitupa* [identity card] [at road-blocks] so what we did was: we hid our *zvitupa* here, before we went to Mozambique, and we produced them when we returned. I then used it when travelling here. When I got to Mutare, I met my husband and talked to him. I pointed out to him that I had to quickly go back for fear that my partner [the junior wife] would be pestered if they discovered my absence. I only slept there for one night …. When I arrived [in Mozambique], they were fast asleep, so I knocked at the door. She [co-wife] could tell, by the way I knocked at the door, that I had returned. – That was quite a problem. Each morning, they [FRELIMO] came to where we were staying. They asked me where I had been the previous day. This other wife had informed them earlier that I had gone to visit my son up there, and that I would be back that same evening. As soon as I arrived, she warned me to say this to them when they came asking where I had been. When they came, I told them this, and they cautioned me against lying. I insisted this was the truth, and they asked whether I would allow them to

search my room. I complied. They told me that they suspected that I had brought things I intended to sell. I denied this. Earlier on, and this I had forgotten, I had taken soap and salt and placed it inside the wardrobe …. When I opened the wardrobe, salt spilled out. [laughter] They did not see it, and so I quickly collected it and hid it.[135] We faced many problems there.

Four months later *sekuru* Moyo joined his wives. He had waited until his employers would give him leave. Initially, he had hoped to return to Mutare after visiting his wives, but FRELIMO did not allow such movement, fearing that people who crossed back into Zimbabwe would report on their activities.

Sekuru remembered that there were no chiefs, but that FRELIMO soldiers maintained discipline among the refugee population:

> In Mozambique, what they did was, if they arrested a person, they did not ask him any questions, but simply beat him up. After assembling the people, they asked them if they knew that person, and if the people said yes, they said they had beaten him, and severely wounded him, but that it was not their [FRELIMO's] fault…. They said so-and-so had informed them that he was saying such-and-such nasty things, or that he was making clandestine trips from there [Mozambique] to here [Zimbabwe] in an effort to buy soap. Soap was a problem there. He was then arrested and beaten.

Sekuru also recollected that he himself was once severely beaten when FRE-LIMO accused him of having crossed the border:

> I was arrested, after someone had sold me out. They were saying that I had a lot of clothes, so they suspected I was going there [to Zimbabwe]. I then produced my receipts and told them to check on them whether the clothes were new; and if that was so, then I was crossing over. These are the scars where I was tied.

He showed his wrists, which still bore marks of the rubber strips used to tie him up during the beatings. *Sekuru* felt mistreated: 'I can say we were looked after, but our upkeep was not without an element of cruelty. They treated us with the mind that our *bhururu* [relatives; ZANLA] were giving them problems.' Here he is probably referring to the difficulty that the huge influx of youths and refugees from Zimbabwe caused the newly independent Mozambican government, something that was aggravated once the Rhodesian government started carrying out cross-border attacks.

Mbuya Moyo emphasised that while FRELIMO looked after her and her co-wife, she also perceived FRELIMO as strict and at times unjust in their conduct. When asked what FRELIMO did for them, she stressed their guardianship:

> If, say, I and this second wife had a quarrel, they took us to their camp where we would be punished.

She added:

> They looked after us very well. … They passed through our place on their way to the well. Each time they checked on us … and they wanted to find if any men were coming to us, since there was no male. They knew our husband was away.'

Hence FRELIMO took the role of monitoring women's sexuality in the absence of men who were migrant workers or fighting, in all likelihood in order to sustain male support and minimize conflict in the refugee settlements. This kind of control stopped after her husband joined them. *Mbuya* also complained:

> They simply killed people's cattle. After killing such cattle, they would then call whoever they wanted, to collect the meat. If you misbehaved, or if, say, I quarrelled with my husband, he would be taken away under arrest. [The husband would then be beaten.]

> Interpreter: But then you were given meat.

> *Mbuya*: Ah, would you love to die for that? You could get the meat, but life was horrible!

Both FRELIMO and ZANLA rustled cattle in the Honde Valley to feed the refugees in Mozambique. Such actions led to resentment by those who stayed towards those who had left.[136]

Mbuya further insisted that the Zimbabwean refugees had minimal interaction with Mozambicans because they perceived the latter as backward. Her account might reflect her views as somebody who grew up in Matabeleland and who later in life joined the frontier society: 'The local people [refugees from Katiyo area] stayed together in one group, and those from there stayed together in another group. Some of the people there do not wear clothes. Just like this cloth. [indicates her wrapper, i.e., no western-style clothing].'

Sekuru emphasised that there was no inter-marriage, but he conceded that the refugees socialised, particularly at beer parties. Land was no problem: 'We were given enough land to plough. One could choose where one wanted to plough.' But the Mozambican liberation war, in particular the revenge actions by the retreating settlers, had destroyed the infrastructure and subsequently few facilities were available. As a result, living conditions were difficult.

> Mbuya: The growing of crops [maize and rice] sustained us, and nothing else. We did not get anything. In any case, what could we have gotten? There were no stores there ….. One of the problems we faced there was a shortage of salt, sugar, soap. For this we used a certain muti [part of a tree] we found in the forest. This muti was dug from the ground and used for washing.

Although the Moyos had 'run away from war', they were nevertheless directly affected by living in a country that was just gaining independence after a protracted struggle and by residing within a major infiltration route for every army that operated in the area: FRELIMO, ZANLA, the Rhodesian Security Forces, and the Mozambican Resistance Movement (RENAMO). This showed not only in the treatment they experienced from FRELIMO and the poor living conditions, but the Rhodesian air-raids on refugee camps that the Moyos also witnessed. *Sekuru* explained about FRELIMO and ZANLA: 'The comrades … did not have their camps in the same areas', and that they therefore rarely saw ZANLA fighters. And *mbuya* Moyo added:

> *Mbuya*: We saw them when they were on their way to join. While we were there, we never saw them. No …

> H.S.: During the war, did you ever see any other soldiers than FRELIMO?

> *Mbuya*: Yes. We saw *matsangas* [RENAMO], the recent ones – the ones who have

been butchering us here. They arrived while I was there. And they fought against the FRELIMO, despite that they were one and the same [Mozambicans]. They were fighting against themselves, and they did not kill civilians then. They only fought against the FRELIMO. If [FRELIMO] came to a homestead, they told us that if we saw [RENAMO] coming, we had to tell them …. The FRELIMO were afraid of them, and so they did not follow them. [laughter] I do not know where they came from, but whenever they moved, they carried a lot of goods.

Later, however, RENAMO bandits did attack civilians in Mozambique:

> They [Mozambicans] felt … the *matsangas* [RENAMO] were nasty because they killed indiscriminately; they did not mind whether those were the *kamaradha* [FRELIMO] or simply civilian women.

Both *mbuya* and *sekuru* Moyo stressed repeatedly that life in Mozambique was very hard and that there had been no question that they would return to the valley at the earliest opportunity. Repatriation finally came during Zimbabwe's ceasefire period, from 28 December 1979 to independence 18 April 1980. *Sekuru* recalled that FRELIMO instructed the refugees to return to Zimbabwe after surrendering their Mozambican registration certificates: 'Just before we came here, we were all assembled and told that since we had come from Zimbabwe, we had to go back there since the war was over. This was in 1980…. We were overjoyed! The prospect of going back home was quite a joy.'

Asked how she crossed the border back into Zimbabwe, *mbuya* said that she did so at night: 'It was *mainini* [the junior wife] and myself. My husband had escaped alone and left us there [clicks her tongue in disapproval].' The wives returned to the Honde Valley only with what they could carry and were forced to leave their goats and all other possessions behind. They walked as far as the next military camp, from which they were ferried to Ruda Protected Village (PV). Reunited with their husband, they were told to move to Chisuko PV, where their *sabhuku*, Katiyo, was located. There they lived for about one month, after which they were allowed to return to the Katiyo area, having to abandon their freshly planted crop.

> Mbuya: We then stayed in that keep [vernacular for PV] for quite some time. We used to tend our fields from there. After we had started growing crops there, we were told that the country was now independent so we had to leave the keep, and each family had to go to their respective villages.

The Moyo family's return was part of the larger repatriation during the ceasefire period.

Mbuya: Nobody remained there. All those from this side came back.

Interpreter: And some Mozambicans joined them.

Mbuya: Ah, yes, they came with us.

Interpreter: Because there was war between FRELIMO and *matsanga* [RENAMO]. So some of the Mozambicans had to move.

Mbuya: Even today, some of them are here. [pause] There are a lot of them here.

Mbuya and her co-wife re-established a household in the Katiyo area and their husband left for migrant labour as soon as independence came. Yet their life was soon disrupted by further violence. In 1985 the family was forcibly evicted from Katiyo estate, where they were then considered to be 'squatters' by the government, and between 1989 and 1990 they took refuge at a nearby school after *mbuya* witnessed a RENAMO attack. By the early 1990s, the Moyos were among the poor, with *sekuru* elderly and living at home now and *mbuya* lending a hand to neighbours in return for food. The youngest co-wife was struggling: she had the affection of her elderly husband, but no close bond with her two senior co-wives. They in turn cherished their partnership, forged through their shared suffering that was further deepened when their husband had left them behind in Mozambique in 1980.

Conclusion

The settler government became present on the ground in the Honde Valley in the early 1950s and the response to its interventions, particularly the implementation of the Native Land Husbandry Act, conservation measures, and the introduction of tea, were resentment and resistance. Women spearheaded the protests, while land husbandry measures were usually opposed by entire communities, often under the leadership of chiefs and *masabhuku*. Tea outgrowing was rejected by most valley inhabitants, though not by all, and with opposition particularly firm, tensions arose within the communities.

Several arguments regarding violence emerge from the history of the valley in the 1950s and 1960s. Actions directed against the settler government were not necessarily nationalistic, they were often an expression of a threshold of suffering that was crossed: the frontier people felt that their way of life was under threat and they took steps accordingly. Hence, much of the non-cooperation and opposition was shaped by a radically local agenda, although nationalist parties were present and did find a following. The literature on nationalism has made much of age as a factor, it being angry young men, born of an 'age of improvement',[137] who stood in the limelight of nationalist discourse as they protested against colonialism. In contrast, the history of the valley demonstrates the significant role women played, and not merely as supporters of male nationalists. In the valley, men did at times address their wives', sisters', and mothers' grievances, but most often women let their voices be heard and fought their own struggles.

When the young men with guns arrived, first FRELIMO in 1974, then ZANLA in 1975, they presented both dangers and opportunities, and thus contributed further to the frontier character of the valley at a time when its inhabitants were already fighting to sustain their independence from state interference. Against the existing historiography, what is perhaps most surprising is again the prominent role women played, even if they were merely reacting to FRELIMO's request to relocate to Mozambican territory. At the same time, for co-wives to make such major decisions in the absence of their husbands counterbalances the notion of the overpowering presence of the young men with AK-47s and the role of youth in guerrilla warfare. It is certainly remarkable that *mbuya* Moyo managed to cross the border twice under cover of night in order to travel to Mutare, and even to bring contraband back to her new home while the Rhodesian forces and FRELIMO were on high alert. The Moyos did experience much hardship and found themselves pressured from more than one side in Mozambique, but at least, from 1975, they lived in an independent African country. Those who stayed in the Honde Valley bore the full brunt of the insurgency and counter-insurgency campaigns, the topic of the following chapter.

Notes

1   *Flame*, 1996 feature film directed by Ingrid Sinclair and produced by Joel Phiri and Simon Bright.
2   See, for example, Ranger's studies on state intervention that represent two periods of historiography, *Peasant Consciousness and Guerrilla War in Zimbabwe: A Comparative Study* (London, 1985) and *Voices from the Rocks: Nature, Culture and History in the Matopos Hills of Zimbabwe* (Oxford, 1999).
3   Norma Kriger, *Zimbabwe's Guerrilla War: Peasant Voices* (Cambridge, 1992), p. 51, passim. For Kriger's critics, see, Kenneth Manungo, 'The Peasantry in Zimbabwe: A Vehicle for Change', *Cultural Struggle and Development in Southern Africa*, Preben Kaarsholm (ed.) (Harare, 1991), pp. 115-24; David Moore, 'Zimbabwean Peasants: Pissed on and Pissed off', *Southern African Review of Books*, 4, no. 6 (1994), pp. 5-6; the review of Kriger's book by Terence Ranger, *African Affairs*, 93, no. 370 (1994), pp. 142-4.
4   Umtali District, Annual District Report, 1955, S2827/2/2/3, 1955, NAZ.
5   For a different view of rural Zimbabwe women's politicisation, see Eleanor O' Gorman's insights on 'the lives of women lived between revolutionary resistance and survival'. She focuses entirely on the liberation war itself. *The Front Line Runs through Every Woman: Women and Local Resistance in the Zimbabwean Liberation War* (Woodbridge, 2011), p. 150. Except for Susan Geiger's pioneering and Elizabeth Schmidt's seminal studies, a women's or gender history of nationalism in Africa is still very much a lacuna in historical research. Susan Geiger, *TANU Women: Gender and Culture in the Making of Tanganyikan Nationalism, 1955–1965* (Portsmouth, NH, 1997); Elizabeth Schmidt, *Mobilizing the Masses: Gender, Ethnicity, and Class in the Nationalist Movement in Guinea, 1939–1958* (Portsmouth, NH, 2005), and especially her path-breaking 'Top Down or Bottom Up? Nationalist Mobilisation Reconsidered, with Special Reference to Guinea (French West Africa)', *American Historical Review*, 110, no. 4 (2005), pp. 975-1014. See also Aili Mari Tripp, *Women and Politics in Uganda* (Madison, WI, 2000).
6   Henry Moyana, *The Political Economy of Land in Zimbabwe* (Gweru, 1984), pp. 70, 77; Anna Weinrich, *Black and White Elites in Rural Rhodesia* (Manchester, 1973), p. 15; Kriger, *Zimbabwe's Guerrilla War*, p. 59.
7   John Lonsdale and Donald Low, 'Introduction: Towards the New Order 1945–1963', *History of East Africa*, vol. 3, Donald Low and Alison Smith (eds) (Oxford, 1976), p. 54.
8   For detailed treatment of the NLHA, see William Munro, *The Moral Economy of the State: Conservation, Community Development, and State-Making in Zimbabwe* (Athens, OH, 1998), chapter 3; Ian Phimister, 'Rethinking the Reserves: Southern Rhodesia's Land Husbandry Act Reviewed', *Journal of Southern African Studies*, 19, no. 2 (1993), pp. 225-39; Jocelyn Alexander, *The Unsettled Land: State-Making and the Politics of Land in Zimbabwe, 1893–2003* (Oxford, 2006), chapter 2.
9   In the early 1980s, the majority of households in the valley, probably more than the estimated share of sixty-one per cent in Manyikaland as a whole, were female-headed. International Labour Organisation, 'Project Idea, Project Title: Rural Development and Rural Energy in Communal Areas, Manicaland Province, Starting Date: July 1986', vol. 2, PAO.
10 NC Umtali to PNC, 15 September 1959, box number 57577, NRC.
11 Umtali District, Annual Report, 1955, S2827/2/2/3, NAZ.
12 The land shortages were so severe that even the 880 acres for a township at Ruda were released. Umtali District, Annual Report, 1960; also Annual Report, 1962, box number 62328, NRC.
13 Umtali District, Annual Report, 1960, box number 62328, NRC; also Umtali District, Annual Report, 1961, S2827/2/2/8, NAZ.
14 NC Inyanga to PNC, 20 February 1956, box number 103986, NRC.
15 It is unclear whether Mugarbi was from the area. Ibid. In 1952, the NC Umtali reported that Chief Mutasa and his people favoured the 'Rhodesian African Association' over Burombo's 'African Voice Association'. Umtali District, Annual Report, S2827/2/2/1, 1952, NAZ; Michael West, *The Rise*

of an African Middle Class: Colonial Zimbabwe, 1898–1965 (Bloomington, IN, 2002), pp. 130, 185, passim. For the competition between the two organizations in Manyikaland, see Ngwabi Bhebhe, *Burombo: African Politics in Zimbabwe, 1947–1958* (Harare, 1989), p. 74.

16 Inyanga District, Annual Report, 1955, S2827/2/2/3; also Inyanga District, Annual Report, 1956, S2827/2/2/4, NAZ.

17 Inyanga District, Annual Report, 1960, box number 62328, NRC.

18 DC Inyanga, 'Evidence Pachije', 21 December 1964, box number 103986, NRC.

19 Umtali District, Annual Report, 1958, S2827/2/2/6, NAZ. In 1961, the DC Umtali observed about the NDP: 'The method of approach was to contact small groups of known malcontents and to endeavour by this means to spread the pernicious doctrines.' Umtali District, Annual Report, 1961, S2827/2/2/8, NAZ.

20 Inyanga District, Annual Report, 1961, S2827/2/2/8, NAZ.

21 Inyanga District, Annual Report, 1962, S2827/2/2/8, NAZ.

22 Umtali District, Annual Report, 1960, S2827/2/2/8, NAZ.

23 Rudo Gaidzanwa, 'Women's Land Rights in Zimbabwe', *Issue: A Journal of Opinion*, 22, no. 2 (1994), pp. 12-16.

24 Extension Officer Holdenby and Manga TTLs to DC, 23 March 1967, PER5 Headman Zindi, DAO.

25 Umtali District, Annual Report, 1960, box number 62328, NRC.

26 In 1992, I observed the DA Chimanimani calling his colleague in Mutasa asking for advice. He was besieged by women who had stripped and he was at a loss at what to do. Such women's protests bring the well-researched Aba women's war of 1929 in Nigeria to mind. See, for example, Misty Bastian, '"Vultures of the Marketplace": Igbo and Other Southeastern Nigerian Women's Discourse about the Ogu Umunwaanyi (Women's War) of 1929', *Women and African Colonial History*, Jean Allman et al. (eds) (Bloomington, IN, 2002), pp. 260-81; Judith van Allen, '"Sitting on a Man": Colonialism and the Lost Political Institutions of Igbo Women', *Canadian Journal of African Studies*, 6, no. 2 (1982), pp. 165-81.

27 Pafiwa Mutasa to DC Umtali, 6 May 1970, PER5 Chief Mutasa, DAO.

28 Case numbers 206-27, 1956, District Court Inyanga, S2221/5, NAZ.

29 Umtali District, Annual Report, 1961, S2827/2/2/8, NAZ.

30 Ibid.

31 Extension Officer Holdenby/Manga TTLs to Group Officer DC Inyanga, 17 November 1966; PER5 Headman Zindi, DAO.

32 Extension Officer Holdenby and Manga TTLs to DC, 23 March 1967; PER5 Headman Zindi, DAO.

33 Inyanga District, Annual Report, 1966, box number 88459, NRC.

34 DC Inyanga to attorney Peck, Salisbury, 24 March 1970. Box number 115133, NRC.

35 Plowes to PNC, 2 March 1961, box number 57577, NRC.

36 Kriger, Zimbabwe's *Guerrilla War* and 'The Zimbabwean War of Liberation: Struggles Within the Struggle', *Journal of Southern African Studies*, 14, no. 2 (1988), pp. 304-22.

37 The DC listed the following as experimental crops: ginger, turmeric, pepper, curry leaves, coriander, chinchona, black gram, oranges, naartjies, avocados, bananas, papaw, pineapples, and granadillas. Inyanga District, Annual Report, 1952, S2827/2/2/1 and 1956, S2827/2/2/4, NAZ.

38 Personal communication with Mark Igoe, 15 July 2007.

39 'Special Purpose Crops Report', 1959, p. 34, box number 57577, NRC.

40 Ibid., p. 41. In contrast, Joseph Mtisi maintains that the scheme was started with four families: *Origins and Development of Tea Outgrowers* [sic] *Schemes in Colonial Zimbabwe*, Economic History Seminar Paper (Harare: University of Zimbabwe, 1993).

41 Inyanga District, Annual Report, 1961, S2827/2/2/8, NAZ; 'Special Purpose Crops Report'.

42 'Special Purpose Crops Report', pp. 9-17, 34-5, 41-2.

43 Interview #84.

44 Inyanga District, Annual Report, 1960, box number 62328, NRC.

45 NC Inyanga to PNC, 'Working Party D.3: Third Report: District Survey', 9 August 1962, box number 103987, NRC. Mtisi, *Tea Outgrowers Schemes*, p. 22.

46 Inyanga District, Annual Report, 1966, box number 88459, NRC; 'Holdenby Outgrowers Development Report', 1982, PPE.

47 Inyanga District, Annual Report, 1967, box number 62328, NRC.

48 Interview #88; also Mtisi, *Tea Outgrower Schemes*, pp. 13; 17.

49 Interview #88.

50 Inyanga District, Annual Report, 1966, box number 88459, NRC.

51 Interviews #123, #80, #86, #88. For resistance against the Wattle Company, see also Heike Schmidt, *Muredzwa Superwoman: Mapping Areas of Female Power in the Mutasa Mamboship, Eastern Zimbabwe*, Institute of Commonwealth Studies Collected Seminar Papers (London, 1993).

52 Interview #84.
53 PNC to CNC, 2 February 1956, box number 55619, NRC.
54 Interview #91.
55 Ibid.
56 Interview #84.
57 Coffee outgrowing is not without its problems either. The specific burden is the care the coffee bush requires, which include money-demanding inputs like artificial fertiliser and pesticide. Moreover, the quality of the harvest tends to differ greatly depending on rainfall patterns and other environmental influences. Interview #126.
58 Interview #84; the interviewee began growing tea after 1980.
59 Interview #90; also #84.
60 Mtsi, *Tea Outgrowers Schemes*, p. 12. For the outgrower scheme in the early twenty-first century, see Joseph Mtsi, 'Green Harvest: The Outgrower Tea Leaf Collection System in the Honde Valley, Zimbabwe', *Delivering Land and Securing Rural Livelihoods: Post-independence Land Reform and Resettlement in Zimbabwe*, Michael Roth and Francis Gonese (eds) (Madison, WI, 2003), pp. 57-80.
61 In 2005, around seventy Vapostori and Zionist church leaders in Zimbabwe agreed to abolish polygyny. World Wide Religious News, 'Zimbabwe Sect Issues Call to Abandon Polygamy', 19 September 2005.
62 Interview #94.
63 Interview #67 with a Methodist woman and #84 with a Vapostori man; see also Donna Pankhurst and Susan Jacobs, 'Land Tenure, Gender, and Production: The Case of Zimbabwe's Peasantry', *Agriculture, Women, and Land: The African Experience*, Jean Davidson (ed.) (Boulder, CO, 1988), pp. 202-27.
64 See Lloyd Sachikonye, *The State and Agribusiness in Zimbabwe: Plantations and Contract Farming*, Leeds Southern African Studies Series, 13 (Leeds, 1989), pp. 9-14.
65 Interview #84. Sabotage against cash crops also occurred elsewhere in the district. For cotton, see Principal Information Officer, Rhodesian Information Service, to Director of Information, 'Summary of Field Research Reports Week Ending 20th March 1965: No. 15', 25 March 1965, box number 88399, NRC.
66 Interview #2.
67 Provincial Agricultural Officer Plowes knew Baxter in Kenya. Ibid.
68 Government of Rhodesia, Ministry of Internal Affairs, J.G. Baxter, An Assessment of the Tea Growing Potentials of the Manga and Holdenby Tribal Trust Lands and Recommendations for its Development as a Tea Scheme (Salisbury, 1969), NAZ.
69 Interviews #1, #2; also TILCOR, 'Project Report on Katiyo Tea Estate', March 1971, p. 1, PPD; S. Manase, 'Communal Land Reorganization and Development: Honde – Pungwe Valley Communal Lands, Initial Report, by the Department of Rural Development (Derude)', October 1990, pp. 18-21, DERUDE.
70 TILCOR, 'Project Report', p. 7.
71 Ibid.
72 Ibid., pp. 7, 8.
73 Hansard, Parliament of Zimbabwe, House of Assembly, 15 July 2009; Golden Sibanda, 'ARDA, Tea Estates in Joint Venture', *Herald*, 3 September 2009.
74 In this arrangement ARDA holds fifty-one per cent of the shares. *Herald*, 6 March 2011.
75 Holdenby Tea Estate, Monthly Report, August 1969, PPD.
76 Ibid., November 1969.
77 Ibid., September 1970; also October 1970.
78 TILCOR estimated the population based on a pilot survey, backed up by aerial photography and discussions with estate staff. TILCOR, 'Project Report', p. 6; also interview #53 with a *sabhuku* in the Chikomba area; see also 'list of "kraals" in the district', [n.d., 1983], PER5 GEN, DAO; 'Possible PV Sites (Following D.C. Mutasa's Meeting of 4.4.1974)', PPF.
79 Umtali District, Annual District Report, 1955, S2827/2/2/3, NAZ.
80 Terence Ranger, 'African Politics in Twentieth-Century Southern Rhodesia', *Aspects of Central African History*, Terence Ranger (ed.) (London, 1968), p. 243.
81 'The Crocodile Gang', *Black Fire! Accounts of the Guerrilla War in Zimbabwe*, Michael Raeburn, (Harare, 1986 [1978]), pp. 1-22; Terence Ranger, 'Violence Variously Remembered: The Killing of Pieter Oberholtzer', *History in Africa*, 24 (1997), pp. 273-86.
82 For a study of FRELIMO and RENAMO in Manica Province, see Mark Chingono, *The State, Violence and Development: The Political Economy of War in Mozambique, 1975–1992* (Aldershot, 1996).
83 DC Mutasa to PC, 17 October 1975, 15 August 1975, PER5 Headman Muparutsa, DAO.

84 Extension Officer to DC Inyanga, 20 September 1967, PER5 Headman Muparutsa, DAO.
85 DC Mutasa to PC, 5 July 1977, PER5 Headman Muparutsa, DAO.
86 Extension Officer to DC Inyanga, 20 September 1967; P. Muparutsa-Pfete to Secretary for Internal Affairs, 17 April 1974, PER5 Headman Muparutsa, DAO.
87 P. Muparutsa to DC Inyanga, 20 September 1967, PER5 Headman Muparutsa, DAO.
88 PC to Secretary for Internal Affairs, 8 August 1970, PER5 Headman Muparutsa, DAO. Chief Muparutsa's predecessor and several *masabhuku* had already been prosecuted in 1962 for delaying the land census through 'strong opposition'. NC Inyanga to PNC, 'Working Party D.3'.
89 DC Mutasa to PC, 17 May 1974, PER5 Headman Muparutsa, DAO.
90 DC Mutasa to PC, 17 October 1975, PER5 Headman Muparutsa, DAO.
91 Ibid.
92 DC Mutasa to PC, 5 July 1977, PER5 Headman Muparutsa, DAO.
93 Secretary for Internal Affairs to PC, 30 October 1967 and DC Inyanga to PC, 12 November 1969, PER5 Headman Chikomba, PAO; DC Inyanga to DC Sinoia, 10 November 1969 and DC Sinoia to DC Inyanga, 21 November 1969, PER5 Headman Chikomba, DAO.
94 DC Inyanga to attorney Peck, 24 March 1970, PER 5 Headman Chikomba, DAO.
95 Peck to DC Inyanga, 27 February 1970, PER 5 Headman Chikomba, DAO.
96 DC Inyanga to Peck, 24 March 1970, PER 5 Headman Chikomba, DAO.
97 Peck to DC Inyanga, 14 August 1970, PER 5 Headman Chikomba, DAO.
98 DC Inyanga to Peck, 25 August 1970, PER 5 Headman Chikomba, DAO.
99 Ibid.
100 See, for example, Inyanga District, Annual Report, 1966, box number 88459, NRC. In 1967, the DC Umtali urged that because children were crossing into the Honde Valley and Penhalonga, birth certificates should be issued 'in all classes in an effort to keep aliens out'. Umtali District, Annual Report, 1967, box number 88399, NRC.
101 Tea Officer Holdenby Tea Scheme to Estate Manager Katiyo, 9 September 1975, PPD.
102 Peck to DC Inyanga, 27 February 1970, PER5 Headman Chikomba, DAO.
103 DC Inyanga to PC, 11 March 1971, PER 5 Headman Chikomba, DAO.
104 Peck to DC Inyanga, 27 February 1970, PER 5 Headman Chikomba, DAO.
105 Ibid.
106 Ibid.
107 DC Inyanga to PC, 3 March 1971, PER 5 Headman Chikomba, DAO.
108 Ibid.
109 TILCOR, Minutes of the 84th Projects Staff Meeting, 21 January 1974, PPD.
110 DC Inyanga to PC, 22 November 1968, PER5 Chief Mafi, PAO; Katiyo Tea Estate, Monthly Report, April 1971, PPD.
111 Katiyo/ADF, Minutes of the Liaison Committee, 7 March 1974; DC Mutasa to Secretary TILCOR, 4 April 1974, PPD. Chiwanza was finally resettled and compensation was paid in March 1975. Katiyo/ADF, Minutes of the Liaison Committee Meeting, 6 March 1975, PPD.
112 Katiyo/ADF, Minutes of the Liaison Committee Meeting, 6 June 1974, PPD.
113 PC to Secretary for Internal Affairs, 11 September 1974, PER5 Headman Chikomba, PAO. *Ishe* Chikomba disappeared with his six wives; it is unclear what happened to all of them. At least one of his widows returned to live not far from her former homestead. Secretary for Internal Affairs to PC, 6 September 1974, PER 5 Headman Chikomba, DAO; interview #71.
114 Secretary for Internal Affairs to all PCs and DCs, 'List of Chieftainships and Headmanships Revised to 15th November 1978', 20 November 1978; Secretary for Internal Affairs to all PCs and DC, November 20, 1978, Secretary for Local Government and Town Planning to all DAs and all Under Secretaries (Development) at Province, 14 June 1982, PER5 GEN, DAO; PC Manyikaland to Secretary Internal Affairs, September 11, 1974, PER5 Headman Chikomba, PAO.
115 See, Kriger, Zimbabwe's *Guerrilla War*, pp. 196-206 and 'Popular Struggles in Zimbabwe's War of National Liberation', *Cultural Struggle and Development in Southern Afric*a, Preben Kaarsholm (ed.) (Harare, 1991), pp. 140-5. For the argument that colonial chiefs were 'decentralised despots' see Mahmood Mamdani, *Citizen and Subject: Contemporary Africa and the Legacy of Late Colonialism* (Princeton, NJ, 1996), chapter 2.
116 According to the former ZANLA detachment commander in the Honde Valley, in 1974 FRELIMO fighters also received food, clothes, and medicine in the Kairezi area, north of the Honde Valley. Interviews #27, #28. The Rhodesian *Herald* reported that one hundred and fifty FRELIMO and ZANLA forces executed a combined attack at a tea estate in Chipinge District in 1977. 'D.A. Is Killed in Action', 25 May 1977.
117 Interview #14.
118 Ibid., and interview #69.

149

[119] The historiography on women who joined the liberation armies during the Second Chimurenga is still amazingly weak. Josephine Nhongo-Simbanegavi, *For Better or Worse? Women and ZANLA in Zimbabwe's Liberation Struggle* (Harare, 2000); Tanya Lyons, *Guns and Guerrilla Girls: Women in the Zimbabwean National Liberation Struggle* (Trenton, NJ: 2004); also, Eleanor O' Gorman, *The Front Line Runs through Every Woman: Women and Local Resistance in the Zimbabwean Liberation War* (Woodbridge, 2011).

[120] Kriger, 'Popular Struggles', p. 126 and *Zimbabwe's Guerrilla War*, passim.

[121] 'Justice must be done' to DC Inyanga, 14 November 1973, PER5 Chikomba, DAO; also S.A.O. Mutasa to DC Mutasa, 19 September 1974, PPF.

[122] S.A.O. Mutasa to DC Mutasa.

[123] Interview #94.

[124] Interview #85.

[125] S.A.O. Mutasa to DC Mutasa; interview #96. For broader resentment by local people against government employees, see Priest-in-charge Bonda Mason to NC Inyanga, 14 December 1956, box number 103986, NRC.

[126] DC Mutasa to Member-in-charge BSAP Penhalonga, 5 December 1975, PER5 Chief Mutasa, DAO. The letter had an envelope and a translation attached. Hostility against Mutasa escalated, with several people from the immediate vicinity of his homestead killed and their bodies exhibited at the roadside. In 1977, the acting *mambo* moved to Mutare for safety reasons. DC Mutasa to Fuel Rationing Officer Umtali, 14 February 1977, PER 5 Headman Chikomba, DAO; interview #67.

[127] The letter further reads: 'we are here in SALISBURY, BULAWAYO, GWELO, RUSAPE, UMTALI and here in MOCAMBIQUE'. DC Mutasa to Member-in-charge BSAP Penhalonga, 5 December 1975, PER5 Chief Mutasa, DAO.

[128] Interview #87.

[129] Interview #85.

[130] S.A.O. Mutasa to DC Mutasa.

[131] Ibid.

[132] Interviews #94, #146.

[133] Interview #53; also 'Chikomba's Councillors', [n.d., 1974] and 'Justice must be done' to DC Inyanga, 14 November 1973, PER5 Headman Chikomba, DAO; Katiyo/ADF, Minutes of the Liaison Committee Meeting,' 24 September 1974 and 6 March 1975, PPD.

[134] Interview #75.

[135] During Nigeria's civil war (1967–1970), women crossed the frontier at night to secure foodstuffs for the beleaguered Biafra, a practice referred to as 'attack trade'. Axel Harneit-Sievers and Sydney Emezue, 'Towards a Social History of Warfare and Reconstruction: The Nigerian/Biafran Case', *The Politics of Memory: Truth, Healing, and Social Justice*, Ifi Amadiume and Abdullahi An-Na'im (eds) (New York, 2000), p. 117.

[136] Interview #53.

[137] John Iliffe, *Tanganyika Under German Rule, 1905–1912* (Cambridge, 1969), chapter 8.

5

War Rages Hot
Insurgency & Counter-insurgency

The Second Chimurenga, Zimbabwe's liberation war of the 1970s, is a prime example of guerrilla warfare, both of how it was fought by each side and how it affected the non-combatant population. This chapter examines these questions in unprecedented detail and in so doing addresses major queries that have been at the core of debate since the end of the Cold War, namely: What is political violence and how is it enacted, and how can a state legitimately counter insurgent violence? Eric Hobsbawm's challenge to the historical study of nationalism, to examine the phenomenon from both above and below, provides the necessary approach to gain a new understanding of guerrilla warfare.[1] The Honde valley, as one of the most hotly contested areas of the entire conflict, is pertinent to this discussion. For this study, and for the first time, it was possible to gain access to the necessary evidence to reconstruct in detail the strategies and tactics employed by the guerrilla fighters and by the Rhodesian counterinsurgency initiative, as well as gain insight into the experiences of the affected rural population.[2] The sources encompass the minutes of all the defence committee meetings for the Honde Valley and interviews with those having been involved in the conflict in a range of capacities. What transpires is a liberation war with a political agenda and daily tactics which were enacted in shifting microcosms of local support structures and the presence of the enemy. The counter-insurgency effort was devised as a total war from its outset. As a result, the valley population experienced a harsh period of suffering between 1976 and 1980, but at the same time individually and communally forged new means of incorporating the ever-changing situation into their frontier identity and of sustaining social cohesion.

Guerrilla warfare is political in nature, but guerrilla tactics can be employed in a range of contexts; since the end of the Cold War they have become the most common military approach used by insurgent groups. The philosophical and existential response to the most violent period in world history so far, the twentieth century, has often been to denounce violence altogether. In his 1993 essay, to which there was a broad response, Hans Magnus Enzensberger voiced his deep frustration that the end of the Cold War did not bring peace, but rather a new world order of small wars.[3] He was concerned with what he

9. Entrance to the Honde Valley, 1978: District Commissioner Higgs and African staff member (Source: Private Papers H)

calls 'molecular wars' characterised by groups of young males who struggle to assert their manliness and who fight *'wars that are about nothing at all'* (emphasis in the original).[4] Violence is thus a means to an end, used in gang warfare and the destruction of playgrounds in western cities to warlordism and drug trafficking in developing countries. Today's molecular war, according to Enzensberger, 'has freed itself from ideology'.[5] He wrote his essay in an angry voice, spitting venom at the failure of the twentieth century. His insightful observations about the significance of small wars, de-provincialising the west by showing that this violence is omnipresent and recognising the role of the crisis of masculinity, culminate in the problematic statement that insurgent violence is no longer politically motivated. Enzensberger even goes so far as to apply his view to past aggression when he concludes that 'only since the end of the Cold War have we been able to see [conflicts] for what they really are'.[6] The first decade of the twenty-first century with more small wars than ever before, including major insurgencies, raised fundamental questions about whether a conventional army can overcome guerrilla fighters, indicating the continuing relevance of Enzensberger's concerns and raising the question of what constitutes 'just' violence.

Political thinkers such as Hannah Arendt, despite her loathing for violent youth protest and the Cold War expressed in her *On Violence*, published in 1970, differentiated between the legitimacy and justification of violence even

152

at that point. Arendt explained that violence can never be legitimate, because that requires arguments drawing on the past, as is the case in revenge kill-ings.[7] 'Just' violence, on the other hand, projects a future goal, such as national liberation, and she herself, newly arrived in New York in 1941, had called for a Jewish army to participate in the war against Nazi Germany.[8] Arendt's observation that the use of violence in conflict situations can be justified has far-reaching relevance for insurgencies and counter-insurgencies. By contrast, Immanuel Kant, in his essay 'On Perpetual Peace' (1795), in which he pre-sented his reflections on Enlightenment, the nation state, the new world order, and conflict, wrote the following about soldiers in conventional armies: 'paying men to kill or be killed appears to use them as mere machines and tools in the hands of another (the nation), which is inconsistent with the rights of human-ity'.[9] Something Kant could not have foreseen was that with the revolutionary era creating the first nation states, guerrilla warfare also came into being as a common counter-force against conventional armies through the insurgents' engagement of the Napoleonic troops in Spain – a watershed in the early nine-teenth century.

Guerrilla fighters may be involved in highly profitable enterprise, historical studies of which go back to Eric Hobsbawm's *On Bandits* (1969),[10] but soldiers in liberation armies do not receive pay, and economic gain is usually prohibited by army regulations. Even so, Enzensberger would still deny the possibility of political mobilisation and thus Arendt's justification of violence in the context of insurgencies.[11] New revisionist studies of guerrilla warfare in Africa argue along similar lines: Morton Bøås and Kevin Dunn observe of contemporary Africa that 'people take up arms because they are angry and scared and see no other solutions or opportunities'.[12] Georg Elwert correctly observed that the boundary between politically motivated insurgents and warlords and their followers can be permeable and shifting. However, the Honde Valley demon-strates that the choice to 'take up arms' is not necessarily one of desperation and aimlessness or of material aspiration. A sense of adventure certainly played a role for many, but unbearable suffering and the concerted effort towards a just political goal stood at the centre of mobilisation.

Conventional armies are not well suited to oppose insurgents, not least because there has been reluctance to recognize the practical problems. The United States army only published their first *Counterinsurgency Field Manual* in 2003 and famously used the film *The Battle of Algiers* for military and stra-tegic training for urban counter-insurgency at West Point and the Pentagon with the onset of the Iraq War in 2003.[13] The mounting pile of publications by veterans, soldiers, and embedded journalists about the conflicts in Iraq and Afghanistan that are often autobiographical and attempt to address the still unresolved question of how a conventional army can successfully coun-ter insurgent violence bears testimony to the fact that little progress has been made in that regard since the Malaya Emergency (1948–1960) and Mau Mau in Kenya (1952–1956).[14] The problems remain the same – separation of com-batants from civilians, population control, winning hearts and minds, and the ethical question of how far a conventional army and a possibly democratic gov-ernment will go in fighting what is perceived as a terrorist onslaught, while the supporters of the insurgents celebrate them as freedom fighters or follow them as warlords. Such strategic, humanitarian, ethical, and legal issues have been addressed in studies in the last few years.[15]

During the Chimurenga, the Catholic Commission for Justice and Peace (CCJP) in Zimbabwe coined the term 'men in the middle' to highlight the suffering of the civilian population who were harassed and tortured by the army during the day and coerced by the fighters to provide supplies and support at night.[16] However, the full extent and immorality of the government atrocities which the commission admirably documented is not reflected in the metaphor 'men in the middle', nor the fact that often girls and women found themselves caught between guerrilla and government forces' demands. In the Honde Valley, it emerges clearly that 'taking sides' in the political struggle became a necessity in the 1960s, as chapter four showed. Once the insurgency and counter-insurgency campaigns began, however, the everyday experience of violence and the threat thereof became significantly more complicated.

This chapter examines how the Zimbabwe African National Liberation Army (ZANLA) and the Security Forces fought the Second Chimurenga and how Honde Valley inhabitants perceived these intrusions. The first section examines what marked the beginning of war to the frontier people and how they distinguished between legitimate and illegitimate combatants. Thereafter, the focus will move to insurgency. It will be shown how ZANLA fighters used a range of appeals to establish themselves in different parts of the valley upon their arrival in 1975, and an account of the insurgent attacks will be given. The focus will then shift to counter-insurgency, first by laying out the initiatives the settler government took, then by looking specifically at cross-border attacks. The final aspect of counter-insurgency examined here is forced villagisation, a contribution to the debate triggered by Caroline Elkins' controversial study of such counter-insurgency measures during Mau Mau in Kenya.[17] The final section discusses the RENAMO war that so severely impacted the Honde Valley after independence that villagisation was temporarily reintroduced.

Seeing War: On Historical Structuration

On the surface, dating a war and naming the armies involved may appear to be one of the more simple aspects of reconstructing a violent past. Reinhart Koselleck makes the observation that historians process 'natural chronology' through 'structuration' and so create 'historical chronology'.[18] Such chronology, he posits, has to be partisan because it is the result of analysis and interpretation. When Koselleck first made his epistemological contribution it was pathbreaking – most historians still believed in the objectivity of their reconstruction of the past. The purpose here is to draw attention to the notion of 'natural chronology'. There are no 'natural' facts waiting to be discovered by a historian to structure them into an analytical narrative.

Traces left by the past become historical sources because they had meaning to those who created, shaped, or experienced them, something Koselleck himself observes. He coined the term *geschichtliche Zeit* (historical time), which is constituted through the tension between past and future, between experience and expectation.[19] Historical time is experienced time, inextricably linked to 'social and political actions, with concretely acting and suffering human beings and their institutions and organisations'.[20] It is this linkage between experience and history that is enacted in memory. At the same time, it may also express 'futures past', remembered expectations.[21] An example of this embedded meaning is differences in contemporaries dating and naming actors and events that provide a patchwork which together creates an intricate and layered perspective on the past without any meta-narrative. Once the historian adds process to the consideration, what emerges is not a timeline or glossary that artificially codifies past occurrences, but rather a palimpsest. The Second Chimurenga illustrates this argument. The aspects that need examining are the dating of the beginning and end of the war, and terms used in reference to the combatants.

Even in the national narrative dating the Second Chimurenga varies. The beginning of the conflict either dates from the 'Battle of Chinoyi' on 28 April 1966, the first major direct military confrontation (and since independence celebrated as Chimurenga Day), or the Altena farm attack in northern Zimbabwe on 21 December 1972, the initial ZANLA assault following Maoist tactics, as recorded in several of the semi-official histories of the conflict.[22] Likewise, the war ended either with the ceasefire on 28 December 1979 or with political independence on 18 April 1980. On the national level, this dating can be further contested given that insurgent activities date back to 1964 and independence was followed by years of dissident activities.

For the inhabitants of the Honde Valley, the Chimurenga began when their suffering became unbearable, while the war ended with their recovery of mobility and relative security. Consequently, the dating differs. Most recall that the war began when they were resettled into Protected Villages (PVs). A female elder remembered: 'We first saw the war when we were put behind the fence.'[23] Similarly, an old man recalled: 'When we were put into the keeps, we had heard that war would be starting. After the fence was erected.'[24] The drastic impact of the sudden forced resettlement of the entire valley population into PVs explains that for those who underwent this radically dislocating experience, this marked a turning point. Even so, not everybody identified the same event with the start of the war, and the villagisation programme was introduced over the course of almost two years.

David Pratten, in his study of the leopard hunt murders, a series of killings that occurred in south-east Nigeria in the 1940s in Annang society, is in part concerned with vernacular knowledge. Pratten emphasises that in Annang there is a distinction made between historical knowledge, or wisdom, for which one term is used, and 'to know', which translates as 'to see something'.[25] Accordingly, when Honde Valley inhabitants related that they first saw the war on a certain occasion, this knowledge was acquired from personal experience and not through social memory, the radio, the government, or school. Seeing war meant that one's livelihood and wellbeing was now driven in the context of conflict. *Mbuya* Moyo's account in the previous chapter demonstrated that rarely did valley inhabitants perceive the guerrilla fighters as bringing war: almost always it was the Security Forces. A female elder explained:

> The recent war? We had not realized it until we saw *mabhunu* [Boers; here: European soldiers] dropping from airplanes. They flew to this place. We were surprised to see these

airplanes, and we wondered what they were for. They came to us and asked whether we had seen any *magandanga* [bandits, here: guerrillas]; we asked what *magandanga* were, and they insisted we knew where the *magandanga* were.[26]

Young men who had left the valley to join the liberation army frequently recalled that the war started the day a particularly harsh injustice pushed them to take the radical step to cross the border, such as a beating at school or the austere actions by a work supervisor on the tea plantations.

Public discourse on insurgencies has progressed little since the days of the Chimurenga. Rhodesians, that is, the government, white citizens, settlers who supported the Unilateral Declaration of Independence and the war effort, called their own army Security Forces and referred to the soldiers of the liberation armies as terrorists or terrs, and, as the war progressed, CTs – communist terrorists, a term introduced by Vietnam veterans.[27] For most Zimbabweans, the young men with AK-47s were liberation fighters and children of the soil. However, just as not every white citizen of the country agreed with the government and did not necessarily use the derogatory terminology, the split also ran deep within the African majority. During the 1970s, four armies were operating in the Honde Valley at various times: the government troops, most of whose soldiers were African men, from 1974; FRELIMO from 1974 to 1975, ZANLA from 1975 to 1979, and RENAMO from 1976 to 1979, then again 1984 to 1992. The latter used it as a corridor to infiltrate Mozambique in order to fight the newly independent government in the 1970s and to carry out attacks in Zimbabwe from Mozambique in the 1980s and early '90s.

The terms valley inhabitants used in reference to these soldiers denotes whether they remembered them as just in their cause and demeanour, or whether they saw them as violent intruders. Very rarely would people refer to the combatants by referencing the armies; if they did, it was usually in response to a direct question. Instead, most often the following terms were used: *vana vangu* (our children) or *vana vemuno* (those who grew up here) for ZANLA and FRELIMO; *vakomana* (boys) mostly for ZANLA; *macomrades* or *kamaradha* (comrades) mostly for FRELIMO, rarely for ZANLA; *mangezi* and *mabhunu* (Europeans, Boers) or *masoldiers* for members of the Security Forces; *matsanga* (after RENAMO's first leader Andre Matsangaissa)[28] and most frequently *magandanga* (savage person) for RENAMO. *Magandanga* was initially introduced by the Security Forces as a derogatory label for guerrillas. A woman recalled the army interrogating her father: 'They asked him whether he knew a thing called *gandanga*, to which he replied no…. They saw this place as the sanctuary for *magandanga*, and they made frequent visits to hunt down *magandanga*.'[29] In situations where civilians felt terrorised by combatants, they labelled them accordingly. Hence a male elder explained about ZANLA's request for support: 'If you gave them food and the white soldiers got to know of it – you were killed. If the white *magandanga* came and asked for food and you gave them, you were killed by the comrades if they got to know of it. What then could we do?' [laughs].[30] *Magandanga* is clearly a derogatory term and thus could be used in reference to soldiers of any of these armies in order to emphasise that they were not considered just in their actions.

While the usage of such a breadth of terms can be confusing, it neatly expresses the ambiguity of violence and a sense of either violation or support and belonging. In one interview a male elder explained how his household had supplied fighters with food:

> As for me, I can say *vana vemuno* [those who grew up here] arrived at my place and put up there …
>
> Interpreter: Are you talking about *vana vedu* [our children]?
>
> *Vana vedu*, yah! They then left. The FRELIMO came later and asked who had put up there and I said the comrades had put up there.[31]

Here the research assistant became confused and had to verify whether he had understood the elder by using the most commonly applied term during the war, *vana vedu*. In this regard, David Lan, in his study of the Dande area in northern Zimbabwe, was the first to show in a somewhat idealised schematic model that ZANLA guerrillas were incorporated into local communities as *vana vevhu* (children of the soil). Forming an alliance with senior spirit mediums (*mhondoro*) allowed the fighters to gain legitimacy and political authority; despite being young men, they could then exercise authority over elders.[32] In the valley, the more common use of *vana vemuno* (those who grew up here) for ZANLA allows for a distinction from FRELIMO, who, though strangers, were ideologically *vana vedu* (our children) because they supported the local political agenda and took on the responsibility as guardians over women in the absence of husbands and fathers.

In short, from the perspective of valley inhabitants, their own suffering drew the line between crisis and war and between perceiving a soldier's actions as just or not. At this point, a vernacular chronology emerges that sets the Chimurenga as a watershed in the valley's history. The chronology is highly individualised and marks the beginning of the liberation war in each person's memory as suffering experienced at the hands of soldiers of any of the four armies. The first war in the Honde Valley was the Makombe War of 1917–1920. Although this war was not seen in the area, it became part of social memory through the accounts of its refugees. State intervention from the 1950s caused sufficient grievances to politicise and eventually militarise the frontier people, but it was with the beginning of the Chimurenga that life appeared to be reduced to survival. It was then, when combatants acted as *magandanga*, that war became 'unbearably hot', a time when flight became a response of choice. As a male elder explained: 'When the war became hot … a lot of people ran away into Mozambique. They fled the war, which had become unbearably hot.'[33]

Insurgency

After several years of ill-fated attempts to fight the settler regime, and a few unevenly successful years of insurgency from December 1972, 1975 would prove a major strategic turning point for the Second Chimurenga. It was in that year that Mozambique gained political independence from Portugal, and hence the long border between the two countries became fully available for infiltration. Strategically, geopolitics had hampered the two liberation armies – ZAPU's armed wing, ZIPRA, and ZANU's ZANLA. Zimbabwe is bordered to the south by South Africa, a country at the time also under white minority rule that sided with the Rhodesian settler regime, and to the south-west by Botswana, a country politically sympathetic but one that did not condone insurgent actions. Zambia, the neighbour to the west and north-west, did welcome the liberation armies, but at times closed the border naturally formed by the Zambezi River and Lake Kariba, both of which were difficult to cross without detection. Finally, Mozambique offered a crucial frontier, with its 765 mile-long border, sections of which provided ideal cover in Manyikaland. After a difficult interim period, the new Mozambican government under President Samora Machel decided to allow ZANLA to base their military operations in that country, and in the Honde Valley the fighters spent the rest of 1975 preparing the ground for the full military onslaught, which began in 1976.

MOBILISATION AND SUPPORT STRUCTURES

Norma Kriger, in her study on the Second Chimurenga, emphasised the importance of appeals and support structures for understanding insurgencies.[34] By the very definition of guerrilla warfare, relations between combatants and civilians are crucial in allowing success for such small wars against the overwhelmingly stronger conventional opponents. The classic authors on guerrilla warfare, Mao Zedong and Che Guevara, differ on the exact role of the insurgent army in the struggle, but all strategists emphasise one aspect, namely the 'absolute co-operation of the people'.[35] ZANLA fighters were usually trained in Tanzania or China in Mao-style tactics that prescribed the relationship between 'the people and the troops' as follows: 'the former may be likened to water and the latter to fish who inhabit it. How may it be said that these two cannot exist together? It is only undisciplined troops who make the people their enemies and who, like fish out of its natural element, cannot live'.[36] It is not surprising therefore that ZANLA's rules of conduct towards the civilian population were almost identical to those propagated by Mao, albeit adapted to the particular challenges of the Zimbabwean conflict.[37] In the valley, the collaboration between combatants and civilians, a distinction that is deceptive in its clarity, was so successful that until the ceasefire in December 1979 the area continued to provide a major infiltration route for fighters, even when the Rhodesian government made an intense effort to implement counter-insurgency measures.

Guerrilla–civilian interactions from ZANLA's arrival in 1975 through the changes that villagisation introduced in the Honde Valley demonstrate that the different models of mobilisation as developed in the Zimbabwean historiography by Kriger, Lan, and Ranger are not exclusive, nor even contradictory.[38] The sociopolitical geography of an area and its strategic opportunities or limitations can at times be so small-scale that it is more useful to acknowledge complex constellations of politicisation and mobilisation than it is to develop meta-narratives of political violence and insurgency. One way of breaking down such persuasive narratives – important as they are being part of nationalist discourse and later post-colonial nation-building – is to take a radically local perspective. This same argument accounts for some of the difficulties of counter-insurgency success during warfare. ZANLA strategies varied over time and within different parts of the Honde Valley. Between 1975 and 1977, two distinct patterns of interaction between guerrillas and the valley population emerged. In the northern part, Holdenby Tribal Trust Land (TTL), local appropriations of guerrilla violence characterised their relationship, while in the south, in Manga and Mutasa North TTLs, ZANLA units employed violence to intimidate local communities.

In Holdenby, several factors facilitated ZANLA's efforts to organise supply structures. Even after the increased Rhodesian military presence from the second half of 1974, it was relatively easy for insurgents to move within the area, as the territory provided excellent cover and abundant fruit and water to help sustain the fighters. Moreover, FRELIMO's presence in 1974 had prepared the ground for further guerrilla activities. As one ex-combatant who had operated there as detachment commander recalled: 'the people in Honde Valley, they knew the comrades earlier than those who were inside [the country]. They were already motivated; they were ready to receive us'.[39] ZANLA was particularly successful in infiltrating the western part of Holdenby because the rainforest on the slopes provided ample opportunity to hide. Once counter-insurgency measures such as defoliation made this more difficult, the importance of having local support increased. The tea estate manager who had wanted to see *ishe* Zindi sent to shovel coal at Hwange in 1954 as punishment for his obstinacy was not the last person to be incensed by the chief. Zindi's capacity to undermine the settler state was continually underestimated, as he kept the administration on its toes. He helped ZANLA units find hiding places at sacred sites, including the ancestral graveyard which is remembered to have been safe throughout the war.[40] At the end of 1975, the District Commissioner (DC) Mutasa regarded *ishe* Zindi as 'old and sick' and in need of a deputy, but it was only in March 1976 that the Security Forces found him feeding guerrillas at his homestead and failing to report their presence, something for which he was charged, detained, and subsequently sentenced to two years in prison. He was released after 16 months and in July 1978 he was reinstated as chief by the government. Although he then lived in Zindi PV under close government supervision, he appears to have continued to actively support guerrilla units in his area.[41]

ZANLA's approach in Holdenby deviated from its principal strategy of never deploying guerrillas in their home areas and that of mobile insurgency.[42] Instead, with the help of local young men, the area became a training ground within the country.[43] This enabled the building of much closer relationships with the civilian population compared to other areas. Consequently, the local units succeeded in mobilising support through appeals rather than coercion. In 1975, ZANLA, like FRELIMO before, directed violence primarily at people who were locally resented, such as tea outgrowers.[44] The former detachment commander recalled the importance of winning male elders – community leaders, and in particular chiefs – first so that efficient mobilisation would follow: 'Those are influential leaders. And you've got to win them. And when you win an *ishe*, the chief and the kraalhead, you've won the people.... So if the chiefs say these are our children and we've got to support them, no-one will go against that.'[45] Even in areas where it was impossible to gain legitimacy through 'winning' the elders, logistical and material support was forthcoming. The guerrillas knew to focus on specific households, such as those of businessmen and migrant labourers, who, because of their cash income, would be in a better position to provide supplies.

Women were most directly involved in supporting the fighters as providers of food and as heads of household in the absence of men in migrant labour, as was the case with *mbuya* Moyo and her co-wife in their interactions with FRE-LIMO. One ex-combatant even claimed that women were more committed to the struggle. He asserted:

> Women were more determined than men.
>
> H.S.: Why do you think that is so?
>
> Well, well, I say so, because even when the tough gets tougher, the women could sacrifice and bring food, even when the fighting is taking place, to get to us. I mean, I think, perhaps it's motherhood. That they feel it. You see what I mean? That our sons are fighting, our sons and daughters are fighting, they spend the whole day fighting, they must be hungry.... And you find that during the struggle, if there is an attack, men seem to run away, leaving the family behind, and the woman would die with her children. You see, there is that boldness in women. That's my observation.[46]

As shown in chapter four, women reasoned that they were merely doing their duty by providing for the fighters. But many were undoubtedly politicised, as the women's resistance against the Native Land Husbandry Act (NLHA) in the 1960s proved, and some women crossed the border in order to become combatants.[47] The depoliticised view of women's roles during the struggle is due to a regression in gender relations after independence, as has been the case in many post-war situations, and also reflects strategies of 'hidden struggles'.[48] Their apparent conformity, whether in women's claims or men's interpretations of their behaviour, 'hid' the subversiveness and political character of their actions, albeit recognised here by the veteran as 'that boldness in women'.

ZANLA guerrillas' organisation of support took a different course in the southern part of the Honde Valley. The close proximity to the military and police base at Ruda, together with less favourable cover and escape routes, was responsible for guerrilla coercion. Possibly the fast-changing presence of guerrillas, who mainly used the area as an infiltration route into the country and therefore had no longer-term relationships with local people, also contributed to uneasy relations. It appears that here, against the background of imminent danger of a counter-attack and problems of mobilising support in contested areas, Kriger's model of guerrilla coercion is applicable.[49]

From 1975, the newly arrived ZANLA units asked the local population about their grievances and drew up 'hit lists' of those who were perceived as socially harming in their behaviour, including *varoyi* (witches and wizards, sing. *muroyi*).[50] The fighters saw them as potential collaborators and realised that public beatings and assassinations would draw support and at the same time set an example of the power they wielded.[51] However, elders who helped the fighters to draw up such lists of 'bad people' often caused individuals to be victimised because of personal grievances. An elder explained:

> Some were innocent, you know? Like – if there is somebody who has got many oxen, so

I can list him up! If there is somebody I had asked to give me something and he refused, I can also list him up! So many people died here.… Now we knew what would be done to bad people.[52]

Subsequently, the phrase 'bad people' quickly became synonymous with those who were seen as dangerous to their neighbours and to the struggle and who were thus in danger of being punished by the fighters. The choice of individuals against whom guerrilla violence would be directed was mediated through individual and local interests, and thus for some, it was possible partially to appropriate this violence, while others were its victims. At the *pungwe*, the nightly meetings, disciplinary beatings and killings were publicly carried out. An ex-combatant recalled how local people were forced to sing the Chimurenga song *Vanamukoma vanouraya*, which he translates as 'Comrades, they kill!' He remembered: 'The people they started singing. Then we started hitting.'[53]

On the basis of this initial campaign of intimidation, which must have heightened tensions within communities, support structures were set up to provide the guerrillas with information, food, money, and other items. But in 1976 and 1977, until villagisation, violence continued to occur. As elsewhere in the country, rural entrepreneurs became a target because their exposed economic position made them conspicuous as collaborators yet at the same time obvious as potential suppliers for guerrilla needs. In 1977, for example, at a business centre in Mutasa North TTL, a group of guerrillas threatened to kill one of the local businessmen. This man had, since his youth, worked as a migrant labourer with the intention of setting up some kind of business. Finally, the Manyika resettlement in the 1950s afforded him the opportunity to accumulate sufficient capital for a store. When it transpired that packing material for household items was not available, the businessman-to-be had the idea of buying second-hand empty bags from a company in the provincial capital Mutare to sell to the families that were to be resettled. He then followed them into the Honde Valley and, after raising more money through working as a hawker, mainly selling spices, he set up a store. From the late 1950s, he prospered by supplying the newly established tea estates in Holdenby, transporting goods at first in a canoe across the Honde River and later, by lorry.[54]

This man vividly recalled the incident when guerrillas accused him of being a *mtengesi* (sell-out) because of his alleged contacts with Europeans:

When we were trading there, all our goods were being taken and we were lucky not to be killed. Some other business people were killed and then some time they wanted to kill me also. They said: 'You got the petrol, you got the diesel [he ran a filling station], you've got the store. How did you get it? It's part of the Europeans' property! So we are fighting the Europeans and you are in for them.' They [local people] witnessed me being killed. But then there was another one who said: 'First, he must confess!' During that time … the Zimbabwean guerrilla fighters used to come and say: 'Confess and tell the truth before we kill you!' They said: 'Put him down onto the floor, so that it's easier!' Then I was down on the floor and everybody was called in to come and hit me and kill me. Then this other one said: 'Say now what it is! How did you get the money to start the business? Who owns the business? Who is supporting you?'[55]

When he explained how he had set up his business, the guerrillas asked onlookers whether the account was true: 'They said: We did not see any Europeans coming to his shop and organise anything. But if it is a secret, we don't know!'[56] The guerrillas then threatened to burn the fuel at the filling station. However, they gave in to the owner's reasoning that the explosion would probably be fatal to all of them and also would attract the attention of the Security Forces. Thus they resigned themselves to robbing and destroying the store, and urging the owner not to sell out. Because of this episode and from being excluded from local intelligence, such as warnings about landmines, he left the area in 1978 and lived in Mutare for the rest of the war.[57] The phrase 'being killed' does not necessarily mean put to death, but frequently denotes an unbearable degree of suffering, as in this interview in reference to violent and humiliating interrogation.

Despite such violent episodes of torture and killings when the young men with AK-47s asserted their authority, it should not be underestimated how much they depended on the local population. Arendt observed that where violence is absolute, power is absent and that no government based on force alone can last.[58] If fighters pushed the use of intimidation too far, they could easily lose their civilian support, and in the valley even a single disgruntled person could prove disastrous because the Security Forces were always within reach and ready to retaliate. Also, for many fighters, being young and living their lives so precariously, spiritual protection was crucial. The government observed that spirit mediums were particularly influential in Mutasa South TTL, where they prevented the local ZANLA units from laying landmines and using coercion.[59] Militarily, ZANLA would not have persevered as they did in the valley after 1977 had they not found spiritual support, particularly in the Zindi and Muparutsa areas. When the army created no-go areas, they deforested the slopes of the valley, probably using Agent Orange,[60] but it was still possible for the fighters to keep base camps at spiritual sites, as elders shared their vernacular knowledge of cosmologically mapped places beyond the reach of the military. The frontier character of the valley, however, did not only afford insurgents some protection, it also caused them problems.

The detachment commander remembers that when he first took his unit into the valley and called the initial *pungwe*, the purpose was to introduce themselves to the local population and create an impression of strength that would leave no doubt who was in charge, while at the same time communicating their political message, that they had come as sons of the soil to liberate the country. Everybody was rounded up and the meeting commenced with songs. The crowd became apprehensive when the commander stepped back and the political commissar took over to explain their mission. As he began his speech, introducing the slogans of the struggle, he soon found himself interrupted as an elderly and frail man began shifting on the ground. The elder became more and more agitated, and the fighters had to decide whether to punish him for the disturbance. At that point it became clear that a spirit was in the process of manifesting itself in the man's body. Eventually the frail elder rose and began dancing a warrior's dance like a young man, stabbing an invisible spear in different directions, and singing a song in a language nobody understood.[61] Everyone appeared baffled, and eventually the ZANLA fighters asked whether anybody understood what the spirit, who had by then fully emerged, was saying. One man stepped forward, explaining that he had learned Zulu when working in South Africa, and that this was one of the *madzviti*, a fighter from the olden days whose spirit had returned as a *ngozi* (avenging spirit) because he, the most powerful warrior of his day, had been killed by valley inhabitants. Then the spirit left the elder's body and he returned to his frail self.[62]

This incident upstaged the young guerrilla fighters in more ways than one. In the process of attempting to enforce their authority as young men with guns, embodying the potential of violence, they were challenged by the heroic stories which the warrior spirit told and performed through song and dance, using a local elder as his vessel. Moreover, they could only come to an understanding of what was going on with the help of another experienced and older man who interpreted for them. Worse still, when the *ngozi* spoke, he admitted that he had been defeated by the ancestors of the same people the ZANLA fighters saw as meek civilians. The guerrillas had to abandon their attempt to impose their narrative onto the local population and instead were forced to listen and to pay tribute to memories rooted in the locality and embodied by the local medium.

So far it has been shown that guerrilla–civilian relations were not simply a matter of the fighters enforcing their agenda. Mobilisation approaches varied in different parts of the area, with appeals and sustained supportive relationships between the local ZANLA units and the civilian population largely successful in Holdenby, but the southern part of the valley characterised by coercion and reliance on settling local scores. The latter is the context in which the residents at Honde Mission and Industrial School found themselves.

MISSIONS AND THE WAR

By 1970, the Ziwe Zano Society was facing serious internal disagreements and financial problems that caused the temporary closure of Honde Industrial School. A few years later, however, under the leadership of one of the founding fathers, S.M. Kanyenze, who became President of the society after Katsidzira's death, the situation improved.[63] Paradoxically, the deteriorating political situation in the country indirectly helped Ziwe Zano for a short while, as non-governmental and church organisations became interested in financing indigenous self-help projects in the context of colonial deprivation and struggles for liberation. International funding from a range of sources became available.[64] But with the war of liberation heating up, it became increasingly difficult to access foreign aid, the government being concerned that the funds might be channelled to the insurgents.[65] At the same time, Ziwe Zano lost most of its local European benefactors, as in the case of one who 'stopped [giving support] the time politics began'.[66] A long-standing supporter, W.R. Cruickshank, a Mutare businessman who had been treasurer of Ziwe Zano from 1970 to December 1976, was willing to continue his work but could no longer visit Honde Mission because of the deteriorating security situation.[67] Here, the rapid succession of dramatic events between 1975 and 1977, which culminated in the closure of Honde Mission, will be examined in order to show that in the end, the members' insistence on their outsider status made their situation precarious during the war.

In 1974, Honde Industrial School was thriving, with a total enrolment of 293 students (125 male and 168 female), of whom fifty per cent came from

Manyikaland, thirty-five per cent from Mashonaland, ten per cent from Mata-beleland and five per cent from other areas. In 1975, 464 students applied for the 107 available places, and the total enrolment amounted to 350 students.[68] In 1973, school inspector Rondozai had reported that discipline was excellent, but only two years later he found 'an element of hopelessness', with fifty-seven male students leaving for Mozambique.[69] During the night of 3 July 1975, eighteen male students crossed the border, and thirty-nine more the following night. The headmaster immediately reported this to the police, and the Security Forces intercepted a third group of eighteen boys. The school inspector investigated the incident and found that:

> Although the rest of the school appeared to be running 'normally', it was clear that there was an undercurrent of confusion, fear, frustration and an element of hopelessness in everyone concerned. There was no apparent reason why and how the 57 boys left, except perhaps a bunch of adolescents looking for a bit of adventure.[70]

The remaining students were sent home on the following day. It appears that none of the fifty-seven boys returned before the end of the war.[71] The school inspector reported that they had 'left the centre on their own'.[72] However, a woman who lived at the mission at the time remembered:

> They [the students] had been having a debating session that afternoon in that hall when the boys [guerrillas] arrived. The boys then politicised those boys and girls who were in the hall. By the end of the session, most had made up their minds, and the following day we woke up to find that all the boys had gone.[73]

She explained that guerrillas frequented the mission to meet the students. Two of her brothers left with them, one of whom died, and the other returned after independence; she said that her family did not know about their plans.[74] Despite the contradictory evidence regarding the presence of ZANLA at Honde Mission, both accounts tally in their classic portrayal of youth mobilisation that excluded elders.[75]

One of the biggest firefights of the war, 'the mother of all battles', occurred in the immediate vicinity of Honde Mission, at Chiwawadzira Mountain in November 1976. According to the Rhodesian press, 'it was the most spectacular kill by Security Forces in the war to date'. Allegedly, thirty-one guerrillas and only one Security Force member were killed in a twelve-hour firefight. 'Vast amounts of material' were recovered from arms caches on the mountain.[76] By 1976, ZANLA had established a base camp on Chiwawadzira Mountain and an infiltration route along which guerrilla units moved from Mozambique through Mutasa North TTL to other parts of the country.[77] A young woman from the mission recalled the event:

> That night, the white soldiers came to put up here. It so happened that the vakomana [boys] were passing through on their way to that mountain. They had come from Mozambique. The white soldiers spotted those comrades as they passed. As soon as they spotted the comrades, the white soldiers sent a signal into the sky – their signal to summon fighter planes. As the comrades proceeded, the planes had already come here. It was then that the comrades rushed towards the mountain. There was much bombardment in that mountain, and more reinforcement for the soldiers came. The whole area was covered with soldiers.[78]

The soldiers displayed the corpses at the mission and arrested and interrogated Ziwe Zano's elderly President Kanyere. They stayed for a week in order to pursue follow-up operations[79] and later closed the mission. At a time when the government usually assumed the worst and asked questions later, the police and administration nevertheless accepted that the former pioneers who had insisted on their outsider status from their arrival in 1938 were innocent bystanders. The Minister of Education was even prepared to write a supportive letter for Ziwe Zano's fund-raising campaign in October 1975.[80] It seems plausible that the elders at Honde Mission had no detailed knowledge about guerrilla activities before 1976. However, it is surprising that they did not appear to have known that a major guerrilla base was situated nearby, on a mountain which had been used for prayer meetings by mission members before the Chimurenga. This can only be explained by the generational crisis in the church and their exclusion from local discourses about landscapes of violence and war.

The situation at Honde Mission finally peaked in 1977. On 30 January, when the school was about to re-open, guerrillas arrived, assembled everybody, and accused the students of being government informers before killing two of them. A third student survived, but with serious injuries. A few days later, the police charged several Ziwe Zano members with supporting the guerrillas and arrested them. Although they pleaded not guilty, this time they were sentenced to death. This was later commuted to imprisonment, and they were subsequently released at independence.[81] Meanwhile, in the valley, government soldiers looted the mission on several occasions.[82] When a plan to establish 'Honde Mission PV' was abandoned, the mission remained closed.[83] Some younger Ziwe Zano members who had roots in the valley moved into PVs, but the majority left for Mutare, where they attempted to continue their work.[84] Despite the death penalties handed down to some Ziwe Zano elders, Kanyenze, 'the pioneer of the Honde Valley Trade School and hospital', was decorated with a Meritorious Service Medal in 1979.[85] This account of Ziwe Zano elders and students illustrates that the metaphor of 'men in the middle' greatly simplifies the experience of the Second Chimurenga, at least in the Honde Valley.

In general, relations between missionaries and guerrillas varied greatly,[86] depending on the local standing of the missionaries and their incorporation into the local support structures. In the 1960s St Peter's Mandeya had been served by Father Lewis, an outspoken supporter of the Rhodesian regime, and in May 1977 the Anglican station 'was abandoned as being militarily indefensible' during the villagisation exercise. The mission was then looted and burnt down.[87] The contrast between Honde Mission and St Peter's with St Columba's, a Roman Catholic mission at Hauna, none far from each other, is striking (see map 4). Even in 1976 and 1977, when incidents were at their height, the Carmelite sisters, catechist John Sunwa, and Father Michael Hender still travelled to their brethren, albeit now by bicycle, because that made it easier to avoid landmines.[88] During the war, some Carmelites were injured but none were killed.[89] From their arrival in the country in 1946, the order positioned itself within liberation theology, as described in their recent self-portrayal:

Carmelites, however, from the beginning, were not happy with the laws of discrimination which were in force against Africans in their own country. Other conditions in Zimbabwe were not dissimilar to the situation that had prevailed in pre-Independence Ireland, such as ownership of land, commerce, education and administration of justice. That is why they could understand the struggle of Africans to gain their independence, eventually by force, when all avenues to meaningful negotiations for them were closed.[90]

Despite the proximity of the nearby police station and military base at Ruda, the resident Irish priest even held regular meetings with the local ZANLA unit, exchanging information and providing them with food, medical supplies, and other items.[91] St Columba's had reached this accommodation with the guerrillas that escaped both Honde Mission and St Peter's until an unfortunate incident in 1977. On 31 May, members of the local ZANLA unit were visiting the priest when they were surprised by an off-duty police reservist and his 'girl friend'.[92] A shoot-out ensued, during which Father Gerry Galvin was wounded. He subsequently had to leave the country.[93] Later that year, St Columba's became part of Hauna PV. Just how significant being part of local networks was for survival is illustrated by another incident that occurred in November 1977. In October, catechist John Sunwa and Father Michael Hender were ambushed in the Mutasa area, on the plateau. The guerrilla fighters took Hender and another father to St John's Mission in Mutare, where they were to be executed on the veranda. They barely managed to escape.[94] This stands in stark contrast to the position only a few months before, when Hender had been able to ride his bicycle through the heavily mined Honde Valley quite freely.

HIT AND RUN: KILLING FOR LIBERATION

Late in the evening of 28 February 1976, a group of five to seven guerrillas approached the Rambanayi 'hotel' – it functioned as a brothel – at Zindi Business Centre. They called the customers outside and asked if any of them were policemen or members of the Criminal Investigation Department (CID). Suddenly, the sound of an approaching vehicle was heard and when the fighters recognised it as a police Land Rover, they shouted: 'These are the enemies of Zimbabwe, are they not?' When the Land Rover stopped, 'fire started regardless of the nearness of the crowd. A rocket was fired setting the vehicle aflame. Everybody panicked and started running wildly.' Three policemen were killed, as well as a son of the hotel owner, who was hit by a stray bullet.[95] Over the course of the following months, 'security incidents' became an almost daily occurrence. ZANLA mined the roads heavily, and it became dangerous for government and tea estate employees to move without a convoy or mine-proof vehicles.[96]

From 1976, most of the guerrilla activities in Holdenby were directed against the three plantations, Katiyo, Aberfoyle, and Eastern Highlands Tea Estates (EHTE), as well as the Rumbizi tea scheme.[97] Katiyo was less affected, despite its location immediately on the border; as a parastatal it was equipped with better security facilities provided by Internal Affairs, National Servicemen, District Assistants, and the Security Forces. It also had a guarded and fenced labour compound.[98] Typical of guerrilla warfare, the main objective was to attack 'soft targets' – tea workers, technical equipment, and infrastructure –

in order to stop production, further damage the economy, which was already under UN sanctions, and thus weaken the enemy. The tea fields themselves could not be sabotaged through neglect, by fire, by driving livestock into the fields, or similar measures. Once full-grown, the closely planted bushes are resistant to any such activities, an advantage which Geoff Baxter, a tea expert, foresaw in 1974: 'terrorists will gain little satisfaction from trying to damage 13,500 plants in every hectare, although the sabotaging of the pump installations might prove an attraction to them.'[99] Attacks against the tea processing factories were also next to impossible, because they were heavily guarded. With the tea plants and larger technical installations out of reach, the fighters focused on tea workers and on sabotaging road transport. Accordingly, the second major attack in the valley after the Rambanayi 'hotel' incident, was the 'Pimayi massacre' of 10 May 1976, in which an African Development Fund (ADF) lorry carrying workers detonated a landmine near Pimayi business centre, leaving two Rumbizi tea workers dead and eight injured. The Rhodesian African Rifles (RAR) commander-in-charge later argued that this ambush was a retaliatory measure against labour working for less than one Rhodesian Dollar per day.[100] In 1976, ZANLA fighters frequently attacked transport facilities and told the workers either to quit their employment or to demand higher wages.

During May and June 1976, ZANLA specifically targeted the Rumbizi tea scheme. An eyewitness of the raid on the labour compound and headquarters during the night of 28 May recalled that one aspect the guerrillas objected to was the involvement of local women with resident tea staff. They instructed the former not to wear 'European' clothes and adornments: 'girls had been prohibited from doing certain things. For example, mini-skirts, trousers, wigs and make-up were all prohibited'.[101] During the Chimurenga, guardianship over civic virtue, such as women's morals and the rejection of western consumer goods and mimicry, were typical demands through which local units attempted to assert their authority as sons of the soil, their political agenda, and the ancestors' prohibitions.[102] By this time *muzvare* Muparutsa was supporting the war effort in her role as *mhondoro* (senior spirit medium) and, after crossing the border with her followers in December 1976, she cleansed fighters before and after they went into battle.[103] The Rumbizi attack and Pimayi massacre in May and the deteriorating security situation left the resident staff rattled and led to increased alcohol consumption. They were said to have 'made sure that each alone had enough drinking stock for every night as they thought it better to die drunk … as was the custom those days.'[104]

On the plantations, the situation was not much better. Until villagisation, few men from the Honde Valley worked on the tea estates. The management relied on migrant labour with the majority of workers coming from Malawi, Zambia, and Mozambique. The first two countries having gained independence in the 1960s, those workers had the reputation of being more politicised than others, which resulted in strikes, as in 1960, 1961, 1974, and 1975.[105] In the latter half of 1976, guerrillas began to frequent the labour compounds at Aberfoyle and EHTE, where they told workers to leave their employment, a request hundreds followed. Towards the end of the year, the fighters became increasingly daring. During one of the nights preceding the Aberfoyle massacre, when a ZANLA unit visited a labour compound at EHTE, they fired shots into the air.

This alerted the Security Forces to their presence and six members of the units were killed. The guerrillas showed some nerve when they stayed long enough to celebrate by singing liberation songs with the assembled workers.[106]

On the evening of 19 December 1976, the single most deadly attack against the civilian population during the Chimurenga inside the country occurred, that is, the so-called 'Aberfoyle massacre'. The fighters had been drinking with the workers all day, but had remained unrecognised and undetected.[107] Several witnesses testified that these men were drunk when they identified themselves as guerrillas at approximately eight p.m. and assembled forty male workers with their wives and children. According to the official government report, the guerrillas then proceeded to take valuables and money from the workers and their homes. They told the assembly that they intended to kill the men, because they had continued to work for the estate, despite their warnings. The captors walked the group along the road through two other labour compounds to the Nyawamba Bridge, where two men jumped into the river and escaped. The fighters then proceeded to the floodlights at the Wamba factory gate on the major estate road. There they told the women and children to move aside and to sit with their heads between their legs and then instructed the men to lie down. They opened fire and used their bayonets, killing twenty-seven of the thirty-eight men and wounding eleven. Of those who died, ten were Zimbabwe-ans, nine Mozambicans, and eight Malawians.[108] Aberfoyle closed for a month thereafter.[109]

The massacre caused a national and international outcry.[110] Whereas the Rhodesian government blamed ZANLA for the incident, both liberation movements claimed the Selous Scouts, a notorious elite unit of the Security Forces that used pseudo gang tactics, was responsible.[111] Since then it has been widely believed that ZANLA carried out the attack, although there is contradictory evidence.[112] The free reign the fighters had that night is certainly astounding, and in the aftermath of the massacre the guerrillas appear to have lost no legitimacy with local communities. This could be attributed to the fact that most of the workers killed came from elsewhere.[113] In addition, the attackers followed typical ZANLA procedure in the area, ensuring the safety of women and children, as happened at an incident at Luleche workshop, EHTE, where the women and children were 'guarded by one of the guerrillas in case of crossfire with the Security Forces', while the men were forced to participate in burning vehicles.[114] In the end, it is relevant for the analysis of guerrilla warfare that either party could have been responsible and that each in fact blamed their opponent. This reflects a typical insurgency/counter-insurgency situation.

1976 was a year when the military initiative was with the insurgents and the administration acknowledged that the valley had become a semi–liberated area. DC Peters summarised the events of the year in a radio interview:

> Up until earlier this year the situation was that the Honde Valley was to a very large extent overrun by terrorists. The entire economy of the valley had virtually collapsed, and we had lost the ability to be able to administer or govern. The terrorist was in a situation where he was carrying out administration of his own type.[115]

The DC further characterised the security situation: 'Intaf [Internal Affairs] and the Security Forces constantly having [had] to react to terrorist incidents rather than the C.T. reacting to our own administrative procedures.'[116] Thus, during 1976 the Honde Valley had become a major ZANLA infiltration route from Mozambique and a training ground inside the country, with the tea industry specifically targeted and subsequently paralyzed due to lack of labour. In May 1977, the tea estates tabled and adopted a paper that summarised their economic crisis:

> During the crop year now approaching its end, barely 20% of [the] potential has been realised. Some 80% of the total tea lands have grown so out of hand through lack of labour during the year that it will require a colossal effort to rehabilitate these lands before they can be made productive again. Such have been the economic hardships suffered by the estates that there now exists a genuine danger that if called upon to suffer another year like the last they will not survive. The problem has now reached a most critical stage.[117]

After the string of security incidents in 1976, the situation was desperate. The government stepped up their efforts and swiftly introduced villagisation from December of that year.

Counter-insurgency

In 1977, when the liberation war had fully escalated, the government portrayed the relationship between the white and African population in the country as follows: 'Now as then … co-operation is a feature of Rhodesian life.'[118] In an attempt to boost the morale of the troops and their families, issue four of the magazine *Rhodesian Fighting Forces*, published by the Department of Information, opened with this editorial message, which continued:

> In all of Africa, possibly in all the world, there may not be another country where relations between the races – white, black, coloured and Asian – are as harmonious as in Rhodesia.
>
> On the farms, in the mines, in shops, offices, factories and workshops, in Government offices, in the Army, Air Force, and Police, the races work alongside each other toward the common goal of welding a nation.[119]

The 'harmonious' relation and the 'working alongside' of the neatly listed 'races' is further illustrated by an image of an Ndebele scout pointing towards the horizon, assisting a white solider during the First Chimurenga of 1896-97. Their relationship is clearly marked by the African man being barely visible in the background, and on foot, while the soldier towers over him, heavily armed, sitting on a horse with impressive proudly pointed ears.

From a minority government point of view it was crucial to uphold the myth of harmony and cooperation with the majority population, some of whom were allegedly seduced or coerced by barbarous CTs into supporting their cause. Such propaganda, together with the image of a happy home front,[120] underlines the success of the insurgency which brought a great sense of vulnerability into settlers' everyday life, including their very own homes, as distrust of their

NOW AS THEN . . .

. . . CO-OPERATION IS A FEATURE OF RHODESIAN LIFE

*In all Africa, possibly in all the world,
there may not be another country where
relations between the races — white, black,
coloured and Asian — are as harmonious
as in Rhodesia.
On the farms, in the mines, in shops,
offices, factories and workshops, in
Government offices, in the Army, Air Force
and Police, the races work alongside each
other toward the common goal
of welding a nation.*

DEPARTMENT OF INFORMATION
P.O. Box 8150, Salisbury, Rhodesia.

10. Editorial page, Rhodesian Fighting Forces, *no. 4, 1977* servants soured even this last resort.[121] Many of the Rhodesians who supported the war effort thought of themselves in various ways as either victimised by terrorists, heroic, or as merely fulfilling their duty. While this persuasive racial discourse prevailed among a large part of the white population, the reality was a government that was waging total war against the African majority.

Rhodesian war efforts, typical for a counter-insurgency initiative, were both all-encompassing and limitless. Boundaries between military, private, and civil structures and interests became permeable or were removed entirely and the attempt was made to maintain authority over, at the very least, those African communities located on the border with Mozambique in the totality of their lives. The initiative entailed a hearts-and-minds campaign directed at the various sections of the population, the militarisation of the administration, close cooperation between economic and state interests, and, in terms of tactics and strategy, a major effort to control the borderlands, in particular through villagisation, while also pursuing the enemy into neighbouring countries. In what follows, the focus at first will be on the early war years and the ruthlessness of the government initiative, followed by a discussion of the cross-border offensives the Security Forces executed through the Honde Valley in order to raise the question of ethics and just violence. The final section will examine villagisation.

A TOTAL RESPONSE TO TOTAL WAR

In March 1977, at the height of hostilities in the country, the government created a Ministry of Combined Operations (ComOps) that included the prime minister, several members of the cabinet, and army, police, and air force commanders.[122] This signifies not only the severity of the military situation at the time, but also the seamless collaboration between civilian and military interests and the merging of the legislative, executive, and judiciary branches, something that is, in varying degrees, a normal state of affairs for any country involved in a counter-insurgency effort. Central elements of guerrilla strategy include making it impossible to distinguish between combatant and civilian and fighting a mobile, responsive, and spontaneous war in which small units adapt to local circumstances, carrying out hit-and-run attacks on soft targets, while avoiding direct confrontation or battle with army units. ZANLA followed Mao's strategy, and combatants usually did not wear uniforms, which meant they were not protected by the Geneva Convention of 1929. Security Forces could often only identify guerrillas by bangles and bracelets which spirit mediums and healers gave them for their protection or because they wore several layers of clothing so they did not have to carry baggage.[123] By contrast, a conventional army is trained to fight on a battlefield in uniform and is expected to obey the laws of their country and international law. Asked to compare his experience as a World War II veteran with the Chimurenga, an elder responded:

> [The Second World War] was conventional warfare; one party informed the other, and battle-lines were drawn. … And the war was then fought. This guerrilla war is different in that you are not prepared, and, while carrying that gun, you may be struck without

warning. … It is different in that the recent Chimurenga was a guerrilla war. The enemy stalks his adversary and shoots.[124]

The elder pinpointed the difference between conventional and guerrilla warfare: the latter is a war without boundaries. Responding to this challenge during the Second Chimurenga, the minority government fought a total war against its majority population.

Strategically, 'dirty' war tactics are militarily advantageous to the state. The abandonment of lawful pursuit through the merging of the powers was a crucial step in that direction taken by the Rhodesian government early in the conflict. After the attack on Altena Farm in December 1972, and subsequent ZANLA and ZIPRA insurgent operations, the government began its counter-insurgency offensive in 1973, part of which was to ensure farm and estate security and to implement villagisation. In order to pre-empt further infiltration by guerrillas, particularly in the north-eastern border area, these security measures were then extended to areas hitherto unaffected by the war.

In the Honde Valley, the war effort was driven by an alliance between military, administrative, political, and tea industry interests. District administration had raised the security alert even before ZANLA arrived in the area. As early as March 1973, DC Umtali warned the chiefs and *masabhuku* that 'No excuses will be tolerated if terrorists do enter through the Mutasa North TTL' and the Ministry of Internal Affairs distributed a circular to rural commercial areas drawing attention to the danger of potential attacks.[125] The combining of civil and military efforts was carried out swiftly, beginning with the creation of Mutasa District, consisting of the Honde Valley, the New Reserve, and Watsomba. Thus, the administrative problem dating back to the beginning of settler rule, namely of having had to deal with an inaccessible frontier area split between two districts, was finally resolved under the banner of unity of command. District headquarters were located on the plateau close to the main road between Mutare and Nyanga, and staff accommodation, overlooking a valley towards the west, was built with the ongoing war in mind, even though it had not yet reached that area. The houses were built with walls in front of the windows to avoid mortar attacks, floodlights in the yard, and higher-ranking staff houses each had a bunker. The feeling this left long after independence was one of claustrophobia.[126] Despite the precautions, once ZANLA began operating in the area, they attacked the buildings from a hill nearby.

In May 1974, the DC Mutasa was instructed to provide the European farmers with circulars that provided advice for 'safe' farm management, including the necessity to keep 'good labour relations' in order to avoid being attacked: 'Labour relations appear to have a direct bearing on the attitude taken by the terrorists. The better the relationship the less likelihood there is of attacks. All employers of labour should, therefore, endeavour to have, and retain, good relationships with their labour.'[127] This shows that while the government officially insisted on portraying the liberation armies as communist barbarians who coerced the rural population into liberation activity, politicians and the administration had clearly recognised the political character of the insurgency. The DC was to establish a 'Civil Defence Co-ordinating Committee' for his district that added business and settler interest directly to the war effort.[128] The minutes of the committee meetings provide extraordinary testimony, not least because they illustrate how close cooperation was between civilian interest and the military effort. Even from March 1974, security issues had been treated as confidential and relevant documents were subsequently removed from running files at the plantations in the valley.[129]

By the end of 1974, part of the border with Mozambique was fenced between Honde River and Panga Mountain,[130] and the government built an airstrip for light aircraft at Hauna and an excellent tar road that runs through the valley to the tea plantations. In December of that year the first steps were taken to improve security at management staff housing at Aberfoyle, followed one month later with the introduction of Agric Alert, a call-system that eventually connected all the commercial tea and forestry estates, individual European households, the District Office, the police camp, and the Security Force camp in Mutasa district with each other.[131] The district defence plan was also drawn up in January 1975, detailing the responsibility of European residents in the area and liaison structures in case of attack.[132] In short, by the beginning of ZANLA's insurgency campaign in 1976, preparations to create 'civil' defence structures as a forum for settler and business interest and a combined civilian/government military effort were complete.[133] These measures played a vital role in shaping the lives of valley inhabitants.

The government initiated its military counter-insurgency campaign in the Honde Valley in response to Chief Tambudzayi Chikomba's abduction. A new Security Forces base camp was opened near Rumbizi and in order to stabilise the political situation an uncle of Tambudzayi's, Mpota, was appointed as acting chief in August 1974, as the abducted office holder was apparently still alive at the time.[134] Chief Mpota strongly supported the government, and in 1977 the DC praised his commitment when he wrote that since in office, '[he] has been regarded as one of our more loyal tribal leaders in the face of tremendous pressures from both within the area and from across the border.'[135] Mpota's swift appointment can only be explained by the fear of losing administrative and political control, something the government exercised in rural areas through 'tribal authority', especially during the war.[136] Between 1974 and 1978 the number of chiefs in the country was increased by five and headmen by sixteen, of whom three were introduced in the southern part of the Honde Valley.[137] After Chikomba's abduction, Mpotedzi, Sahumani, and Nyamandwe, who so far had been 'unrecognised headmen', now became formally appointed in order to fill 'a gap' in the local government's 'line of tribal control'.[138]

Despite the government's measures, in 1976 the military initiative was clearly with ZANLA, which operated from Holdenby, now a semi-liberated area. Things started to change, however, when Operation Crusader got under way in that same year. The RAR 'C' Company 2, under the leadership of a young, already highly decorated commander, Nick Fawcett, set out to bring the security situation in the valley under control.[139] The commander introduced a longer duty call than the usual six weeks in order to provide continuity and to achieve better knowledge of the operational area.[140] Another measure the administration took was to relieve DC 'Chick' Fowle from his post in January 1976. He was not highly regarded by European men in the district, in whose view he was 'too soft' and did not take the insurgency threat sufficiently seriously. In

11. Major Nick Fawcett of the Rhodesian African Rifles, 1976: officer in charge of the counter-insurgency campaign in the Honde Valley (Source: National Archives of Zimbabwe; detail of the original)

contrast, DC Hamish Peters, who would serve in Mutasa District in 1977, was a man who apparently saw his task as a family tradition, as his grandfather had been Native Commissioner (NC) during the First Chimurenga, 1896-97.[141] By June 1977, the RAR commander summarised the security situation as 'most favourable'.[142] In early 1978, a *Sunday Mail* article celebrated the success of the counter-insurgency campaign: 'The taming of the Honde Valley, on the border with Mozambique, is regarded as a remarkable success to Internal Affairs, working in co-operation with the Security Forces.'[143] The cornerstone in the turn of events from the onslaught of ZANLA attacks in 1976 was the villagisation of the entire valley population and will be examined below. First though, the focus will be on the role the valley came to play in the larger war effort.

NO BORDERS, NO BOUNDARIES

Contrary to the statement in the *Sunday Mail*, the concerted attempt by the Security Forces towards the 'taming of the Honde Valley' continued to fall short, not least because ZANLA continued to use the area as an infiltration route from Mozambique. Ironically, the valley was also serving two armies as a corridor into Mozambique: the Security Forces and the

Mozambique Resistance Movement (RENAMO). Part of the total war strategy deployed by the minority rule government was to attack the liberation movements and their armies in neighbouring countries through so-called 'hot pursuit', by deploying the air force and even ground troops, mostly in Mozambique and Zambia in an attempt to destabilise these 'frontier states'. Such strategies included the founding and support of RENAMO on Rhodesian soil. The prolonged liberation struggles in Lusophone Africa came to a successful end when the coup in Lisbon suddenly led to independence of the Portuguese colonies, including Mozambique, in 1975. This new majority rule left some settlers so disgruntled that, supported by the Rhodesian government, they founded RENAMO, on a tobacco farm in the Odzi area not far from the valley, in order to destabilise the newly independent government via cross-border attacks, claiming that their bandit movement was really a liberation army to free the people from the socialist government. ZANLA endured RENAMO crossing through their operational area, while they focused on their own struggle. [144]

The Honde Valley also became an ideal route into Mozambique for the notorious Selous Scouts, a Rhodesian unit that operated largely independently, often through pseudo-gangs. [145] A tactic adopted from Mau Mau in Kenya, where pseudo-gangs were introduced and run by police officer Ian Henderson, the approach was usually to capture enemy combatants, brain-wash them, add these men to their operational units, and then either pose as the enemy to gather information or stage violent incidents for which the enemy could then be blamed. [146] Katiyo, as a parastatal and with its airstrip, became a base for some of these operations between 1977 and 1979. Tea estate employees remembered that on one occasion two captured 'CTs' turned out to be well-disguised white Selous Scouts who had got lost during one of the operations in Mozambique and been given orders not to reveal their identity. Among the reasons the valley was chosen for cross-border operations were its location, the tea estates that provided European-controlled safe havens, and most importantly, once villagisation had been introduced, almost complete control over the movement of the civilian population. As a consequence, Selous Scouts were referred to as 'Eskimos', because they could freeze the valley at any given time, particularly at night, imposing curfews that even affected European staff and members of the Security Forces to enable the Scouts to operate in secrecy. [147] They carried out the ground attack on Chimoio from the valley, which was part of one of the war's most notorious 'hot pursuit' incidents. In November 1977, the Rhodesian air force bombed Chimoio, a ZANLA refugee and army camp in Mozambique, killing at least 1,200 men, women, and children. Freezing the Honde Valley was crucial, so that no warning of an impending attack could be given. The Selous Scouts then crossed the border from Katiyo to kill survivors of the air attack and to retrieve any useful materials. They transported even heavy armoury and other material back through the valley. [148]

Among the elders in the Honde Valley memories of hot pursuit attacks are vivid. *Mbuya* Moyo, whose war experiences were related in chapter four, remembered hearing the planes fly overhead and seeing the yellow napalm clouds over Chimoio. Others, embodying the unspeakable horror of the past by shuddering and shaking, the women clicking their tongues, recalled seeing

Mount Zaramira, the location of a refugee camp and the ZANLA base, on fire when fighter planes dropped napalm.[149] In 1990, the first time I stayed in the Honde Valley for a few days, I asked people for the names of landmarks. I referred to Mount Zaramira respectfully, not pointing my finger; that cultural insight was surprising to valley inhabitants when they first met me, but initially I could not understand why it was such a special site. Only once people came to trust me did they talk about the Chimurenga, and only when I witnessed conversations did I realise how deep a mark that mountain has in personal and social memory, and in the sense of belonging and community today. Zaramira is a mnemotope for war becoming hot, for unbearable suffering.

During a long interview session with a former administrator in Harare, his wife, apparently feeling somewhat excluded, and after interrupting numerous times, brought out the family photo album from the war years. She proudly showed a photograph of herself as a young woman carrying an FN rifle, and explained that she knew the war too, as she had served her country as an emergency clinic nurse on one of the tea estates. While telling her story somewhat defiantly, her voice changed as she recalled that she once faced a difficult situation. She became agitated, explaining that she could not understand why the army had wasted their resources on airlifting in an African teenage boy who had napalm burning into his flesh. Shifting to a slow and quiet voice, she described the severity of the injuries, her helplessness witnessing the unbelievable pain the boy went through. Quickly she became boisterous again and said that she was surprised that those 'people' – she used a derogatory term – could feel pain at all!

The moral, ethical, and legal implications of attacking an enemy on the territory of a foreign country with whom the government is not at war are obvious, and the position of the civilian population was debated as the war was going on. As is the norm for most forces involved in a counter-insurgency campaign, the Rhodesian government and its army argued that the enemy was cowardly for placing refugee camps next to military sites, and that their insistence of not distinguishing between civilian and combatant was responsible for the casualties. At that point, the term 'collateral damage' was not yet in use. From a humanitarian standpoint, it is clear that the government failed the standards of modern times. But the question remains unanswered whether a conventional army needs to draw a principled line in their pursuit of an insurgent enemy or whether the total war approach is acceptable in legal and moral terms.

Villagisation

In the Honde Valley, in 1977, Operation Rivet commenced. The goal was to resettle the entire valley population into so-called 'Protected Villages'. The villagisation programme was the most drastic counter-insurgency measure the government adopted vis-à-vis the civilian population during the liberation war. It caused tremendous suffering and is an example of the creativity of violence, with frontier people having to adapt to forced conditions. According to official estimates, approximately 750,000 people were resettled into more than 200 PVs throughout the country between 1974 and 1979.[150] In the Honde Valley, the

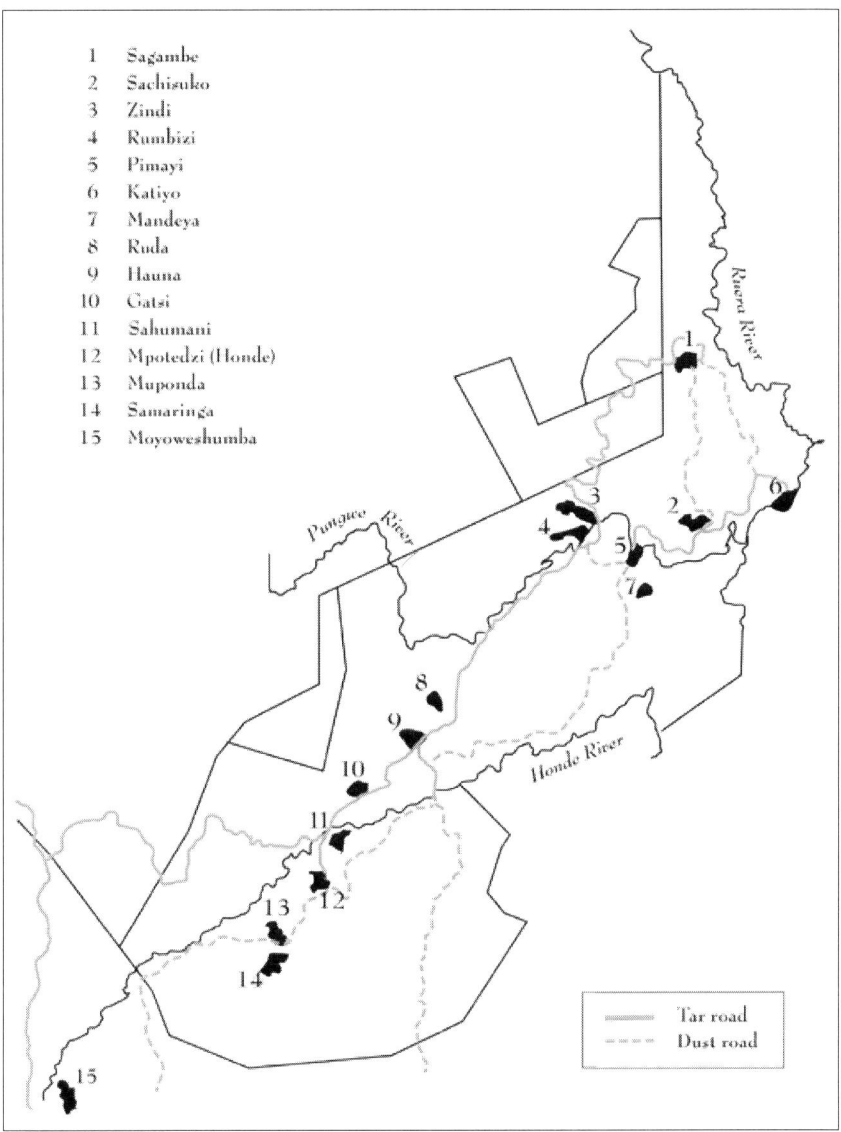

1   Sagambe
2   Sachisuko
3   Zindi
4   Rumbizi
5   Pimayi
6   Katiyo
7   Mandeya
8   Ruda
9   Hauna
10 Gatsi
11 Sahumani
12 Mpotedzi (Honde)
13 Muponda
14 Samaringa
15 Moyoweshumba

Map 3 Honde Valley: Protected Villages, c. 1978

population temporarily dropped from 60,000 to 20,000 people, although eventually two-thirds of the population were forcibly resettled.[151] What the government called 'Protected Villages' the villagers referred to as 'keeps', and in the valley also as 'the fence'. This section of the chapter will first look at how the programme was implemented and then examine the impact on villagers' lives and on the course of the war. What transpires is that villagisation caused tremendous suffering and at the same time provides an example for the creativity of violence, as the frontier people adapted to the forced conditions.

SEPARATING THE FISH FROM THE WATER

The collaboration between civil and military interests in the counter-insurgency campaign is most obvious with the villagisation programme in the Honde Valley. Prussian General Carl von Clausewitz famously postulated in 1832 that a state may deploy its troops in conventional war as 'a mere continuation of policy by other means'.[152] As important as villagisation was militarily to regain the initiative in the confrontation with ZANLA, much of the programme can only be understood as a continuation of economic policies by other means. The implementation of the NLHA and the tea outgrower scheme that had been so fervently resented and resisted from the 1950s, as well as measures to address the lack of a local labour supply to the plantations, were now executed with military force.

The strategic rationale of villagisation was that the programme would allow a clear distinction between civilian and combatant and also undercut support structures, to separate the fish from the water, to use Mao Zedong's phrasing. In the words of Internal Affairs: 'The essential aim is to deny wandering bands of terrorists the opportunity to live off rural settlements and intimidate the inhabitants.'[153] A ZANLA commander explained that a battlefield was created and asserted: 'We now met the enemy straight',[154] or, in the words of former PC Noel Hunt, who was instrumental in designing the Rhodesian villagisation programme, 'the army could have the area in between to act as a killing ground'.[155] In addition to the regular curfew hours from 6 p.m. to 6 a.m., and the occasional 'freezes', population movement was curtailed at all times and no-go areas, such as the western slopes of the valley and the Mapokana hills, covered approximately sixty per cent of the valley. The army was given orders to fire at anyone not a member of the Security Forces spotted in a no-go area or outside a keep during curfew. The Indemnity and Compensation Act, passed in 1975, but retroactive from 1972, protected all government employees, including the armed forces and police, from the consequences of any acts carried out in the course of duty, such as injuring or killing an innocent non-combatant; this measure escalated violence against civilians.[156]

Officially, the government claimed that villagisation had the benefit of providing safety in the PVs and of making crossfire unlikely. Accordingly, DC Mutasa explained local reactions to villagisation in 1977:

> Initially they didn't like the idea and they were very concerned about it, but gradually they realized that there were advantages in moving into the PVs, and that, contrary to

what the terrs [terrorists] said, they were protected, and they weren't subject to being knocked off, either by Security Forces or by the terrs.[157]

However, incidents involving civilians occurred frequently, for instance when a soldier on patrol opened fire on a woman who was collecting wood in the Mapokana Hills.[158] Moreover, when the villagisation exercise shifted the military balance in favour of the government troops, guerrillas specifically targeted PVs in an attempt to force the army to abandon the programme and to directly confront the Security Forces. According to government sources, ten per cent of the country's 200 Protected and Consolidated Villages were destroyed between September 1976 and October 1977, with more than seventy attacks in the first five months of 1977.[159] The most severe incident of that kind occurred in 1978, when ZANLA guerrillas attacked the military and police base in Ruda.[160] Such attacks necessarily created crossfire, as the Security Forces were stationed at the centre of the PV, and any fire exchange had to pass over the villagers who in effect became a buffer between guerrillas and the soldiers, thus making the actual keep housing the villagers' alleged protectors the safest part of the structure.

In Mutasa District, preparations for villagisation date back to April 1974 when, as part of the larger security exercise along the borders, the DC was instructed to identify possible PV sites.[161] During the same month, the Department of Conservation and Extension produced a pamphlet titled *Protected Farm Villages* that detailed necessary security installations for farmhouses and their labour compounds and was distributed to all commercial farmers. The government impressed on the settlers that labour compounds were to be arranged following the example of villagisation, already introduced in the Zambezi Valley, the site of the infiltration leading up to the December 1972 attacks in the north of the country.[162]

The army made an initial attempt to establish Ruda PV, close to their base camp, in December 1976, and after the Aberfoyle massacre during the same month, the government stepped in with full force. DC Peters, interviewed at the time, explained: 'The Honde Valley represents one of the most valuable areas of Rhodesia. We simply can't afford to lose this area – and we won't.'[163] Technocrats were brought in swiftly to plan PVs for the entire valley and were instructed to complete their task in three months, taking into consideration the plantations' labour demands, and basing their plans on blueprints of the PVs already established along other border sections.[164] Those blueprints in turn drew on the similar exercise carried out during Mau Mau in Kenya by the British colonial government, which in turn was informed by villagisation during the Malaya Emergency. Also, in the Honde Valley at least, some of the technocrats had background experience from having participated in the counter-insurgency efforts during Mau Mau. In short, villagisation in Zimbabwe was very much an exercise in the transfer of imperial, military, and scientific knowledge. Still, without further training and little assistance, apart from African DAs and members of a Coloured Protection Unit who were supposed to ensure the planner's safety in the valley, the task proved to be difficult.[165]

The person in charge of planning the valley's villagisation programme remembered that he had to work in a great rush and that 'the planning period

12. *'Adoption' of the Rhodesian African Rifle 'C' Company 2 by the Tea Estates, Aberfoyle 1978* (Source: Private Papers B)

13. *Lay-out of a Protected Village with the keep in the centre, 1975: Masawu keep, Mudzi area* (Source: National Archives of Zimbabwe)

14. Guard Force receive uniform and equipment, Honde Valley 1977 (Source: National Archives of Zimbabwe)

15. Forced villagisation, Honde Valley 1977 (Source: National Archives of Zimbabwe)

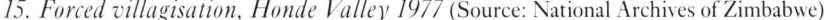

and setting were quite impossible'.[166] The operational headquarters frequently overruled agricultural and social considerations on military grounds. Although PV inhabitants were officially supposed to adopt intensive agricultural methods on fields in the vicinity of the keep, there were neither enough time nor resources to allocate land before the resettlement exercise. Despite the rush, the planning officer spent considerable time in the area surveying sites, but never consulted valley inhabitants. Even if they asked, he did not inform local people about his task, although, he recalled, they might have had their suspicions.[167] Indeed, a female elder said of Sagambe PV:

> So, when they established a keep here, they told us they would look after us and whatnot, but they did not tell us it was a keep. People were just told there would be the Native Commissioner's [sic] office here so as to serve the people – yet actually this was the keep. They did not want everybody to know that this was a keep, since they feared people might panic, as I have already mentioned that the people were afraid of getting into the keep, thinking they would then be killed.[168]

A group of men who recalled the move into Gatsi PV said: 'They were never given notice that they shall be in PVs. So these people thought the government is preparing camps for soldiers. Instead they were the ones who were put in those Protected Villages. They were never given notice.'[169] In the course of two day-long interviews, the technocrat emphasised that he had merely followed orders, and that he had done a perfect job under the circumstances by applying scientific knowledge to the best of his abilities. At the end of the two days spent poring over maps, he emphasised that I would have come to the same conclusions, had I had to apply myself to the problem.[170]

The resettlement exercise for the Honde Valley was codenamed 'Rivet'. According to DC Peters, the objectives, suitably reflected by the name, were:

> Together with the army, the police and the Ministries of Water Development, Roads, Health, African Education and the Veterinary Department it is our intention to forcibly re-locate the civilian population in the protected villages where they will be programmed to adapt to a new, though somewhat restricted way of life.[171]

Both the acknowledgment of forced resettlement and the technical language – 'programming' villagers – were characteristic also of similar operations elsewhere, such as the pipeline system and detention during Mau Mau.[172] Still, as in Kenya, this dehumanising language and practice contradicted official policies of 'winning the hearts and minds' of rural Africans. DC Mutasa argued that necessitated by 'the virtual total subversion of the local population by CT's … extreme measures' were to be taken in order to relocate the population.[173] He explained, 'We have to be seen to be strong.'[174]

The movement of people into the PVs was a military exercise co-ordinated by RAR Commander Fawcett. Operation Rivet lasted from March 1977 to the beginning of 1978 and resulted in sixteen PVs with an average population of 1,500 to 3,000 inhabitants.[175] The implementation moved largely from north to south, beginning with Zindi and Rumbizi PVs, followed by Sagambe, Sachisuko, Pimayi, Mandeya, Fenga, Ruda, and Hauna, all of which were occupied by August 1977.[176] From September, seven more PVs were planned for Manga and Mutasa North TTLs: Sahumani, Honde, Muponda, Samaringa, Gatsi, Samanga, and Moyoweshumba.[177] About a third of the valley population managed to flee across the border to Mozambique or move to urban areas.[178] Of the remainder, many people were forcibly resettled, although some moved voluntarily, hoping for greater security and less harassment from guerrillas and Security Forces. A villager recalled: 'We felt we had nowhere else to go.'[179] The PC claimed that 'the people are not unwilling to go into them [PVs], but, for their own safety, they wish it to be clearly seen that they are under compulsion by the Army'.[180] One area where there was unwavering resistance against resettlement was the Muparutsa chieftaincy.

DC Mutasa assembled Chief Muparutsa and his eighteen *masabhuku* on 8 November 1976. He instructed the latter to report to the chief on a daily basis about guerrilla activities in the area, a reflection on the security situation. When the *masabhuku* pleaded with him to relax the order, the DC agreed to reduce the frequency to every third day.[181] The DC also notified the men to prepare to move to Ruda PV 12 December. However, four days before the scheduled move, Security Forces surrounded the chief's homestead and forcibly moved him to Ruda:

> The soldiers were ordered to carry the chief's belongings aboard the army trucks. The chief left his home in a few minutes time. There was no-one else in the protected village. Two tin huts were immediately erected for the chief but these were too small to accommodate all his belongings. Some of the things are still in the open today, 1½ months after the incident of the forced transfer. The chief's wife, who had been at church on the Sunday morning when the chief was moved to the protected village, came back home to find it empty. She walked to the protected village to join her husband. Apart from the D.C. and army personnel, the chief and his wife are the only inhabitants of the Muparutsa [Ruda] P.V.[182]

This pre-emptive measure was probably designed to ensure that the Muparutsa people could be resettled easily a few days later. However, when they learnt what had happened, they left the valley. Some remained in the country and stayed with relatives in towns and other rural areas, but most crossed the border with *muzvare* Muparutsa, much to the embarrassment of the army, whose base camp was located close to the keep.[183]

Ruda PV continued to remain vacant, and subsequently the government first threatened to and then actually did destroy the Muparutsa people's property:

> Because the people in this part of Honde Valley refused to live in a protected village, the Security Forces combed the area on 7 January 1977, burning down the people's houses, huts and granaries. People who witnessed the burning describe the palls of smoke that covered the area as the soldiers went on rampage from home to home.[184]

Still, in February 1977, the PC had to admit that Ruda PV was virtually empty 'due to voluntary departure from the area of most of the inhabitants', although he did expect them to return.[185] But by June the situation had not changed: whereas other PVs in the valley had populations of up to 3,000 people, only 250 lived at Ruda.[186] The government made a last and unusual attempt by issuing an order for them to return to the Honde Valley in two newspapers, the *Umtali*

Post and the *Rhodesian Herald.* Some came to collect their movable property, but still rejected villagisation.[187] The local RAR commander summarised the situation accordingly when he stated that the Muparutsa people made Ruda PV a 'white elephant'.[188] Even Chief Muparutsa left the PV in December 1976 under the pretext of visiting relatives in Harare for Christmas, but then refused to return.[189] The DC appears to have been infuriated by this, and in July 1977 he recommended the chief's suspension, which was confirmed:

> Despite all efforts to get Headman Muparutsa to move into Ruda protected village he has continued to disobey all instructions and orders to move…. The Muparutsa people have scattered, a mere 250 remaining in the area and our intelligence shows they have no intention of returning to the Valley.
>
> Today in the presence of Acting Chief Mutasa, Headman Muparutsa formally refused to go and live in Ruda PV and in view of his political history I have no intention of forcing him to do so.[190]

The government and the army were helpless in countering resistance against villagisation in the Muparutsa area. The chief later lived at Old Mutare Mission, where he died in 1982; his people only returned after independence.[191] Those from other parts of the valley who stayed suffered in the keeps, and acts of sabotage were common even post-resettlement. Meanwhile, after the ZANLA incident of February 1976 at Zindi Business Centre, the managers of the tea plantations started to become directly involved in the villagisation exercise, which was driven by business interest as much as it was by strategic concerns.

THE CONTINUATION OF LAND POLICIES BY OTHER MEANS

Security concerns became part of everyday life in the Honde Valley and tea plantation management requested protective measures, such as armed presence at strategic points, twice-daily mine-sweeping on bus routes, and tarring of the access roads to the estates.[192] When help was only partly forthcoming due to strained government resources,[193] the estates asked for further assistance in establishing labour PVs on their land: 'We are now of the opinion that the time has come to ask Government to consider our main [sic] compounds "protected villages": Fenced with horizontal barbed wire, plus vertical strands, to a height of 8', AND [sic] protected by fire [-power]'.[194] In August, another request followed for PV-style labour compounds with protection by the Guard Force, a unit created specifically for the purpose of serving PVs, and for further villagisation throughout the valley in order to secure local labour supplies, with the expectation that the workers would mostly be 'girls'.[195] However, in September, tea management found that 'the labour force would resign rather than live behind security fencing'.[196] The April 1974 pamphlet to farmers had already proposed labour committees,[197] and once villagisation was under way, such a body was implemented.

The Honde Valley Labour Committee met thirty-three times between March 1977 and April 1980.[198] The constitution of the committee stated that the meetings should be attended by two representatives from each plantation, the manager of Rumbizi tea scheme as the ex-officio government representative, and a member of the local Joint Operations Command (JOC). Even at the founding meeting the central questions of labour supply, the standardisation and uniformity in labour relations that resulted in reduced wages, and the allocation of tea fields to PVs were discussed. While some emphasised that labour had to come forward voluntarily, the EHTE manager, who stood out with his especially austere views towards the African population, pointed out that three months after resettlement villagers would be so desperate for food they would be forced to work on the estates. He expressed regret that 'school children could not put in a full day's work due to their school commitments'.[199] The collaboration between the tea industry and the military was very close, though opinions were not always unanimous. Notwithstanding the tea industry's implication in the counter-insurgency efforts, in 1992, an article in the *Air Zimbabwe* magazine celebrated the 'romantic history of tea'.[200]

Once the PVs were established, private business and the government's investment in Katiyo and Rumbizi continued to profoundly shape the lives of the villagers, initially causing much resistance. Plans to use the war effort to generate a local labour supply dated back to 1974, when a Tribal Trust Land Development Corporation (TILCOR) report envisaged the villages as nuclei settlements, with Rumbizi as a nucleus estate; outgrower tea block cultivation, named 'village tea blocks'; and minimal food crop production.[201] In 1976, even before ComOps was in place, the Ministry of Internal Affairs instructed TILCOR to draw up a land use plan for the PVs,[202] with the advice that villagers should not be allowed to cultivate arable land in excess of absolute minimum subsistence requirements.[203] Implementation of these measures became crucial after the Aberfoyle massacre, when the labour position on the plantations became disastrous, as summarised by one of the managers: 'The serious deterioration of the security situation in the Honde Valley during the 1976/77 season, brought the tea industry to a standstill.'[204] Despite the labour crisis, the tea management conceded that recruitment should only begin once the villagers had completed the construction of basic facilities in the keeps.[205]

Initially, resistance against plantation labour continued, even though most villagers had lost access to their fields and were tightly controlled in their access to the production areas. The villagers demanded one Rhodesian Dollar per day, instead of the standard wage of 60 cents paid to male workers (50 cents for women and 45 cents for juveniles, with increments for uninterrupted service) that the plantations had raised uniformly to that level only in April. Again, management turned to the military, but when the locally based RAR Company was assigned to assist labour recruitment from the PVs in May 1977, Commander Fawcett made clear that he and his men did not wish to be involved in 'extortion':

> [He] stated that his men were not happy with their role in the operation. They too considered that for the amount and type of work 60 cents was inadequate and they felt they were being unwilling accomplices to extortion. He said he had misgivings about daily payments as it tended to accentuate a daily payment that hardly met the cost of 5 kilos of mealie meal in the local shops.[206]

Despite this temporary obstacle, relations between the tea estates and the military were very cordial. The management expressed their appreciation by 'adopting' the RAR 'C' Company 2 through forming a welfare fund in July 1977, and later they arranged a reunion and parties for the soldiers at the estates for which Rhodesian 'girls' were brought in for troop entertainment.[207] More importantly, when the labour shortage continued, the estates eventually increased the wages in June to 85 cents per day plus a bonus. Clearly, the bargaining power still tipped in favour of the workers.[208]

Another measure that affected the labour situation was Operation 'Turkey', first introduced in January 1977 and designed to prevent villagers from assisting guerrillas by providing them with food. The civil defence committee also expected Operation 'Turkey' to push the villagers into tea estate employment in order to cover their households' most basic needs. The operation entailed strict regulations for store-owners, and no villager was allowed to 'have in his possession more than seven kilograms of food at any time', or to take food outside the PV, even when working in the fields during the day.[209] The latter order caused hardships, particularly for small children and pregnant women who had to spend the entire day without food.[210]

Initially, the impact of villagisation on household income was drastic. Villagers lost access to their fields and there was tight control of the newly allocated production areas. An EHTE employee stated that he had left his employment after the Aberfoyle massacre. However, by mid-1977 he saw no alternative but to return:

> It is true that we were all warned before to stop work [by the guerrillas] because of low wages but we could not stop work because we want to earn our living. I returned two weeks ago for work because there is nothing else that I can do since the soldiers destroyed our property burning our huts. I am working in order to support my family. War is everywhere and we have to put up with it.[211]

Despite the tremendous economic pressure on the villagers, during the early months of 1977, seeking employment on the tea plantations was still the exception. Overall, resistance against plantation labour continued.

In May 1977, the DC acknowledged the desperation of the villagers' situation: 'There is still food in the lands but it does not take long for the weeds to grow here and the baboons will have the mealies before too long. By June there will be nothing left.'[212] This prediction proved true when the severe shortage in foodstuffs peaked in June, during the dry season. RAR commander Fawcett, however, when investigating reactions to the recruitment exercise in Zindi PV, found that detailed demands were made to improve working conditions on the estates and that 'none liked to be forced to work'.[213] Finally, the implementation of the TILCOR plan made resistance against labour recruitment impossible. The PVs in Holdenby were zoned between the four estates and the villagers were transported to and from them each day.[214] The de facto forced labour system began to work, and by May 1978 '[p]eople were being turned away daily.'[215]

In sum, the villagisation program in the Honde Valley, Operation Rivet, was successful in restoring the commercial capacity of the area for a government that saw itself increasingly under economic pressure because of the war effort and economic sanctions. In Holdenby, technocrats planned the specifics of the PVs primarily to satisfy the labour demand of the tea industry, but strategic considerations were also important. Operation Rivet transformed the valley from a frontier area that was almost beyond state access in the early 1950s into one where, by mid-1977, both population and territory were under sufficient control to ensure that ZANLA attacks were limited to rare occasions. As a consequence, the valley became an ideal corridor for counter-insurgency operations across the border into Mozambique, but it still remained a militarily contested area. Operation Rivet though was of limited success, as the regime failed to win the villagers' hearts and minds.

LIFE BEHIND THE FENCE

At least during the initial sweep, the soldiers rounded up the valley population at night without giving notice. They burnt the homesteads and all possessions and foodstuffs that were left behind in order to discourage people from returning and at the same time to destroy potential shelter for guerrillas. The soldiers 'escorted' the villagers to the PV sites.[216] There, they found themselves inside a perimeter fence, encircling more or less cleared ground and the actual keep, the heavily fortified area, at the central and most strategic point of the PV, where the administrative buildings and staff quarters were located. The European keep commander was instructed to tell them upon arrival that from now on they would live inside the security fence and to brief new arrivals on procedures and security precautions, such as curfew regulations within the PVs themselves. Villagers were locked inside until the exercise was completed, and movement would be restricted thereafter, as anybody entering or leaving the PV would be searched at the gates, which would be closed at all times. The commander then sorted the newcomers into 'kraal groups', registered them, and assigned blocks to the *masabhuku*, who were supposed to continue their duties as 'tribal leaders' in the new location. The keep commander was to allocate later a stand of 15 metres by 25 metres inside the PV to each married woman and ideally one hectare of arable land per family outside the fence. Finally, the villagers were instructed to settle in, fetch water, collect firewood, and prepare their 'shelters', for which sheeting was distributed in this high rainfall area: 'Issue to each head of family black polythene sheeting at the rate of 1 metre per person over the age of 2 years. Some flexibility may be permitted regarding the assessment of ages.'[217]

On their first day in the keep, the DC delivered a 'Psychological Action' address. Villagers were then classified according to age, sex, and physical ability and each group was assigned tasks. 'Young and old women capable of work' and young men would then return to their villages as 'collection parties' under army escort and be allowed to collect building materials, food, and movable property before rejoining their families and constructing facilities and their huts in the PV. Only after this was completed were community and woman advisers, agricultural extension staff, and development workers supposed to help people to restructure their lives in the new environment.[218] The resettlement exercise was formalised by precise administrative procedures, including notices signed by the respective *sabhuku* and witnesses (in triplicate) that ordered the destruction of all property outside the PVs seven days after their arrival. DC Peters insisted that: 'Firmness and fairness must be the key to all our dealings with the local population.' In contrast to his successor, Bundock, who claimed that PVs were 'just like an English village system', the terms for the villagers were made clear: 'Following the destruction of all kraals, dwellings, property etc. abandoned in terms of orders issued by the Protecting Authority all persons will be advised that the return to their villages will mean that they will be shot as terrorist collaborators.'[219]

Villagisation conventionalised the war by drawing a spatial and conceptual line between civilians living inside PVs and the outside battlefield, and it affected guerrilla tactics significantly. Without doubt, Operation Rivet dealt a blow to ZANLA operations in the Honde Valley. One ex-combatant remembered: 'Apart from the war now, the direct confrontation with the enemy, there was another war that we were fighting – for survival! We wanted food and these people had been pushed with their food into keeps![220] But despite the difficulties, when asked to compare his experience in the valley with other areas where he had operated, he insisted: 'Honde was sweet to me, very sweet!'[221] The government had spatially separated the fish from the water – the insurgents from the civilians – but the valley remained an operational area because ZANLA succeeded in modifying support structures.[222] Previously, units had introduced themselves to chiefs and *masabhuku*, had held *pungwes*, and solicited supplies from specific households. When the valley inhabitants were moved behind the fence, this was no longer possible. Consequently, the fighters created communal organisation networks through the chiefs and *masabhuku*, with each family contributing food, clothes, cigarettes, and other goods. A *sabhuku* recalled: 'I used to order them [villagers] to make *sadza* to take there [to the guerrillas].'[223] Women would then prepare and carry the food, hidden on their bodies or among their belongings to the fields, and child messengers took the supplies to the ZANLA fighters. Children played a greater role after villagisation because it somewhat limited the role of *mujibhas* and *chimbwidos*, the juveniles assisting the guerrillas. Their mobility outside the keeps was severely confined. Also, the local ZANLA commander maintained that youths were not trusted in organisational positions, as they were 'too ambitious', whereas 'married and old people were more careful with what they said',[224] something that was crucial with the Security Forces always close by.

Guerrilla appeals probably also became more successful for two additional reasons. First, to an unprecedented degree, the villagers set themselves apart from the migrant labourers on the plantations. After the Aberfoyle massacre in December 1976, attempts to recruit labour from Chipinge District, the other tea-producing area in the country, met with some success. These were usually skilled labourers and personnel who held supervisory positions, whereas the villagers were employed mainly as tea pickers, and under semi-forced conditions.[225] Not surprisingly, tensions arose, further exacerbated because the Chipinge workers usually were chiNdau speakers, seen as the ethnic group that supported RENAMO at the time, and associated with the *madzviti* raids of the nineteenth century.[226] Resident labour on the tea estates became increasingly discredited amongst villagers when guerrillas explained to them that the estates generated capital that was invested in the war effort and thus had to be sabotaged. They promised that the plantations would be nationalised after independence and that villagers would become plot-holders.[227] One of the men from Chipinge who had started work at Aberfoyle at the onset of the war remembered how things changed in 1977. Even though he was married to a local woman, he now found himself forced to visit her secretly in her village:

> We [resident labour] used not to go to places. Because if you go there, otherwise you would disappear. That was the problem. So it was a boundary. Those in the communal area, they used to stay there, those in the compound, they used to stay here .... Even to visit, it was difficult.[228]

A second factor strengthening guerrilla–civilian relations was that after villagisation coercion decreased. It might appear surprising that even outgrowers were targeted less frequently after 1977. By the beginning of 1976 there were 75 outgrowers under TILCOR who, by 1978, were cultivating 116 ha of tea.[229] They had their green leaf collected under army protection and were therefore directly implicated in the war effort.[230] Nevertheless, ZANLA units recognised that these outgrowers – and storekeepers – had cash incomes and were more likely able to provide material support in these difficult times.[231]

Aspects specific to the valley further facilitated the reorganisation of support structures. First, due to the abundant environmental resources, it was possible for guerrillas to survive on fruit and roots, which meant they could reduce the frequency of contact with villagers.[232] Second, villagisation and hardships in the PVs even alienated those who had moved voluntarily. Villagers voiced complaints about the harsh living conditions: the strict controls at the gates, curfew regulations, the keeps being locked down for long periods after a contact, and being prohibited from taking food to the fields, without exceptions even for small children.[233] Despite these tight controls, however, villagers found various ways to maintain support for the guerrillas, as one man remembered: 'Each time we went out of the keep, they [guerrillas] told us they were hungry. All the foodstuffs were in the keep. We did not want to see them hungry, since we wanted to be liberated. We devised methods to bring them food.'[234] Usually, women smuggled supplies out, but at times the fence was cut by guerrillas or food was thrown across. Fighters even entered PVs by swopping clothes with male villagers, carrying their identity cards, while those they were masquerading as spent the night at the guerrilla base. If the fighter vaguely resembled the photograph on the identity card, it was unlikely that the guards would notice the difference. These collective support structures appear to have continued even throughout the challenging period of 1978/79, when increasingly 'rogue guerrillas' were operating in the valley: young and often untrained men who were less disciplined than those in previous units.[235]

The PV programme was a dramatic intervention in the valley landscape and everyday life. ZANLA effectively adjusted the support structures, while most villagers experienced severe everyday suffering. For a few, PVs did provide some social and material success, and at a younger age than was usually possible. Such achievement is reflected in the life of a man, born in 1957.[236] He had only attended school for one year when he started his professional life at the age of eleven. For the following nine years he engaged in a variety of casual labour in the valley and adjacent areas. He married his first wife in 1974 and by 1976 he had learnt to be a builder. The establishment of the keeps marked the beginning of his career. He first constructed buildings at the newly established sites and then made buckets and dishes for the villagers. This earned him and his family enough money to open a store in one of the PVs.[237] The young man therefore benefited from the initial keep period, as well as the controlled flow of goods that privileged the few store owners. He also profited later from the end of villagisation and subsequent reconstruction efforts. During the ceasefire period, he drove a lorry which he used to access regional markets.[238] In 1982 to 1984, when most people left the PVs and re-established their homesteads, he worked as a builder and carpenter and raised a considerable income.[239] His success can be explained by the economic opportunities villagisation introduced and by the absence of older, better-qualified men.

Another example of a 'new big family' is that of Mpota Chikomba. From a young age, in the 1910s, he had been a migrant labourer in South Africa, where he had become a leader of one of the Vapostori churches.[240] In 1968, he decided to retire to the Honde Valley with his South African wife and their six surviving children, all of whom had been born in South Africa.[241] The government's choice to name him acting chief following Chief Chikomba's abduction came as a surprise to people in the area, and from then on the family fate took an unexpected turn.[242] Mpota and his family became deeply drawn into the politics of war. He supported the villagisation programme and thus, from the government's point of view, turned out to be the ideal appointment: 'Headman Chikomba has recently spoken out strongly in support of the Government and the need for protected villages. The stability of Sagambe P.V. is an example of how strong tribal leadership can influence the population into a peaceful and co-ordinated adjustment to a new way of life.'[243] But it was his wife Emily, *mbuya* Mpota, who played a particularly significant role in this process. Her husband was already elderly and feeble when he came to office and the Ministry of Internal Affairs asked her to visit PVs in Chiweshe in order to prepare her for her new role as a community leader in Sagambe PV, and at a time when nobody else had even been forewarned of the impending villagisation.[244] She remembered glowingly how she advised her husband and that she herself presided over court cases, because he was blind and therefore, as she argued, unable to assess testimonies. It was not unusual for journalists to interview her and portray her as an outspoken woman, as did war reporter Chris Ashton in 1978:

> Emily Chikomba, mother, wife of the headman and herself a trade store owner and tea farmer asks: 'Do you know why we want development here? Because it will keep our children close to us. In the past they have grown up and gone away to the towns. They have become delinquents, some of them. We have lost them. We want development so they will stay and work here.[245]

The years in the keep represented a period of personal empowerment for her; the prosperity and rising importance of the family continued after independence.

Mbuya Mpota claimed that even after her husband's death in 1984 some people asked her to continue hearing cases.[246] The newly independent government assessed the chief as having influence merely over the '60- and 80 year-old people', while the administration praised his wife for her development efforts: '[She] is a powerful, intelligent, influential and active woman who has taken a lot of initiative in development activities generally connected with women, not only in her area but in other parts of the District.'[247] It appears that Mpota Chikomba's and his wife's war-related career enabled their eldest son to also become a big man. At Sagambe PV he was the local World Vision represent-ative, and by the early 1990s, when he contested the chieftainship, he was a well-established businessman, living at the former keep site in what was locally referred to as 'the palace'.

KEEP ETHNICITY

The Rhodesian government claimed that the PVs served to protect the civil-ian population from terrorist intimidation and that villagisation would pro-vide higher living standards and even generate rural prosperity.[248] At the time, human rights organisations and scholars feared that the often harsh living conditions would cause social disruption.[249] In the Honde Valley, at least, the opposite was true: the villagers were ever more vulnerable to violence and dep-ravation, and the pressure of living behind the fence under constant observation by the Guard Force, while the local ZANLA units still demanded support, made social cohesion crucial for surviving these trying times. Consequently, the frontier ethnicity underwent yet another, if temporary, transformation, as a new sense of community was created and a distinctive keep ethnicity emerged.

In a PV, a certain degree of social control, interdependency, and organisation was required to transform guerrilla support from a household and neigh-bourhood matter into one of collective responsibility. This reflects the most significant element of this new sense of community and belonging: support for ZANLA and absolute silence about the war and internal grievances became civic virtues, crucial elements of the keep ethnicity that was crafted under extreme duress. The safety of everybody involved depended on the certainty that not a single villager would raise an alarm about guerrilla support.[250] There is no evidence of sell-out accusations and community-based violence, because the slightest suspicion could have led to drastic collective punishment by the Security Forces.[251] Moreover, part of the hardship in the PVs was the extreme spatial constraint: in contrast to the privacy afforded by the scattered home-steads in the TTLs, the proximity of neighbours made life very public. An elder explained his keep experience: 'We live so closely together. When I turn in my bed and cough, my neighbour wakes up.'[252] Consequently, collaboration could barely be kept a secret.

Such social control, however, was double-sided. It was exactly because of this transparency and intimate knowledge of each other that it became almost impossible to chide one's neighbour for his or her annoying, suspicious, objec-tionable, or dangerous behaviour. Accordingly, grievances brought to *mbuya* Mpota's attention related to hardship caused by the Security Forces, but rarely involved other villagers. Also, despite the tightening communal control, social gaps and niches emerged that enabled challenges to the established consensus on social roles and status. It became possible to contest gender, age, and social hierarchies. This was further facilitated by the striking demographic impact of the villagisation programme. Not only did the valley population drop dramatically from 1974, the age and gender composition also changed. It was mostly men who left the valley and few of the male migrant labourers who were absent at the time returned before the end of the Chimurenga.[253] An ex-combatant pointed out that the war provided an opportunity for some men to escape obligations such as debts, whereas mothers with their children were less mobile. He argued: 'And all the dangers that were created by the war, mostly, they were directed to women, because they are the people who are mostly caught in between, you see. I know of quite a number of comrades who just left their wives and disappeared.'[254] Initially, young women and girls also left as a sense of social and military instability prevailed, but by September 1977, 'a large number of young girls were returning to the Valley now that there was safety in the Villages'.[255] In 1978, with many young people escaping in order to join ZANLA,[256] PV populations consisted largely of women of all ages, youths, children, and old men. The population of Zindi PV, for example, comprised 248 men, 553 women, 78 juvenile males, and 143 juvenile females in April 1977. In June of the same year, Rumbizi PV was inhabited by 184 men, 360 women, and 786 juveniles.[257] This demographic transformation had a three-fold impact on gender relations in the keeps.

First, women and juveniles seized the increased sexual and other opportunities in the absence of their male guardians and under the enforced silence. Even before the Chimurenga, male workers and employees of the tea estates provided a chance for women to enter sexual relations outside their communities. Some lived with men as *mapoto* (common law) wives, literally wives 'who share the cooking pots'. In such arrangements on the plantations, a woman lived with a man in single quarters, usually illegally. However, when fenced and guarded labour compounds were established on the estates, these women were evicted and the management observed that this generated problems: 'restlessness has been noticed.… It was felt it was a social problem amongst the single males who were cut off from female company …. There appeared no solution and while married men were preferred because of the element of family stability, the strain on available accommodation was considerable.'[258]

Another indicator of increasing sexual mobility is that in the keeps cases of adultery escalated and sexual abuse on part of the Guard Force became common.[259] By April 1978, one outcome that had been observed by the tea management was the rise of venereal diseases 'at a dramatic rate' among young women. The women blamed this development on the Guard Force; this was confirmed by the Provincial Medical Officer.[260] The management complained that: 'Many working days were being lost by female tea pickers at Rumbizi and Katiyo while they underwent treatment. The villagers blamed the present high incidence of V.D. on the guards whose approaches they could not reject without risking reprisals.'[261] By July 1978, the issue had escalated so far that a tea estate representative asked ComOps to look into the matter.[262] Despite the spread of diseases and their suffering, many young people also saw positive elements in life behind the fence, as they had the opportunity to escape parental control. A young man recalled that the proximity of other young people and the township character of keep life made it interesting.[263]

A second effect of villagisation and the demographic shift was that some women began engaging in sex work. The centre of such activities was the Rambanayi 'hotel' at Zindi Business Centre, and later PV, in the vicinity of Rumbizi and EHTE. Women had solicited clients there before the war, but it appears that with the large increase of paying customers and a lack of local male control, sex work became fully commercialised during the Chimurenga. The attack at the hotel in February 1976 was, in fact, a carefully planned ambush helped by the sex workers, who supported ZANLA. One night, when they expected police customers, they signalled to the fighters, who assembled the men 'from the bedrooms' for execution.[264] In 1977, an African representative of TILCOR who inspected PVs from which labour was drawn for Rumbizi estate wrote about the 'hotel' rather appropriately, under the heading 'Life':

> The Pungwe Hotel [is] locally named 'RAMBANAYI' which literally means 'DIVORCE'. This name did not only exist to be called but to put things in practice. Young girls also had to know from others what happens in big cities, being not family controlled they bore many illegitimate children. Many men did not like it because they thought men died in numbers to leave women to more freedom.[265]

Apparently, the combination of the increase in the number of potential customers with spending power, together with relaxing social control due to keep life, led to such a development.[266] Finally, the incidence of polygyny and the number of women married to one man increased in the PVs. Young women realised that their personal safety was threatened and that they were facing economic hardship. With few young men present, it was mostly the male elders, many of whom were members of the Vapostori churches, who became patrons of women through marriage. An old man maintained that the Vapostori churches became popular 'because there are many women to be married. If one fails to get a woman to marry, he joins the Vapostori church.'[267] A female elder remembered that there were few Vapostori before the war and that villagisation 'marked an era of much marriage'.[268]

Life in the keeps challenged not only gender relations, but also age status. Some male elders gained seniority by marrying women, but their authority was undermined by shortcomings in their guardianship over females whom they could not efficiently protect from the Guard Force in the keeps or from ZANLA outside. The often-humiliating treatment by government employees and soldiers affected older men in particular.[269] Their loss of authority is reflected in the account of a PV in the Honde Valley in a pro-government magazine that reported men resisting orders to clear undergrowth along the fence line:

> Nineteen-year-old Internal Affairs cadet Erica Jones of Bulawayo had summoned a meeting of the villagers to hear their grievances, channel them to the proper authorities and persuade them on the basis that it was a security hazard to clean the fenceline.
>
> They didn't have the time, the tribesmen replied. The Government should do it because it had built the fence. Alternatively, it should pay the villagers to clear it.[270]

Even though cadet Jones listed all the benefits the government provided as part of villagisation, she did not succeed in her task:

> The meeting broke up with the issue unresolved. Internal Affairs was adamant that the

fenceline would be cleared even if a little arm-twisting was necessary. Beer brewing, which requires Government permission, could be banned and the PV gates closed all day to bring the villagers round.[271]

It was exactly such measures as this 'arm-twisting', in this case employed by a female teenager, which corrupted male elder authority.

In sum, the government pursued villagisation as a crucial counter-insurgency measure along its border with Mozambique in response to the December 1972 attack in Centenary District. With the plans already at hand, and the plantation management's interest articulated after the Aberfoyle massacre of December 1976, Operation Rivet could get underway quickly and efficiently, not least because of the transfer of imperial knowledge from Malaya to Kenya and Zimbabwe. This war effort in the Honde Valley was without doubt a military and economic success, but as the Security Forces never managed to extinguish entirely relations between the villagers and the local ZANLA units, the area remained a crucial infiltration route into the country. Ironically, becoming a war frontier during the Chimurenga severely undermined the frontier character of the valley once the PVs were created, simply because they constrained valley inhabitants' mobility. However, despite the severe hardships of keep life, villagers succeeded in creating a keep ethnicity that generated a sense of identity and belonging. After the war this led to tension between those who had remained and those who had left the valley. In fact, with independence, when villagers had the option of leaving the PVs, many did not do so immediately, and some even decided to stay indefinitely. Thus forced communities turned into chosen ones. But that was not the end of villagisation programmes in the Honde Valley – they were reintroduced in the late 1980s when RENAMO operations in the area became so severe that the post-colonial government implemented counter-insurgency measures based on the same blueprints.

Another War: RENAMO

Zimbabwe gained independence in April 1980, but peace in the Honde Valley did not last for long. *Mambo* Abishai Mutasa, talking about the Honde Valley in the late 1980s, remarked: 'They were still at war, while others had peace.'[272] RENAMO, at that time referred to in Zimbabwe by the English acronym 'MNR', had begun their operations in the 1970s by infiltrating Mozambique across the border,[273] using the Honde Valley as their major route, but in 1980 had to relocate to South Africa. Soon, RENAMO angered their hosts by attacking the power line from Mozambique's Cabora Bassa Dam that provides South Africa with electricity. After the Nkomati Accord of 1984, RENAMO shifted their base to Mozambique, at which point their strength was estimated to be as high as 20,000.[274] That same year, 1984, the first fighters were sighted in Mutasa District, apparently in search of food,[275] but it was only after RENAMO declared war against Zimbabwe in 1986, because the latter supported the FRELIMO government's war effort, that their main onslaught across the border commenced. The war lasted until the signing of the Rome Accord on 4 October 1992.[276] The areas most affected were Chimanimani, Chipinge, and Rushinga Districts – and the Honde Valley.[277] The day the ceasefire was declared in Rome, RENAMO troops came down to the Pungwe River at Katiyo estate, jubilantly holding up their AK-47s.

While it was going on, valley inhabitants emphasised that the effects of the RENAMO war were worse than the Chimurenga, because of the insurgents' cruelty and indiscriminate killing. A female elder who recalled her suffering during the liberation war when she lived in a PV concluded her account by saying: 'But *matsangas* [RENAMO] were worse.'[278] Another emphasised the fact that RENAMO caused much anguish: 'We really feared the axe!'[279] The fighters frequently used machetes to chop their victims' spines, particularly those of children, and during the conflict women commonly used the chopping motion to express their fear or to signal that RENAMO might be close.

At the beginning of the offensive in 1987, attacks were concentrated on representations of the Zimbabwean state, as, for example in July, when RENAMO bombed the Katiyo tea factory, a parastatal.[280] A newspaper article pointed out the irony that RENAMO, initially a Rhodesian creation, was now attacking the tea industry, something the Rhodesian state had made every effort to defend during the Chimurenga.[281] Even more bizarrely, Katiyo was one of RENAMO's main infiltration points into Mozambique in the 1970s.[282] The period of recovery from the Chimurenga was brief for the valley, as the violence soon spread. Bus services were not yet fully re-established by 1984 and three years later ambushes, landmines, and abductions of children necessitated the renewal of restrictions, such as the re-introduction of a dusk-to-dawn curfew, because the security situation deteriorated rapidly.[283] Recruitment was at times voluntary, as in the case of a chief's son, but the relationship between youths and RENAMO was ambiguous, because the latter frequently abducted boys and killed children.[284] Between July 1988 and January 1989 alone, 420 RENAMO-related incidents, including the murder of 93 Zimbabweans and 139 abductions, were reported throughout the country.[285]

In 1990, when RENAMO activities reached their peak in the area, stores outside the plantations and former keep sites were closed and the burnt remains of huts scattered the northern part of the valley. In February, in the Chikomba area, RENAMO killed four people in one incident and in another attack on a homestead left five members of a family axed to death and the father paralysed; only one child who was hiding survived unharmed.[286] A less visible effect of the long-term destabilisation was the drop in school enrolment and overall deteriorating education; experienced teachers refused to work in the area, forcing the government to post mostly young women teachers.[287]

On Sunday 23 September 1990, the Katiyo soccer team and a lorry full of fans travelled to Aberfoyle for a Honde Valley cup game. Everybody was merry, the game was great fun. The return journey had been planned for the afternoon, but it was delayed as the game had started late. Most men were drunk and everybody on the lorry sang until dusk fell, after which there was silence, which appeared to deepen once the journey commenced on the dust road. Despite the short distance, the drive took one and a half hours, as the lorry was old, travelled very slowly around the hairpin bends and to avoid detonating land mines, and took a long route in order to drop workers from Holdenby as close to their homesteads as possible. When people reached their homes, the driver stopped and shone the headlights into the bush to light their way. Every time the driver slowed down or stopped, the silence became even more pronounced given our increased vulnerability to an ambush. The silence was broken as some people repeated over and over that there would be a RENAMO attack and that everybody would die; both women and men cried with fear. When the driver stopped for a bathroom break, nobody dared to leave the immediate vicinity of the lorry for fear of landmines or abduction. Everybody got off and urinated standing next to each other, men at the back, women at the front of the lorry. Finally, after passing through the security gates of Katiyo estate, guarded by Zimbabwe National Army (ZNA) soldiers, the singing commenced.

RENAMO insurgents brought terror to the valley, but the presence of these armed men was not only feared and at times resisted, but also accommodated, as was that of other young men with guns in the previous decade. From the late 1980s, RENAMO operations in the Honde Valley shifted from political insurgency to warlordism and banditry, and increasingly focused on establishing trading and bartering networks with valley inhabitants.[288] At the peak of the war in 1990, local MP Oppah Rushesha, a ZANLA ex-combatant, harshly accused the local inhabitants of collaborating with RENAMO when she addressed people at Sagambe: 'I would also like to tell you, the people in this area, that you are to blame for the activities of the MNR bandits because you collaborate with them. You give them food and other goods in exchange for *mbanje*, rhino horns and elephant tusks.'[289] Her speech seemingly had little effect, because just a month later, on 28 September 1990, a major barter transaction allegedly took place in the same area, with RENAMO exchanging more than 200 kilograms of *mbanje* (cannabis) for clothes.[290] That the ZNA participated in such deals was widely spoken of, such as one night when an army truck was allegedly used to transport a major shipment to the plateau. Most of the transactions, however, involved small-scale bartering, with RENAMO fighters exchanging *biltong* (dried meat), *kapenta* (dried fish), and *mbanje* (cannabis) for clothes and mealie meal; gold nuggets, rhino horn and elephant tusks were also in circulation.[291] Towards the end of the war, RENAMO increasingly exchanged weapons for goods, and during the drought in 1991/92 barter activities accelerated when RENAMO even acquired, through drought relief, some yellow mealie meal colloquially referred to as 'Kenya'.[292] In 1990, the government targeted young people in an effort to undercut the trade with the insurgents by creating employment opportunities. However, it was reported that 'the majority of the ruling party youths are not interested in working at tea estates.'[293] Apparently, not much had changed between the war and post-war valley generations.

In 1991 the security situation began to calm down, displaced people returned to their homesteads, and reconstruction commenced. This development was partly due to the successful employment of the ZNA in the valley and in Mozambique. In many aspects, the counter-insurgency campaign against RENAMO resembled the Rhodesian war effort.[294] In 1988, the valley was a militarily restricted area, again under a dusk-to-dawn curfew with restricted access, the entry controlled by roadblocks, army units occupying former bases, and with a joint operations command as had existed less than a decade earlier. Civil defence structures were re-established, with the army, local government, and the tea industry regularly convening security meetings; Agri Alert, the call-system, was also re-introduced.[295] In addition, much attention was paid to 'screening of aliens' and to 'cleaning' the border area.[296] The government assumed that the massive influx of war refugees that depopulated the Mozambican border area attracted further incursions and that some of the refugees were active RENAMO supporters.[297] Consequently, people who could be identified as Mozambicans were moved into refugee camps. The distinction, however, was often difficult, because in the border region it was common to carry identity documents for both countries. For example, valley inhabitants who had crossed into Mozambique during the Chimurenga had been given, and kept, Mozambican identity cards, while Mozambican refugees were apparently issued Zimbabwean identity cards so that they could vote for the ruling party in the 1985 elections.[298]

A central counter-insurgency measure was the re-introduction of a villagisation programme in the affected border areas. These so-called Planned Village Settlements (PVSs) militarily and politically closely resembled the Rhodesian PVs. The programme was supposed to implement agricultural policies through a military framework. The main gist of the intervention in rural production was to address the pressure for land and to modernise agriculture. In Mutasa District, the first attempts to centralise land allocation on a voluntary basis were made in 1985.[299] The official policy prescribed: 'With the establishment of the new Social Order which requires the transformation of our society from a capitalistic orientation to an egalitarian socialistic society, it is imperative that there be a supportive socialistic [sic] infrastructure in the rural areas, where 80% of our population reside.'[300] MP for the Honde Valley, Lazarus Nzarayebani interpreted the programme as follows: 'It is a question of sacrifice to accept the new socio-economic order. That is what scientific socialism entails. It is for the good of all our masses.'[301]

Land reform entailed three components which manifested continuity with colonial agricultural policies: block cultivation, growth points, and resettlement of Communal Land dwellers into 'lines', or, as a planning officer called it, 'settlement in an orderly manner':[302] 'The Communal Area replanning programme is therefore aimed at creating well-defined arable blocks, well-defined grazing blocks and consolidated villages. The rationale behind this is to maximise agricultural production from Communal Areas which should provide a base for Agro-industries in the same areas.'[303] This second villagisation programme implemented in Zimbabwe's borderlands with Mozambique resembled other socialist resettlement attempts, such as collectivisation in the Soviet Union and *ujamaa* villagisation in Tanzania, the latter witnessed by ZANU and ZANLA during their exile in East Africa. All three governments' interests were to modernise agriculture and raise the standard of living for rural communities, and at the same time to increase the legibility of their citizens. In Zimbabwe this became part of the counter-insurgency campaign against RENAMO.

Clearly, the Zimbabwean government used the Rhodesian blueprints to implement the PVSs. In Mutasa District, 'communal land re-organisation' began in June 1988,[304] and due to the RENAMO incursions, in 1990 it was decided to combine this land reform with the villagisation programme.[305] Some valley inhabitants had already begun 'self-villagisation' as a result of the RENAMO terror. Inhabitants of *ishe* Mandeya's area, where the security situation was described as 'threatening', abandoned their homes as early as 1988.[306] People from the most northern part of the valley moved to the old PV site at Sagambe and built a small shanty town close to the soldiers' quarters.[307] In the Katambarare area, local people feared retaliation from RENAMO after several incidents in which some fighters died drinking insecticide and one insurgent was killed with an arrow. Eventually, after a family massacre, people spent the night at the local school under a self-imposed dusk-to-dawn curfew.[308]

Despite voluntary displacement, however, the frontier people were just as unwilling to permit state intervention as they and their parents had been in previous decades.[309] A senior government employee involved in the resettlement exercise explained that the PVSs reminded people of their unpleasant experiences of PVs during the Chimurenga.[310] In 1987, the government found that 'the people totally refused' to comply.[311] In the adjoining Nyanga District, the DC found three reasons for resistance to villagisation: one, uncertainty that every member of the community would be accommodated at the site; two, objection to the concentration of people from different areas under one *sabhuku*; and three, uncertainty about grazing and arable rights.[312] In the Honde Valley, resistance delayed the full implementation of the programme right through to 1992, when it was abandoned. At Katambarare village, one saw a number of homesteads put into a straight line which appeared to suddenly explode into scattered settlement patterns. Despite the limited success of government policies, with independence, the Honde Valley never again became a frontier area beyond state intervention, as the nation state had come to stay.

Conclusion

In 1975, ZANLA arrived in the Honde Valley to establish support structures before beginning their offensive in the following year. The area became a major infiltration route into the country, and a training ground, while the fighters targeted the tea industry. With the initiative clearly with the insurgents in 1976, the government responded with a counter-insurgency campaign, driven by security and economic concerns, and by governmental as well as private interests, that focused on the forced resettlement of the entire resident valley population into PVs. The liberation war added another layer to the frontier character of the valley: it became the most contested area in the country.

The course of the Second Chimurenga in the Honde Valley and how it is remembered by inhabitants throws an important light on some of the central questions surrounding guerrilla warfare and counter-insurgency: the justness of violence, the legitimacy of fighters, and the ethics of a conventional army engaging guerrilla troops. Here, it is clear that the white minority government gave up any pretence of ethical concerns, and sought out men and women who would carry out the required actions on the ground, whether African, Rhodesian, soldiers, mercenaries, technocrats, nurses, or administrators. It also transpires that in such a geographically small area there was a wide range of guerrilla–civilian interactions that cannot be seen to be wholly characterised by coercion, although that did also occur. In the Honde Valley, chiefs, portrayed in the literature as overwhelmingly loyal to the government and targeted by the insurgents, often played a crucial role in organising support structures. Those frontier people who could not, or would not, resort to flight for survival and subsequently found themselves spatially controlled to an extreme degree in the PVs emerged with a transformed identity and supported ZANLA throughout the Chimurenga. This was mainly to do with their specific grievances, and in the end, this support provided an important building block for liberation. However, it rapidly became clear, as early as the ceasefire period, that while the war might have ended as far as military interventions were concerned, political conflict would continue for some time.

Frederick Cooper observed that decolonisation is a process of both change and continuity.[313] Insurgency and counter-insurgency operations in the Honde Valley during the Chimurenga and the RENAMO conflict illustrate this well and highlight three aspects in particular: political legitimacy, just violence, and the transfer of knowledge. As the settler regime utilised imperial knowledge, which in turn informed Zimbabwean counter-insurgency after independence, the rupture of historical turning points and distinction between perspectives blurred. Such ambiguities played out further, as social healing and reconciliation became central to the project of the new nation state, as chapter six discusses.

Notes

1 Eric Hobsbawm, *Nations and Nationalism Since 1780: Programme, Myth, Reality* (Cambridge, 1990), p. 10. One of the few studies that has successfully employed the top down and bottom up approach to nationalism is Elizabeth Schmidt, 'Top Down or Bottom Up? Nationalist Mobilization Reconsidered, with Special Reference to Guinea (French West Africa)', *American Historical Review*, 110, no. 4 (2005), pp. 975–1014 and *Mobilizing the Masses: Gender, Ethnicity, and Class in the Nationalist Movement in Guinea, 1939–1958*, (Portsmouth, NH, 2005).

2 For the past twenty years Rhodesian veterans have felt ever more comfortable publishing their war memoirs and posting on nostalgic websites. Academic research, however, still suffers from lack of access to the relevant primary sources. Since the initial research for this study, the Rhodesian Army Archive Project was started at the University of Western England; the papers have not been accessible to researchers. See Paul Moorcraft, *Fireforce: One Man's War in the Rhodesian Light Infantry* (Boulder, CO, 2007 [1988]); Dennis Croukamp, *The Bushwar in Rhodesia: An Extraordinary Combat Memoir of a Rhodesian Reconnaissance Specialist* (Boulder, CO, 2007); Faan Martin, *James and the Duck: Tales of the Rhodesian Bush War (1964–1980): Based on the Truth, The Memoirs of a Part-Time Trooper* (Central Milton Keynes, 2007); Douglass Hubbard Jr, *Bound for Africa: Cold War Fight Along the Zambezi* (Annapolis, MD, 2008).

3 Hans Magnus Enzensberger, 'Civil War', *Civil Wars: From L.A. to Bosnia* (New York, 1994 [1993]), pp. 11–71.

4 Ibid., p. 30.

5 Ibid., p. 20.

6 Ibid., p. 17.

7 Hannah Arendt, *On Violence* (New York, 1970), p. 52; also, Johan Degenaar, 'The Concept of Violence', *Political Violence and the Struggle in South Africa*, N. Manganyi et al. (eds) (Basingstoke, 1990), pp. 70–86. For the current discussion of just war, see Barack Obama, *Nobel Peace Prize Lecture* (Stockholm, 2009).

8 Elisabeth Young-Bruehl, *Hannah Arendt: For Love of the World* (New Haven, CT, 1982), p. 173.

9 Immanuel Kant, 'To Perpetual Peace: A Philosophical Sketch [1795]', *Perpetual Peace, and Other Essays on Politics, History, and Moral Practice* (Indianapolis, IN, 1983), p. 108.

10 Eric Hobsbawm, *Bandits* (New York, 2000, new rev. ed. [1969]); see also Donald Crummey (ed.), *Banditry, Rebellion and Social Protest in Africa* (London, 1986); Georg Elwert, 'Markets of Violence',

Dynamics of Violence: Processes of Escalation and De-Escalation in Violent Group Conflicts, Georg Elwert et al. (eds), *Sociologus Supplement* 1(1999), pp. 85-102.

11 Kant, *To Perpetual Peace*, p. 61.

12 Morten Bøås and Kevin Dunn, 'African Guerrilla Politics: Raging Against the Machine?' *African Guerrillas: Raging Against the Machine*, Morten Bøås and Kevin Dunn (eds) (Boulder, CO, 2007), p. 37.

13 United States, Department of the Army, *Counterinsurgency Field Manual* (Chicago, IL, 2003); *The Battle of Algiers*, feature film, Italy and Algeria, 1966.

14 John Nagl, *Learning to Eat Soup with a Knife: Counterinsurgency Lessons from Malaya and Vietnam* (Chicago, IL, 2002); Thomas Hammes, *The Sling and the Stone: On War in the 21st Century* (St Paul, MN, 2006); Donovan Campbell, *Joker One: A Marine Platoon's Story of Courage, Leadership, and Brotherhood (New York, 2009)*; Philip Bobbit, *Terror and Consent: The Wars for the Twenty-First Century* (New York, 2008); Dexter Filkins, *The Forever War* (New York, 2008).

15 David Kennedy, *Of War and Law* (Princeton, NJ, 2006); Philip Gourevitch and Errol Morris, *Standard Operating Procedure* (New York, 2008).

16 CCJP in Rhodesia (ed.), *The Man in the Middle: Torture, Resettlement and Eviction* (London, 1975).

17 Caroline Elkins, *Imperial Reckoning: The Untold Story of Britain's Gulag in Kenya* (New York, 2005).

18 Reinhart Koselleck, *Futures Past: On the Semantics of Historical Time* (New York, 2004), p. 106.

19 Reinhart Koselleck, *Vergangene Zukunft: Zur Semantik geschichtlicher Zeiten* (Frankfurt/Main, 1979), p. 12; *Futures Past* (New York, 2004), pp. 1-3, passim.

20 Koselleck, *Futures Past*, p. 2.

21 Jim Giblin impressively shows how members of a rural community accommodated their lives with the Tanzanian colonial and post-colonial states by re-imagining and practicing belonging and normativity in multiple and complex ways, inadvertently utilising what Koselleck calls the multiple layers of historical time. James Giblin, *A History of the Excluded: Making Family a Refuge from State in Twentieth-Century Tanzania* (Oxford, 2006). See also Reinhart Koselleck, *The Practice of Conceptual History: Timing History, Spacing Concepts* (Stanford, CA, 2002), p. 110.

22 David Martin and Phyllis Johnson, *The Struggle for Zimbabwe: The Chimurenga War* (London, 1981). For dating in conflict, see Heike Behrend, *Alice Lakwena and the Holy Spirits: War in Northern Uganda 1986-97* (Oxford, 1999), p. 151.

23 Interview #89.

24 Interview #119.

25 David Pratten, *The Man-Leopard Murders: History and Society in Colonial Nigeria* (Bloomington, IN, 2007), p. 340.

26 Interview #78. The Carmelites, in their remembrance volume of their work in Manyikaland, also date the beginning of the Chimurenga as 1974. Leo Gallagher, *The Catholic Church in Manicaland, 1946–1996* (Harare, 1996), pp. 32-43. For the presence of guerrilla fighters marking the beginning of the war, see interviews #56, #45, #127.

27 The absorption of foreigners, especially US American veterans, into the Rhodesian army, is a sensitive topic, and Rhodesians insist fervently that these were not mercenaries. The current military engagement of the United States in Iraq and Afghanistan is the first time in modern history that a democratic government deploys more soldiers of a private army than regular troops in formal conflict. Jeremy Scahill, *Blackwater: The Rise of the World's Most Powerful Mercenary Army* (New York, 2nd ed., 2008) and 'The Secret US War in Pakistan', *The Nation* (21 December 2009), pp. 11-18.

28 Alex Vines, *Renamo: Terrorism in Mozambique* (London, 1991), p. 74.

29 Interview #133.

30 Interview #111.

31 Ibid.

32 David Lan, *Guns and Rain: Guerrillas and Spirit Mediums in Zimbabwe* (London, 1985), p. 164, passim.

33 Interview #84.

34 Norma Kriger, *Zimbabwe's Guerrilla War: Peasant Voices* (Cambridge, 1992), chapters 3 and 4.

35 Ernesto Guevara, *Che Guevara On Guerrilla Warfare* (Lincoln, NE, 1998 [1961]), p. 16, passim; see also Mao Zedong, *On Guerrilla Warfare* (Chicago, IL, 2000 [1937]), p. 43, passim.

36 Mao Zedong, *On Guerrilla Warfare*, p. 93.

37 ZANU's 'Operational Rules' from 1978 reflect the specifics of the course of the Chimurenga, in particular the increasing problem with the discipline of the troops deployed within the country due to their declining age and less thorough training. Henrik Ellert, *The Rhodesian Front War: Counter-insurgency and Guerrilla Warfare, 1962–1980* (Gweru, 1989), pp. 155-7; Mao Zedong,

Quotations from Chairman Mao Tsetung [The Little Red Book] (Peking, 1966 [1947]), pp. 256-7; 'Kenya Land Freedom Army Directives', *Kenya's Freedom Struggle: The Dedan Kimathi Papers*, Maina wa Kinyatti (ed.) (London, 1987), pp. 21-2.

38 Kriger, *Zimbabwe's Guerrilla War*; Lan, *Guns and Rain*; Terence Ranger, *Peasant Consciousness and Guerrilla War in Zimbabwe: A Comparative Study* (London, 1985). More recent research on the Chimurenga has added case studies but not significantly shifted the understanding of the conflict as developed by the above cited studies. See, for example, Jocelyn Alexander et al., *Violence and Memory: One Hundred Years in the 'Dark Forests' of Matabeleland* (Portsmouth, NH, 2000).

39 Interview #28.

40 Interviews #124, #28.

41 DC Mutasa to Officer Commanding, Central Criminal Bureau, Salisbury, 30 December 1975; DC Mutasa to Secretary for Internal Affairs, 23 June 1977; DC Mutasa to Smith, n.d. [1978]; DC Mutasa to PC, 17 July 1978, DAO.

42 Interview #121.

43 Interviews #27, #28, #30; both interviewees were trained in the valley.

44 Interview #54.

45 Interview #28; also #53, #110, #124.

46 Interview #28.

47 Interviews #69, #133.

48 For the concept of hidden struggles see William Beinart and Colin Bundy (eds), *Hidden Struggles in Rural South Africa: Politics and Popular Movements in the Transkei and Eastern Cape 1980–1930* (London, 1987).

49 Kriger, *Zimbabwe's Guerrilla War*, pp. 11, 94, 101-9. For a case of the Security Forces burning down a homestead in the valley because they suspected guerrilla support, see 'Incident in Hauna in June 1976', CCJPZ. For guerrillas carrying out 'disciplinary killings' after each contact with the army in Chiweshe District, see, 'Report on the Conducted Tour of the Chiweshe TTL on 5th September, 1974', Protected Villages, CCJPZ.

50 Interview #127. Kriger provides examples of killings and incidents of coercion of specifically targeted groups such as chiefs and headmen, government employees, 'better-off farmers', people using government services, farm labourers, storekeepers, and people with the 'wrong' party card. *Zimbabwe's Guerrilla War*, pp. 101-9, 179-86.

51 Interview #28.

52 Interview #127.

53 Interview #116.

54 Interviews #32, #23. See also CNC to NC Inyanga, 26 March 1949, S2588/1977, NAZ.

55 Interview #32.

56 Ibid.

57 In order to support the frequently targeted rural business people, the government made a concession regarding the Group Area Act and for the first time allowed African-owned stores to open on Mutare's main street. Interview #69.

58 Arendt, *On Violence*, pp. 56, 42-56.

59 Secretary for Internal Affairs to all PCs and DCs, 'Intelligence Summary: Terrorist Tactics: January, 1978', 20 February 1978, PPG.

60 Personal communication with forester, Chimanimani, May 1987.

61 For the description of a woman becoming possessed by a *madzviti* spirit in the Honde Valley in the 1920s, see Denis Shropshire, 'A Journey in Mashonaland', *African Affairs*, 51, no. 202 (1952), pp. 54-5.

62 Interview #26.

63 John Pafiwa Katsidzira, no title [history of Ziwe Zano Society] (n.p. [Honde Mission], ms., n.d. [1976]), vol. 2, chapter 41, PPA.

64 Organisations that supported Ziwe Zano were Brot für die Welt and Evangelische Zentralstelle für Entwicklungshilfe in Germany, the Conference of British Missionary Societies London in Britain, Meals for Millions in the USA, War on Want, and the British Ministry of Overseas Development. See Katsidzira, vol. 3, chapters 69, 78; S. Kanyenze to K. Mutasa, 24 July 1964; Minutes of 'The Joint Meeting of Management and Advisory Board Honde Industrial Mission', 11 May 1974; Memorandum 'Honde Creditors Control Committee', 30 May 1975; Rondozai to Cruickshank, 30 January and 22 September 1975; Honey and Blanckenberg to Cruickshank, 16 June 1978; Cruickshank to Honey and Blanckenberg, 19 June 1978, PPA.

65 Katsidzira, vol. 3, chapter 74.

66 Ibid., vol. 1, chapter 36.

67 Cruickshank to Honey and Blanckenberg, 19 June 1978 and to the Officer Commanding, Military

Forces, Honde, 14 December 1977, PPA.

68 Rondozai, 'Honde Craft Centre: 0008, Report on Manager's Visit', 5 August 1974 and 22 January 1975; Rondozai to Deputy Provincial Education Officer, 18 October 1974, PPA.

69 Rondozai to Deputy Provincial Education Officer, 18 October 1974; Rondozai, 'Manager's Report: Honde Craft Centre 0008', 24 October 1973, PPA. Abduction as well as voluntary recruitment of groups of students occurred occasionally during the Chimurenga. Between June and October 1977 alone, an estimated 700 students crossed the border to Mozambique. David Caute, *Under the Skin: The Death of White Rhodesia* (Harmondsworth, 1983). In June 1975, the government imposed a curfew on twenty-three mission stations countrywide, including Honde Mission and St Columba's in the Honde Valley. In July the curfew was extended to the eastern border, from the Ruenya to the Sabi River. 'Umtali Curfew Area Defined', Bulawayo *Chronicle*, 26 June 1975, 'Curfew Put on 500 km Strip down E. Border', *Sunday Mail*, 25 July 1975.

70 Rondozai, 'Honde Craft School: 0008, Notes on Manager's Visit', 17 July 1975, PPA.

71 Ibid., 19 September 1975.

72 Ibid., 17 July 1975.

73 Interview #133.

74 Ibid.

75 Rondozai, 'Honde Craft School: 0008, Notes on Manager's Visit', 17 July 1975 and 5 August 1974, PPA; also 'Moment of Truth for Merchants of Kukwanisa', *Umtali Post*, 10 June 1977.

76 'Forces Bag 31 in One Battle', *Rhodesian Herald*, 18 November 1976.

77 Interviews #30, #28.

78 Interview #133.

79 Ibid.

80 Minister of Education to Cruickshank, 6 October 1975, PPA.

81 Interview #22. Michael Bratton discussed special laws within the emergency legislation that were introduced to deal with civilians. See 'Settler State, Guerrilla War and Rural Underdevelopment in Rhodesia', *Issue: A Journal of Opinion*, 9, nos. 1/2 (1979), p. 60; also CCJP in Rhodesia, *Civil War in Rhodesia: Abduction, Torture and Death in the Counter-Insurgency Campaign* (London, 1976), pp. 85-9. For the British approach during Mau Mau, see David Anderson, *Histories of the Hanged: The Dirty War in Kenya and the End of Empire* (New York, 2005), pp. 151-77, 289-93, passim.

82 Cruickshank to Officer Commanding, Military Forces, Honde, 14 December 1977, PPA.

83 Minutes of Honde Valley Tea Growers' Liaison Committee Meeting, 22 November 1977, PPF; Rondozai to Cruickshank, 6 December 1977, PPA.

84 Interviews #133, #21; 'Honde Mission School to Re-open in City', *Umtali Post*, 4 May 1979; 'Go ahead for Craft School', *Umtali Post*, 27 April 1979.

85 'Manicaland Awards for Brave, Loyal Service', *Umtali Post*, 27 April 1979.

86 For a range of guerrilla–missionary interactions, see Janice McLaughlin, *On the Frontline: Catholic Missions in Zimbabwe's Liberation War* (Harare, 1996); Michael Bourdillon and Paul Gundani, 'Rural Christians and the Zimbabwe Liberation War: A Case Study' and Ngwabi Bhebe, 'The Evangelical Lutheran Church in Zimbabwe and the War of Liberation, 1975–1980', *Church and State in Zimbabwe*, Carl Hallencreutz and Ambrose Moyo (eds) (Gweru, 1988), pp. 147-61 and 163-94. See also Caute, *Under the Skin*, passim.

87 Arthur Lewis, *Too Bright the Vision? African Adventures of an Anglican Rebel* (London, 1992), pp. 227, 268. For Lewis' political role outside the valley, see Julie Frederikse, *None But Ourselves: Masses vs. Media in the Making of Zimbabwe* (London, 1982), pp. 48, 189-93, 227, 341.

88 Gallagher, *The Catholic Church*, p. 36. Businessmen and others who were excluded from information also cycled to avoid detonating landmines. Interview #32.

89 Gallagher, *The Catholic Church*, pp. 34, 36.

90 Ibid., p. 11.

91 For another incident in the area at the time, see, 'Five in Terror Case to Ruda for Sentence', *Umtali Post*, 2 April 1976.

92 Interviews # 97, #127. The incident was prominently reported in the press as an example for the insurgents' victimisation of missionaries until the priest's role came to light. See, 'Priest Is Hurt, Terrorist Killed at Mission', *Umtali Post*, 1 June 1977; 'Mission Heroes Tell the Story', *Umtali Post*, 3 June 1977. A similar crossfire incident occurred at St Augustine's in Penhalonga, the southern part of the Mutasa mamboship, where the priest-in-charge, Father Keble Prosser, tolerated ZANLA presence on the mission premises. See Caute, *Under the Skin*, pp. 149-54, 311-15. In Penhalonga, even some Rhodesians who opposed the war provided supplies to ZANLA in exchange for safety. See Tom Wigglesworth, *Perhaps Tomorrow* (Harare, 1982).

93 Gallagher, *The Catholic Church*, p. 37.

94 Ibid.

95 Memorandum on the security situation in the Honde Valley by a tea estate employee, 19 May 1978, PPG; interview # 101. A former District Assistant claimed that he was the only person at Ruda base camp who risked driving to Zindi in order to recover the corpses during that night. He recalled the incident as particularly savage, because the policemen did not expect an ambush. Interview # 132. This is the only African man who served the Rhodesian government during the war who was prepared to talk about his experiences in the context of this study.

96 Rumbizi's manager survived detonating a landmine. Interview #98. For a discussion of training African combatants in the use of weapons and the discourse about guns in both the Rhodesian army and ZANLA, see Luise White, '"Heading for the Gun": Skills and Sophistication in an African Guerrilla War', *Comparative Studies in Society and History*, 51, no. 2 (2009), pp. 236-59.

97 Tea estates in Chipinge District were also targeted. See 'Mortar Raid on Tea Estates', *Umtali Post*, 11 May 1977; 'D.A. Is Killed in Action', *Rhodesian Herald*, 25 May 1977; 'Tanganda Profit down by 79 Percent', *Rhodesian Herald*, 27 September 1979.

98 Tea Growers' Liaison Committee Meeting, 10 June 1976; Manager EHTE to Sutton-Pryce, Deputy Minister, Department of the Prime Minister, 13 August 1976, PPF.

99 TILCOR, 'Holdenby Tea Scheme, Proposals for further Development of the Tea Potential of the Pungwe Valley', 1974, 25, PPD.

100 Tea Growers' Liaison Committee Meeting, 1 June 1977.

101 'Memorandum on the security situation'. Andrew Ivaska examines gendered prohibitions as part of nation-building in post-colonial Tanzania. Andrew Ivaska, *Cultured States: Youth, Gender, and Modern Style in 1960s Dar es Salaam* (Durham, NC, 2011), chapter 2.

102 Lan, *Guns and Rain*, p. 189.

103 Interview #134, #135. For details on spirit mediums supplying guerrillas with charms and information and influencing guerrilla tactics, see Internal Affairs, 'Intelligence Summary'.

104 'Memorandum on the security situation'.

105 Inyanga District, Annual Report, 1960, box number 62328, NRC; Inyanga District, Annual Report, 1961, S2827/2/2/8, NAZ; 'Points Arising from the Labour Unrest at Aberfoyle Saturday, 3rd August to Saturday 10th August, 1974' and 'Labour Unrest: Aberfoyle 1st Quarter 1975', 18 April 1975, PPC.

106 'Events Preceding the Massacre', Aberfoyle Massacre, CCJPZ.

107 This account of the massacre is based on CCJPZ sources. The file 'Aberfoyle Massacre' contains evidence compiled during an investigation the following day, eye-witness testimony which was collected in June 1977, the official security report, various press cuttings, and some information gathered in January 1977.

108 Ibid. It is not known whether the nationality of those men who were killed had any relevance in the course of events. If one is to believe Raeburn's account of the Whistlefield farm attack on 23 December 1972, Zimbabwean farmworkers used the opportunity to burn down the huts of their Malawian counterparts and the mosque of the Mozambican workers in the labour compound. See Michael Raeburn, *Black Fire! Accounts of the Guerrilla War in Zimbabwe* (Harare, 1986 [1978]), p. 166. For an ethnography of farmworkers, see Blair Rutherford, *Working on the Margins: Black Workers, White Farmers in Postcolonial Zimbabwe* (London, 2001).

109 Interview #45. When most workers refused to return after the massacre, attempts were made to recruit a new labour force. See advertisement in the *Sunday Mail*, 'Tea Pickers Aberfoyle Plantation', 23 January 1977.

110 See *Rhodesian Herald*, 'Terrorists Massacre Workers: Wives, Children Watch 27 Die', 20 December 1976; 'Terrorists Massacre Workers: Mozambique Nationals among the Victims', 21 December 1976; 'Atrocity Featured in U.K. Press', 22 December 1976; Caute, *Under the Skin*, pp. 78-9.

111 *Rhodesian Herald*, 'Nkomo Calls for an Inquiry', 22 December 1976; 'Government Blamed for Atrocities'; 'Comment: Smear Tactics', 23 December 1976.

112 The issue was still hot in the 1990s: staff at the estates did not wish to talk about the massacre, and the author's suggestion of the Selous Scouts' responsibility enraged former members of the Rhodesian administration.

113 A member of the CCJP found by June 1977 that in the valley 'everybody believes Selous Scouts did it'. Aberfoyle Massacre, CCJPZ.

114 'Events Preceding the Massacre', CCJPZ.

115 Radio broadcast transmitted from Salisbury in English, 1 August 1977; International Defence Fund (IDF), MS308/52, NAZ.

116 DC Mutasa, 'Operation "Rivet", Honde Valley, Holdenby TTL', 2 March 1977, PPF.

117 Secretary of the Honde Valley Labour Committee, 'The Economy of and the Labour Position in the Pungwe Valley', April 1977, PPF. For a contrasting view, see the official statement by Baily, the chairman of TILCOR, 'Tilcor Worries Will Slow', *Rhodesian Herald*, 6 October 1976.

118 Rhodesian Fighting Forces, no. 4 (1977), n.p. Note that 'white' is here used as a category of self-reference among Rhodesians.
119 Ibid.
120 See, for example, the Lion Lager beer ad that shows soldiers on leave enjoying a braai (barbecue) by the pool in the company of young women. Ibid.
121 This is brilliantly reflected in David Caute's *Under the Skin*.
122 Paul Moorcraft and Peter McLaughlin, *The Rhodesian War: A Military History* (Barnsley, 2008 revised ed. [1982]), p. 61.
123 Interviews #36, #38, #96; Internal Affairs, 'Intelligence Summary'; 'Guerrillas to Alter Tactics', *Rhodesian Herald*, 3 June 1971; Wigglesworth, *Perhaps Tomorrow*, p. 34; Terence Ranger, 'Bandits and Guerrillas: The Case of Zimbabwe', *Banditry, Rebellion and Social Protest in Africa*, Donald Crummey (ed.) (London, 1986), pp. 379-86.
124 Interview #56.
125 'Meeting on 23rd March, 1973 Re: Terrorist Infiltration: Mutasa North TTL', PER5 Headman Muponda, DAO; Ministry of Internal Affairs, 'Protective Security Hints for the Rural Resident', 12 March 1973, PPF.
126 The desolate set-up of the district centre apparently did not prevent a 'happy valley' culture in the first years of the district's existence, given the wife-swapping parties among European staff. Interview #34.
127 DC Mutasa to all members of the (proposed) Mutasa District Civil Defence Committee, 7 September 1974, PPF.
128 The direct collaboration between economic interest and the military effort appears to be one significant difference in the counter-insurgency campaign in Zimbabwe compared to Mau Mau in Kenya, unless such an approach remains undiscovered for the latter conflict. Some of the parallels are nevertheless notable, including the presence of a tea plantation sector in the war-affected areas, as well as continuity in personnel that had left Kenya at independence and moved to southern Africa.
129 TILCOR, 'Minutes of the 32nd Meeting of Services Division Staff', 8 March 1974, PPD.
130 District Assistants were instructed to introduce the development cautiously to local people: 'The reason for the fence is to try and stop people crossing the boundary by mistake.' Memorandum by Assistant DC Mutasa, 31 October 1975, PER 5 Headman Nyamaende, DAO.
131 Minutes of tea estate management committee meetings, 4 December 1974 and 15 January 1975, PPC. The problem of the costs of such installations soon became clear. See DC Mutasa to Rumbizi Tea Estate, 22 July 1975, attached: Secretary for Internal Affairs to all Civil Defence Committees, 'Assistance to Farmers in Designated Areas', 23 June 1975; DC Mutasa to all civil defence zone representatives, 20 November 1975, PPF.
132 DC Mutasa to the manager Rumbizi tea scheme, 14 February 1975, PPF.
133 Members of 'civil defence' structures were exclusively Europeans. Africans benefited only in so far as farm workers and domestic servants were included in security planning.
134 DC Mutasa to PC, 23 August 1974, PER5 Headman Chikomba, DAO. Typically about one year after the death, the *chenura* (*kurova guva*) burial ceremony is performed to allow the spirit of the deceased to pass on and become an ancestral spirit before a successor is appointed and the property is distributed. Kriger argued that when guerrillas killed chiefs, they did not usually allow such a ceremony to take place. *Zimbabwe's Guerrilla War*, p. 105.
135 DC Mutasa to PC, 23 May 1977 and DC Mutasa to PC, 23 August 1974, PER5 Headman Chikomba, DAO.
136 DC Mutasa to PC, 11 February 1975, PER5 Headman Chikomba, DAO.
137 Secretary for Internal Affairs to DC Mutasa, 'List of Chieftainships and Headmanships, April 1974', 1 April 1974; Secretary for Internal Affairs to all PCs and DCs, 'List of Chieftainships and Headmanships Revised to 15th November 1978', 20 November 1978; also, DC Mutasa to Chief Mutasa, 'The Involvement of Tribal Leaders in Winning the War Against the Terrorists', 17 May 1977, PER5 GEN, DAO.
138 Mpotedzi is a chieftaincy reserved for female office holders in vernacular understanding, and it was likely due to the security situation that the government recognised her against general policies of rejecting women in that capacity. DC Mutasa to PC, 30 September 1974 and PC to Secretary for Internal Affairs, 10 October 1974, PER5 Headman Mupotedzi, PAO.
139 Fawcett had been awarded the 'Bronze Cross of Rhodesia' for his deployment in the Zambezi Valley in 1968, followed by the 'Officer of the Legion of Merit' medal in 1977 for his successful role as commander of operations in the Honde Valley. John Lovett, *Contact: A Tribute To Those Who Serve Rhodesia* (Salisbury, 1977), p. 160; Major General MacIntyre to Smith, 6 October 1977, PPF.
140 'Minutes of the Eighth Meeting of the Honde Valley Labour Committee', 23 June 1977, PPF.
141 Interviews #95, #38, #59; 'Internal Affairs Men Now Learn the Arts of War', *Sunday Mail*, 26

February 1978.

142 'Minutes of the Eighth Meeting of the Honde Valley Labour Committee', 23 June 1977, PPF.

143 'Internal Affairs Men Now Learn the Arts of War', *Sunday Mail*, 26 February 1978.

144 Interview #28. Another ex-combatant claimed that he was once captured by RENAMO in Mozambique. Interview #121.

145 For the Selous Scouts, see the hagiographic account by its commanding officer, Ron Reid-Daly, *Selous Scouts: Top Secret War*, as told to Peter Stiff (Johannesburg, 1982); also Caute, *Under the Skin*, pp. 46-9, 140-2.

146 Ian Henderson (with Philip Goodhart), *The Hunt for Kimathi*, (Bristol, 1958).

147 Interview #38; see also Alexandre Binda, *Masodja: The History of the Rhodesian African Rifles and Its Forerunner, the Rhodesia Native Regiment* (Johannesburg, 2008), p. 286.

148 Interviews #35, #38, #128, #129; see also Goswin Baumhögger, with the assistance of Telse Diederichsen and Ulf Engel, (eds), *The Struggle for Independence: Documents on the Recent Development of Zimbabwe (1975–1980)* (Hamburg, 1984), vol. 2, pp. 123-5, 477-80. For the hot pursuit attacks in Chimoio and Nyadzonia, see Fay Chung, *Re-Living the Second Chimurenga: Memories from Zimbabwe's Liberation Struggle* (Uppsala, 2006), chapter 8.

149 Interviews #89, #149, #150.

150 'Let's Build Zimbabwe Together: ZIMCORD', Conference Documentation, Zimbabwe Conference on Reconstruction and Development, Salisbury, 23-27 March 1981, p. 25, DERUDE. By the end of the war, the PVs were guarded by approximately 7,000 men. Jakkie Cilliers, *Counter-Insurgency in Rhodesia* (London, 1985), p. 95. From 1975, less fortified Consolidated Villages and unprotected sub-offices were also established. 'New Concept in Fighting against Terror', *Rhodesian Herald*, 3 June 1975; Elvis Muringai, 'The Socio-Economic Impact of Concentration Camps on the Peasantry During the Second Chimurenga: The Case of Madziwa Area 1974–1980' (BA Hons thesis, University of Zimbabwe), 1985, pp. 9-10. For an account of the experience of villagisation in Chiweshe District, albeit entirely based on interviews, see Eleanor O' Gorman, *The Front Line Runs through Every Woman: Women and Local Resistance in the Zimbabwean Liberation War* (Woodbridge, 2011), chapter 5.

151 As early as two weeks after Operation Rivet commenced, it was noticed that 'a large number of people' had left the valley. Later, the total population of the valley increased to 40,000 to 50,000 people. Minutes of a 'Meeting Held to Discuss the Implications and Effect of Current Military and Administrative Policies in the Holdenby T.T.L., Mutasa District', 16 March 1977, PPF; 'Internal Affairs Men now Learn the Arts of War', *Sunday Mail*, 26 February 1978; interview #59.

152 Carl von Clausewitz, *On War* (Phoenix, 2008 [1832]), p. 42.

153 F. Du Toit to DA Mutasa, received 24 August 1974, PPF. João Coelho shows that in post-independence Mozambique RENAMO bandits perceived the FRELIMO government's socialist villagisation programme as a threat to their insurgency campaign. See 'State Resettlement Policies in Post colonial Rural Mozambique: The Impact of the Communal Village Programme on Tete Province, 1977–1982', *Journal of Southern African Studies*, 24, no. 1 (1998), pp. 61-91.

154 Interviews #27, #28.

155 Interview with Noel Hunt, 27 November 1983, p. 52, ORAL/240, NAZ.

156 Government of Zimbabwe, Honde–Pungwe Valley: Integrated Rural Development Plan, vol. 1: Project Environment (Rome, 1985), p. 34, PAO; Jakob Chikuhwa, *A Crisis of Governance: Zimbabwe* (New York, 2004), p. 67; Martin and Johnson, *The Struggle for Zimbabwe*, pp. 103-4.

157 Radio interview with DC Peters, transmitted in English from Salisbury, 1 August 1977, IDF, MS308/52, NAZ.

158 This is remembered as a particularly cruel incident by a member of the district staff. Interview #95.

159 'Terrorists Burn Down Villages', *Sunday Mail*, 9 October 1977; 'Terrorists Getting Cross with the PVs', *Rhodesian Herald*, 30 May 1977; also interview #59; DC Mutasa, 'Operation "Rivet"'.

160 Interview #96; ZANLA publication, 'Ruda Base Pounded'.

161 'Possible PV Sites', April 1974. For details on planning and purpose, see PAO to all DCs, all Agricultural Officers, PC, Director of African Agriculture, 5 July 1974, PPF.

162 F. Du Toit to DA Mutasa.

163 'Moving Lock, Stock and Barrel into the Honde PVs', *Umtali Post*, 13 April 1977.

164 Bratton, 'Settler State, Guerrilla War', p. 61; Cilliers, *Counter-Insurgency*, pp. 17, 82-7. For the official view on the PV programme, see, A. Hamilton, 'Intaf: Here for "Keeps"', *Fighting Forces of Rhodesia*, 4 (1977), pp. 23, 25, 29.

165 The person in charge of planning had direct experience of Mau Mau. Interview #59; also Lewis Gann, *The Struggle for Zimbabwe: Battle in the Bush* (New York, 1981), p. 74; Thomas Hodges, 'Counterinsurgency and the Fate of Rural Blacks', *Africa Report*, 22, no. 5 (1977), p. 18; Anna Weinrich, 'Strategic Resettlement in Rhodesia', *Journal of Southern African Studies*, 3, no. 2

(1977), p. 207. Government propaganda compared the Rhodesian PV programme with villagisation in independent African countries such as Mozambique and Tanzania. See *The North East News* (January 1974), pp. 2-3. For state-sponsored villagisation, see James Scott, *Seeing Like a State: How Certain Schemes to Improve the Human Condition Have Failed* (New Haven, CT, 1998), chapters 6 and 7.

166 Interview #60.

167 Ibid. He resigned in early 1977 because of deep frustration. He had envisaged the PV programme as an important step in the long-term effort to transform TTL agriculture, but felt hampered in his task by the inefficiency of Intaf, in particular that of the current DC, who was 'despised by virtually every member of that staff'. Letter of resignation by Agricultural Officer, Mutasa District, 31 January 1977, PPH.

168 Interview #75.

169 Interview #13. At the time, the valley was a militarily restricted area and the interview had to be conducted in the presence of a government official, with soldiers close by.

170 The comparison with Hannah Arendt's notion of the banality of evil and her observations about technocrat perpetrators comes to mind. It is astounding that critical studies on counter-insurgency usually forget the role of the Eichmanns. *Eichmann in Jerusalem: A Report on the Banality of Evil* (New York, 1963).

171 DC Mutasa, 'Operation "Rivet"'; also, 'New Homes for 7,000 in Honde Valley', *Rhodesian Herald*, 25 April 1977.

172 Anderson, *Histories of the Hanged*, chapter 7; Elkins, *Imperial Reckoning*, chapter 4, passim. For a contemporary discussion of the dehumanisation of the enemy in counter-insurgency campaigns, see Gourevitch and Morris, *Standard Operating Procedure*.

173 DC Mutasa, 'Operation "Rivet"'.

174 'Moving Lock, Stock, and Barrel'.

175 Tea Growers' Liaison Committee Meeting, 11 May 1977, PPF.

176 Tea Growers' Liaison Committee Meeting, 11 May, 23 June, 17 August 1977.

177 Tea Growers' Liaison Committee Meeting, 17 August, 28 September 1977; 'Lion-Hearted Bid to Resettle Villagers', *Sunday Mail*, 1 January 1978.

178 This was the case in Chief Mandeya's area. 'PVs: Minutes of a Meeting Held at the Office of the PC, Manicaland', 7 February 1977, PPF.

179 Interview #81. Voluntary resettlement apparently increased as villagisation proceeded. Tea Growers' Liaison Committee Meeting, 8 February 1978.

180 'PVs: Minutes of a Meeting Held at the Office of the PC, Manicaland', 7 February 1977, PPF. The same argument was put forward by a government employee who had witnessed the resettlement of people into PVs in the valley. Interviews #37,#38.

181 With the support of ZANLA, Chief Nyamaende crossed the border in August or September 1976. He was subsequently removed from office and was reinstated in 1980, after his return to Zimbabwe. DC Mutasa to PC, 22 October 1976, PER5 Headman Nyamaende, DAO; Secretary for Internal Affairs to PC, 1 February 1977, DC Mutasa to PC, 14 October 1980, PER5 Headman Nyamaende, PAO.

182 Unnamed [Chief Muparutsa], CCJPZ.

183 Interviews #134, #135. For details on spirit mediums supplying guerrillas with charms and information and influencing guerrilla tactics, see, Internal Affairs, 'Intelligence Summary'.

184 Unnamed [Chief Muparutsa].

185 'PVs: Minutes of a Meeting Held at the Office of the PC, Manicaland', 7 February 1977, PPF.

186 DC Inyanga to Secretary for Internal Affairs, 17 November 1977, PER5 GEN, DAO.

187 Tea Growers' Liaison Committee Meeting, 17 August and 28 September 1977.

188 Ibid., 23 June 1977.

189 Unnamed [Muparutsa]; Waddilove Institute Marandellas to DC Mutasa, 10 January 1977, PER 5 Headman Muparutsa, DAO.

190 DC Mutasa to PC, 5 July 1977, PER 5 Headman Muparutsa, DAO.

191 Muparutsa was re-appointed on 31 August 1980. DA Mutasa to Secretary (Development) Manicaland, 10 March 1982; DA Mutasa to PC, 2 September 1988; DA Mutasa to PA, 18 July 1988, PER 5 Headman Muparutsa, PAO.

192 First Honde Valley Tea Growers' Liaison Committee Meeting, 8 March 1976, attached: manager of EHTE to Minister of Internal Affairs, 3 March 1976; managing director, Aberfoyle, to Minister of Internal Affairs, 21 May 1976; 'Minutes of a Meeting Held between Intaf and Tilcor', 17 September 1976, PPF.

193 Minister of Internal Affairs Mussett to the manager, EHTE, 25 March 1976, PPF.

194 Manager, EHTE, to Minister of Internal Affairs, 13 May 1976, PPF. Eleven days later a meeting

between the Minister of Law and Order, the police, and a representative of the estates was arranged to further discuss security matters. 'Memorandum of Discussion Held at Ruda Police Post, Honde Valley on 24th May, 1976', PPF.

195 Manager, EHTE, to Deputy Minister, Department of the Prime Minister, 13 August 1976, PPF.

196 'Minutes of a management meeting', Aberfoyle, 3 September 1976, PPC.

197 Attached pamphlet, F. Du Toit to DA Mutasa, PPF.

198 'Minutes of the Inaugural Meeting of the Honde Valley Labour Committee', 16 March 1977; Chairman, National Co-ordinating Committee, Ministry of Agriculture, to all Area Civil Defence Committee Chairmen, 3 April 1980, PPF.

199 'Minutes of a Meeting Held to Discuss the Implications and Effect of Current Military and Administrative Policies in the Holdenby T.T.L., Mutasa District', 16 March 1977, PPF.

200 Merna Wilson, 'Tea Break', *Skyhost*, 4, no. 3 (1992), p. 33.

201 J.G. Baxter, *An Assessment of the Tea Growing Potentials of the Manga and Holdenby Tribal Trust Lands and Recommendations for its Development as a Tea Scheme* (Salisbury, 1969), pp. 2, 24-6, NAZ. TILCOR became increasingly instrumental to the war effort. In mid-1978, the parastatal, together with ADA and the Sabi-Limpopo Authority, was transferred to the Ministry of Lands, Natural Resources, and Rural Development; the renamed Agricultural Rural Development Agency (ARDA) became the parent body. C. Butcher, 'The Tribal Trust Land Development Corporation: An Evaluation', July 1980, p. 2, Ministry of Agriculture.

202 Ministry of Internal Affairs, 'Pungwe Valley Development Draft Report', 29 July 1977, PPD; S. Manase, 'Communal Land Reorganization and Development: Honde–Pungwe Valley Communal Lands, Initial Report, by DERUDE', October 1990, pp. 18-22, DERUDE.

203 Ministry of Internal Affairs, 'Pungwe Valley Development Draft Report', p. 24; 29 July 1977, Projects Manager Rumbizi to the Honde Valley Labour Committee, 31 August 1978, PPF; interview #60.

204 Projects manager Rumbizi to TILCOR Regional Manager Manicaland, 1 August 1978. One of the tea estates was 'forced to progressively abandon planted areas from 1074 ha to 33.6 ha'. Manager EHTE to the Honde Valley Labour Committee, 4 September 1978, PPF.

205 DC Mutasa, 'Operation "Rivet"'.

206 Tea Growers' Liaison Committee Meeting, 18 May 1977.

207 'Tea Estates Show Their Appreciation', *Umtali Post*, 29 November 1977, 4; interview #128; Minutes of the Honde Valley Tea Growers' Liaison Meeting, 21 November 1979, PPF.

208 The DC advised that in contrast to the situation in Chipinge, it was almost impossible to entice outside labour because of the valley's bad reputation in terms of security. Minutes of the Honde Valley Labour Committee Meeting, 7 April and 18 May 1977, PPF; Minutes of a tea estate management meeting, Aberfoyle, 17 June 1977, PPC.

209 Order in Terms of the Emergency Powers (Maintenance of Law and Order) Regulations, as Published in Govt. Notice 204 of 1976, as Amended by Govt. Notice 75 of 1977, PPG; also Cilliers, *Counter-insurgency*, pp. 158-60.

210 Interviews #75, #89.

211 The homesteads were burnt as part of the PV programme in order to discourage people from returning and at the same time to destroy potential shelter for guerrillas. Aberfoyle Massacre, CCJPZ.

212 'Moving Lock, Stock, and Barrel'. On impoverishment due to villagisation, see interview #13.

213 One of the tea managers claimed that workers wanted guerrillas to witness them being forced to work by soldiers. Minutes of the Honde Valley Labour Committee Meeting, 1 June 1977, PPF; interview #37, #38.

214 DC Mutasa, 'Operation "Rivet"'.

215 Minutes of a tea estate management meeting, Aberfoyle, 4 May 1978, PPC.

216 DC Mutasa, 'Operation "Rivet"'; also, interview #13.

217 DC Mutasa, 'Operation "Rivet"'.

218 Ibid.

219 'Lion-Hearted Bid to Resettle Villagers'; DC Mutasa, 'Operation "Rivet"'.

220 Interview #28.

221 Ibid.

222 Secretary for Internal Affairs to all PCs and DCs, 20 February 1978, PPG.

223 Interview #110; also, #117, #124.

224 Interview #28. It appears, therefore, that Kriger's model of guerrilla coercion and abuse of power by their messengers does not apply to areas where villagisation was implemented.

225 Interview #45; also, 'Minutes of a Meeting of the Executive Committee of the Rhodesian Tea Growers' Association', 17 June 1975, PPD.

226 Interviews #17 and #19 with a young Ndau woman.
227 Interview #53.
228 Interview #45.
229 Secretary of the Honde Valley Labour Committee, 'The Economy of and the Labour Position'.
230 Ibid.
231 Interview #88.
232 Interviews #27, #28.
233 Interview #9. In 1974, it was observed in Chiweshe TTL that tensions arising from PV life led to an increase of alcoholism among men, even in communities where Christian churches had prohibited the consumption of alcohol by their members. 'Report on Chiweshe TTL', 26 August 1974, Protected Villages, CCJPZ.
234 Interview #81.
235 Interviews #67, #69, #56. For the term 'rogue guerrilla' and a similar dynamic of the war elsewhere in Zimbabwe, see,' Ranger, 'Bandits and Guerrillas', p. 383. Muringai' in his study on villagisation in Madziwa TTL, noticed during his research in 1985 a 'spirit of communalism' which he attributed to the keep experience. Muringai, 'The Socio-Economic Impact', p. 32. Surprisingly, O'Gorman comes to the opposite conclusion for the same district. *The Front Line*, chapter 5.
236 The following account is mostly based on the entrepreneur's own testimony, interview #88.
237 Operation Rivet required that all installations and facilities outside the keeps be abandoned and destroyed, business centres included. Most, but not all, stores were rebuilt behind the fence. See 'No Humans Stir Among the Mud Huts: Martin Dickson Reports on Rhodesia at War in Town and Country', *Financial Times*, 6 May 1978.
238 Interview #88.
239 Ibid.
240 'Report: Headman Chikomba', n.d. [198?], PER5 Headman Chikomba, DAO.
241 *Mbuya* Mpota gave birth to two more children in the valley. Interview #9.
242 'Chief's and Headman's Meeting: Tuesday 3rd July 1979', PER5 GEN, DAO.
243 DC Mutasa to PC, 30 June 1977, PER5 GEN, DAO. Mpota Chikomba was not paid any allowance until his appointment as substantive Chief Chikomba in 1979. DC Mutasa to PC, 18 July 1979, PER5 Headman Chikomba, PAO.
244 In the keep, *mbuya* Mpota distributed powdered milk to mothers on behalf of the Red Cross. Interview #9.
245 Chris Ashton, 'Protected Villages: Chris Ashton Visits the Honde Valley', *Illustrated Rhodesia*, 11 May 1978, p. 9.
246 Interview #9; DA Mutasa to Under Secretary (Development) Manicaland, 7 February 1984, PER5 Headman Chikomba, PAO.
247 'Report: Headman Chikomba', n.d. [198?], PER5 Headman Chikomba, PAO
248 See 'Resettled Tribesmen will be Better Off – Minister', *Rhodesian Herald*, 24 May 1973.
249 See CCJP, *The Man in the Middle*, p. 12. Anna Weinrich argued that life in the PVs threatened the 'kinship ideology of the Shona'; 'Strategic Resettlement in Rhodesia', p. 226.
250 Interviews #88, #86, #47, #26.
251 Hunt (PC Manyikaland during the 1970s) had lobbied for introducing collective punishment for years, but he was only given the permission to draw up an applicable act in the context of the villagisation exercise in Chiweshe TTL in 1973. Interview with N.A. Hunt, pp. 52-3; also, 'Rhodesians Warned of Guerrilla Danger', *The Times*, 19 January 1973.
252 Interview #119.
253 A female elder remembered: 'Some ran away to Harare, and they eat up their families there.' Interview #75. Migrant labourers who did return for visits were at times robbed by the guards or not allowed to return to work. Interview #13.
254 Interviews #28, #133, #69.
255 Minutes of the Honde Valley Tea Growers' Liaison Committee Meeting, 28 September 1977, PPF.
256 Interview #120.
257 'Circular from Defence Committee Chairman to Honde Valley Labour Committee', 18 April 1977 and Minutes of the Honde Valley Tea Growers' Liaison Committee Meeting, 1 June 1977, PPF.
258 Tea Growers' Liaison Committee Meeting, 8 February 1978.
259 Interview #75.
260 Tea Growers' Liaison Committee Meeting, 8 February and 28 April 1978, PPF.
261 Minutes of the Honde Valley Labour Committee Meeting, 14 July 1978, PPF.
262 Ibid. Venereal diseases appear to have been prevalent among tea workers prior to the war, though to a much lesser degree. See the directive of one estate, 'Clinic Treatments', 12 August 1971, PPD.
263 Interview #76.

264 'Memorandum on the security situation'.

265 TILCOR representative, 'Report of 1st Visit to Rumbizi, Zindi and Pimayi 11th Oct. 1977–21st Oct. 1977', PPE.

266 Interview #113, with a sex worker, and interviews #99, #101, #59, #60, #38.

267 Interview #111, with a Vapostori. For the prevalence of Vapostori churches in the Honde Valley, see also Simon Gregson et al., 'Apostles and Zionists: The Influence of Religion on Demographic Change in Rural Zimbabwe', *Population Studies*, 53 (1999), pp. 179-93.

268 Interview #75.

269 For an interpretation that differs in most aspects, see Mike Kesby, 'Arenas for Control, Terrains of Gender Contestation: Guerrilla Struggle and Counter-insurgency Warfare in Zimbabwe 1972-80', *Journal of Southern African Studies*, 22, no. 4 (1996), pp. 561-84.

270 Chris Ashton, 'Protected Villages', p. 8.

271 Ibid.

272 Interview #7.

273 For the RENAMO war in Manica Province, see Mark Chingono, *The State, Violence, and Development: The Political Economy of War in Mozambique, 1975–1992* (Aldershot, 1996).

274 Malyn Newitt provides a concise overview of RENAMO's insurgent years in *A History of Mozambique* (Bloomington, IN, 1995), p. 564.

275 Mutasa District, Monthly Report, December 1984, Chitepo District Council, PAO.

276 The considerable body of literature on RENAMO has paid little attention to its operations in Zimbabwe. For a comprehensive overview, see Vines, RENAMO, pp. 61-6, passim.

277 '200 Families Displaced in Mutasa', *Herald*, 24 September 1990.

278 Interview #75.

279 Interview #67.

280 'Victor Mallet Reports on the Increasing Threat of Incursions by Mozambique Guerrilla: MNR Returns to Haunt Zimbabwe's Borders', *Financial Times*, 22 September 1987; interviews #43, #41, #56.

281 'MNR Returns to Haunt Zimbabwe's Borders', *Financial Times*, 22 September 1987. The deteriorating security situation again caused labour problems on the tea estates. 'Minutes of a tea estate management meeting', 6 April 1990, PPC.

282 Interview #92. In addition to the Katiyo estate, Chikomba, Mandeya, and Zindi, as well as the Nyamukwarara Valley, south-east of the Honde Valley, were particularly affected. Protection officer to the security officer Harare, 'Report on my Visit to Stapleford Forestry Commission on 31st May 1988', 6 June 1988, PPB.

283 Mutasa District, Monthly Report, February 1984, Chitepo District Council, PAO; 'Minutes of the JOC Meeting Held at Ruda', 14 July 1987, PPB.

284 Women were also specifically targeted and frequently used as porters. Interviews #139, #39.

285 Moven Mahachi, Minister of Home Affairs, 'Motion: Renewal State of Emergency', *Hansard*, Parliament of Zimbabwe, House of Assembly, 24 January 1989, p. 2139; also pp. 2140-58.

286 Interviews #73, #71; 'Minutes of a tea estate management meeting', 23 February 1990, PPC.

287 Interview #62; Mutasa District, Monthly Report, November 1988, Chitepo District Council, PAO.

288 For the connection between violence and enterprise, see Elwert, 'Markets of Violence'.

289 'Warning to Stop Helping MNR Bandits', *Herald*, 24 August 1990; see also 'Minutes of a JOC Meeting Held at Hauna (Ruda)', 20 April 1990, PPB. A man from Manyikaland appealed to the governor: 'The RENAMO is operating from within. The RENAMOs are within … these people are fed by their parents', ZANU(PF) member to the Provincial Governor, 17 September 1988, establishment of Vidcos, Wadcos, PAO. Afonso Dhlakama, President of RENAMO, apparently promised that if the chiefs assisted the movement in coming to power, the Mutasa mamboship would be reinstalled in its 'traditional' boundaries between Marondera in Zimbabwe and Beira on the Mozambican coast. Interviews #39, #25.

290 'Police Net 202 Kg of Mbanje Destined for SA Market', *Herald*, 11 October 1990.

291 Interviews #47, #51, #139. RENAMO appears to have aimed violence at families with whom they traded and whom they suspected of reporting or defrauding. Interviews #39, #62; 'Fears Grow Over Villagers' Links with MNR Bandits', *Herald*, 13 February 1990.

292 The relief mealie meal was referred to as 'Kenya' because the word was printed on the bags, but few realised that this was the country of origin. Most people considered this yellow flour as unfit for human consumption. Frequent complaints were that even dogs refused to eat it and that it would only 'make the chickens happy'. During the 1991/92 drought, local trade further diversified when women went to the large, second-hand clothes market in Chimoio. Another commodity smuggled across the border and sold on plantations and commercial farms was relief food such as tins of sardines. Interviews #99, #105, #71, #51, #25, #56; also, 'Minutes of a JOC Meeting Held at

Hauna (Ruda)', 1 June 1990, PPB.

293 'Minutes of a Sub JOC Meeting Held at Ruda', 9 October 1990, PPB.

294 See, C. Morna, 'Schutzdörfer in Zimbabwe für RENAMO-Opfer', *IZ3W*, no. 159 (1989), p. 55; 'Planned Villages for MNR Victims', *Herald*, 28 April 1989.

295 Minutes of a tea estate management meeting, 8 October 1987, PPC; Memorandum from 62 Infantry Battalion Ruda to all SUB JOC Members, 'Attendance to Sub JOC Meetings: Ruda', 2 August 1989, PPB.

296 'Minutes of a Sub JOC Meeting Held at Ruda', 9 October 1990, PPB; Mutasa District, Monthly Report, February 1988, Chitepo District Council, PAO.

297 'Minutes of Sub JOC Meeting Held at Ruda', 17 September 1988, 26 January, and 18 May 1990, PPB; Mutasa District, Monthly Report, November 1988, PAO.

298 Interviews #41 and #147 with a senior civil servant; 'Minutes of a JOC Meeting Held at Hauna (Ruda)', 18 May 1990, PPB.

299 'Minutes of the Mutasa District Development Committee Meeting', 17 October 1985, PPD. Four years later, DA Mutasa stated that 'people to be villagised have to first of all agree before they are driven out'. 'Minutes of the JOC Meeting Held at Ruda', 18 August 1989, PPB.

300 Provincial Community Development Officer Manicaland to PA, 8 November 1988, establishment of Vidcos, Wadcos, PAO.

301 Lazarus Nzarayebani, MP Mutare East, to Katiyo, 8 September 1986, PPD.

302 Interview #137, with a DERUDE employee.

303 'Land Use Planning – A Paper Presented at a Provincial Development Committee Meeting, 25-26 June, 1987', 23 June 1987, establishment of Vidcos, Wadcos, PAO; see also K. Nyamapiena, 'Proposals for Communal Land Re-organization in Zimbabwe', 1990, a FAO consultancy report, DERUDE. For earlier attempts to introduce block cultivation at Katiyo tea estate, see 'Proposed Tenancy Plan', 21 January 1972, PPD.

304 DA Mutasa to Agritex Mutasa, 11 July 1988, establishment of Vidcos, Wadcos, PAO; Mutasa District, Monthly Report, December 1989, Chitepo District Council, PAO; 'Minutes of a JOC Meeting Held at Hauna (Ruda)', 18 May 1990, PPB.

305 Chief Development Officer DERUDE, 'Mutasa Villagization Manicaland: June 1990-June 1991', 12 June 1991; Manase, 'Communal Land Reorganization', pp. 25-26; 'Local Government Promotion Officers' Monthly Report for September 1990, Mutasa District', Chitepo District Council, PAO; in the *Herald*, 'Border People to Move in Settlements Soon', 15 April 1989; 'Planned Villages for MNR Victims', 28 April 1989; 'Rushinga Sets Up Security Villages to Counter MNR', 21 May 1989; 'State in Village Protection Drive', 19 October 1989; Richard Carver, *Zimbabwe: A Break with the Past? Human Rights and Political Unity: An Africa Watch Report* (New York, 1989), p. 82.

306 Mutasa District, Monthly Report, November 1988, PAO.

307 Interview #78; 'Minutes of a JOC Meeting Held at Hauna (Ruda)', 20 April 1990, PPB; Mutasa District, Monthly Report, May 1990, Chitepo District Council, PAO.

308 Interviews #14, #71.

309 Interview #25, with a DERUDE officer; interview #28.

310 Interview #25; Security Officer Eastern Districts, 'Annual Report: Security Operation Return on Estates: Financial Year 1989/90', 20 July 1990, PPB; minutes of a border security meeting, Chipinge, 1 June 1989, establishment of Vidcos, Wadcos, PAO. A former ZANLA fighter who had been operational in the valley and had attacked PVs was now a civil servant involved in convincing people to move into PVSs. Interview #26.

311 Mutasa District, Monthly Report, May 1988, Chitepo District Council, PAO.

312 DA Nyanga to PA, 18 February 1988, establishment of Vidcos and Wadcos, PAO; also the reader's letter from a Honde Valley man: 'Against Linear Settlement', *Parade* (February 1992), p. 5.

313 Frederick Cooper, *Africa Since 1940: The Past of the Present* (Cambridge, 2002), p. 4, passim.

6

After Violence
Healing the Wounds of War

The Second Chimurenga came to an end with a negotiated ceasefire period that lasted from 28 December 1979 to 4 January 1980, followed by the first democratic elections in Zimbabwe in February 1980. Under the Lancaster House Agreement of 1979, the 100 parliamentary seats were divided as follows: 20 for a white electoral roll, all of which went to the Rhodesian Front, the former ruling party, and 80 for the common roll. These seats were distributed as follows: ZANU(PF), under the leadership of Robert Mugabe, won 57 (63 per cent), all in their operational areas during the Chimurenga, with the exception of one constituency; ZAPU, under the leadership of Joshua Nkomo, came to the poll as the Patriotic Front (PF) and won 20 seats (26 per cent) along the same lines, while three seats went to the United African National Council, led by Bishop Abel Muzorewa.[1] During the transition period, the territory known as Zimbabwe–Rhodesia between June and 12 December 1979, temporarily became a crown colony and was renamed Southern Rhodesia, with Lord Soames as its Governor. He announced the election results on 4 March, and the country erupted with celebrations that culminated on independence day, when at midnight 17 April 1980, the British flag was lowered and the new Zimbabwean flag was hoisted in Rufaro Stadium on the outskirts of Harare.

The newly elected government faced tremendous political, social, and economic challenges, not least because the Chimurenga had caused much destruction throughout the country. Taken together with the legacy of the discriminatory policies of the settler state, this made it necessary to focus on reconstruction and development. The most immediate tasks at hand in April 1980 were the rebuilding of infrastructure and services, assistance for returning refugees and displaced people, and food security.[2] In all, 250,000 refugees from neighbouring countries, 400,000 people internally displaced, and 750,000 people in Protected Villages (PVs) required help.[3] Moreover, attacks on 'soft targets' in rural areas, such as farmsteads and infrastructure, had been central to insurgency operations during the Chimurenga and scorched-earth tactics were part of the counter-insurgency villagisation programme and the creation of no-go areas, all of which had resulted in further deprivation.[4] At the end

16. Pungwe Gorge before the 1980 elections (Source: National Archives of Zimbabwe)

of the war, the situation in rural areas was desperate: 180 out of 243 clinics, 23 out of 59 mission hospitals, and 90 out of 147 privately owned secondary schools were closed,[5] while 2,000 out of 2,500 primary schools, 9,600 kilometres of roads, 64 causeways and bridges, 70 out of 109 cattle marketing pans, and 1,300 cattle dip tanks had been damaged or destroyed. Furthermore, 41 out of 59 irrigation schemes were closed or had been directly affected by the war and there were 750 square kilometres of minefields to be cleared.[6] In addition, well over one million head of African-owned cattle, one third of the pre-war count, had died as a result of disease, been hamstrung, or simply stolen.[7] Despite this daunting legacy of war, the early 1980s saw Zimbabwe become a success story, with the government providing unprecedented access to services for the majority of the population. At the Zimbabwe Conference on Reconstruction and Development (ZIMCORD) in 1981, the government suggested that 45 per cent of the total reconstruction budget should be allocated to rural infrastructure alone.[8] The costs of the development effort, however, were tremendous.[9]

This chapter demonstrates that despite the joy over national independence that swept through the country, the birth of a renamed nation state, the election of a majority rule government, enacting a new constitution, and raising a new flag did not bring overnight peace and social healing, nor did it guarantee that every Zimbabwean would recognise the government as legitimate. This chapter shows first that immediately after independence, the Honde Valley once again became a frontier to state authority. The second section examines spiritual healing and reconciliation, beginning with mapping post-conflict tensions and discussing spiritual and social healing. The argument put forward is that while healing practices and spiritual affliction often indicate suffering, they may also generate a sense of empowerment, as in the case of *chikwambo*, male spirits that affect females, and *madzviti* (here: warrior spirits) that afflict men. The last part of this chapter shows how once peace arrived in the early 1990s, the inhabitants of the Honde Valley attempted to reclaim their frontier landscape in a manner that interlaced the spiritual, political, social, and economic spheres. In the end, however, the tremendous effort of recovering from war and of undoing the geography of racial dispossession brought the state into the Honde Valley as a permanent presence and so ended its frontier career.

Dissidents & Political Legitimacy

Throughout the colonial world, the transformation process of nationalist parties or liberation movements into ruling parties was never instantaneous and was often difficult. In Zimbabwe, the task of transforming the war economy and socio-political structures of the Rhodesian state into a stable, post-settler society involved reconciling liberation ideology with material and planning needs on the ground. Frederick Cooper succinctly observed that decolonisation turned empires into nation states.[10] In metropoles such as France or Germany, whose populations had for centuries been nations, the transition to nation states was seamless. However, in the former colonies, political independence did not give birth smoothly to nations when colonial subjects became citizens. Ernest Renan's 1882 classic definition of the nation as a 'community of interest', the membership of which requires a 'daily plebiscite' that reinforces the notion of a shared past, a 'sentimental side', 'present day consent', and both memories and the promise of sacrifice and suffering[11] suggests that societies which gain their country's independence through a liberation struggle would be in an ideal position to rise as strong nations. However, the nationalist ideology that emerges from such constellations is often one of post-revolutionary, hyper-nationalism as became manifest in Zimbabwe from 2000, when Robert Mugabe, still president, declared a Third Chimurenga for the recovery of lost lands.[12]

During the ceasefire period, the Rhodesian government ordered all sensitive files to be destroyed by their own offices and parastatals, and in some cases the same was done by private companies. At times, the materials survived due to sentimentality and pride in one's work on the part of those who took them home, as well as the attempt to preserve documentation during a period when a sense of insecurity was widespread. Another reason why so many, especially security-related, written documents evaded destruction is that in the Mutasa area, for example, as soon as the ceasefire was declared, guerrilla fighters appeared in public, announcing that they had won the war. One such incident occurred at one of the forestry estates. The files had been taken down to the sawmill to be burnt when a Land Rover suddenly arrived, carrying ZANLA ex-combatants holding up their AK-47s and shouting liberation slogans. The staff only just managed to shove the papers out of sight, stowing most in a big wooden box; some files were later used as insulation material for the roof.[13] This incident, telling as it is regarding the casualness with which the Lancaster House Agreement that prescribed disarmament of the liberation armies was breached, illustrates that the beginning of the ceasefire at the end of 1979 set off a period of ambiguity of power and authority. One symptom of this uncertainty is that even after independence the plantations in the Honde Valley decided to retain the regular liaison meetings they had established during the war, but now without the army, despite government directives to abandon such actions by the end of June 1980.[14] In the Mutasa area, as elsewhere in the country, some fighters did not disarm. While they never posed a military threat, their presence and actions nevertheless directly challenged the state's monopoly on violence and the legitimacy of the new government. As a consequence, they were officially referred to as dissidents.

The turning point that marked the end of the war for most was not the ceasefire, the first democratic elections, or independence day, but rather the return home, the moment of recovering a deep sense of belonging. Those who had stayed in the PVs during the war were allowed to leave after the elections. During the ceasefire period, they were joined by repatriated refugees from Mozambique, while most of the internally displaced returned from April 1980 and settled directly on land.[15] 1980 was a time of homecoming for most, but men who had joined the Security Forces or the police typically did not return for some time, fearing hostilities. As one man related: 'They came later, after some years, when things had cooled down. The comrades here did not want to see those who had been soldiers.'[16] Returning home was a process that imposed a substantial strain on communities, with neighbours comparing experiences, and competition over resources, especially land, erupting for the first time. The combatants' return, however, appears to have been the most difficult part of the transition to peace.

Youths who had left to fight the Chimurenga with ZANLA were welcomed upon their arrival. A commander who had been operational in the valley and who returned in the early 1980s as a government bureaucrat recalled that some people who recognised him said: 'You are now grown up!'[17] Sadly, a number of those tea estate workers who had joined the struggle because of poor working conditions and low pay saw no alternative after independence but to resume work for their former employers.[18] This was the case with a young ex-combatant who related, with pride, how he had joined up as a young boy because he could not bear the conditions on the tea estate and had subsequently been trained as a fighter. He explained, with tears in his eyes:

> We looked forward to the government addressing our plight. If I sit and wonder, I end up chiding myself for going to war. As for me, I now have a troublesome leg, a legacy from war, and no doctor can cure it. Today, if I thought about it, I became mad. An employer can chuck me away because of this leg, which makes me unable to do work …. Because of war, I was not able to attend school, and I'm being [too] old now to go back to school. – I now find that death is the only way to ebb this pain away.[19]

Yet this young man had somehow persevered, and there were also good things in his life – he truly beamed when he insisted that I take a photograph of him with his wife and child, who had been born that very day.

Most ex-combatants soon had to realise that their heroes' welcome would not last long. One man remembered that the change took place in 1981/82: 'It is different now. Way back, during the war, my mere presence as a comrade made people shiver. Today, the same people are no longer afraid of me. They now see me as their equal.'[20] A young man present during this interview observed: 'They are now toothless, barking dogs.' The ex-combatant went on to complain that:

> They talk about reconciliation. Reconciliation indeed! Those who killed people at Nyadzonia [a ZANLA camp in Mozambique that fell victim to hot pursuit] and also beat up our parents are said to be good soldiers today, and they are given good jobs. As for those who fought for the country, well, they say they are not educated. They seem to forget that we fought those whites.[21]

More than a decade after learning of their disempowerment, not every ex-combatant had managed to move on. This veteran, also working at a tea estate in the Honde Valley, recovered from his bitter rant by revelling in his heroic days as a liberation fighter. Even so, he did not recall his idealism and political hopes; instead his reverie culminated in an account of his unit torturing a chief whom they suspected of having passed information to government troops:

> We went to that chief. We took him and we said: 'Tell us, what you have done.' He tried to say this and this. We said: 'My friend, say what you have done.' 'Ah,' he said, 'ah, nothing.' Said 'ah'. 'Today we are going to fix you.' We cut him into pieces. We cut his fingers. I took a knife and one eye came out. And again – the other …. He just said: 'I have done nothing *vana vangu* [my children']…. We beat him, but he was still alive. We put him in a chicken run, poured paraffin on it, and set it on fire, with him locked inside. At the end of it, he came out unscathed. This threw us into confusion – until a comrade, Gamba Muhondo, chose to shoot him, and that's when the wizard died. After we had cut him into pieces and set him on fire, he came out alive and apparently unscathed, so we had to shoot him dead![22]

The other young man present during the interview reminded the ex-combatant that 'a white woman' was present, but he continued gleefully with his narrative. Later he concluded that it would take him only two days to be dangerous again. All he needed was an AK-47.[23] Stories circulated that he abused women, and not long after the interview, it was believed he raped a young girl.[24] His example is not typical of Chimurenga veterans, but it illustrates the horror the combatants went through, usually as teenagers or while in their early twenties, and the difficulty this brought to reintegration after the war. The fear of being rendered powerless without their AK-47s might well be one reason why thousands of fighters did not report to the Assembly Points. Some of these men apparently turned to banditry in 1980.

Two other interviewees, one a fighter originally from the Honde Valley and the other who had been based there, both recalled that their superiors were sceptical of the ceasefire and the election arrangements at the time. Under the Lancaster House Agreement, all liberation fighters had to report to one of sixteen Assembly Points, supervised by the Commonwealth Monitoring Force, by 4 January 1980 as part of the ceasefire provisions and to be recognised as legitimate combatants. But many guerrillas feared that the arrangements were no more than pre-arranged ambushes and expected air attacks.[25] They also objected to the often humiliating process of having to submit, at least temporarily, to the authority of their former enemy, having to prove that they were combat-trained and not merely posing as fighters, and to the prospect of amalgamation into a regular army after independence. One ex-combatant – a ZANLA commander – pointed out that he still kept in contact with his superiors in Mozambique after he had entered an Assembly Point, and that he was called back across the border in order to be instructed in conventional warfare to prepare for possible deviations from the peace plan. He remembered that he was instructed to hide inside the country with his platoon until the elections. He found their roles unexpectedly transformed when he and his men had to take over some of the women's chores in order to support the democratic process:

> We were really looking after the children, you know, cooking *sadza* for the children while the mothers had gone for voting.
>
> H.S.: Really? [laughter]
>
> And looking after their *mombes*, the cattle, herding them.[26]

Norma Kriger estimates that as many as two thirds of ZANLA's 30,000 fighters entered the country after the ceasefire and thus did not go through the regular disarmament and rehabilitation process.[27]

During this period, when a sense of insecurity and political uncertainty prevailed, violence returned to the Honde Valley. Officially, the incidents were labelled 'dissident activity' because the armed men had no legitimacy in the eyes of the government, but from a local perspective they were initially regarded as social bandits. Eric Hobsbawm defines social bandits as outlaws who use violence or the threat thereof to challenge power in social, political, and economic spheres and thus find support among the marginalised. When such backing falls away, they become mere bandits.[28] At first, the young men who used their guns to settle scores and continue politicisation in the aftermath of the Chimurenga had legitimacy in the eyes of valley inhabitants, much like FRELIMO and ZANLA had during the Chimurenga, but as time passed, intimidation replaced authority.

In the valley, during the initial phase of the Chimurenga, FRELIMO, and then ZANLA, addressed the radical local agenda of a recovery of the frontier identity from state intervention by attacking the tea plantations, state institutions, and individuals perceived as a threat to social cohesion and wellbeing. Such grievances were carried into the post-independence period. The perception of independence as a break with the past was further undermined by the continuity of district staff from Rhodesian times who enforced land allocation and agricultural policies. Examples include the retention of Europeans as Provincial Administrator Manyikaland, District Administrator (DA) Mutasa and Nyanga, and the appointment of African men as District Assistants who had served in a similar role before independence.[29] In addition, the attempt to radically revise local government policies met with obstinate rejection. Although the newly formed District Councils were now officially responsible for land allocation, for example,[30] they were rivalled by grassroots village committees organised by returnees from Mozambique and by chiefs and *masabhuku*, who claimed their ancestral right to allocate land.[31] Against this background, support for the young men with guns carried on at first, and met with their continued appeals, such as the intention to parcel up the estates and reallocate tea fields to valley inhabitants.[32] The ex-combatants were, however, no longer in a strong enough position to fight socio-economic inequality. The early independence period, when disempowered, if not always demobilised, fighters found their way back into civilian life and the new government took up its responsibilities, left a deep mark in personal and social memory in the valley.

The young men's initial actions show a sense of euphoria over having won the war and they limited themselves to a minimal use of violence. Several episodes support this view. In March 1980 'an armed group of ZANLA', including 'Comrade James Bond 007' and 'Comrade Black Label' (a beer brand),[33] confiscated cars owned by a storeowner at Rumbizi. Some of these men went to the Katiyo clubhouse and demanded 'drinks and accommodation without payment' and called on workers to celebrate rather than work. The relatively insignificant material loss to the company indicates that this was not an act of sabotage: 3,500 Rhodesian Dollars (loss of revenue due to workers not attending work), plus eight bottles of beer, one packet of meat pies, nine packets of Madison cigarettes, six cases of beer, one-and-a-half bottles of brandy, eighteen bottles of 'minerals' (fizzy drinks), and seven litres of petrol.[34] Even so, the 'dissidents' also continued to politicise tea workers. For example, one occasion saw three men, armed with Chinese stick grenades, take the bus from Sagambe PV to Katiyo. They gathered workers at the beer hall:

> The crowd was apparently told that the country was now free and that everybody should work together. They also instructed the workers that they were to return to work as soon as possible after the gathering. ... It is interesting to note that every night since Monday most of the compounds on the Estate have been singing songs and drinking until early hours of the morning. This has not happened for some time and is obviously a direct result of dissident influence as the songs are of a political nature.[35]

Three days later, eight 'dissidents' returned in the afternoon. One of them, Comrade Samora, introduced himself to a member of the management and asked for permission to hold a meeting in a labour compound that evening. He was recognized as a former estate worker who had crossed into Mozambique in 1975.[36]

The actions of armed men did not always take the innocuous form of asking permission or travelling by bus, nor did they stop with mobilisation and celebration. Some old scores were settled, for instance, when a landmine was planted in the driveway of the house of one of the European staff at EHTE.[37] On another occasion the 'dissidents' attracted a 'small crowd' at Katiyo who began singing. They then demanded a Guard Force member join in, something which caused him 'to be ridiculed and suffering humiliation'.[38] Finally, the habit of intervening in local politics also continued from the Second Chimurenga, as in July 1980, when a 'ZANLA element' interrupted a meeting convened to formalise the appointment of the loyalist Mpota as Chief Chikomba.[39]

At the end of 1980, when this initial period of celebration and ambiguous

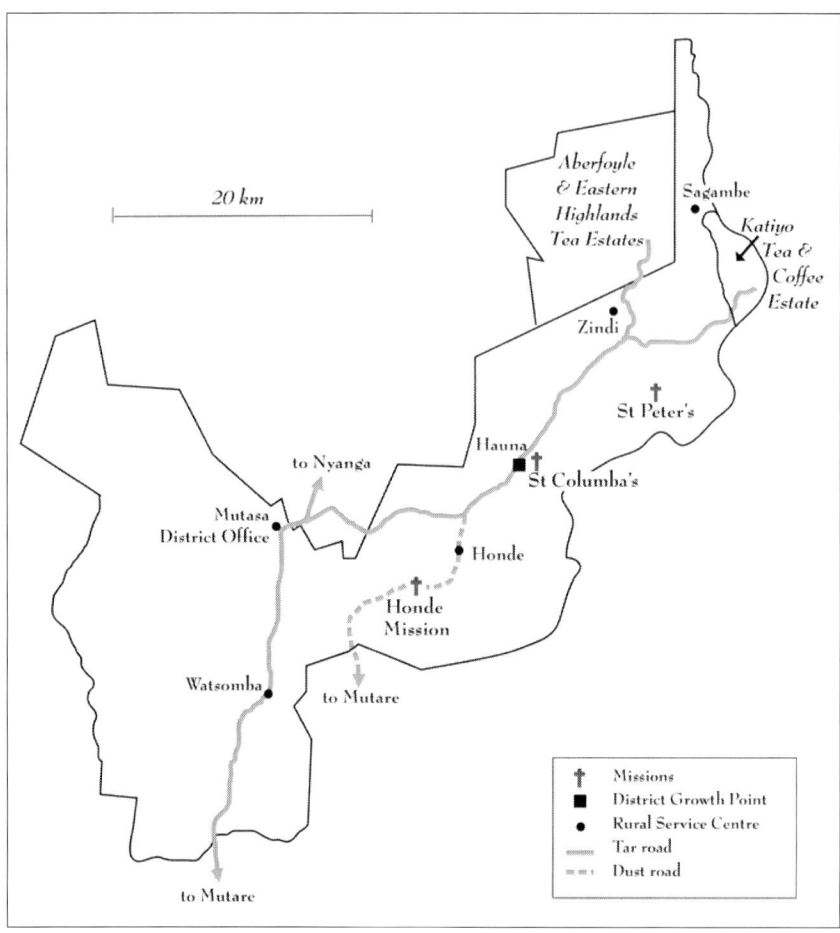

Map 4 Mutasa District, 1982

power relations came to an end and the ex-combatants had dropped their approach of social appeal, a different pattern of 'dissident' activities emerged. A spate of domestic crimes and murders had already been reported during that year[40] and facilitated by access to large numbers of weapons some men turned to banditry. This development escalated with armed hold-ups, robberies, and youth gangs on the tea estates in early 1981, and it was reported that a gunman who killed five people in several attacks in the Nyamaende area caused 'so much panic that some of the people in the area are deserting their homes'.[41] This bout of violence ended in late 1982, when the last 'dissident', 'an armed man on whose gun butt was written "Mbuya Nehanda" was seen somewhere in the Honde Valley.[42]

Even before the *Gukurahundi* (1982–1987), the government's violent campaign in Matabeleland, officially directed against 'dissidents' that caused the death of up to 20,000 Zimbabweans and foreshadowed events of the early twenty-first century, the government took steps to fight opposition and dissent in Manyikaland. Here, the administration, police, and army of the newly independent state had failed to gain legitimacy through elections and independence alone, and it is telling that some valley inhabitants also referred to members of the National Army (ZNA) as dissidents.[43] As late as 1981, the officer in charge at Ruda police camp explained that 'his Ministry was involved in the keeping of Law and Order and making every citizen happy and not frighten[ing] them. He said that in certain areas, some people were still suspicious of their role and could not assist them in providing information on criminal elements in the district'.[44] The government was clearly concerned about the security threat the young men with guns in the valley posed by undermining the state's monopoly on violence:

> Had [the] Police made a direct approach to armed and drunken dissidents this would have resulted in armed conflict. This, in turn, would have culminated, not only in the loss of life and limb, but could have had a ripple effect in other dissidents becoming more militant. Their attention would have been drawn to soft target areas of the tea estates.[45]

The fear of insurgent activity reached into late 1981, when local government discussed a proposal to employ ex-combatants together with the army and police 'to address the locals in the security affected areas'. While the understanding of the problem appears to have been present, so too was colonial discourse – a European officer added 'that there was no danger from the Army as long as the locals complied with orders given to them, e.g., if asked for identification card one must produce it'.[46] By November 1981, Prime Minister Robert Mugabe made internal security in border areas the army's responsibility and deployed three units operating along the border in the Honde Valley.[47] Nevertheless, the security situation was such that weapons were still being recovered and government employees working in the area continued to request army protection. It being crucial to gain control, the government adopted a new strategy that would successfully end 'dissident' activities in the valley by the end of 1982.

In a twist on insurgency and counter-insurgency tactics, merging support structures and hearts and minds, in November 1981 the army began to work hand-in-hand with ex-*mujibhas*, the male youths who had assisted the combatants during the Chimurenga, and focused on ensuring cooperation between 'security people and the locals' in Mutasa District.[48] This co-opting of youths into communal responsibility – and hence party structures – achieved success within six months[49] and was crucial in undermining 'dissident' activities in the valley. The boys and young men who previously had passed information about troop movements to ZANLA now reported on armed activities to the government; this was a step towards the role youths would later play in merging violence and politics during the so-called Third Chimurenga in many areas of Zimbabwe. In 1990, a ZANU(PF) representative at a district meeting reported on the valley and concluded that 'the youths were all theirs'.[50]

In short, the ceasefire did not bring the end of violence to the Honde Valley, as young armed men branded by the government as 'dissidents' carried out their activities. The first two years after independence were a period in which initial enthusiasm and political and social instability as experienced by the newly re-united valley communities was partly expressed, and then increasingly overshadowed by violent events. By the end of 1982, however, the post-colonial state had established its presence in the valley through the army and party organisation.

Reconciliation: Remembering & Forgetting

The impressive body of literature on violence and war addresses the question of individual and communal experiences of conflict, usually through the lens of responses to and victimisation by state-sponsored violence, guerrilla movements, and warlordism.[51] Turning the focus to questions of social cohesion and the sense of belonging, and doing so from a radically local perspective, allows a more complex understanding of identity and violence beyond both the old-fashioned paradigm of false consciousness and the more pragmatic considerations of guerrilla support structures and anti-government resistance. What emerges is that communities under duress can seldom afford to voice or even show discord. Once security returns, however, multiple layers of memory and forgetting signifying identity, belonging, and past experiences emerge. Space is invested with meaning, creating landscapes of violence that crystallise a sense of belonging, serve as mnemotope, and become a home for both spiritual security and danger. This part of the chapter examines how the frontier society recovered from the Chimurenga, both in its aftermath under the strain of the RENAMO insurgency and then with an outlook towards reconciliation during peace.

In 1992, an elderly woman declared: 'If there is one place in Zimbabwe where reconciliation is taking place, then it is here. The valley is a place of true reconciliation!'[52] Yet, at the same time, it was striking that even by the early 1990s inhabitants of the Honde Valley still frequently associated geographical locations with violent events: a schoolyard where the Security Forces had displayed dead ZANLA fighters; a tree under which guerrillas had killed supporters of Bishop Abel Muzorewa, the leader of the United African Council and Prime Minister of the internal settlement government in 1979; a clearing where RENAMO had axed a family to death. Thus the valley was mapped as a landscape of violence, albeit expressed in a tension between forgetting and memory, the foundation upon which reconciliation was built through healing processes.

RIFTS EMERGE

In the Honde Valley, some individuals, especially government employees and business people, perceived the Second Chimurenga as a period of total victimisation, but for most it was a time of both suffering and liberation. When the displaced started to return during the ceasefire period, a complex reintegration and reconciliation process began that brought together those who had stayed and those who had left: villagers and the displaced; parents and their children who had run away to join the war; siblings who found that they had fought on both sides of the conflict; and rural African communities with staff of the administration and police who continued to work in that capacity, at least for some time, now serving the post-colonial government. Inevitably, the reconstitution of communities caused tensions.

A decade after the war ended, ideological differences still manifested themselves in the form of competing claims about whose fate had brought more suffering. A group of men who had lived in a PV emphasised that 1980 had been a very difficult year for those who had been forcibly resettled. Their spokesman summarised their view that they had yet to recover pre-war living standards as follows: '1980 was a very hard year for them and since they had to rebuild houses – and some of their property was lost during the war – and find and buy property to put in houses; even today, they are saying, some haven't finished building what they want to build.'[53] In contrast, a male elder who had left for Mozambique in 1976 recalled the solitude experienced and the material loss caused by displacement:

> You do not pack much before fleeing: you simply collect your blankets and cross over. Each man takes his family and flees. You do not invite others to join you in running away…. We fled the war. We had no happy moments. We came back here with neither property nor wealth.[54]

Dissent over hardship and suffering added to struggles over land and other resources after the war. In November 1980, the administration in Zimunya Communal Land (CL) found that the distribution of fertiliser, seed, and ox-drawn ploughs was causing problems with local communities: 'They think it is a thank you for supporting the war whereas it is for the refugees.'[55]

A sense of entitlement and the necessities of war recovery, together with the heightened land pressure, at times even resulted in open strife. The legacy of the villagisation programme, the increasing influx of refugees displaced by Mozambique's RENAMO war now seeking refuge on the Zimbabwean side of the border, and favourable agricultural conditions in the valley which attracted immigrants, including staff and workers from the tea and adjacent forestry estates, led to land scarcity for the very first time, especially in Mutasa North and Manga CLs.[56] The reoccupation of arable land in the Honde Valley unfolded unevenly. Most valley inhabitants who had spent the war years in

Mozambique returned to the Honde Valley in early 1980, but were initially forced to stay in PVs under military control and remembered the keep experience as alienating. They were the first to return to their old homesteads when the keeps were opened at independence.[57] Others who had made a living in the PVs, and who stayed there until as late as 1984 before leaving, usually found their land occupied by those who had returned earlier. Finally, according to estimates, 'less than a quarter' of the PV populations decided to stay, in part because of the infrastructural advantages such as grinding mills and marketing facilities.[58] These households kept the land close to the keeps that they had begun cultivating during the war. However, it was often the case that this land had been previously farmed by others before the Chimurenga, which caused further problems.[59] As a result, the valley underwent a major transformation in land use patterns, and the unevenness in the process of returning from war caused a brief scramble for land that left some aggrieved.

A number of resident plantation staff acquired land in the CLs because they were not allowed to keep livestock on the estates. One man explained that he had not attempted to become local; instead of entering reciprocal relationships, he had 'bought' land in the valley in 1981, before most of the previous occupants of the area had returned from the former PVs. He gave a chief money and livestock that far exceeded the usual *hombera* (paying of tribute and respect) to the local chief upon a newcomer's arrival.[60] Land cannot be acquired as property in CLs as title deeds do not exist, rather members of the community gain land use rights. Only if an allocated plot contains cash crops and structures is some payment expected. The member of estate staff who wanted to rear a herd of cattle reasoned: 'One needs to think about the future. It is important. Some time I will be old and I need a place I can go to. It is better to just eat food now, but have something later.'[61] He settled his family on the land so that they could look after the property. But he faced problems with his neighbours: 'When people returned from the keeps, they were envious. Things started to happen.'[62] He recalled three incidents in which his livestock – cattle and goats – was stolen or killed, and even his homestead was burnt down. Although he felt bitter about the attacks, he continued to develop his property.

The scramble for land went hand in hand with its commercialisation. Cash transactions were the exception, though in one case a Vapostori household paid more than 30,000 Zimbabwe Dollars for a developed tea field.[63] Tea and coffee in particular created capitalised land claims. As in earlier times, development efforts arrived in the valley in the usual, modernist guise of land reallocation and the improvement of land use practices, with the revival and reintroduction of cash crop production especially. The 1985 development plan for the valley praised the area as the 'best farming region in the whole country' and identified an impressive planning list that included coffee, dairy, deciduous fruit, barley, tobacco, grazing, garden, honey, and health projects. In addition to eight ministries, several NGOs were involved in this effort: UNICEF, the Lutheran World Federation, SIDA, the International Red Cross, the EEC, Christian Care, and Oxfam. In this way, the 1956 Native Land Husbandry Act found a post-colonial reincarnation.[64]

In 1986, local leadership appealed to the government: 'Comrade Ministers I strongly appeal to you to work tirelessly and use your good office to assist this mountainous and densely populated District to develop. The Potential [sic] is here, money we don't have, save our souls in the name of development.'[65] In this regard, a significant difference can be observed compared to earlier efforts. After independence, most households with sufficient labour and access to suitable land started to grow tea in Holdenby.[66] The adoption of coffee thrived from 1985 with the establishment of the Coffee Growers Co-operative Society that runs pulperies, where the beans are graded and processed. By 1992, the 360 founding members had expanded to 2,000 growers cultivating 820 hectares of coffee,[67] supported since the mid-1980s by EEC funds.[68] After 1980, land use and settlement patterns represented a solid expression of differences in war experiences, moral, economic, and political choices, and the sense of belonging on the ground.

FORGETTING

Memory or forgetting of violence, its presence or absence as shared past in the Honde Valley after the Chimurenga, manifested itself in social healing and was shaped by strategic survival when RENAMO began operating in the area once more. Valley inhabitants witnessed, experienced, and perpetrated violence during the Chimurenga, but these were occurrences they could not talk about in the presence of armed men. The caution that had helped villagers live through their years in the PVs, all the while sustaining support structures for the ZANLA fighters, continued after the war, necessitated first by the uncertainty of the initial post-independence period and, after a brief peaceful interlude, the return of war with RENAMO infiltration from 1984. A valley inhabitant explained:

> The people around here can keep secrets. They can even kill a person here and dig him under, covering him up with soil and so on, but nobody will utter a word. I don't know why it is this way. They learnt during the war, and during the war you were not allowed to speak too much – you can see but not talk.[69]

One example of such silence is the case of a policeman who had his throat cut by guerrillas in 1977, when he took the risk of visiting his rural home because his child had died. Although the incident was known to the police, his parents did not dare to admit that they knew of the killing or to identify the burial site.[70] In short, until the Mozambican ceasefire in October 1992, the discourse about the Chimurenga was driven by forgetting, silence, and absence – 'you can see but not talk'.

In interviews and conversations, older male valley inhabitants and, once they felt comfortable doing so, women spoke in depth about their war experiences, whereas those who had been teenagers or in their early twenties during the Chimurenga tended to be vague. The only exceptions were ex-combatants. A striking example of almost universal forgetting is the silence on the roles individual members of their communities had played during the Chimurenga, and in particular on the subject of *mujibhas* and *chimbwidos*, the male and female children and youths who had assisted the liberation fighters during the war as intermediaries between them and the civilian population. One male elder, a *sab-huku*, recalled how a neighbour and contestant for his office had sent *mujibhas* to report him to the guerrillas. The incident could have easily cost him his life, but he claimed not to remember the neighbour or who these young boys were.[71] A *ñ'anga* (healer) explained that many young women had relationships and children with either guerrillas or members of the Security Forces during the war and that some came to consult him. When asked what had happened to these women, he maintained that they and their children died.[72] It is not unreasonable to assume that such deaths had occurred, as the HIV rate in the area was particularly high. In 1992, 75 per cent of those females aged between 15 and 35 were HIV-positive.[73] Also, there are complications in the healing of children if their totem, which is identical with their father's, is not known to the *ñ'anga*. This is often the case with children born out of forced or casual encounters, events which became much more common with the presence of armed young men.[74] Still, it is striking that alleged death or the claim of forgetting about ex-*mujibhas* and *chimbwidos* turned out to be the common answer from the parent generation.

No full study has been done on young women (or men) and their fate after the war, but accounts by female ex-combatants support the view that their reintegration into civilian life often resembled social death. Having escaped male guardianship and parental control for months or even years, these women were viewed as prostitutes, outcasts who struggled to regain an acceptable status that would allow them to marry.[75] According to Norma Kriger's evidence, and supported by the *sabhuku*'s account above, *mujibhas* in particular had often been directly involved in punitive actions, whether as informants or by inflicting beatings. Once the valley communities were reunited and newly constituted after 1980, forgetting these actions proved to be crucial for social healing, preventing the break-up of communities, and even of families, some of which were divided between members who had supported the various antagonists of the war and challenged the age and gender norms of peacetime society. Forgetting and absence can signify the presence of knowledge, such as painful memories or those that may cause conflict in the community. However, in the Honde Valley, once peace came and drought caused renewed suffering, these memories resurfaced.

REMEMBERING

1992 was a year of joy and of suffering in the Honde Valley, and both contributed to the resurfacing of memories. October saw the Mozambican ceasefire and thus the cessation of RENAMO's presence in the area, but the country's worst drought in living memory took its toll. The contrast between forgetting and remembering was stunning. Silence was deeply enshrined, and a woman from the valley insisted that people still do not shake hands. She reasoned that during the war one was easily accused of being a sell-out if one appeared to be friendly with strangers: 'We used to shake hands, but with the war, no! During the Chimurenga it used to happen that you shook hands with a stranger, next thing you were taken into the bush and beaten to death.'[76] Less than a year after the ceasefire, however, valley inhabitants expressed their disbelief that RENAMO could have ever caused so much terror and began to talk about their experiences. In 1993, as part of RENAMO's integration into the Mozambican army, Britain implemented a training exercise for soldiers of both armies at the military base in Nyanga District. In the Honde Valley, the story circulated that most RENAMO soldiers were physically so weak that they had to be fed before they could embark on any military training. People joked that during the war, they had had to feed the RENAMO insurgents before they could be dangerous. Such stories simultaneously ridiculed RENAMO and emphasised the importance of civilian support structures. [77]

The joy over peace went hand in hand with renewed suffering. The 1991/92 famine shook the valley population to its core, as a *sabhuku* explained: 'We love this area because we have good rains each year. If there is famine elsewhere, we do not suffer here, as there is food. No wonder many people admire this area and are coming to settle here.'[78] One chief emphasised: 'We have never experienced such a drought in our time, we don't have such a thing! This is strange to us.'[79] Even at the peak of the drought in November 1992, Holdenby appeared lush in comparison with other parts of Mutasa District and the rest of the country.[80] Still, the consequences of the lack of rainfall were severe. In Mutasa North and Manga CLs, there was widespread crop failure, and in Holdenby the full brunt became apparent when production at the three plantations was affected, as was the tea industry countrywide, seeing a drop in the total production of tea from the 18,000 tons of 1991 to 11,000 tons in the following year.[81] Katiyo could partly absorb the impact of the drought, because of the Pungwe River-fed irrigation system, although the plantation still recorded a production loss of thirty-five per cent in mid-1992, but Aberfoyle and EHTE depended entirely on rainfall. In response to the drought, management implemented changes which directly affected the workforce: contract labour was laid off, part-time employment was introduced for permanent workers, working conditions generally deteriorated, and Aberfoyle and EHTE had to close for a few weeks.[82] These measures had an impact on resident labour, tea workers from the valley, and the broader community.

A female staff member of one plantation explained that in normal circumstances workers could feed their families from the produce of their small gardens in the labour compounds, supplemented with local produce from the 'green market' and a few store-bought items, namely mealie meal, sugar, milk powder, tea, salt, and *kapenta* (dried fish). But as wages became more volatile, life changed; she said:

> One is now working for the mealie meal only.... Bread, tea, eggs – ah! – are unnecessarily expensive, a luxury. Then it will be just *sadza* [mealie meal porridge], vegetables, no cooking oil, no tomatoes, just plain vegetables; just take a plain cabbage, boil it, cook the *sadza* and go on with it. At times some even go without the *sadza* itself. Yes! Some are even taking green pawpaws, green mangoes, eating wild roots…. If you think of eating then you have to buy everything, almost everything.[83]

The already strained living conditions in the labour compounds deteriorated further. The quarters became crowded with school-age children whose parents could no longer afford the fees and with unemployed or part-time male and female labourers biding their time.[84] Domestic violence increased, and accusations of theft and drunken brawls became common. At the peak of the drought, alcohol consumption seems to have risen to unprecedented levels. A young woman commented upon the workers' behaviour: 'The less they get, the more they drink!'[85] While vegetable producers lost their tea estate customers, incidents of theft and armed robberies increased throughout the valley, affecting Hauna township, business centres, and schools. Women even accused their neighbours of stealing from their gardens.[86] Other aspects of drought management further exacerbated tensions. Problems of the quality and distribution of drought relief were widely discussed at the time, as was its allocation.[87] Initially the responsibility of the Ministry of Welfare, it was now the DA who was in charge of establishing who was entitled to food relief.[88] The urgency of the situation and lack of resources led the district staff to rely on local notables for this exercise, a decision which in turn triggered competition for this responsibility as well as irregularities.[89] As a result, fracture lines surfaced.

One of the main characteristics of this frontier society had been that newcomers were introduced to the values, practices, and meaning of the community they joined. Passing on vernacular knowledge was an important part of this process, but some aspects were known only by the descendants of earlier inhabitants. In this ecologically unique area that had not experienced a famine in living memory, knowledge of drought-resistant food plants suddenly set people apart as a gap emerged between those whose ancestors had settled in the valley and more recent immigrants. Once rifts appeared, the claim to belonging could determine access to food and even lead to allegations of witchcraft.[90]

Social cohesion became ever more brittle, as at the height of the drought different explanations for the crisis were voiced and blame was variously assigned. In the Zindi area, it was widely believed that the rains had failed because of the quarrel over the ancestral graves between the chief and EHTE management, and the famine was thus a consequence of the conflict between moral and commercial claims to land.[91] In the Hauna area, *muzvare* Muparutsa and her *masabhuku* complained that people had refused to donate *rapoko* (millet) for the rain rituals, which thus could not be held and that this had caused the famine.[92] In the New Reserve, just outside the valley, the drought was attributed to a struggle over local authority. Anger at the *mambo*'s appointment of Chieftainess Muredzwa was voiced, for with *ishe* Nyamandwe demoted to being the *muzvare*'s *nehanda* (here: follower), he had lost the authority to perform proper rain rituals.[93] In two other areas, supporters of rival contestants thought that the rains failed because the chief was wrongly appointed and was not in possession of the office insignia; the ongoing struggle between *mambo* Mutasa and the government over ownership of land regarding the Osborne Dam was also understood to be a cause of the drought.[94]

The famine brought into the open a controversial political debate about difference, responsibility, and authority to which unintended consequences of the Mozambican ceasefire contributed: self-repatriation and emigration. The sudden peace in Mozambique did not only allow refugees of that country to return home but it also caused emigration from the valley. People were attracted by environmental resources; as one man put it: 'In Mozambique, there is a big land.'[95] The result was intense border traffic consisting of daily crossings to access Mozambican markets, such as the town of Chimoio, or repatriated refugees heading to the valley to access services such as grinding mills. Some valley inhabitants left to try their luck in that 'big land', though they usually returned, emaciated, after a few months, as post-war recovery took its time in Mozambique.[96]

When the rains eventually arrived at the end of 1992, drought recovery further deepened distress. Due to the dry conditions, the government had refrained from spraying gullies and other mosquito breeding places, and the onset of the rainy season subsequently caused a malaria epidemic.[97] The increased prevalence of malaria-carrying mosquitoes combined with clinics running low on medicines and the poor nutritional state of toddlers and smaller children, in part due to the high HIV rate among mothers who therefore were weakened and unable to look after their children properly, caused the mortality rate among young children to spiral. By the dry season of 1993, these deaths were frequently interpreted in terms of spirit affliction. It was often argued that a *ngozi* (avenging spirit) was the reason for a specific death, the spirit of a person unjustly murdered during the Chimurenga or the RENAMO war seeking revenge. Also, for the first time, a witchcraft discourse emerged, expressing a sense of spiritual insecurity permeating everyday life.[98]

One story illustrates just how radical the shift from forgetting to recollection was. In September 1993, the police arrested an elder for weapons possession. It was not uncommon for muzzleloaders to be stored in the roofs of cooking huts, and with five armies having operated in the area in recent years, modern weapons were also present, albeit well hidden.[99] What makes the case unusual is the outbreak of witchcraft accusations. Just after the end of the Chimurenga, a young boy walked down to the river in the morning where he discovered human remains and an AK-47 close to the water. He left the corpse untouched and took the gun home to his grandfather, who stowed it away.[100] It was that same boy who took a bus to the police base at Ruda to report his grandfather more than a decade later. What transpired was that during the previous months, families in the area were trying to understand why so many young children were dying. The scientific explanation that connected drought-related malnutrition, the failure to spray DDT, the upsurge in the mosquito populations and malaria with the increase in child mortality did not satisfy. The loss was personal but it also appeared to be understood as a communal punishment, and by September 1993, in one area an explanation had been found: the old man had accepted the AK-47 but failed to rebury the remains of the guerrilla fighter, thus spiritually endangering the entire community. He had to be a wizard. Once the accusation began to circulate, the grandson reported his grandfather to the police in an attempt to protect him by having him removed from what might have escalated to a violent confrontation. What is astonishing about this occurrence are two aspects: one is that despite the strength of social coherence, as soon as the constraints of war loosened, assigning responsibility and blame became possible. More surprising, though, is that there is no evidence of even a single allegation of witchcraft in the valley during the war. This underlines that forgetting, silence, and absence can be crucial in living through periods of duress. Now the time for healing had arrived, as forgetting turned into remembering and old wounds opened.

Healing: The Question of Just Violence

The first step in spiritual healing is to recognise that there is a problem that requires such treatment. A string of events, perhaps involving the destruction of field crops, the death of a chicken, or sickness among children, might to one family be bad luck, while another assumes that affliction might be the cause. Symptoms such as swollen legs and fatigue may, for one person, indicate spirit affliction that requires ritual healing, while another might suffer from the same symptoms and address them through biomedicine or Christian exorcism. Once an individual, often with his or her immediate social group, acknowledges that a ritual expert is necessary for diagnosis and remedy, the healing process is set into motion and makes sense of the past retrospectively. It is not uncommon for the afflicted person to consult several *ñ'anga* and possibly healers of independent churches before a diagnosis is accepted. Part of the moral universe that maps suffering and healing is the notion of just violence.

Both civilians and ex-combatants make a clear distinction between killing in combat and murder; only the latter has repercussions for the culprit and his or her family. In other words, only unjust violence causes problems, hence the saying '*hondo haina pfukwa*', 'war does not lead to haunting'.[101] It is widely believed that the spirit of a person who was murdered or inadequately buried can afflict members of the lineage to which the person responsible belongs.[102] Such an 'aggrieved spirit or the revenge inflicted by such a spirit' is referred to as a *ngozi*.[103] An elder explained that fighters are not afflicted by *ngozi* for violence which they committed in combat: 'There is no *ngozi* in war …. During the war, when you fight and kill each other, there is no *ngozi* – but when you go astray, *ngozi* occurs, if you just kill innocent people.'[104] An ex-combatant argued along similar lines: 'If, say, someone wanted to sell us out, we killed him. This was within the spirit of war – no repercussions occurred. Suppose you murdered in cold blood, then the spirit of the murdered person would surely come back to haunt you.[105]

An elder illustrated the difference between just and unjust violence by comparing the Gaza warrior raids of the nineteenth century with the Chimurenga:

> The war of the *madzviti* has got *pfukwa* [haunting] because they simply invaded and killed – without waging war. It is quite different from this recent war of the comrades. If you are a comrade and I am a comrade, if one kills the other then there is no *ngozi*. But not if you invade and kill people while they are just seated.[106]

Kriger has pointed out that *mujibhas* and *chimbwidos* were frequently responsible for reporting, beating, and even killing alleged sell-outs and that they often abused their position.[107] In the Honde Valley they are remembered – or rather forgotten – in this ambiguous position of power. In the early 1990s, *mujibhas* were reported to be suffering because of their wrongdoings:

> In most cases here you find that a lot of *mujibhas* now have *ngozi*. Yes, they are now possessed by the avenging spirits. But the real comrades are not being affected …. Some of them are now mad. You see what's happening in towns, you can find one madman

brandishing an imitation of a gun. [laughter] You then see that this is *ngozi* at work. And if you ask him closely, you find he was not a comrade, but a *mujibha*.[108]

This account portrays those young people not merely socially dead, as argued above, but also in spiritual peril. Kriger interprets the youths' abuse of power as an expression of generational struggles.[109] But apparently there was also another reason for their involvement in acts of violence: the fighters' self-protection. One ex-combatant explained that guerrillas encouraged civilians who accused others of being sell-outs to punish them themselves:

> The thing was, some of them fabricated stories against others.... During the war, we were led by *midzimu* [ancestral spirits], who forewarned us against spilling innocent blood as a result of listening to lies. So, if a *chimbwido*, or anybody told us that so-and-so was a sell-out, we gave you a gun to kill the sell-out, since we did not have evidence of him selling out. So, if you killed an innocent person, his spirit would come back to haunt you.[110]

Rightful and wrongful killing is therefore distinguished according to whether it occurred during war, and, if it did, whether it was just. This understanding of violence caused a moral ambiguity for participants and observers, an ambiguity that left a remaining tension between the parent and children generations. Likewise, the fighters in the various armies that fought in the Honde Valley, even if convinced they were doing right, could never be absolutely certain that they were safe from haunting. Closure about individual killings can only be achieved when a *ngozi* manifests him- or herself and, through a process of healing, is appeased. This spiritual vulnerability was the reason why cleansing rituals before and after combat became crucial.[111] The fear of *ngozi* affliction represents a moral interpretation of the past and a manner of accommodating past suffering in the present. These important layers of the meaning of affliction in the context of conflict are further articulated during the process of diagnosis, which itself is a simultaneous commentary of the present as the lifeworld of the afflicted is mapped. This practice is illustrated by a *ngozi* case from the Honde Valley, as heard by a chief.[112]

A woman from the Honde Valley had fallen ill and eventually, when the symptoms became so severe that she could no longer fulfil her duties in the house and fields, she consulted a *ñ'anga*. Through numerous consultations with several healers, she came to realise that she was suffering from spiritual affliction. What initially appeared to be unconnected occurrences now became a narrative of the past. The spirit had first caused harm at the margins of her lifeworld when some of her household's livestock became sick or simply disappeared and a cow eventually died. Then, as if in concentric circles, the spirit had proceeded to approach her by making a distant relative ill, then one of her children, and then herself.

When she experienced the affliction as suffering, the woman initiated the healing process. Once the symptoms were identified, the *ñ'anga* called upon the spirit, which manifested itself in speech, something that does not always happen, and the woman learned that this was her husband who had disappeared during the Chimurenga and had returned to trouble her because he had not been properly buried. However, the healer failed to help the widow find her husband's remains. At this point she decided to ask the chief to mediate. He explained his role in such a case: first, he held meetings with the afflicted person and his or her immediate social group, then he called on the deceased person's family. He continued in this way, drawing wider and wider social circles until everybody involved was present.[113] This healing practice resembles mapping connections that eventually embed the afflicted person within his or her social environment.

At the meetings, everybody kept assuring the chief that the husband had disappeared mysteriously during the war, and that nobody knew what had happened or could identify the whereabouts of his remains. In this case, eventually with family and former neighbours present, what transpired was that during the Chimurenga the local ZANLA unit had suspected the deceased to be a *mtengesi* (sell-out). The fighters then held a meeting, had him publicly executed by a relative, and instructed the community to leave the remains at the site unburied. Most who were present at the hearing had witnessed the killing, and everybody knew exactly what had happened, including the afflicted widow herself. Even so, shared silence continued for months through the healing process until all those involved were present and memory could be articulated. It was only when the chief mediated a discourse about the context of the killing within the community involved that the story finally surfaced via this communal process in the arena of a healing practice. The story was told. Past experience gained meaning. The bones were found and re-buried. No compensation was paid. The *ngozi* was appeased.

In this case, the spiritual manifestation shifted from affliction to possession, making the widow his vessel and providing a spoken narrative. What was left to be done was to reconstruct his murder. This is not always the way situations are resolved, for the diagnosis often involves identifying the spirit by reconstructing how the spirit manifested him-, her-, or itself, moving closer to the centre, usually from inanimate, to animal, to humans. The remedy requires reversing that movement in the opposite direction. The practice thus maps the patient's social and moral world, and in the process spiritual healing provides a narrative of the past and a debate over the meaning of community, belonging, and responsibility across time.[114] Even though such healing focuses on individual suffering, it is thus crucial for making sense of the past and of remaking the community and can be seen as part of John Lonsdale's arena of moral ethnicity.[115] Part of this practice is the forging of connections through the actual appeasing of the spirit, the final step of the healing process.

Typically, *ngozi* cases involve two lineages, that of the deceased and that of the murderer. The spirit makes him- or herself felt by afflicting a family member or descendant of the latter, through whom compensation is demanded, usually in the form of livestock and a young girl. The girl is given to a male descendant of the *ngozi* in order to bear a child of the same sex as the deceased. After the child is born, bride-price is often paid and the girl remains with the deceased's family.[116] A chief explained that there is no specific term for the girls who are pledged, only for their role: 'If you hear that one was *berekerwa* [given to bear offspring] then one was given to appease avenging spirits.'[117] He clarified the procedure as follows:

> In most cases, when the spirit of *ngozi* manifests itself, you have to quickly appease it, so as to send it away from the family …. When you go to *ñ'angas* to find out the cause of this spate of deaths, you are told that there is *ngozi* in your family – you killed so-and-so and he needs to be compensated. That is when you take a small girl and give to the family of the deceased as compensation.[118]

In the aftermath of the Chimurenga, as was previously the case with migrant labourers, alternatives had to be found if the origins of the spirit could not be established. An ex-combatant explained the challenge:

> Taking myself for example – I went to Mozambique without the knowledge of my parents, and I had even told them they were not going to see me again. Now, if I had died in Mozambique, my spirit would have come to manifest itself in anybody here, telling them that I had died. The manifestations of my spirit would then tell them the truth about what would have happened to me, and if possible they would come and take me for burial back home. There is no other way.[119]

He continued to explain that he did not suffer from *ngozi* from his actions during the war, but that he had been possessed by the spirit of his brother, a civilian who had been 'sold out for harbouring comrades'. The spirit had guided him and his family to his brother's remains.[120] However, especially with casualties of war, it is not always possible to bring the families of perpetrator and victim together.[121] The chief who had heard the case above explained that even policemen, to whom he would normally refer such cases, would concede that as the murder had been committed during the Chimurenga, it was a case 'for the chief and the spirit'.[122]

People in search of healing do not pursue healing practices exclusively, but as a hierarchy or as a patchwork of possibilities, and at times as both. Frequently, patients consult different healing churches and cults or biomedical facilities according to their specific problem and whether help is forthcoming.[123] A *ñ'anga* explained that people who became Vapostori because they were afflicted by *ngozi* would nevertheless brew beer for their ancestors if the church failed to help them.[124] A multiple approach even applied to some Ziwe Zano members. Kasambira, for example, who since 1938 had been involved in Honde Mission, in 1955 turned to Mai Chaza's Guta raJehova church, where he and his wife sought healing because she had failed to conceive sons.[125] Terence Ranger pointed out that Christian healing became prevalent in Zimbabwe after the Chimurenga,[126] and in the Honde Valley this was all the more so after the Mozambican ceasefire. The number of churches in the valley had increased after independence, and in the early 1990s probably more than seventy were active, many of them healing churches.[127] Gregson et al. counted twenty-seven 'distinct churches' among 346 adults in the Zindi area alone.[128] A turning point was an aggressive, self-proclaimed 'crusade' which the Zimbabwe Assemblies of God Africa (ZAOGA) conducted on both sides of the border, including the refugee camps. Non-members often perceived ZAOGA as a 'hard church' because of its crusades that involved the destruction of cave paintings and ancestral graves and because it demands tithes.[129] ZAOGA addressed pertinent issues: in the valley, the message at prayer meetings focused on exorcisms of evil spirits and on marital relations. The pastors preached that husband and wife should make household decisions together in order to ensure peace, security, and upward mobility of their families. At this time of crisis this message was welcomed by women in particular, and many people joined the church.[130] Christian practices differ greatly from spiritual healing; exorcism usually involves calling out the spirit, but it is then forcibly removed not through creating a narrative of the past, but by confession and by affirming one's Christian beliefs. When ZAOGA carried out their crusade, many people said they were attracted to this church because it helped you 'lose your spirits' in just one night at a prayer meeting.

In short, widespread healing only became possible once peace arrived in the valley, after which two changes occurred: existing cults were re-interpreted and new cults and churches became prominent. Moreover, 'healing the wounds of war' involved three processes: spiritual healing provided an important arena for individuals and communities who were attempting to make sense of past events in the aftermath of war.[131] Second, the practice turns experience and forgetting into memories of the past and hence it creates meaning. From this follows, third, that spiritual healing is necessarily social, as it connects experience, memory, personhood, and belonging. The search for a diagnosis as well as for healing resembles a socially embedded negotiation process: in this case, it allowed valley inhabitants to address tensions that arose from their different memories and experiences of war by making sense of violence.

Affliction as Empowerment

Affliction is usually associated with suffering because a spirit troubles a person's being to a point where the afflicted becomes a mere vessel during full possession. At the same time, this surrendering to the spirit can be experienced not just as violation and risk that requires healing, but also as empowering, because it can explain and thus legitimise the sufferer's divergent behaviour. Two gendered spiritual practices in the Honde Valley, both of which are directly connected to violence, illustrate this argument: *chikwambo* and *madzviti*.

A *chikwambo*, like a *ngozi*, is the spirit of a person, usually a man, who was killed and who takes revenge by afflicting the perpetrator's kin group.[132] In cases of *chikwambo*, healing and resolution are impossible because the deceased person was a stranger and thus the bringing together of the two lineages cannot take place.[133] Instead, the spirit can only be appeased. By the 1990s, women of all ages were afflicted by *chikwambo*, and the common explanation was that their male ancestors had killed and robbed returning migrant labourers who used the Honde Valley as a route home in the 1930s and 1940s. As one woman explained: 'They trapped them like wild animals with nets.'[134]

A *chikwambo* can only be appeased when the perpetrator's lineage gives him a young girl as his wife – or the spirit may choose her himself, through affliction. She then becomes known by the same term, as *chikwambo*. Similar to girl-pledging in *ngozi* cases, a girl can be promised to or chosen by the spirit before she is even born, or at a very young age; often she will be unaware of her role until she is of child-bearing age. However, since the spirit's lineage cannot be located, as can be done with resolved *ngozi* cases, the girl cannot be given in compensation. Instead, she becomes the spirit's wife, and once she is grown up, her father will usually allocate her some land, so that she has her own homestead or, at the very least sleeping hut.[135] A young woman explained what happens:

> Suppose my father long back, or my grandfather, would have killed somebody and after some time that person starts to cause problems in our family, they will go to see a *ñ'anga*. Then they will be told, your grandfather has killed somebody, a man. So the man wants a wife and a house. So my parents will have to build a hut, put some utensils there, a pot and a rack, find a virgin girl, say: 'This is now your wife. Don't trouble us anymore!'[136]

As a spirit wife, the woman will be unable to fulfil her expected gender role among the living.[137] The *chikwambo* may not allow her to get married or to work in the fields, and, as a young woman observed, he can make life difficult: 'The *chikwambo* can say, "I don't want her to work or a man to go near her." Then she will have a problem. Because as soon as she doesn't obey, she will get ill. She can get very ill. She will have a lot of problems.'[138]

Should the woman marry, the *chikwambo* will seek revenge with her lineage and that of her in-laws: she might not get along with her husband, remain barren, even death can occur.[139] On the other hand, the spirit will usually permit sexual relationships with men, since any resulting children bear the spirit's totem and not that of the biological father and are thus considered his offspring: 'You can have partners, it all depends on the *chikwambo*. At times he wants the woman to have children. They won't belong to that person, they will belong to the *chikwambo*. And that one just makes the children for him.'[140] One young woman maintained that those afflicted are 'seeing everybody' but also insisted that there is no stigma attached to the women's conduct.[141] This was the case with a woman who had become a sex worker during the war. In contrast to others who were ostracised in the early 1990s, this woman appeared to participate in the social life of the community. She explained that she had not chosen her occupation 'for the fun' or the money, but because she was afflicted by *chikwambo*. As a result, she could not relate to men in a way accepted by the standards of her community and therefore had to enter into commercial sexual relations.[142]

According to vernacular cosmology, *chikwambo* affliction forces young women to break with their prescribed gender role of entering a virilocal marriage at an appropriate age and instead allows them to gain land use rights, and even property, independent of a male guardian. When asked whether some of the afflicted might enjoy their condition, one woman said: 'For example, if you have problems, if you don't have a child, now, in our custom, if you are married and you don't bear a child, then they will say, "No, you go! We didn't get you just to feed you! We want children! You go back!"'[143] In other words, if a young woman fails in her expected gender role, she might experience it as liberating to find an explanation in her affliction. Such spiritual practice then allows women to claim their position in the moral community, which, because of the challenges to age and gender status during the Chimurenga, was probably crucial in the aftermath of the war.

By contrast, the *madzviti* cult has male membership. Some young men are possessed by the Gaza warriors who were killed in the Honde Valley in the nineteenth century. In the 1990s, this possession cult appeared to play no role in the wider community because, as the elders contended about the *madzviti*, 'we don't know where they come from';[144] they are alien and not ancestral spirits. 'There is little purpose they are serving. They only want to enjoy, to remember their past,' they said.[145] This celebration of young warrior masculinity is performed at night, when men come together, share beer brewed for the spirits, and dance. A member of a Vapostori church explained the *madzviti* cult:

> It just manifests itself so as to have beer, have war dances and adopt that attire they used to wear then. [laughter] As for us – the Manyika – I would like you to understand what purpose the *madzviti* serves. If one is possessed by the spirit of our forefathers, he acts just like they did then. Similarly, if, say, I am possessed by the Ngoni spirit, I act in the same manner the warrior must have done, dictating the type of attire to be worn, the type of beer and also the type of dance – just as the Ngoni did. When the person is possessed, he announces the attire he wants to adopt. Yes, and this is made from animal skin. The headgear is made of feathers, and he carries a knobkerrie and a spear.[146]

Seventy years earlier, in the 1920s, Denis Shropshire observed a strikingly similar performance by a female *madzviti* medium in the proximity of the valley:

> Her dancing dress consisted of the skin of a monkey, a wild cat skin, ostrich feathers, coloured headdress, white sash, two pieces of black cloth, two spears, a shield of hide, and a knobkerrie …. She said that her possessing spirit desired this particular form of dress, and would be offended if she omitted any part of it.[147]

Two young men, one an ex-combatant, related that the spirits of guerrilla fighters afflict young men in a comparable manner. They explained that 'the spirit makes its medium act the same way the host did during the war'. Accordingly, the afflicted 'will be dressed like those people – they were like the freedom fighters, dressed in jeans, then they would be carrying sticks like guns. Then they will act like those comrades.' They further maintained that such affliction was responsible for the so-called 'dissidents'.[148]

John Rennie traces the first case of possession by a *madzviti* spirit to as far back as 1888, during the reign of the Gaza polity.[149] His description of the possession rituals tallies in some aspects with those in the Honde Valley, but his case concerns a female Ndau medium. The female *madzviti* medium whom Shropshire observed in the area just east of the Honde Valley, in the 1920s, had her affliction divined by a *ñ'anga* who had also outfitted her with the necessary paraphernalia. Shropshire emphasised that she herself was not a healer and interpreted her role as that of a 'minstrel' who earned a living by performing dance and song in the neighbouring villages with her ritual assistants, young girls.[150] The most striking difference to the Honde Valley is that these earlier accounts are examples of female mediums. Either this significant difference in the possession practice is due to regional variation or the phenomenon changed over time. It may have become a male practice due to the experience of war, as the *madzviti* cult came to serve as a celebration of male prowess from the margins. This is the case with cult members who are ex-combatants who had to face sudden disempowerment at independence and young men threatened by the RENAMO incursions during that conflict. This connection between masculinity, military prowess, and empowerment resonates also in the story of the ZANLA unit upstaged by an incident of *madzviti* possession that asserted civilian power, as told in chapter five. It was certainly noticeable that after the ceasefire of 1992, most nights the valley resonated with *ngoma* (drums and song) calling the spirits at meetings of spirit cults and healing churches. During daylight, however, the re-appropriation of landscape that had begun during the RENAMO war continued along its way.

Reclaiming the Frontier:
Spiritual Landscape & Story-Telling

A spiritual landscape is a place invested with meaning that expresses the local cosmology in practices, prohibitions, and narrative that are part of the making of and debate about community. It is also a location of ambiguity – characterised by a tension between danger and belonging, much as the Honde Valley had been for a long time until its hitherto most radical landscape transformation: the villagisation exercise during the Chimurenga. Still, even then, spiritual and political leaders succeeded in undermining state authority by advising the ZANLA fighters to base themselves at sacred sites and fortifying them for daring to do so by welcoming them as the children of the soil. The cooling down of the RENAMO war opened more opportunities for such defiance.

In the Honde Valley, sacred landscape includes mountains, namely Nyangani, the Mahemasimike rock formations, and the forest on the slopes of the escarpment, with some sites carrying specific ritual meaning, for example, ponds and ancestral graveyards. The spatial aspect hence unfolds between the apparent and the hidden, with the mountains visible from large parts of the valley, but the forest prohibited and the sites concealed inside. In vernacular cosmology mountains command respect from near and afar. One may, for example, not point a finger at a mountain, as much as that would be considered rude towards another person, and mountains should not be climbed frivolously. In the absence of any *mhondoro* (spirit medium) in his area, Chief Zindi is, he explained, the spiritual guardian of Mount Nyangani, Zimbabwe's highest mountain (8,504 feet).[151] If circumstances force one to ascend Nyangani, no inauspicious words should be uttered. A complaint on how steep the ascent is can lead to disappearance; Nyangani takes that person, who might be allowed to return to the world of the living, if appropriate sacrifices are made through Chief Zindi and ritual experts.[152] A well-known case was the disappearance of the Masaya sisters, two teenage girls, in the 1980s while they were climbing the peak with friends, who gave the alarm. One of the parents, Victoria Chitepo, a cabinet minister, called the army, which moved in swiftly, but the girls were not found, despite a thorough search. Initially, the parents sought solace and retained hope through other channels, but, according to Chief Zindi, the father, MP Masaya, eventually asked for his assistance to appease the mountain. Even so, the girls remained lost.[153] It was on the lower slopes of Mount Nyangani that

ZANLA had managed to retain their base camp with the chief's spiritual forti-
fication, even during the height of the counter-insurgency campaign.

A less dramatic example pertaining to sacred landscape is that of the Mahemasimike rocks. This conflict, however, went right to the roots of authority
and power in rural post-colonial Zimbabwe. During the drought of 1991/92,
ecological and spiritual prohibitions relating to the landscape were negotiated
in order to allow access to more resources. These changes were highly contested
and the question arose of who could legitimately make such decisions. Should
it be the District Council, the Village Development Committees, the chiefs,
or the spiritual leaders?[154] This debate surfaced in a court case when *masabhuku* of the Muparutsa chieftaincy challenged the *muzvare*, the guardian of
the spiritual landscape, who had ruled that fields could be opened close to the
Mahemasimike formation, a hitherto protected sacred space.[155]

The forest bordering the valley to the west constitutes a multi-layered sacred
landscape. The ancestral burial ground of the Zindi Chieftainship is located
there, the ritual site that became hotly contested between Zindi and his followers and the EHTE management in 1992, as well as the ancestral graves of the
Chikomba chieftainship. This part of the forest is also a sexualised landscape,
one where trees can acquire sexual features so that men entering it illegiti-
mately can be lured into mistaking 'trees with breasts' for attractive women. An
elder, a *ñ'anga* and *sabhuku*, explained the dangers:

> All this area; if you walk through there, and you see, say, a tree – if you say something
> nasty about that tree, you get lost …. There are strange trees there, which you might
> mistake for a person, and if you then say 'look at that girl' when actually it is a tree, you
> get lost.[156]

The forest is not only sexualised, it is also gendered. Entering it posits danger to
both men and women, but men are harmed through their manliness, or even dis-
appear, although no stories circulate about the exact punishment women would
receive if they contravened the prohibitions. On the contrary, in the Zindi area
women would gleefully joke about the dangers for men, while post-menopausal
women would perform the annual rain ceremony with the chief and roam the
forest for a day, sexually liberated, stripped to a loin cloth, singing, dancing, and
enjoying themselves, the men having to stay indoors, not allowed to so much as
catch a glimpse of them.[157]

Ponds that form at the bases of waterfalls on the western slopes of the Honde
Valley are another important part of the spiritual landscape. Newcomers tried
to take advantage of such vernacular mapping in a religious competition over
landscape.[158] After the ceasefire, as healing churches swept through the valley,
a Vapostori church insisted on holding a baptism in one of the sacred Pungwe
ponds. Non-church members clicked their tongues at that folly, and the story
of what happened was told over and over again. The preacher had entered the
pond, and as he submerged the first believer during the baptism ceremony, suddenly there was much commotion in the water, and the preacher disappeared.
Divers were swiftly brought in and found the corpse, so the story went, tucked
under a stone. Outsiders suggested that this is how crocodiles kill their prey,
but the local discourse clearly circulated around the question of authority and
sacredness.

An important layer of spirituality in the forest is the presence of *njuzu*, female water spirits.[159] They are believed to live in some of the ponds formed by streams and run-off from the escarpment that in places create waterfalls. *Njuzu* appear to men as beautiful young women. Should a man show sexual interest, the *njuzu* will usually take him with her and give the man the option of being trained as a *ñ'anga*. If he agrees, he will live with the spirits at the bottom of the pond for a few days, or even for years, until he completes his training and then returns to the surface. If the man declines her offer, he will remain lost to the world of the living. The most sacred of these ponds is Pungwe Pool. One story that circulated about the pool demonstrates the importance of spiritual landscape and belonging in asserting authority over armed men with guns. An aspect of the military campaign against RENAMO, the government declared part of the western slopes of the Honde Valley a no-go area, one where interlopers would be shot on sight by patrols, as had been the case during the Chimurenga. From the military's point of view, the forest was a zone of potential danger as an infiltration route into mainland Zimbabwe and a hiding place for insurgents, but at the same time it was a symbol of ultimate state control.[160] This control was undermined in mid-1992.

Two ZNA soldiers were patrolling the forest close to Pungwe Pool when they saw a beautiful young woman collecting firewood in the distance. That appeared odd to them, as the local population was well aware of the no-go area. The men followed the woman for a while, but as far and as long as they walked, they failed to catch up with her. Eventually, one soldier confronted the other, pointing out that she did not present a security risk and that they should return to the base camp at Ruda. The other soldier, however, intrigued by the woman, did not want to give up the pursuit. So they split up, one man turning back to Ruda, while the other stayed in the forest. This soldier eventually caught up with the woman, who was indeed very beautiful. Inevitably, they had sex. While he was 'pumping away',[161] he suddenly noticed that he was merely pushing on the ground – the woman beneath him had disappeared. And then he realised that not only was the woman gone, his 'vital parts' had disappeared as well!

Slowly it dawned on him that he had had intercourse with a *njuzu*, who had punished him for defiling the sacred landscape. He came to realise that there was nothing he could do but to return to base camp. Accosted by the guard for reporting late, he immediately went to the sick bay, where he presented his problem to the medical orderly, who could not help him. After a few days, during which his penis remained missing, he was given permission to travel on sick leave to Mutare, the closest city, to consult a *ñ'anga* there. It is not known whether his castration was reversed. The story was widely told, spread quickly through the valley and was enjoyed a lot, especially by women. There was much mocking of the soldier, who should have known better than to lose what was so important to him by disobeying the rules of the land.

Four years later, in mid-1996, another story circulated about Pungwe Pool. For quite some time, going back to plans from the colonial period, in fact, the state had intended to construct a water pipeline feeding off the pond to supply the provincial capital, Mutare.[162] The severe drought of 1991/92 appeared to justify the implementation of the project, but chiefs and elders confronted the DA and demanded respect for the sacred site.[163] State and moral claims to land clashed, and for a while it appeared that the frontier people might be able to re-appropriate their landscape. A surveyor was sent to the Honde Valley in order to prepare the construction work. He arrived with a team of men who were supposed to carry his equipment into the forest. When the group reached Pungwe Pool, all the men, except for the surveyor himself, disappeared. He went to the next settlement for help, only to be told that surely the *njuzu* took the men. The surveyor failed to recruit labour locally. The account was passed on excitedly from neighbour to neighbour and celebrated as a victory over state intervention. However, the project was merely delayed. The pipeline was eventually constructed, when an agreement had been reached with Swedish donors in February 1996, despite the prospect of ecological disaster and non-feasibility.[164] President Mugabe opened the pipeline in March 2000, three months before crucial parliamentary elections, and in his speech reportedly threatened that 'Those who try to cause disunity among our people must watch out because death will befall them.'[165]

These stories about the dangers that emanate from spiritual landscape provide examples of the collision between vernacular knowledge and state power. They illustrate the confrontation between the frontier people and state agents – soldiers, technocrats, administrators, and politicians. But clear-cut and concrete as these conflicts might appear, they are located in complex layers of competing perceptions of the past and present and imaginations for the future, and thus also throw light on internal moral debate. From a valley perspective, the forest represents a fragile moral equilibrium. It is highly ambiguous, as it not only provides protection – in this case from state intervention – and a source of social wellbeing, but also presents potential danger to anyone who enters the forest, most prominently to sexually active men. Moreover, the mocking of the Zimbabwean soldier frequently led to continued story-telling about valley inhabitants' experiences with ZANLA guerrillas during the Chimurenga. This provided an opportunity to relate personal memories within families and between neighbours, and to share social memory with immigrants who had only settled in the valley after 1980 and thus had no first-hand local experience of the Chimurenga. In short, while the stories were celebrated as tales of victory over state intervention, they also more generally illustrate landscape as a contested field, a place of identity practice and discourse, and a multi-layered landscape of violence.

Conclusion

In its first decade in power, the government of the newly independent Zimbabwe not only faced economic and social difficulties, but also political and military challenges. These included gaining legitimacy in the eyes of its citizens, recovery from war destruction, the implementation of development measures to raise the standards of living and expand the life chances of the majority population that had been severely curtailed under ninety years of settler rule, not to mention the RENAMO insurgency, as discussed in chapter five. Liberation movements that knew what they were fighting for – majority rule – overnight became ruling parties that faced the difficulties of nation-building in a country where not everyone considered being a citizen a priority, or agreed that the government had any business in interfering with their everyday lives. Basil Davidson eloquently referred to the legacy of the nation state inherited by the nationalists and the challenges of governance as the 'black man's burden',[166] though one may well argue that the true burden was building the nation, while the political legitimacy of the newly independent state could not be taken for granted, but had to be locally made.

In African societies, processes of making sense of violence in the aftermath of conflict are often negotiated in religious healing practices. For survivors inhabiting a world both of the living and the dead, spiritual healing can provide an understanding of unspeakable experiences and memories within known systems of knowledge. It is crucial to investigate the complex negotiation and mapping process through which identities and appropriations of violence, or at times also the surrendering to its dislocation and rupture of personhood, are established. The Honde Valley provides a crucial example of the importance of social healing and community. Its frontier identity, however, was finally undermined by the post-colonial state, whose presence transformed rapidly from reconstruction to alienation and, finally, repression. By the twenty-first century, the frontier people of the Honde Valley had lost part of their spiritual landscape to the expansion of Nyanga National Park, the Mutare pipeline, and a dam, and it also became one of the areas much affected by the state-sponsored, anti-opposition violence that characterised the so-called Third Chimurenga. Nevertheless, the people of this area are an extraordinary example of the perseverance of community and the insistence on moral debate in the face of suffering and dispossession.

Notes

1   Tom Lodge et al., *Compendium on Elections in Southern Africa* (Johannesburg, 2002), p. 442.
2   'Zimbabwe's Post-War Recovery Programme', document prepared for the Zimbabwe Conference on Reconstruction and Development, 23-27 March 1981, DERUDE.
3   'Let's Build Zimbabwe Together: ZIMCORD', Conference Documentation, Zimbabwe Conference on Reconstruction and Development (ZIMCORD), Salisbury, 23-27 March 1981, p. 25, DERUDE; see also Stella Makanya, 'The Desire to Return: Effects of Experiences in Exile on Refugees Repatriating to Zimbabwe in the Early 1980s', and Jeremy Jackson, 'Repatriation and Reconstruction in Zimbabwe during the 1980s', *When Refugees Go Home: African Experiences*, Tim Allen and Hubert Morsink (eds) (London, 1994), pp. 105-25 and 126-66.
4   Interview #14, with a man who was an extension worker in Makoni District during the Chimurenga. Michael Bratton, *Beyond Community Development: The Political Economy of Rural Administration in Zimbabwe* (London, 1978), p. 35, Michael Evans, *Fighting Against Chimurenga: An Analysis of Counter-Insurgency in Rhodesia 1972-9* (Salisbury, 1981), p. 25.
5   No more than 57 of these schools were closed at any one time. Most of the 400 schools in Manicaland needed reconstruction. 'Minutes of the Umtali District Team Meeting', 6 October 1980, PPD.
6   'Zimbabwe's Post-War Recovery Programme', pp. 6-37.
7   Ibid., p. 5. Surprisingly, the impact of the Second Chimurenga, or guerrilla warfare more broadly, on cattle husbandry has largely been overlooked. R. Norval, Department of Veterinary Sciences, Ministry of Agriculture, 'The Effects of a Break-Down of Dipping in Tribal Areas in Rhodesia', n.d. [1979], Ministry of Agriculture; Heike Schmidt, 'The Impact of Zimbabwe's Liberation War 'Second Chimurenga' (1972–1980) on the Rural Population in the Tribal Trust Lands', MA thesis, University of Hannover, 1989, chapter 2.4.

8 'Zimbabwe's Post-War Recovery Programme', p. 5. The challenges of overcoming the legacy of white minority rule regarding services and infrastructure are comparable in post-apartheid South Africa.

9 See Diana Auret, *A Decade of Development: Zimbabwe 1980–1990* (Gweru, 1990).

10 Frederick Cooper, *Colonialism in Question: Theory, Knowledge, History* (Berkeley, CA, 2005), chapter 6.

11 Ernest Renan, 'What is a Nation? [1882]', *Nation and Narration*, Homi Bhabha (ed.) (London, 1990), pp. 8-22.

12 Robert Mugabe, *The Third Chimurenga: Inside the Third Chimurenga* (Harare, 2001).

13 It was possible to recover all those files with the permission of the management in the 1990s, even those used as roof insulation, although a European woman standing on a ladder in the sawmill pulling out materials from the roof appeared sufficiently suspicious to some workers to alarm the party youth, who in turn informed the Central Intelligence Office.

14 Chairman National Co-ordinating Committee, Ministry of Agriculture, to all ACC Chairmen, 3 April 1980, PPF; Honde Valley Tea Estates Liaison Committee, Constitution and Modus Operandi, n.d. [1980], Secretary to all members Honde Valley Area Co-ordinating Committee, 21 April 1980, PPD.

15 Interview #83.

16 Interview #111.

17 Interview #26.

18 Despite the significant improvement of working conditions during the 1980s, strikes occurred frequently. Zimbabwe Tea Growers' Association, 'Aide Memoire: Tea Industry – Industrial Relations – Assistance Required from Government', 24 September 1980, PPD; Minutes of a tea estate management meeting, 17 February and 2 July 1986, PPC; Mutasa District, Monthly Report, September 1985, DAO.

19 Interview #117. For a brief but very useful insight into ex-combatants' perceptions, see Teresa Barnes, 'The Heroes' Struggle: Life after the Liberation War for Four Ex-combatants in Zimbabwe', *Soldiers in Zimbabwe's Liberation War*, Ngwabi Bhebe and Terence O. Ranger (eds) (London, 1995), pp. 118-38. One of the four men interviewed came from the Honde Valley.

20 Interview #112.

21 Ibid. For the politics of veterans, see, Norma Kriger, *Guerrilla Veterans in Post-war Zimbabwe: Symbolic and Violent Politics, 1980–1987* (Cambridge, 2003) and Zvakanyorwa Sadomba, *War Veterans in Zimbabwe's Revolution: Challenging Neo-Colonialism and Settler and International Capital* (Woodbridge, 2011).

22 Interview #112.

23 Ibid.

24 Interview #100.

25 Caute points out that the danger of Rhodesians sabotaging the ceasefire was imminent. David Caute, *Under the Skin: The Death of White Rhodesia* (Harmondsworth, 1983), p. 389.

26 Interview #26.

27 Norma Kriger, *Guerrilla Veterans*, p. 46; also Caute, *Under the Skin*, pp. 389-90.

28 Eric Hobsbawm, *Bandits* (New York, 2000 new rev. ed. [1969]), Terence Ranger, 'Bandits and Guerrillas: The Case of Zimbabwe', *Banditry, Rebellion and Social Protest in Africa*, Donald Crummey (ed.) (London, 1986), p. 381.

29 PC to the DCs Manicaland, 15 September 1980; DC Inyanga to DC Mutasa, 4 November 1980; DC Mutasa to PC, 14 October 1980, PER5 GEN, DAO; DC Mutasa to PC, 17 February 1981, PER5 Headman Samanga, PAO; interview #128.

30 'Minutes of the Mutasa District Team Meeting', 19 July 1984, PPD. Another challenge Mutasa District administration faced throughout the 1980s was that no DA stayed for more than one year. Interview #27 with a former DA Mutasa.

31 Interviews #44 and #46.

32 Interview #51.

33 ZANLA required the use of *noms de guerre*. James Bond, Che, Samora (Machel) were among those most commonly chosen.

34 Manager, Katiyo, 'Report on Incidents at Katiyo Estate, 26-27 March 1980', PPF.

35 Ibid.

36 Ibid.

37 Interviews #35, #140.

38 Manager, Katiyo, 'Report on Incidents'.

39 Acting DC Mutasa to PC, 4 July 1980, PER5 Headman Chikomba, PAO.

40 'Minutes of the Umtali District Team Meeting', 1 December 1980, PPD.

41 'Minutes of a tea estate management meeting', 4 March 1981, PPC; 'Minutes of the Mutasa District Team Meeting', 19 November 1981, PPD.
42 Mbuya Nehanda was and is revered as mhondoro and a leader of the First Chimurenga of 1896-97. 'Minutes of the Mutasa District Team Meeting', 7 October 1982, PPD.
43 Ibid.
44 'Minutes of the First Mutasa District Team Meeting', 9 July 1981, PPD. Civil servants also struggled to establish legitimacy. 3 November 1980, PPD.
45 BSAP, Manicaland Provincial Headquarters, Umtali, to the Managers Tilcor Rumbizi Estate, Katiyo Estate and Aberfoyle Plantations, 22 May 1980, PPF.
46 'Minutes of the Mutasa District Team Meeting', 19 November 1981, PPD.
47 Ibid.
48 Ibid.
49 'Minutes of the Mutasa District Team Meeting', 17 June 1982, PPD.
50 'Minutes of a Sub JOC Meeting Held at Ruda', 9 October 1990, PPB.
51 In his study on the RENAMO war in Manica Province, Mark Chingono took the approach of examining the impact of war on and responsive coping mechanisms by the civilian population. See *The State, Violence, and Development: The Political Economy of War in Mozambique, 1975–1992* (Aldershot, 1996).
52 Interview #64.
53 Interview #12.
54 Interview #80.
55 'Minutes of the Umtali District Team Meeting', 3 November 1980, PPD.
56 Interviews #64, #66. At the peak, in 1990, 150,000 Mozambicans were located in refugee camps in Zimbabwe, 30,000 of whom lived in Nyamgombe camp in Nyanga District. Fuelwood Crisis Consortium on Behalf of the Agricultural Sub-Committee of the Mozambican Refugee Programme, 'An Assessment of the Environmental Damage in the Areas Surrounding the Mozambican Refugee Camps in Zimbabwe, (September 1994), pp. 6, 10, MMZ/MZI 23.1 FUE, RSC.
57 Interviews #82 and #83.
58 Government of Zimbabwe, Honde–Pungwe Valley: Integrated Rural Development Plan, vol. 1: Project Environment (Rome, 1985), p. 34, DAO; interview #88.
59 Interview #24.
60 Interview #41.
61 Ibid.
62 Ibid.
63 Interview #88.
64 ZIMCORD, 'Index: Land Settlement and Rural Agricultural Development', p. 18; DA Mutasa to PA, 14 May 1986, Rural Development, PAO.
65 'Mutasa Constituency Seminar Planned Development of the Mutasa District', n.d. [1986?], Establishment of Vidcos and Wadcos Committees, PAO.
66 Tea outgrower production: 25 ha in 1969–1971, 14.4 ha in 1972, 2 ha in 1975, 29 ha in 1982. 'Holdenby Outgrowers Development Report', 1982, PPE.
67 Interview #122 with a coffee expert; Mukondiwa, ADA Coffee and Fruit Project (EEC), 'Agricultural Development Authority: Agrobascd Rural Dcvclopmcnt Projects: Organisational Experiences', 15 July 1992, p. 9; 'Memorandum to the Project Manager from the Coffee Field Supervisor, Subject: Spraying Gang', 13 July 1992, ADA.
68 S. Manase, 'Communal Land Reorganization and Development: Honde–Pungwe Valley Communal Lands, Initial Report, by the Department of Rural Development', October 1990, p. 24, DERUDE.
69 Interview #49; also #104.
70 Internal Affairs Running Diary, BSAP, 22 August 1977, PPG.
71 Interview #106.
72 Interview #115.
73 Interview #98 with Anna Sathiagnanan, resident medical doctor at Aberfoyle Tea Estates during the late 1970s and in the 1990s involved in HIV/AIDS research in Manyikaland. The published project data state a rate of 24 per cent HIV among women attending pre-natal clinics in the Honde Valley in the mid-1990s. See Simon Gregson et al., 'Recent Upturn in Mortality in Rural Zimbabwe: Evidence for an Early Demographic Impact of HIV-1 Infection?', *AIDS*, 11, no. 10 (1997), p. 1273.
74 Interview #92.
75 African women remained legal minors until 1982. Welshman Ncube, 'Released from Legal Minority: The Legal Age of Majority Act in Zimbabwe', *Women and Law in Southern Africa*, Alice Armstrong (ed.) (Harare, 1987), pp. 193-209. For women's post-war struggles, see Kathy Bond-Stewart, *Independence is not only for one Sex* (Harare, 1987), section one; Gay Seidman, 'Women in

Zimbabwe: Post-independence Struggles', *Feminist Studies*, 10, no. 3 (1984), pp. 419-40; Josephine Nhongo-Simbanegavi, *For Better or Worse? Women and ZANLA in Zimbabwe's Liberation Struggle* (Harare, 2000), chapter 6; Donna Pankhurst, 'Post-War Backlash Violence Against Women: What Can "Masculinity" Explain', *Gendered Peace: Women's Struggles for Post-War Justice and Reconciliation*, Donna Pankhurst (ed.) (New York, 2008), pp. 293-320.

76 Interview #21.
77 For the importance of gossip and rumour as moral discourse, see Luise White, *Speaking with Vampires: Rumor and History in Colonial Africa* (Berkeley, CA, 2000).
78 Interview #51.
79 Interview #38.
80 'Swift Rescues Honde Valley Small Farmers', *Financial Gazette*, 8 December 1994.
81 Interview #55; 'Drastic Drop in Tea Production', *Herald*, 11 November 1992.
82 Interviews #13, #136.
83 Interview #135.
84 Interview #43.
85 Interview #135.
86 Interview #49.
87 Interviews #78, #127, #42 with a member of the Mutasa district staff.
88 Interview #42.
89 Interview #49.
90 Drought food included tree fruits and roots, as well as parts of plants not normally eaten, such as the seeds of the wild plantain (*tzoro*), which can be pounded and used as a substitute for mealie-meal. Interviews #99, #13.
91 Interviews #107, #115, #108. For the 'idea of social causation of environmental ills', see Jan Schoffeleers, 'Introduction', *Guardians of the Land: Essays on Central African Territorial Cults*, Jan Schoffeleers (ed.) (Gwelo, 1978), p. 8, 1-46.
92 Interview #8.
93 Interview #127.
94 For the conflict between the *mambo* and government officials, see interviews #4, #6, #142 with a senior government official; Mutasa District, Annual Report, 1992, ADM 6, DAO, 'Osborne Dam: Chief Abisha Mutasa Not Amused', *Parade* (1992), p. 11.
95 Interview #137.
96 Interviews #96, #98, #137.
97 Interview #71.
98 For spiritual revival under the impact of the drought, see Hesekiel Mafu, 'The 1991-92 Zimbabwean Drought and Some Religious Reactions', *Journal of Religion in Africa*, 25, no. 3 (1995), pp. 288-308. For spiritual insecurity and witchcraft, see Adam Ashforth, *Witchcraft, Violence, and Democracy in South Africa* (Chicago, IL, 2005).
99 The armies that operated in the Honde Valley were the Rhodesian Security Forces, FRELIMO, ZANLA, RENAMO, and the ZNA.
100 After the First Chimurenga, at her execution, *mbuya* Nehanda prophesied that her bones would rise again, a metaphor for the presence of the dead in the world of the living. David Beach, 'An Innocent Woman, Unjustly Accused? Charwe, Medium of the Nehanda Mhondoro Spirit, and the 1896-97 Central Shona Rising in Zimbabwe', *History in Africa*, 25 (1998), pp. 27-54; see also Chenjerai Hove, *Bones* (Oxford, 1990).
101 Interview #82. Pamela Reynolds provides a similar account of a haunted ex-combatant. 'Children of Tribulation: The Need to Heal and the Means to Heal War Trauma', *Africa*, 60, no. 1 (1990), p. 14. For the concept of 'just anger' as moral judgement, see Michael Harkin, 'Feeling and Thinking in Memory and Forgetting: Toward an Ethnohistory of the Emotions,' *Ethnohistory*, 50, no. 2 (2003), p. 269.
102 David Lan suggests childlessness as a third reason for a deceased person to become a *ngozi. Guns and Rain: Guerrillas and Spirit Mediums in Zimbabwe* (London, 1985), p. 35.
103 M. Hannan, *Standard Shona Dictionary* (Harare, 1987 [1959]). For *ngozi* caused by killings during the Chimurenga, see Reynolds, 'Children of Tribulation'; Lan, *Guns and Rain*, passim; Richard Werbner, *Tears of the Dead: The Social Biography of an African Family* (Edinburgh, 1991), pp. 151-56, 188-90. For a brief definition of *ngozi* and an excellent study on spirit beliefs, see Peter Fry, *Spirits of Protest: Spirit-mediums and the Articulation of Consensus among the Zezuru of Southern Rhodesia (Zimbabwe)* (Cambridge, 2007 [1976]), p. 129, note 6.
104 Interview #54; also #135.
105 Interview #117.
106 Interview #82.

107 Norma Kriger, *Zimbabwe's Guerrilla War: Peasant Voices* (Cambridge, 1992), p. 179-86.
108 Interview #54; also #65.
109 Norma Kriger, 'Popular Struggles in Zimbabwe's War of National Liberation', *Cultural Struggle and Development in Southern Africa*, Preben Kaarsholm (ed.) (Harare, 1991), p. 127.
110 Interview #117.
111 Pamela Reynolds, *Traditional Healers and Childhood in Zimbabwe* (Athens, OH, 1996) and 'Children of Tribulation'.
112 The following account is based on interview #38.
113 The mapping of social relations involved in spiritual healing resembles Charles van Onselen's method for researching social biography. See 'The Reconstruction of a Rural Life from Oral Testimony: Critical Notes on the Methodology Employed in the Study of a Black South African Sharecropper', *Journal of Peasant Studies*, 20, no. 3 (1993), pp. 494-514.
114 Interviews #135, #47, #48, #71.
115 The communal creation of a narrative of violent past occurrences lies also at the core of *gacaca* courts which functioned between 2002 and 2012 in Rwanda. Lars Waldorf, 'Remnants and Remains: Narratives of Suffering in Post-Genocide Rwanda's Gacaca Courts', *Humanitarianism and Suffering: The Mobilization of Empathy*, Richard Wilson and Richard Brown (eds) (Cambridge, 2009), pp. 285-306 and Phil Clark, *The Gacaca Courts, Post-Genocide Justice and Reconciliation in Rwanda: Justice without Lawyers* (Cambridge, 2010).
116 See Reynolds, 'Children of Tribulation', pp. 14-15.
117 Interview #54. Banning child pledging, which also occurred for other reasons, was a gender concern that united administrative and mission interests in the early twentieth century. See Elizabeth Schmidt, 'Negotiated Spaces and Contested Terrain: Men, Women, and the Law in Colonial Zimbabwe, 1890–1939', *Journal of Southern African Studies*, 16, no. 4 (1990), pp. 628-31.
118 Interview #54.
119 Interview #118.
120 Ibid.
121 Interviews #112 and #30.
122 Interview #38; also #54.
123 For the use of biomedicine, see interviews #16 and #17.
124 Interview #115.
125 Later, Kasambira returned to work for Ziwe Zano at Gatsi primary school. John Pafiwa Katsidzira, no title [history of Ziwe Zano Society] (n.p. [Honde Mission], ms., n.d. [1976]), vol. 2, chapters 41, 49, PPA.
126 Terence Ranger, 'Afterword: War, Violence, and Healing in Zimbabwe', *Journal of Southern African Studies*, 18, no. 3 (1992), p. 705.
127 Interview #87.
128 Simon Gregson et al., 'Apostles and Zionists: The Influence of Religion on Demographic Change in Rural Zimbabwe', *Population Studies*, 53 (1999), p. 188.
129 Interviews #67, #141, with a ZAOGA pastor; see also a history of ZAOGA by David Maxwell, *African Gifts of the Spirit: Pentecostalism and the Rise of a Zimbabwean Transnational Religious Movement* (Oxford, 2006).
130 Interviews #141, #71, with valley inhabitants who joined ZAOGA during the 'crusade'.
131 Heike Schmidt, 'Healing the Wounds of War: Memories of Violence and the Making of History in Zimbabwe's Most Recent Past'. *Journal of Southern African Studies* 23, no. 2 (1997), pp. 301-10, Reynolds, in 'Children of Tribulation', pointed out that the number of afflicted people increased dramatically after the war and that many children were among the patients.
132 For a different view, see Reid, who argued that 'it is called *chikwambo* in Manicaland and *ngozi* in other parts of the country', and that both are merely 'different names for the same type of spirit'. 'The Witch (Muroyi)', n.d. [1977?], RP. For a third interpretation see Michael Gelfand et al., *The Traditional Medical Practitioner in Zimbabwe: His Principles of Practice and Pharmacopoeia* (Gweru, 1985), pp. 71-2.
133 Hannan defines *chikwambo* as a 'faculty, conferred by shave [non-ancestral spirit], of recovering property, and of punishing those who refuse to restore property'. Hannan, *Standard Shona Dictionary*. Lan, in turn, explains that *shave* 'are spirits that emanate from outside known human society' and 'never climax in speech', Lan, *Guns and Rain*, p. 38. Several interviewees used these terms interchangeably and maintained that *chikwambo* as well as *madzviti* may speak through their medium. Interview #61.
134 Interview #135; also #110, #61. At times *ngozi* cases could last for decades, such as in one instance when several girls were pledged between the 1910s and the late 1960s. DC Inyanga to DC Umtali, 22 January 1969, PER5 Chief Mutasa, DAO. Another case continued from the 1940s to the 1970s, see

'The Witch (Muroyi)'.

135 Interviews #141 and #135.

136 Interview #135; see also Heike Behrend, *Alice Lakwena and the Holy Spirits: War in Northern Uganda 1986-97* (Oxford, 1999), p. 132.

137 Interview #82. It is not clear whether, and if so, how deceased women manifest themselves as *ngozi* or *shave* spirits. For literary treatment of the problem, see Alexander Kanengoni, 'The Wo(man) in the Mirror', *Effortless Tears* (Harare, 1993), pp. 101-6.

138 Interview #135.

139 Two young women emphasised that while the afflicted girl and her family may try to find her a stranger as a suitor, because he does not know about her affliction, the spirit will not allow the marriage to be successful. Interviews #135, #61.

140 Interview #135. Another woman maintained that the children have the totem and name of their mother. Interview #63.

141 Interview #63.

142 The young woman spoke while possessed, Zindi, 5 October 1992; for more detail on this incident, see the introduction; see also interview #94.

143 Interview #135.

144 Interviews #54, #107.

145 Interview #77.

146 Ibid.

147 Denis Shropshire, 'A Journey in Mashonaland', *African Affairs*, 51, no. 202 (1952), p. 55.

148 Interview #119.

149 John Rennie, 'Christianity, Colonialism and the Origins of Nationalism among the Ndau of Southern Rhodesia 1890–1935' (PhD thesis, Northwestern University, Evanston, IL, 1973), pp. 157-8.

150 Shropshire, 'A Journey in Mashonaland', p. 55.

151 Interview #4.

152 Interview #2.

153 Interview #3.

154 See Government of Zimbabwe, Report of the Commission of Inquiry into Appropriate Agricultural Land Tenure Systems, vol. 1: Main Report (Harare, 1994), pp. ii, 23, 49-52.

155 Interview #8, followed by a land case hearing; also, Mutasa District, Monthly Report, November 1989, Chitepo District Council, PAO.

156 Interview #106.

157 This story was widely circulated in the Zindi area, and while it may be merely a tale rather than an account of a practice of empowerment today, it is significant that the performative moment of story-telling clearly had meaning in these women's lives. Particularly powerful sites that are of importance for the entire mamboship are Pungwe Pool and a nearby cave whose guardians are prepubescent girls. Denis Shropshire, 'The Mifananidzo of the Mutasa Dynasty', *Man* 30 (1930), p. 5.

158 For spirituality and the importance of landscape and water, see Sandra Greene, *Sacred Sites and the Colonial Encounter: A History of Meaning and Memory in Ghana* (Bloomington, IN, 2002). For competition between spiritual and political authority over land and water against the backdrop of land reform, see Joost Fontein, 'Languages of Land, Water and "Tradition" around Lake Mutirikwi in Southern Zimbabwe', *Journal of Modern African Studies*, 44, no. 2 (2006), pp. 223-49.

159 The similarity between *njuzu* and *mami wata* is striking. See Tobias Wendel, *Mami Wata oder ein Kult zwischen den Kulturen* (Münster, 1991). Abraham Mawere and Ken Wilson examined the 'Mbuya Juliana Cult' which came into existence in southern Zimbabwe in 1992 and lasted for a brief period of time. The cult leader gained her legitimacy from having spent four years in the 1970s living underwater with a *njuzu*. See 'Socio-Religious Movements, the State and Community Change: Some Reflections on the Ambuya Juliana Cult of Southern Zimbabwe', *Journal of Religion in Africa*, 25, no. 3 (1995), p. 254.

160 Interview #89.

161 Zimbabwean women frequently used the term 'pumping' in reference to men having sex, usually accompanied by a corresponding hand gesture.

162 See 'Battle for the Pungwe', 'Pipeline Plan Raises Fears of Bleeding Honde Valley Dry', 'Troubled Waters, Angry Gods', *Horizon* (October 1994), pp. 14-18; DA Mutasa to PA, 14 May 1986, Rural Development, PAO.

163 'Report on a Meeting Held by Traditional Leaders of Mutasa District on Friday 10.04.1992', PER5 Meetings and Assemblies Including Elections of Chiefs, DAO.

164 *Financial Gazette*, 8 February 1996; 'Forget Pungwe', *Herald*, 13 February 1996.

165 *Daily News*, 17 March 2000.

166 Basil Davidson, *The Black Man's Burden: Africa and the Curse of the Nation State* (New York, 1992).

7
Epilogue
Violence That Does Not Haunt

This book calls for a re-examination of the concept of violence by accommodating its ambiguity in a complex understanding of the past. It investigates how those who suffer violence invest experiences of violation with meaning and thus accommodate them in their lives. Such accommodation is not merely a coping strategy or a simple overcoming of a harrowing past. Instead, healing refers to the re-articulation of self and the promise of social harmony in the face of a fractured sense of being and belonging. The three main threads running through the study – violence, memory, and landscape – lead to general conclusions regarding each concept as well as specific insight into the Honde Valley's and Zimbabwe's past.

In an age of accelerated violent conflict that ranges from insurgencies through warlordism, sex trafficking and gang warfare, lessons can be learned from how African men, women, and children make sense of violence in practices and cosmologies alternative to modes common in the western world. Following John Lonsdale's concept of 'moral ethnicity' as a shared set of values that are centred on the notion of civic virtue and debated and articulated in discourse, practice, and everyday encounters,[1] one can locate vernacular knowledge of healing and the importance of social health in the realm of such moral ethnicity. Interpreting memories and experiences of violence within the arena of moral ethnicity and healing reveals the complexity of the concept of violence: it discloses a range of motivations for using, supporting, and opposing violence; it emphasises the potential disconnect between violence and violation; and it shows healing practices which open avenues beyond western-style approaches such as individualised psychological and psychiatric treatment, judicial process, truth and reconciliation commissions, or national apologies. Hence, community, multiplicity, ambiguity, social health, and suffering emerge as elements in the practice and experience of violence.

On one hand, landscapes of violence denote the tension between a sense of belonging and social cohesion generated through an interplay of place being invested with meaning and place in turn informing sets of identities and identity practices. On the other hand, they signify rupture and dislocation through land alienation and enforced land-use practices experienced as violation. Perspective, identity, and practice create landscape, which in turn informs the sense of belonging, shapes identity, and serves as mnemotope, and, in the case of the Honde Valley, as the home for spiritual security and for danger. Communities under duress can often not afford to voice, or even to show, discord. Once security returns, however, multiple landscapes signifying identity, memory, and experience may emerge. It is then that silence can be broken and landscapes of violence as mnemotope, as place invested with memories of past suffering, and as signifiers of belonging, give voice.

Memory – and its opposites, forgetting and silence – is shaped by a given vernacular moral ethnicity. The context of conflict can have a major impact on past experiences being remembered, forgotten or not recalled. Memory is gendered and mediated by other identity traits; it is situational, and informed by violence experienced individually or communally. The process of transforming experience into memory invests the past with meaning. This meaning in turn provides an interpretative framework that reflects and informs identity and fosters or destabilises social cohesion. On the most basic level, memory turns past experiences into a narrative that breaks the silence violation might have imposed. Spiritual healing aims to connect the past and present with imaginations of the future, for it allows the reassertion of personhood through giving meaning to past events.

DESIRE LINES

Desire lines refer to the line of movement between two points, divergent from the trail delineated by landscaping, and reflect the choice and practice of the user, often due to convenience. A lay-out of undulating landscape-gardened paths as much as a geometric grid may hence be interrupted by the traces of short-cuts – or, for that matter, diversions from the master plan. Martin Hall defines 'desire lines' as 'palimpsests of historical experience', and 'contested spaces … challenging the search for order, engaging in a tussle for recognition and difference, and risking disappointment and destruction as the stamp of authority is reasserted'.[2] Taking the concept out of the urban planning context in which it emerged, desire lines open a perspective on spatial practices, the explanation of which is, in terms of African history, more often than not still caught up in the resistance paradigm.

Examining waves of displacement within the Honde Valley, across the tea plantation boundaries, and across the border as movement along desire lines, allows them to be seen as more than dislocation and actions caught up between colonial violence and rural resistance. Such practices may instead be understood as the delineation of a landscape of belonging, as much emotive and driven by desire as they were part of an anti-colonial struggle. As this study hopes to have shown, a perspective reflecting the desire to shape one's life chances and to secure the wellbeing of one's community may well reveal subversive actions against the colonial state and its associated interests, but it does not presume a paradigm of resistance.

THE CREATIVITY OF VIOLENCE

Arthur Kleinman contends that suffering is existential and that it is 'dangers and uncertainties' that 'make life matter. They define what it means to be human'.[3] The common assumption that violence denotes exceptional crises, according to him denies its existential quality in everyday life. Kleinman's notion of a 'moral life' characterised by responsible choices is where his argument connects with Lonsdale's understanding of community. Kleinman, a psychiatrist and anthropologist, focuses on case studies of individuals. Lonsdale's concept of moral ethnicity encompasses the notion of communal debate over identity, danger, and wellbeing. Hence, Lonsdale furnishes what Kleinman identifies as the 'messiness of moral experience' with a communal discursive arena, be that through debate over normativity, through land use or healing practices, or indeed displacement.

The intention here is not to artificially juxtapose western and African societies, but to suggest a change in perspective that opens a new understanding of violence. One important example examined in this study is that of spirit affliction that constitutes a troubling crisis which usually requires a ritual expert to appease the spirit, with the manifestation of the symptoms and their interpretation simultaneously providing a moral commentary on the life of the afflicted and the wider community. It is important to recognise that spiritual healing practices are both a response to a specific crisis as much as part of the ongoing process of recovering and strengthening social health.

The humanistic argument underlying this book is that taking responsibility for oneself and for others, and taking risks to explore and learn, are crucial for the wellbeing of individuals and communities. The notion of life as an ongoing educational experience is more necessary than ever in the twenty-first century. This is a time of unprecedented globalisation, in a world where, ironically, the vast majority suffers from poverty and too many live in conflict situations. Being a 'rooted cosmopolitan', to use Anthony Appiah's term,[4] is a dangerous undertaking, because acknowledging diversity and approaching it with curiosity and the wish to learn – rather than to conquer and change – means risking the realisation that one has to take a critical look at oneself and one's own society; risking having to change oneself. Existentially, Appiah's 'rooted cosmopolitanism' is a dual concept which requires both a locally rooted self with a sense of belonging and the losing's of one's bearings in order to truly engage with diversity and difference. Just as travellers of long ago, departing on a ship and leaving sight of land behind, were literally and metaphorically at sea until their destination was reached, allowing them to regain their cultural bearings, so today's cosmopolitan dares to leave formed understandings temporarily behind to allow for new insights. It is engagement and rootedness that makes us ourselves and allows us to take responsibility in this world. In 1910, E.M. Forster famously wrote in his reflection on personhood and belonging, arguing against the artificial dichotomy of 'prose and … passion' prevalent in Edwardian society, 'Live in fragments no longer. Only connect.'[5] The Honde Valley provides a tremendously illuminating example of such cosmopolitanism and connectedness through periods of great conflict and duress from the mid-nineteenth century to the early 1990s, when it ceased to be a frontier area as the nation state came to stay. Hence, it is appropriate to speak of the creativity of violence.

A FRONTIER LANDSCAPE

Looking at the Honde Valley as a historic place, one shaped and transformed over time, it emerges as a frontier area and borderland that, through historical processes characterised by the tension between danger and opportunity, attracted and displaced inhabitants and hence provided the backdrop against which a specific identity emerged, namely a frontier ethnicity. This began in the 1830s, the time of the Gaza raiders, with the valley serving as a buffer zone between these warriors, the Makombe paramountcy and the Portuguese to the east, and the Mutasa mamboship to which the area politically belongs, to the south and west. The valley's frontier status was transformed but nevertheless solidified with the imposition of colonial rule in the late nineteenth century, which made the area part of the Rhodesian frontier at its border with Portuguese territory. The arrival of African and European self-perceived pioneers with the establishment of an African mission station in 1938, the forced immigration from the highveld when land segregation was fully enforced from 1948, and the establishment of tea estates from 1952 brought more change. Nevertheless, the area remained distant from the central state until the liberation war of the 1970s, when Mozambican liberation fighters first started operating in the area, followed by ZANLA guerrillas, who used the valley as their main infiltration route into the country.

Social and personal memory clearly map the turning points that shaped the frontier ethnicity of the area. The *madzviti* raids from the 1830s to 1880s are remembered as those of predators, while the first war in the valley is that of Makombe, from 1917 to 1920. This conflict was fought elsewhere, but its refugees arrived with accounts of their suffering, and as they became frontier people, their experiences merged with the social memory of the area. Later, the point when the valley inhabitants 'saw' war for the first time differed, just as the degree of suffering delineated the difference between crisis and war: for some it was their initial encounter with guerrilla fighters in 1974, for others the counter-insurgency campaign of forced villagisation from 1976.

The range in dating the beginning of war in the valley reflects the nature of small-scale, mobile warfare that leads to differences in strategy and tactics, even in a geographically small area. More significantly, it also illustrates that two people might experience a similar event differently. However, the important commonality is that valley inhabitants date the Second Chimurenga to their first experience of significant suffering on the hands of armed men. Hence, as a vernacular event, the conflict is not remembered as a liberation war, even though, as a national episode it is understood as the war for lost lands and freedom. Despite the association of the Chimurenga with suffering, it was also a time of reclaiming the spiritual landscape that had been mapped for the guerrilla units' protection. In most parts of the valley social cohesion became more pronounced than ever, disrupted by a brief dissident period after independence, and reinforced again when RENAMO began operating in the area in 1984.

In the early 1990s, with the worst drought in living memory and the Mozambican ceasefire, things began to change: the frontier society loosened and deep rupture lines began to show as Christian churches arrived on crusades and the state began to challenge ownership of the sacred landscape to an unprecedented degree.

Focusing the lens on war and political articulation, several striking aspects emerge. First, a military history of the Honde Valley may characterise this crucial operational area of the Second Chimurenga by its highly politicised inhabitants. While this was indeed the case, demands and actions towards the state and its representatives, settlers, and ZANLA fighters were mostly non-nationalist in nature, being instead an expression of deeply embedded vernacular concerns: the struggle to remain a frontier area beyond state control.

Second, women, chiefs, and youths played a crucial role in actively engaging the changing circumstances of conflict during different periods. As an ex-combatant remembered from the Second Chimurenga: 'There is that boldness in women' – a boldness that maybe became most apparent when women 'roughed up' agricultural extension workers in the 1960s, fed and supported FRELIMO and ZANLA fighters while their husbands were away as migrant labourers, and when they relentlessly mocked sexually compromised men who failed to pay respect to the sacred landscape. Most of the chiefs in the Honde Valley stood at the forefront of protesting their followers' rights to a frontier existence beyond state control, beginning with border movement in the first years of the twentieth century to outright resistance against the settler state during the Chimurenga. The only chief who outwardly disregarded his followers' interests was abducted and executed by FRELIMO, a pattern carried out by Zimbabwe's liberation armies elsewhere in the country. Youths' prominence during the Chimurenga is reflected in part by the resounding silence about them in interviews carried out in the 1990s – with the exception of those with ex-combatants. Such communal silence reflects the spiritual insecurity emanating from some of these youths' actions, such as their responsibility for unjustful killings, especially by those who had acted as intermediaries between the liberation fighters and the elders. At the same time, male and female youths showed tremendous entrepreneurial spirit in the context of forced villagisation, as did one young man who became a successful businessman, enjoyed the liberties of Protected Village life beyond elders' strict control, and crossed the border to fight for freedom.

Third, the counter-insurgency campaign was fought ruthlessly and in particular the 'hot pursuit' attacks and RENAMO's insurgencies constitute major human rights violations. As in Kenya, based on the British expertise gained in the fight against Mau Mau in the 1950s, villagisation was carried out with utmost disregard for the affected African population. In the case of the Honde Valley this tactic was also geared towards the economic gain of the tea industry. Today, civil and international rights issues tend to be at the forefront of critical discussions of counter-insurgency warfare. What the history of the Honde Valley reveals is not merely the merging of civilian and military administration, but the crucial role economic interests played in strategic planning.

In the first decade of the twenty-first century, Zimbabwe plunged into what the government proclaimed to be the Third Chimurenga, which focused on land reform and led to hyper-inflation, bringing with it a hitherto unimaginable daily experience of social injustice for the majority population. Zimbabwe has faced a severe political and socio-economic crisis for some time, although it is blatantly clear that there is no such thing as 'the' Zimbabwe crisis, with conditions changing over time and differing between places. Still, it would be all too easy to subscribe to the perception of Zimbabwe as a poster child of African pessimism. One question raised in the debate about the crisis is why Zimbabwe's civil society has so far failed to seriously challenge or even overcome state repression. An answer may be found in the Honde Valley experience of the twentieth century, where the vested interest in radically local concerns over questions of moral ethnicity largely informed social cohesion, action, and practice, as well as political activism.

Finally, there is much to be learned from how Zimbabweans have made sense of their experience of violence. Healing and the reassertion of social cohesion might be frail and at times fail, but the ideologies and practices delineated in this study offer much insight nevertheless. The most common western approaches of assuming individual injury and addressing it through biomedicine, or an assumption of communal violation that generates hyper-nationalism, contrast sharply with the notions of communal suffering and social healing examined herein. If society offers ways through which experiences, however destructive, gain meaning and can thus be turned into memory, then, as elders in the Honde Valley explained: *Hondo haina pfukwa* – war does not lead to haunting.

Notes

1   John Lonsdale, *Unhappy Valley: Conflict in Kenya and Africa*, Bruce Berman and John Lonsdale (London, 1992), vol. 2, chapters eleven and twelve

2   Martin Hall, 'Afterword: Lines of Desire', *Desire Lines: Space, Memory and Identity in the Post-Apartheid City*, Noëleen Murray et al. (eds) (London, 2007), p. 287.

3   Arthur Kleinman, *What Really Matters: Living a Moral Life Amidst Uncertainty and Danger* (Oxford, 2006), pp. 1, 3; 'The Violences of Everyday Life: The Multiple Forms and Dynamics of Violence', *Violence and Subjectivity*, Veena Das et al. (eds) (Berkeley, CA, 1997), pp. 226-41.

4   Anthony Appiah, 'Cosmopolitan Patriots', *Critical Inquiry*, 23, no. 3 (1997), pp. 617-39; also, Anthony Appiah, *Cosmopolitanism: Ethics in a World of Strangers* (New York, 2006).

5   E.M. Forster, *Howards End* (London, 1989 [1910]), p. 188.

Bibliography

Archival Sources

NATIONAL ARCHIVES OF ZIMBABWE, HARARE

Government Files
A1/6/1-4 Administrator's Office, Manica Reports.
A1/10/1 Administrator's Office, Portuguese Territory.
A3/4/1-9 Administrator's Office, Correspondence Boundaries.
A3/18/38 Administrator's Office, Native Affairs, Portuguese Native Rising.
A3/18/39/16 Administrator's Office, Correspondence, Native Affairs.
L2/1-4 Land Settlement Department, Correspondence.
N3/1-10 Native Department, Chief Native Commissioner.
N9/1/1-26 Native Department, Annual Reports.
N9/2/1-3 Native Department, Half-Yearly Reports.
N9/3/1-3 Native Department, Quarterly Reports.
N9/4/1-38 Native Department, Monthly Reports.
NUC1-2 Native Department, Native Commissioner and Assistant Magistrate Inyanga.
S138 Native Affairs, Chief Native Commissioner, Numerical Series.
S235 Native Affairs, Chief Native Commissioner, Unnumbered Series.
S482/70/43 Office of the Prime Minister, General Correspondence.
S603-604 Native Affairs, Native Commissioner Inyanga.
S1194/190/27/6 Agricultural Department, Secretariat, Correspondence.
S1542/T7 Tete Agreement.
S1561/10 Native Affairs, Chief Native Commissioner, Correspondence, Unnumbered Series.
S2221/1-7 Native Affairs, Chief Native Commissioner, District Courts.
S2588/1977 Native Affairs, Chief Native Commissioner, Correspondence, Land.
S2791/4 Native Affairs, Chief Native Commissioner, Correspondence, Associations and Societies.
S2807/4-7 Native Affairs, Chief Native Commissioner, Correspondence, Land Apportionment Act.
S2810/2371 Native Affairs, Chief Native Commissioner, Missions and Churches.
S2810/4203 Native Affairs, Chief Native Commissioner, Correspondence, Missions and Churches.
S2827/2/2/1-8 Native Affairs, Chief Native Commissioner, Annual Reports.
S2929/1/3 Native Affairs, Delineation Reports Inyanga District.

T2/17/1 Treasury, In-Letters and Correspondence.
ZBJ1-3 Native Production and Trade Commission 1944.

Historical Manuscripts
MA14/1/2 Machiwenyika, Jason. 'The History and Customs of the Manyika People and Manyika'.
MS308/52 International Defence Fund.
WO5 Federation of Women's Institutes .

Government Reports
Baxter, J.G. *An Assessment of the Tea Growing Potentials of the Manga and Holdenby Tribal Trust Lands and Recommendations for its Development as a Tea Scheme.* Salisbury, 1969.
Government of Zimbabwe, Ministry of Internal Affairs, Tilcor. *Pungwe Valley Project Report.* Salisbury: 1976.

Oral Interviews.
ORAL/240 Interview with Noel Hunt, 27 November 1983.

NATIONAL RECORDS CENTRE, HARARE

Box numbers 55619, 57577, 62328, 66721, 88399, 88459, 93785, 93786, 103986, 103987, 150768, 115133.

AGRICULTURAL DEVELOPMENT AUTHORITY, HAUNA

Various papers.

DISTRICT ADMINISTRATOR'S OFFICE MUTASA, MUTASA DISTRICT CENTRE

ADM/6 District Administrator Reports.
PER5 Chiefs and Headmen.
PER 5 GEN.
Establishment of Vidcos and Wadcos Committees, Resettlement.

MINISTRY OF AGRICULTURE, HARARE

Butcher, C. 'The Tribal Trust Land Development Corporation: An Evaluation', July 1980.
Norval, R., 'The Effects of a Break-Down of Dipping in Tribal Areas in Rhodesia', Department of Veterinary Sciences, Ministry of Agriculture n.d. [1979].

MINISTRY OF LOCAL GOVERNMENT, RURAL AND URBAN DEVELOPMENT: DEPARTMENT OF RURAL DEVELOPMENT (DERUDE), MUTARE

Manase, S. 'Communal Land Reorganization and Development: Honde - Pungwe Valley Communal Lands. Initial Report'. Department of Rural Development (Derude), Mutare, 18-21 October 1990.
Nyamapiena, K. 'Proposals for Communal Land Re-organization in Zimbabwe', 1990.
Zimbabwe Conference on Reconstruction and Development, 'Let's Build Zimbabwe Together: ZIMCORD', Conference Documentation, Zimbabwe Conference on Reconstruction and Development, Salisbury, 23-27 March 1981.
— 'Zimbabwe's Post-War Recovery Programme', document prepared for the Zimbabwe

Conference on Reconstruction and Development, 23-27 March, 1981.
Various correspondence.

PROVINCIAL ADMINISTRATOR'S OFFICE, MUTARE

Chitepo District Council.
Establishment of Vidcos and Wadcos Committees, Resettlement.
PER5 Chiefs and Headmen.
PER5 GEN.
Rural Development
Government of Zimbabwe. *Honde-Pungwe Valley: Integrated Rural Development Plan. vol. 1, Project Environment.* Rome: 1985.

CATHOLIC COMMISSION FOR JUSTICE AND PEACE ZIMBABWE, HARARE

Various papers.

OLD MUTARE MISSION ARCHIVES, PENHALONGA

Various papers.

PRIVATE PAPERS

PPA – PPH.
M.G. Reid Papers (RP).

REFUGEE STUDIES CENTRE, OXFORD

MMZ/MZI Mozambicans in Zimbabwe 1-58.

TANZANIA NATIONAL ARCHIVES, DAR ES SALAAM

ACC 155/M5/6 Songea District Office: Miscellanea.

Interviews

The interviews listed below were all conducted by the author, and most were taped. With the exception of prominent members of the community who agreed to be referenced by name, all those interviewed were guaranteed anonymity due to the sensitivity of the issues discussed. The third letter indicates the interviewee's gender – M(ale) or F(emale).

1   J. Geoff Baxter, Mutare, 3 February 1992.
2   J. Geoff Baxter, Mutare, 21 October 1992.
3   *Ishe* Chikomba and his father, Chikomba, 15 August 1992.
4   *Ishe* Zindi and *sabhuku* Gogodi, Zindi, 7 October 1992.
5   *Ishe* Zindi, Zindi, 7 October 1992.
6   *Mambo* Mutasa, Watsomba, 7 March 1992.
7   *Mambo* Mutasa, Watsomba, 8 August 1992.
8   *Mambo* Mutasa, Watsomba, 5 November 1992.

9 *Mbuya* Mpota (Emily Chikomba), Sagambe, 12 August 1992.
10 *Muzvare* Muparutsa, Mahemasimike, 27 October 1992.
11 *Muzvare* Muredzwa, New Reserve, 24 October 1992.
12 *Sekuru* Hwerekwere, Honde Mission, 9 August 1991.
13 Group interview with five communal farmers, Chipupuri, 3 March 1988.
14 Group interview with CBF, BPF, BDM, Chikomba, 13 November 1992.
15 Group interview with CUM, DSM, DTM, Zindi, 10 November 1992.
16 AAM, Hauna, 3 March 1988.
17 AHF, Chikomba, 23 September 1990.
18 AHF, Hauna 19 October 1992.
19 AHF, Hauna, 12 September 1993.
20 AIM, Chikomba, 25 September 1990.
21 AJM and AKM, Honde Mission, 9 August 1991.
22 AKM, Honde Mission, 9 August 1991.
23 ALF, Harare, 27 August 1991.
24 ANM, Penhalonga, 25 January 1992.
25 AOM, Mutare, 31 January 1992.
26 APM, Mutare, 31 January 1992.
27 APM, Mutare, 3 June 1992.
28 APM, Mutare, 21 October 1992.
29 ASM, Mutare, 6 February 1992.
30 ATM, Mutare, 7 February 1992.
31 AUM, Mutare, 28 February 1992.
32 AUM, Mutare, 3 October 1992.
33 AVM, Mutare, 3 March 1992.
34 AVM, Mutare, 6 June 1992.
35 AVM, Mutare, 9 August 1992.
36 AVM, Mutare, 4 October 1992.
37 AVM, Mutare, 17 October 1992.
38 AVM, Mutare, 21 October 1992.
39 AWM, Penhalonga, 7 March 1992.
40 AWM, Penhalonga, 8 August 1992.
41 AYM, Chikomba, 18 May 1992.
42 AZM, Penhalonga, 18 May 1992.
43 BAM, Penhalonga, 19 May 1992.
44 BBM, Mutasa district centre, 2 June 1992.
45 BCM, Zindi, 6 June 1992.
46 BDM, Chikomba, 7 June 1992.
47 BDM, Chikomba, 16 August 1992.
48 BDM, Chikomba, 17 September 1992.
49 BDM, Chikomba, 18 September 1993.
50 BDM, Chikomba, 7 November 1992.
51 BDM, Chikomba, 13 November 1992.
52 BDM, Chikomba, 18 September 1993.
53 BEM, Chikomba, 8 June 1992.
54 BFF, Holdenby, 2 August 1992.
55 BGM and BXM, Chikomba, 9 June 1992.
56 BGM and BXM, Chikomba, 15 August 1992.
57 BHM, Holdenby, 9 June 1992.
58 BHM, Holdenby, 6 November 1992.
59 BIM, Harare, 18 July 1992.
60 BIM, Harare, 19 July 1992.
61 BIM, Harare, 9 September 1992.
62 BJM, Watsomba, 27 July 1992.
63 BKF, New Reserve, 7 July 1992.

64 BKF, New Reserve, 30 July 1992.
65 BLF, Honde Mission, 3 August 1992.
66 BLF and BMF, Honde Mission, 3 August 1992.
67 BMF, Honde Mission, 3 August 1992.
68 BMF, Mutare, 8 October 1992.
69 BMF, Mutare, 28 October 1992.
70 BMF, Mutare, 19 September 1993.
71 BPF, Chikomba, 23 August 1992.
72 BPF, Chikomba, 24 August 1992.
73 BPF and BDM, Chikomba, 13 November 1992.
74 BPF, Chikomba, 18 September 1993.
75 BRF, Chikomba, 12 August 1992.
76 BSM, Holdenby, 12 August 1992.
77 BTM, Chikomba, 12 August 1992.
78 BUF and BTM, Chikomba, 12 August 1992.
79 BUF and BTM, Chikomba, 13 August 1992.
80 BVM, Chikomba, 13 August 1992.
81 BWM, Chikomba, 14 August 1992
82 BXM, Chikomba, 15 August 1992.
83 BZM, Chikomba, 15 August 1992.
84 BZM, Chikomba, 16 August 1992.
85 CAM, Chikomba, 15 August 1992.
86 CBF, Chikomba, 15 August 1992.
87 CBF, Chikomba, 13 November 1992.
88 CCM, Chikomba, 16 August 1992.
89 CDF, Chikomba, 9 July 1992.
90 CDF, Chikomba, 16 August 1992.
91 CDF, Chikomba, 23 August 1992.
92 CEM, Chikomba, 23 August 1992.
93 CFM, Zindi, 24 August 1992.
94 CGM, Chikomba, 18 September 1992.
95 CHM, Harare, 21 September 1992.
96 CHM, Harare, 2 October 1992.
97 CHM, Harare, 1 November 1992.
98 CIF, Mutare, 3 October 1992.
99 CJF and CKF, Zindi, 4 October 1992.
100 CJF and CKF, Zindi, 5 October 1992.
101 CJF and CKF, Zindi, 6 October 1992.
102 CJF, Zindi, 6 October 1992.
103 CJF, Zindi, 11 September 1993.
104 CJF, Zindi, 13 September 1993.
105 CJF and CKF, Zindi, 15 September 1993.
106 CKF, Zindi, 10 November 1992.
107 CKF, Zindi, 15 September 1992.
108 CKF, Zindi, 8 October 1992.
109 CKF, Zindi, 10 November 1992.
110 CLM, Zindi, 5 October 1992.
111 CLM, Zindi, 7 October 1992.
112 CMM, Zindi, 5 October 1992.
113 CNF, Zindi, 5 October 1992.
114 CNY, Zindi, 5 October 1992.
115 COM, Zindi, 5 October 1992.
116 CPM, Zindi, 7 October 1992.
117 CTM, Zindi, 6 October 1992.
118 CUM, Zindi, 10 November 1992.

119 CVM, Zindi, 6 October 1992.
120 CWM, Zindi, 8 June 1992.
121 CWM, Zindi, 7 October 1992.
122 CWM, Zindi, 10 October 1992.
123 CXM, Zindi, 7 October 1992.
124 CZM, Zindi, 7 October 1992.
125 DAF, Mutare, 17 October 1992.
126 DBM, Hauna, 19 October 1992.
127 DCM, Hauna, 19 October 1992.
128 DDM, Mutare, 21 October 1992.
129 DDM, Mutare, 28 October 1992.
130 DEF, New Reserve, 24 October 1992.
131 DFM, New Reserve, 24 October 1992.
132 DHM, New Reserve, 25 October 1992.
133 DIF, Honde Mission, 26 October 1992.
134 DLF, Muparutsa, 27 October 1992.
135 DMF, Muparutsa, 27 October 1992.
136 DNM, Honde Green, 27 October 1992.
137 DOM, Mutare, 28 October 1992.
138 DPM, Mabvuka, 1 November 1992.
139 DQF, Chikomba, 7 November 1992.
140 DQF, Chikomba, 10 November 1992.
141 DRM, Holdenby, 15 September 1993.
142 DSM, Zindi, 10 November 1992.
143 DTM, Zindi, 10 November 1992.
144 DUM, Aberfoyle, 12 November 1992.
145 DVM, Chikomba, 18 September 1993.
146 DWM, Chikomba, 9 September 1993.
147 DXM, Mutare, 20 September 1993.
148 DYF, Chikomba, 24 August 1992.
149 DZM, Zindi, 6 October 1992.
150 EAM, Zindi, 6 October 1992.

Newspapers & Periodicals

Africa Christian Advocate
African Weekly
Bulawayo Chronicle
Fighting Forces of Rhodesia
Financial Gazette (Harare)
Financial Times (London)
Herald
Horizon
Illustrated Rhodesia
Mutare Post
Parade
Rhodesian Herald
Sunday Mail (Harare)
The Times (London)
Umbowo
Umtali Post

Published Sources & Dissertations

Alexander, Jeffrey. 'Toward a Theory of Cultural Trauma', *Cultural Trauma and Collective Identity*, Jeffrey Alexander, et al (eds). Berkeley, CA: University of California Press, 2004, pp. 1-30.

Alexander, Jocelyn. *The Unsettled Land: State-Making and the Politics of Land in Zimbabwe, 1893–2003*. Oxford: James Currey, 2006.

Alexander, Jocelyn, JoAnn McGregor, and Terence O. Ranger. *Violence and Memory: One Hundred Years in the 'Dark Forests' of Matabeleland*. Portsmouth, NH: Heinemann, 2000.

Allina-Pisano, Eric. 'Negotiating Colonialism: Africans, the State, and the Market in Manica District, Mozambique, 1835–1935'. PhD thesis, Yale University, 2002.

— 'Borderlands, Boundaries, and the Contours of Colonial Rule: African Labor in Manica District, Mozambique, c. 1904–1908', *International Journal of African Historical Studies*, 36, no. 1 (2003), pp. 59–82.

— 'Resistance and the Social History of Africa', *Journal of Social History*, 37, no. 1 (2003), pp. 187-98.

Allman, Jean, and Victoria Tashjian. *I Will Not Eat Stone: A Women's History of Colonial Asante*. Portsmouth, NH: Heinemann, 2000.

Ambler, Charles. 'Cowboy Modern: African Audiences, Hollywood Films, and Visions of the West', *Going to the Movies: Hollywood and the Social Experience of the Cinema*, Richard Maltby, Melvyn Stokes, and Robert Allen (eds). Exeter: Exeter University Press, 2008, pp. 348-63.

Anderson, David. *Histories of the Hanged: The Dirty War in Kenya and the End of Empire*. New York: W.W. Norton, 2005.

Anderson, Peter. 'The Human Clay: An Essay in the Spatial History of the Cape Eastern Frontier, 1811–1835'. M.Litt. thesis, University of Oxford, 1993.

— *Report and Protest of the Affairs Occurred at Manica*. Cape Town: Hofmeyr and Regter, 1891.

Andrada, Joaquim Paiva de. *Manica: Being a Report Addressed to the Minister of the Marine and the Colonies of Portugal*. London: George Philip, 1891.

Anonymous. 'Captain Paiva de Andrada's Zambesi Expedition, 1881', *Proceedings of the Royal Geographical Society and Monthly Record of Geography*, New Monthly Series. 4, no. 6 (1882), p. 374.

Appadurai, Arjun. 'The Past is a Scarce Resource', *Man*, 16, no. 2 (1981), pp. 201-19.

Appiah, Anthony. 'Cosmopolitan Patriots', *Critical Inquiry*, 23, no. 3 (1997), pp. 617-39.

— *Cosmopolitanism: Ethics in a World of Strangers*. New York: Norton, 2006.

Arendt, Hannah. *Eichmann in Jerusalem: A Report on the Banality of Evil*. New York: Viking Press, 1963.

— *On Violence*. New York: Harvest Books, 1970.

Armstrong, Nancy and Leonard Tennenhouse. *The Violence of Representation: Literature and the History of Violence*. London: Routledge, 1989.

Ashforth, Adam. *Witchcraft, Violence, and Democracy in South Africa*. Chicago, IL: Chicago University Press, 2005.

Asiwaju, A.I. and Paul Nugent (eds). *African Boundaries: Barriers, Conduits and Opportunities*. London: Pinter, 1996.

Assman, Aleida. *Erinnerungsräume: Formen und Wandlungen des kulturellen Gedächtnisses*, Munich: H.C. Beck, 1999.

Assmann, Jan. 'Collective Memory and Cultural Identity', *New German Critique*, 65 (1995), pp. 125-33.

Auret, Diana. *A Decade of Development: Zimbabwe 1980–1990*. Gweru: Mambo Press, 1990.

Axelson, Eric. *Portugal and the Scramble for Africa, 1875–1891*. Johannesburg: Witwatersrand University Press, 1967.

Barnes, Teresa. 'The Fight for Control of African Women's Mobility in Colonial Zimbabwe,

1900-1939', *Signs*, 17, no. 3 (1992), pp. 586-608.

— '"The Heroes" Struggle: Life after the Liberation War for Four Ex-combatants in Zimbabwe'. *Soldiers in Zimbabwe's Liberation War*, Ngwabi Bhebe and Terence O. Ranger (eds). London: James Currey, 1995, pp. 118-38.

Barnett, Michael. *Eyewitness to a Genocide: The United Nations and Rwanda*. Ithaca, NY: Cornell University Press, 2003.

Bastian, Misty. '"Vultures of the Marketplace": Igbo and Other Southeastern Nigerian Women's Discourse about the Ogu Umunwaanyi (Women's War) of 1929'. *Women and African Colonial History*, Jean Allman, Susan Geiger, and Nakanyike Musisi. Bloomington, IN: Indiana University Press, 2002, pp. 260-81.

Baud, Michiel and Willem van Schendel. 'Toward a Comparative History of Borderlands', *Journal of World History*, 8, no. 2 (1997), pp. 211-42.

Baumhögger, Goswin, with the assistance of Telse Diederichsen and Ulf Engel. *The Struggle for Independence: Documents on the Recent Development of Zimbabwe (1975–1980)*, 4 vols. Hamburg: Institut für Afrikakunde, 1984.

Bay, Edna. *Wives of the Leopard: Gender, Politics, and Culture in the Kingdom of Dahomey*. Charlottesville, VA: University of Virginia Press, 1998.

Bazeley, W.S. 'Manyika Headwomen', *NADA*, 7 (1940), pp. 3-5.

Beach, David. *War and Politics in Zimbabwe 1840–1900*. Gweru: Mambo Press, 1986.

— 'The Uses of the Colonial Military History of Mozambique', *Cahiers d'Etudes Africaines*, 26, no. 4 (1986), pp. 707-13.

— *The Origins of Moçambique and Zimbabwe: Paiva de Andrada, the Companhia de Moçambique and African Diplomacy 1881-91*. History Seminar Paper, 89. Harare: University of Zimbabwe, 1992.

— *Archaeology and History in Nyanga, Zimbabwe*. History Seminar Paper, 97. Harare: University of Zimbabwe, 1995.

— 'An Innocent Woman, Unjustly Accused? Charwe, Medium of the Nehanda Mhondoro Spirit, and the 1896-97 Central Shona Rising in Zimbabwe', *History in Africa*, 25 (1998), pp. 27-54.

Behrend, Heike. *Alice Lakwena and the Holy Spirits: War in Northern Uganda 1986-97*. Oxford: James Currey, 1999.

Beinart, William. 'African History and Environmental History.' *African Affairs*, 99, no. 395 (2000), pp. 269-302.

Beinart, William and Colin Bundy. *Hidden Struggles in Rural South Africa: Politics and Popular Movements in the Transkei and Eastern Cape 1980–1930*. London: James Currey, 1987.

Bender, Barbara and Margot Winder. *Contested Landscapes: Movement, Exile and Place*. Oxford: Berg, 2001.

Berkhofer, Robert. 'The North American Frontier as Process and Context', *The Frontier in History: North America and Southern Africa Compared*, Howard Lamar and Leonard Thompson (eds). New Haven, CT: Yale University Press, 1981, pp. 43-75.

Berman, Bruce and John Lonsdale. *Unhappy Valley: Conflict in Kenya and Africa*, 2 vols. London: James Currey, 1992.

Bhebe, Ngwabi. 'The Evangelical Lutheran Church in Zimbabwe and the War of Liberation, 1975–1980'. *Church and State in Zimbabwe*, Carl Hallencreutz and Ambrose Moyo (eds). Gweru: Mambo Press, 1988, pp. 163-194.

— *Burombo: African Politics in Zimbabwe, 1947–1958*. Harare: The College Press, 1989.

— *The Zapu and Zanu Guerrilla Warfare and the Evangelical Lutheran Church in Zimbabwe*. Gweru: Mambo Press, 1999.

Bhila, H.H.K. *Trade and Politics in a Shona Kingdom: The Manyika and their Portuguese and African Neighbours 1575–1902*. Burnt Mill: Harlow, 1982.

Billington, Ray. 'The American Frontier'. *Beyond the Frontier: Social Process and Cultural Change*, Paul Blog and Fred Bohannan (eds). Garden City, NY: Natural History Press, 1967, pp. 3-24.

Binda, Alexandre. *Masodja: The History of the Rhodesian African Rifles and Its Forerunner, the Rhodesia Native Regiment*. Johannesburg: 30 South Publishers, 2008.

Blennerhassett, Rose and Lucy Sleeman. *Adventures in Mashonaland*. London and New York: Macmillan, 1893.

Bøås, Morton and Kevin Dunn. 'African Guerrilla Politics: Raging Against the Machine?', *African Guerrillas: Raging Against the Machine*, Morten Bøås and Kevin Dunn (eds). Boulder, CO: Lynne Rienner, 2007, pp. 9-38.

Bobbit, Phillip. *Terror and Consent: The Wars for the Twenty-First Century*. New York: Alfred Knopf, 2008.

Bond-Stewart, Kathy. *Independence Is Not Only For One Sex*. Harare: Zimbabwe Publishing House, 1987.

Bonner, Philip and Noor Nieftagodien. *Alexandra: A History*. Johannesburg: University of Witwatersrand, 2009.

Bourdillon, Michael and Paul Gundani. 'Rural Christians and the Zimbabwe Liberation War: A Case Study', *Church and State in Zimbabwe*, Carl Hallencreutz and Ambrose Moyo (eds). Gweru: Mambo Press, 1988, pp. 147-61.

Bozzoli, Belinda. *Theatres of Struggle and the End of Apartheid*. Athens, OH: Ohio University Press, 2004.

Bratton, Michael. *Beyond Community Development. The Political Economy of Rural Administration in Zimbabwe*. London: CIIR, 1978.

— 'Settler State, Guerrilla War and Rural Underdevelopment in Rhodesia', *Issue: A Journal of Opinion*, 9, nos. 1/2 (1979), pp. 56-62.

Brickhill, Jeremy. 'Daring to Storm the Heavens: The Military Strategy of ZAPU, 1976-79'. *Soldiers in Zimbabwe's Liberation War*, Ngwabi Bhebe and Terence O. Ranger (eds). London: James Currey, 1995, pp. 48-72.

— 'Making Peace with the Past: War Victims and the Work of the Mafela Trust', *Soldiers in Zimbabwe's Liberation War*, Ngwabi Bhebe and Terence O. Ranger (eds). London: James Currey, 1995, pp. 163-73.

Brooks, James. *Captives and Cousins: Slavery, Kinship, and Community in the Southwest Borderlands*. Published for the Omohundro Institute of Early American History and Culture, Williamsburg, Virginia. Chapel Hill, NC: University of North Carolina Press, 2002.

Brophy, Alfred. *Reparations: Pro and Con*. Oxford: Oxford University Press, 2006.

Brown, Michael. 'Resisting Resistance', *American Anthropologist*, 98, no. 4 (1996), pp. 729-35.

Brownlie, Ian. *African Boundaries: A Legal and Diplomatic Encyclopaedia*. London: Hurst, 1979.

Burke, Peter. 'Geschichte als soziales Gedächtnis'. *Mnemosyne: Formen und Funktionen der kulturellen Erinnerung*, Aleida Assmann and Dietrich Harth (eds). Frankfurt/Main: Fischer, 1991, pp. 289-304.

Callaway, Hellen. 'Purity and Exotica in Legitimating the Empire: Cultural Constructions of Gender, Sexuality and Race', *Legitimacy and the State in Twentieth-Century Africa*, Terence O. Ranger and Olufemi Vaughan (eds). London: Macmillan, 1993, pp. 31-61.

Campbell, Donovan. *Joker One: A Marine Platoon's Story of Courage, Leadership, and Brotherhood*. New York: Random House, 2009.

Carter, Paul. *The Road to Botany Bay: An Exploration of Landscape and History*. New York: Alfred Knopf, 1988.

Caruth, Cathy (ed.). *Trauma: Explorations in Memory*. Baltimore, MD: John Hopkins University Press, 1995.

Carver, Richard. *Zimbabwe: A Break with the Past? Human Rights and Political Unity: An Africa Watch Report*. New York: Human Rights Watch, 1989.

Casid, Jill. *Sowing Empire: Landscape and Colonization*. Minneapolis, MN: University of Minnesota Press, 2005.

Catholic Commission for Justice and Peace. *Gukurahundi in Zimbabwe: A Report on the Disturbances in Matabeleland and the Midlands 1980–1988*. New York: Columbia University Press, 2007.

Catholic Commission for Justice and Peace in Rhodesia. *The Man in the Middle: Torture, Resettlement and Eviction*. London: CCJP, 1975.
— *Civil War in Rhodesia: Abduction, Torture and Death in the Counter-Insurgency Campaign*. London: CCJP, 1976.
Caute, David. *Under the Skin: The Death of White Rhodesia*. Harmondsworth: Penguin, 1983.
Chabal, Patrick. *Africa: The Politics of Suffering and Smiling*. London: Zed Books, 2009.
Chakrabarty, Dipesh. *Provincializing Europe: Postcolonial Thought and Historical Difference*. Princeton, NJ: Princeton University Press, 2000.
Chapman, Audrey and Hugo van der Merwe. *Truth and Reconciliation in South Africa: Did the TRC deliver?* Philadelphia, PA: Pennsylvania University Press, 2008.
Cherry, David. *Frontier and Society in Roman North Africa*. Oxford: Clarendon Press, 1998.
Chikuhwa, Jacob. *A Crisis of Governance: Zimbabwe*. New York: Algora, 2004.
Chimhundu, Herbert. 'Early Missionaries and the Ethnolinguistic Factor during the "Invention of Tribalism" in Zimbabwe', *Journal of African History*, 33, no. 1 (1992), pp. 87-109.
Chingono, Mark. *The State, Violence and Development: The Political Economy of War in Mozambique, 1975–1992*. Aldershot: Avebury, 1996.
Chung, Fay. 'Education and the Liberation Struggle'. *Society in Zimbabwe's Liberation War*, Ngwabi Bhebe and Terence O. Ranger (eds). Oxford: James Currey, 1996, pp. 139-46.
— *Re-Living the Second Chimurenga: Memories from Zimbabwe's Liberation Struggle*. Uppsala: Nordic Africa Institute, 2006.
Cilliers, Jakkie. *Counter-Insurgency in Rhodesia*. London: Croom Helm, 1985.
Clark, Phil. *The Gacaca Courts, Post-Genocide Justice and Reconciliation in Rwanda: Justice without Lawyers* (Cambridge: Cambridge University Press, 2010)
Clausewitz, Claus von. *On War*. Phoenix: Wilder Publications, 2008[1832].
Coelho, João. 'State Resettlement Policies in Post colonial Rural Mozambique: The Impact of the Communal Village Programme on Tete Province, 1977–1982', *Journal of Southern African Studies*, 24, no. 1 (1998), pp. 61-91.
Cohen, Anthony. 'Boundaries of Consciousness, Consciousness of Boundaries: Critical Questions for Anthropology'. *The Anthropology of Ethnicity: Beyond 'Ethnic Groups and Boundaries'*, Han Vermeulen and Cora Govers (eds). Amsterdam: Het Spinhuis, 1994, pp. 59-79.
— (ed.) *Signifying Identities: Anthropological Perspectives on Boundaries and Contested Values*. London: Routledge, 2000.
Cohen, David William and E.S. Atieno Odhiambo. *Siaya: The Historical Anthropology of an African Landscape*. London: James Currey, 1989.
Cohn, Bernard. *Colonialism and Its Forms of Knowledge: The British in India*. Princeton, NJ: Princeton University Press, 1996.
Cole, Jennifer. *Forget Colonialism? Sacrifice and the Art of Memory in Madagascar*. Berkeley, CA: University of California Press, 2001.
— 'Memory and Modernity'. *A Companion to Psychological Anthropology: Modernity and Psychocultural Change*, Conerly Casey and Robert Edgerton (eds). Malden, MA: Blackwell, 2005, pp. 103-20.
Collier, Paul. *The Bottom Billion: Why the Poorest Countries are Failing and What Can Be Done About It*. Oxford: Oxford University Press, 2007.
— *Wars, Guns, and Votes: Democracy in Dangerous Places*. New York: Harper, 2009.
Collier, Paul, et al. *Breaking the Conflict Trap: Civil War and Development Policy*. World Bank Policy Research Reports. Washington: World Bank, 2003.
Comaroff, Jean, and John L. 'Through the Looking-glass: Colonial Encounters of the First Kind', *Journal of Historical Sociology*, 1, no. 1 (1988), pp. 6-32.
— *Of Revelation and Revolution*. Vol. 2: *The Dialectics on a South African Frontier*. Chicago, IL: University of Chicago Press, 1997.
— *Theory from the South: Or, How Euro-America is Evolving Toward Africa*. Chicago, IL: Chicago University Press, 2012.

Connerton, Paul. *How Societies Remember.* Cambridge: Cambridge University Press, 1989.

Cooper, Frederick. 'Conflict and Connection: Rethinking Colonial African History', *American Historical Review*, 99, no. 5 (1994), pp. 1516-45.

— *Africa Since 1940: The Past of the Present.* Cambridge: Cambridge University Press, 2002.

— *Colonialism in Question: Theory, Knowledge, History.* Berkeley, CA: University of California Press, 2005.

Corbett, Anselm. 'African Encounter 1948–1951', *Celts Among the Shona: Early Experiences of Carmelite Missionaries to Zimbabwe*, Michael Hender (ed.). Dublin: Carmelite Order, 2002, pp. 69-76.

Courcel, Geoffrey de. 'The Berlin Act of 26 February 1885', *Bismarck, Europe, and Africa: The Berlin Africa Conference 1884–1885 and the Onset of Partition*, Stig Förster, Wolfgang Mommsen, and Ronald Robinson (eds). Oxford: Oxford University Press, 1988, pp. 247-61.

Croukamp, Dennis. *The Bushwar in Rhodesia: An Extraordinary Combat Memoir of a Rhodesian Reconnaissance Specialist.* Boulder, CO: Paladin Press, 2007.

Crummey, Donald (ed.). *Banditry, Rebellion and Social Protest in Africa.* London: James Currey, 1986.

Dabengwa, Dumiso. 'ZIPRA in the Zimbabwe War of National Liberation'. *Soldiers in Zimbabwe's Liberation War*, Ngwabi Bhebe and Terence O. Ranger. London: James Currey, 1995, pp. 24-35.

Daniel, E. Valentine. *Charred Lullabies: Chapters in an Anthropography of Violence.* Princeton, NJ: Princeton University Press, 1996.

Darian-Smith, Kate, Liz Gunner, and Sarah Nuttall (eds). *Text, Theory, Space: Land, Literature and History in South Africa and Australia.* London: Routledge, 1996.

Davidson, Basil. *The Black Man's Burden: Africa and the Curse of the Nation State.* New York: Three Rivers Press, 1992.

De Groot, Joanna. '"Sex" and "Race": The Construction of Language and Image in the Nineteenth Century'. *Sexuality and Subordination*, Susan Mendus and Jane Rendall (eds). London: Routledge, 1989, pp. 89-128.

Degenaar, Johan. 'The Concept of Violence'. *Politikon*, 7, no. 1 (1980), pp. 14-27.

— 'The Concept of Violence'. *Political Violence and the Struggle in South Africa*, Noel Manganyi and Andre du Toit (eds). Basingstoke: Macmillan, 1990, pp. 70-86.

Derrida, Jacques. *Of Grammatology.* Baltimore, MD: Johns Hopkins University Press, 1974 [1967].

DeWolf, L. Herold. 'A Do-it-yourself Mission in Rhodesia', *The African Christian Advocate* (July to Sept. 1964), pp. 6-7.

Donham, Donald. 'Staring at Suffering: Violence as a Subject'. *States of Violence: Politics, Youth, and Memory in Contemporary Africa*, Edna Bay and Donald Donham (eds). Charlottesville, VA: University of Virginia, 2006, pp. 16-33.

Döpcke, Wolfgang. *Das koloniale Zimbabwe in der Krise: Eine Wirtschafts- und Sozialgeschichte 1929–1939.* Hamburg: Lit, 1992.

Douglas, Anthony. *Poison and Medicine: Ethnicity, Power, and Violence in a Nigerian City, 1966–1986.* Portsmouth, NH: Heinemann, 2002.

Du Bois, François and Antje du Bois-Pedain (eds). *Justice and Reconciliation in Post-Apartheid South Africa.* Cambridge: Cambridge University Press, 2008.

Dunlap, Thomas. 'Creation and Destruction in Landscapes of Empire'. *City, Country, Empire: Landscapes in Environmental History*, Jeffry Diefendorf and Kurk Dorsey (eds). Pittsburgh, PA: University of Pittsburgh Press, 2005, pp. 207-25.

Durkheim, Emile. *The Elementary Forms of Religious Life.* Oxford: Oxford University Press, 2001 [1912].

Eber, Dena, and Arthur Neal. 'Introduction: Memory, Constructed Reality, and Artistic Truth'. *Memory and Representation: Constructed Truths and Competing Realities*, Dena Eber and Arthur Neal (eds). Bowling Green, OH: Bowling Green State University Popular Press, 2001, pp. 3-18.

Elkins, Caroline. *Imperial Reckoning: The Untold Story of Britain's Gulag in Kenya.* New York: Henry Holt, 2005.

— 'African Idyll', review of *The House at Sugar Beach: In Search of a Lost African Childhood*, by *New York Times Book Review*, 5 September 2008.

Ellert, Henrik. *The Rhodesian Front War: Counter-insurgency and Guerrilla Warfare, 1962–1980.* Gweru: Mambo Press, 1989.

Elwert, Georg. 'Markets of Violence'. *Dynamics of Violence: Processes of Escalation and De-Escalation in Violent Group Conflicts*, Georg Elwert, Stephan Feuchtwang, and Dieter Neubert (eds). *Sociologus*, Supplement. Berlin: Duncker and Humblot, 1999, pp. 85-102.

Englund, Harri. *From War to Peace on the Mozambique-Malawi Borderland.* Edinburgh: Edinburgh University Press, 2002.

Enzensberger, Hans Magnus. 'Civil War'. *Civil Wars: From L.A. to Bosnia*, Hans Magnus Enzensberger. New York: New Press, 1994 [1993], pp. 11-71.

Evans, Michael. *Fighting Against Chimurenga: An Analysis of Counter-Insurgency in Rhodesia 1972-9.* Salisbury: Historical Association of Zimbabwe, 1981.

Fabian, Johannes. *Memory Against Culture: Arguments and Reminders.* Durham, NC: Duke University Press, 2007.

Falola, Toyin and Aribidesi Usman (eds). *Movements, Borders, and Identities in Africa.* Rochester, NY: University of Rochester Press, 2009.

Fanon, Frantz. *Black Skin, White Masks.* New York: Grove, 1963 [1952].

— *Wretched of the Earth.* New York: Grove, 2004 [1961].

The Farming Gazette Supplement. 'Aberfoyle: The Story of a Tea Estate'. 3 May 1985.

Feierman, Steven. *Peasant Intellectuals: Anthropology and History in Tanzania.* Madison, WI: University of Wisconsin Press, 1990.

— 'Africa in History: The End of the Universal Narrative'. *After Colonialism: Imperialism and the Colonial Aftermath*, Gyan Prakash (ed). Princeton, NJ: Princeton University Press 1995, pp. 40-65.

— 'Afrika in der Weltgeschichte: Regionale Konfigurationen des Sozialen', *Afrikanische Geschichte und Weltgeschichte: Regionale und universal Themen in Forschung und Lehre*, Axel Harneit-Sievers (ed.). Berlin: Das Arabische Buch, 2000, pp. 9-22.

Fields, Karen. 'What One Cannot Remember Mistakenly'. *Memory and History: Essays on Recalling and Interpreting Experience*, Jaclyn Jeffrey and Glenace Edwall (eds). Lanham, MD: University Press of America, 1994, pp. 89-106.

Figley, Charles (ed.). *Mapping Trauma and Its Wake: Autobiographic Essays by Pioneer Trauma Scholars.* New York: Routledge 2006.

Filkins, Dexter. *The Forever War.* New York: Alfred Knopf, 2008.

Fontein, Joost. 'Languages of Land, Water and "Tradition" around Lake Mutirikwi in Southern Zimbabwe', *Journal of Modern African Studies*, 44, no. 2 (2006), pp. 223-49.

Forster, E.M. *Howards End.* London: Penguin, 1989 [1910].

Foster, Jeremy. *Washed with Sun: Landscape and the Making of White South Africa.* Pittsburgh, PA: University of Pittsburgh Press, 2008.

Frederikse, Julie. *None But Ourselves: Masses vs. Media in the Making of Zimbabwe.* London: Heinemann, 1982.

Friese, Heidrun. 'Silence – Voice – Representation'. *Social Theory after the Holocaust*, Robert Fine and Charles Turner (eds). Liverpool: Liverpool University Press, 2000, pp. 159-78.

Fry, Peter. *Spirits of Protest: Spirit-mediums and the Articulation of Consensus among the Zezuru of Southern Rhodesia (Zimbabwe).* Cambridge: Cambridge University Press, 2007 [1976].

Gaidzanwa, Rudo. 'Women's Land Rights in Zimbabwe', *Issue: A Journal of Opinion*, 22, no. 2 (1994), pp. 12-16.

Gallagher, Leo. *The Catholic Church in Manicaland, 1946–1996.* Harare: Moate, 1996.

Galtung, Johan. 'Violence, Peace, and Peace Research', *Journal of Peace Research*, 6, no. 3 (1969), pp. 167-91.

Gann, Lewis. *The Struggle for Zimbabwe: Battle in the Bush*. New York: Praeger, 1981.

Geiger, Susan. *TANU Women: Gender and Culture in the Making of Tanganyikan Nationalism, 1955–1965*. Portsmouth, NH: Heinemann, 1997.

Geiss, Immanuel. 'Free Trade, Internationalization of the Congo Basin, and the Principle of Effective Occupation'. *Bismarck, Europe, and Africa: The Berlin Africa Conference 1884-1885 and the Onset of Partition*, Stig Förster, Wolfgang Mommsen, and Ronald Robinson (eds). Oxford: Oxford University Press, 1988, pp. 263-80.

Gelfand, Michael. *The Spiritual Beliefs of the Shona: A Study Based on Field Work among the East-Central Shona*. Gwelo: Mambo Press, 1977.

— *The Traditional Medical Practitioner in Zimbabwe: His Principles of Practice and Pharmacopoeia*. Gweru: Mambo Press, 1985.

Gengenbach, Heidi. 'Truth-Telling and the Politics of Women's Life History Research in Africa: A Reply to Kirk Hoppe', *International Journal of African Historical Studies*, 27, no. 3 (1994), pp. 619-27.

Geschiere, Peter (ed.). *The Perils of Belonging: Autochthony, Citizenship, and Exclusion in Africa and Europe*. Chicago, IL: Chicago University Press, 2009.

Giblin, James. *A History of the Excluded: Making Family a Refuge from State in Twentieth-Century Tanzania*. Oxford: James Currey, 2006.

Giliomee, Hermann. *The Afrikaners: The Biography of a People*. Charlottesville, VA: University of Virginia Press, 2003.

Gillis, John, 'Introduction: Memory and Identity. The History of a Relationship', *Commemorations: The Politics of National Identity*, John Gillis (ed.). Princeton, NJ: Princeton University Press, 1994, pp. 3-24.

Ginzburg, Carlo. 'The Sword and the Lightbulb: A Reading of *Guernica*', *Disturbing Remains: Memory, History, and Crisis in the Twentieth Century*, Michael Roth and Charles Salas (eds). Los Angeles, CA: Getty Trust, 2001, pp. 111-77.

Gordon, James. *Rhodes: A Life*. London: P. Allen and Co., 1927.

Gordon, Robert. *The Bushman Myth: The Making of a Namibian Underclass*. Boulder, CO: Westview Press, 1992.

Gourevitch, Philip. *We Wish to Inform You that Tomorrow We Will Be Killed With Our Families: Stories from Rwanda*. New York: Picador, 1998.

— 'Among the Dead', *Disturbing Remains: Memory, History, and Crisis in the Twentieth Century*, Michael Roth and Charles Salas (eds). Los Angeles, CA: Getty Trust, 2001, pp. 63-73.

Gourevitch, Philip and Errol Morris. *Standard Operating Procedure*. New York: Penguin, 2008.

Government of Zimbabwe, Central Statistical Office. *1982 Population Census: A Preliminary Assessment*. Harare: Government Printer, 1984.

— *Report of the Commission of Inquiry into Appropriate Agricultural Land Tenure Systems*, vol. 1: Main Report. Harare, 1994.

Greene, Sandra. *Sacred Sites and the Colonial Encounter: A History of Meaning and Memory in Ghana*. Bloomington, IN: Indiana University Press, 2002.

Gregson, Simon et al. 'Recent Upturn in Mortality in Rural Zimbabwe: Evidence for an Early Demographic Impact of HIV-1 Infection?', *AIDS*, 11, no. 10 (1997), pp. 1269-80.

— 'Apostles and Zionists: The Influence of Religion on Demographic Change in Rural Zimbabwe', *Population Studies*, 53 (1999), pp. 179-93.

Guevara, Ernesto. *Che Guevara on Guerrilla Warfare*. Lincoln, NE: University of Nebraska Press, 1998 [1961].

Halbwachs, Maurice. *On Collective Memory*. Chicago, IL: University of Chicago Press, 1992 [1941/52].

Hall, Martin. 'Afterword: Lines of Desire'. *Desire Lines: Space, Memory and Identity in the Post-Apartheid City*, Noëleen Murray, Nick Shepherd, and Martin Hall. London: Routledge, 2007, pp. 287-98.

Hamilton, Carolyn (ed.). *The Mfecane Aftermath: Reconstructive Debates in Southern African History*. Johannesburg: Witwatersrand University Press, 1995.

Hammes, Thomas. *The Sling and the Stone: On War in the 21 Century*. St Paul, MN: Zenith Press, 2006.

Hannan, M. *Standard Shona Dictionary*. 1959. Reprint, Harare: The College Press, 1987.

Hansard. Parliament of Zimbabwe. House of Assembly, 24 January 1989 and 15 July 2009.

Hansson, Gurli. *The Rise of Vashandiri: The Ruwadzano Movement in the Lutheran Church in Zimbabwe*. Uppsala: Swedish Institute of Missionary Research, 1991.

Harkin, Michael. 'Feeling and Thinking in Memory and Forgetting: Toward an Ethnohistory of the Emotions', *Ethnohistory*, 50, no. 2 (2003), pp. 261-84.

Harneit-Sievers, Axel and Sydney Emezue. 'Towards a Social History of Warfare and Reconstruction: The Nigerian/Biafran Case', *The Politics of Memory: Truth, Healing, and Social Justice*, Ifi Amadiume and Abdullahi An-Na'im (eds). New York: Zed Books, 2000, pp. 110-126.

Harries, Patrick. *Butterflies and Barbarians: Swiss Missionaries and Systems of Knowledge in South-East Africa*. Oxford: James Currey, 2007.

Henderson, Ian, with Philip Goodhart. *The Hunt for Kimathi*. Bristol: Hamish Hamilton, 1958.

Hobsbawm, Eric. *Nations and Nationalism Since 1780: Programme, Myth, Reality*. Cambridge: Cambridge University Press, 1990.

— *Bandits*. New York: New Press, 2000, new revised edition. [1969].

Hoddeson, Lillian. 'The Conflict of Memories and Documents: Dilemmas and Pragmatics of Oral History'. *The Historiography of Contemporary Science, Technology, and Medicine: Writing Recent Science*, Ron Doel and Thomas Söderquist (eds). New York: Routledge, 2006, pp. 187-200.

Hodges, Thomas. 'Counterinsurgency and the Fate of Rural Blacks', *Africa Report*, 22, no. 5 (1977), pp. 15-20.

Hofmeyr, Isabel. *We Spend Our Years As a Tale That Is Told: Oral Historical Narrative in a South African Chiefdom*. Portsmouth, NH: Heinemann, 1994.

Hoppe, Kirk. 'Whose Life Is It, Anyway? Issues of Representation in Life Narrative Texts of African Women'. *International Journal of African Historical Studies*, 26, no. 3 (1993), pp. 623-36.

— 'Context and Further Questions: Response and Thanks to Heidi Gengenbach'. *International Journal of African Historical Studies*, 28, no. 2 (1995), pp. 359-62.

Hove, Chenjerai. *Bones*. Oxford: Heinemann, 1990.

Howard, Allen and Richard Shain. 'Introduction: African History and Social Space in Africa'. *The Spatial Factor in African History: The Relationship of the Social, Material, and Perceptual*, Allen Howard and Richard Shain (eds). Leiden: Brill, 2006, pp. 1-19.

Hubbard, Douglass Jr. *Bound for Africa: Cold War Fight Along the Zambezi*. Annapolis, MD: Naval Institute Press, 2008.

Hulley, Cecil. *Memories of Manicaland*. Umtali: Cecil Hulley, 1980.

Huntington, Samuel. 'The Clash of Civilizations?', *Foreign Affairs*, 72, no. 3 (1993), pp. 22-49.

— *The Clash of Civilizations and the Remaking of World Order*. New York: Touchstone, 1997.

Iliffe, John. *Tanganyika Under German Rule, 1905–1912*. Cambridge: Cambridge University Press, 1969.

— 'The Age of Improvement and Differentiation (1907–1945)'. *A History of Tanzania*, I.N. Kimambo and A.J. Temu (eds). Nairobi, 1969, pp. 123-60.

Illustrated Rhodesia. 'Protected Villages: Chris Ashton Visits the Honde Valley'. 11 May 1978, p. 8.

Isaacman, Allen. *Mozambique: The Africanization of a European Institution. The Zambezi Prazos 1750–1902*. Madison, WI: University of Wisconsin Press, 1972.

— 'Social Banditry in Zimbabwe (Rhodesia) and Mozambique, 1894–1907: An Expression of Early Peasant Protest', *Journal of Southern African Studies*, 4, no. 1 (1977), pp. 1-30.

— 'Peasants and Rural Social Protest in Africa', *African Studies Review*, 33, no. 2 (1990), pp. 1-120.

— *Cotton is the Mother of Poverty: Peasants, Work and Rural Struggle in Colonial Mozambique, 1938–1961*. Portsmouth, NH: Heinemann, 1996.

Isaacman, Allen and Barbara Isaacman. *Mozambique: From Colonialism to Revolution*. Boulder, CO: Westview Press, 1983.

— *Slavery and Beyond: The Making of Men and Chikunda Ethnic Identities in the Unstable World of South-Central Africa, 1750–1920*. Portsmouth, NH: Heinemann, 2004.

Isaacman, Allen with Barbara Isaacman. *The Tradition of Resistance in Mozambique*. Berkeley, CA: California University Press, 1976.

Ivaska, Andrew. *Cultured States: Youth, Gender, and Modern Style in 1960s Dar es Salaam*. Durham, NC: Duke University Press, 2011, chapter 2.

Jackson, Jeremy. 'Repatriation and Reconstruction in Zimbabwe During the 1980s'. *When Refugees Go Home: African Experiences*, Tim Allen and Hubert Morsink (eds). London: James Currey, 1994, pp. 126-66.

Jackson, Lynette. *Surfacing Up: Psychiatry and Social Order in Colonial Zimbabwe, 1908–1968*. Ithaca, NY: Cornell University Press, 2005.

Jacobson-Widding, Anita. *Chapungu: The Bird That Never Drops A Feather. Male and Female Identities in an African Society*. Uppsala: University of Uppsala, 2002.

Jeater, Diana. *Marriage, Perversion, and Power: The Construction of Moral Discourse in Southern Rhodesia 1894–1930*. Oxford: Oxford University Press, 1993.

Kambudzi, A. 'Zimbabwe–Mozambique Border'. *Zimbabwe's International Borders: A Study in International and Regional Development in Southern Africa*. Vol. 1. *Zimbabwe, Mozambique, Namibia, and South Africa*, Solomon Nkiwane (ed.). Harare: University of Zimbabwe Publications, 1997, pp. 25-41.

Kanengoni, Alexander. *Effortless Tears*. Harare: Baobab Books, 1993.

Kansteiner, Wulf. 'Finding Meaning in Memory: A Methodological Critique of Collective Memory Studies', *History and Theory* 41, no. 2 (2002), pp. 179-97.

Kant, Immanuel. 'To Perpetual Peace: A Philosophical Sketch [1795]', *Perpetual Peace, and Other Essays on Politics, History, and Moral Practice*, Immanuel Kant. Indianapolis, IN: Hackett, 1983.

Kaplan, Robert. 'The Coming Anarchy: How Scarcity, Crime, Overpopulation, Tribalism, and Disease Are Rapidly Destroying the Social Fabric of Our Planet', *The Atlantic Monthly*, 273, no. 2 (1994), pp. 44-76.

Kasrils, Ronnie. *Armed and Dangerous: My Undercover Struggle Against Apartheid*. Portsmouth, NH: Heinemann, 1993.

Katzenellenbogen, Simon. 'It Didn't Happen at Berlin: Politics, Economics and Ignorance in the Setting of Africa's Colonial Boundaries'. *African Boundaries: Barriers, Conduits and Opportunities*, A.I. Asiwaju and Paul Nugent (eds). London: Pinter, 1996, pp. 21-34.

Kennedy, Dane. *Islands of White: Settler Society and Culture in Kenya and Southern Rhodesia, 1890–1939*. Durham, NC: Duke University Press, 1987.

Kennedy, David. *Of War and Law*. Princeton, NJ: Princeton University Press, 2006.

Kesby, Mike. 'Arenas for Control, Terrains of Gender Contestation: Guerrilla Struggle and Counter-insurgency Warfare in Zimbabwe 1972-80', *Journal of Southern African Studies*, 22, no. 4 (1996), pp. 561-84.

Kinyatti, Maina wa (ed.) *Kenya's Freedom Struggle: The Dedan Kimathi Papers*. London: St Martin's Press, 1987.

Kleinman, Arthur. 'The Violences of Everyday Life: The Multiple Forms and Dynamics of Violence'. *Violence and Subjectivity*, Veena Das et al. (eds). Berkeley, CA: California University Press, 1997, pp. 226-41.

— *What Really Matters: Living a Moral Life Amidst Uncertainty and Danger*. Oxford: Oxford University Press, 2006.

Kopytoff, Igor. 'The Internal African Frontier: The Making of African Political Culture'. *The African Frontier: The Reproduction of Traditional African Societies*, Igor Kopytoff (ed.). Bloomington, IN: Indiana University Press, 1987, pp. 3-86.

Koselleck, Reinhart. *Vergangene Zukunft: Zur Semantik geschichtlicher Zeiten*. Frankfurt/Main: Suhrkamp, 1979.

— *The Practice of Conceptual History: Timing History, Spacing Concepts*. Stanford, CA: Stanford University Press, 2002.

— *Futures Past: On the Semantics of Historical Time*. New York: Columbia University Press, 2004.

Kriger, Norma. 'The Zimbabwean War of Liberation: Struggles within the Struggle', *Journal of Southern African Studies*, 14, no. 2 (1988), pp. 304-22.

— 'Popular Struggles in Zimbabwe's War of National Liberation'. *Cultural Struggle and Development in Southern Africa*, Preben Kaarsholm (ed.). Harare: Baobab Books, 1991, pp. 125-48.

— *Zimbabwe's Guerrilla War: Peasant Voices*. Cambridge: Cambridge University Press, 1992.

— 'The Politics of Creating National Heroes: The Search for Political Legitimacy and National Identity'. *Soldiers in Zimbabwe's Liberation War*, Ngwabi Bhebe and Terence O. Ranger (eds). London: James Currey, 1995, pp. 139-62.

— *Guerrilla Veterans in Post-war Zimbabwe: Symbolic and Violent Politics, 1980–1987*. Cambridge: Cambridge University Press, 2003.

Krystal, John, Stephen Southwick, and Dennis Charney. 'Post Traumatic Stress Disorder: Psychobiological Mechanisms of Traumatic Remembrance'. *Memory Distortion: How Minds, Brains, and Societies Reconstruct the Past*, Daniel Schacter (ed.). Cambridge, MA: Harvard University Press, 1995, pp. 150-72.

LaCapra, Dominick. *History and Memory after Auschwitz*. Ithaca, NY: Cornell University Press, 1998.

— *Writing History, Writing Trauma*. Baltimore, MD: Johns Hopkins University Press, 2001.

— *History in Transit: Experience, Identity, Critical Theory*. Ithaca, NY: Cornell University Press, 2004.

— *History and Its Limits: Human, Animal, Violence*. Ithaca, NY: Cornell University Press, 2009.

Lamar, Howard and Leonard Thompson (eds). *The Frontier in History: North America and Southern Africa Compared*. New Haven, CT: Yale University Press, 1981.

Lamb, Sharon. *The Trouble with Blame: Victims, Perpetrators and Responsibility*. Cambridge, MA: Harvard University Press, 1996.

Lan, David. *Guns and Rain: Guerrillas and Spirit Mediums in Zimbabwe*. London: James Currey, 1985.

Landau, Paul. *The Realm of the Word: Language, Gender, and Christianity in a Southern African Kingdom*. Portsmouth, NH: Heinemann, 1995.

Langfur, Hal. *The Forbidden Lands: Colonial Identity, Frontier Violence, and the Persistence of Brazil's Eastern Indians, 1750–1830*. Stanford, CA: Stanford University Press, 2006.

Larémont, Ricardo (ed.). *Borders, Nationalism, and the African State*. Boulder, CO: Lynne Rienner, 2005.

Leverson, Julian. 'Geographical Results of the Anglo-Portuguese Delimitation Commission in South-East Africa, 1892', *The Geographical Journal*, 2, no. 6 (1893), pp. 505-18.

Lewis, Arthur. *Too Bright the Vision? African Adventures of an Anglican Rebel*. London: Covenant Publishing Co., 1992.

Lewis, Martin and Kären Wigen. *The Myth of Continents: A Critique of Metageography*. Berkeley, CA: University of California Press, 1997.

Liesegang, Gerhard. 'Beiträge zur Geschichte des Reiches der Gaza Nguni im Südlichen Moçambique 1820–1895'. PhD thesis, University of Köln, 1968.

— 'Nguni Migrations Between Delagoa Bay and the Zambezi, 1821–1839', *African Historical Studies*, 3, no. 2 (1970), pp. 317-37.

— 'Notes on the Internal Structure of the Gaza Kingdom of Southern Mozambique, 1840–1895'. *Before and After Shaka: Papers in Nguni History*, Jeffrey Peires (ed.). Grahamstown: Rhodes University, 1981, pp. 178-209.

Likaka, Osumaka. *Naming Colonialism: History and Collective Memory in the Congo, 1870–*

1960. Madison, WI: University of Wisconsin Press, 2009.

Lodge, Tom, Denis Kadima, and David Pottie. *Compendium on Elections in Southern Africa*. Johannesburg: Electoral Institute of Southern Africa, 2002.

Lonsdale, John. 'Moral Ethnicity and Political Tribalism'. *Inventions and Boundaries: Historical and Anthropological Approaches to the Study of Ethnicity and Nationalism*, Preben Kaarsholm and Jan Hultin (eds). Roskilde: Roskilde University, 1994, pp. 131-150.

— 'Kikuyu Christianities', *Journal of Religion in Africa*, 29, 2 (1999), pp. 206-229.

— 'Jomo Kenyatta, God and the Modern World'. *African Modernities: Entangled Meanings in Current Debate*. Jan-Georg Deutsch, Peter Probst, and Heike Schmidt (eds). Portsmouth, NH: Heinemann, 2000, pp. 31-66.

— 'Agency in Tight Corners: Narrative and Initiative in African History', *Journal of African Cultural Studies*, 13, no. 1 (2000), pp. 5-16.

— 'Moral and Political Argument in Kenya'. *Ethnicity and Democracy in Africa*, Bruce Berman, Dickson Eyoh, and Will Kymlicka (eds). Oxford: James Currey, 2004, pp. 73-95.

Lonsdale, John, and Donald Low. 'Introduction: Towards the New Order 1945–1963'. *History of East Africa*, vol. 3, Donald Low and Alison Smith (eds). Oxford: Clarendon Press, 1976, pp. 1-63.

Lovett, John. *Contact: A Tribute to Those who Serve Rhodesia*. Salisbury: Galaxie Press, 1977.

Lüdtke, Alf and Hans Medick. 'Einleitung', *SOWI*, 20, no. 3 (1991), pp. 155-6.

Lugard, Frederick. *The Dual Mandate in British Tropical Africa*. London: William Blackwood, 1922.

Luig, Ute and Achim von Oppen. 'Landscape in Africa: Process and Vision. An Introductory Essay', *Paideuma*, 43 (1997), pp. 7-45.

Lyons, Tanya. *Guns and Guerrilla Girls: Women in the Zimbabwean National Liberation Struggle*. Trenton, NJ: Africa World Press, 2004.

MacGonagle, Elizabeth. *Crafting Identity in Zimbabwe and Mozambique*. Rochester, NY: University of Rochester Press, 2007.

Mafu, Hesekiel. 'The 1991-92 Zimbabwean Drought and Some Religious Reactions', *Journal of Religion in Africa*, 25, no. 3 (1995), pp. 288-308.

Maier, Charles. '"Being There": Place, Territory, and Identity'. *Identities, Affiliations, and Allegiances*, Seyla Benhabib, Ian Shapiro, and Danilo Petranovi (eds). Cambridge: Cambridge University Press, 2007, pp. 67-84.

Makambe, Elioth. 'The Nyasaland African Labour "Ulendos" to Southern Rhodesia and the Problem of the African "Highwaymen", 1903–1923: A Study in the Limitations of Early Independent Labour Migration', *African Affairs*, 79, no. 317 (1980), pp. 548-66.

Makanya, Stella. 'The Desire to Return: Effects of Experiences in Exile on Refugees Repatriating to Zimbabwe in the Early 1980s'. *When Refugees Go Home: African Experiences*, Tim Allen and Hubert Morsink (eds). London: James Currey, 1994, pp. 105-25.

Mamdani, Mahmood. *Citizen and Subject: Contemporary Africa and the Legacy of Late Colonialism*. Princeton, NJ: Princeton University Press, 1996.

Manungo, Kenneth. 'The Peasantry in Zimbabwe: A Vehicle for Change'. *Cultural Struggle and Development in Southern Africa*, Preben Kaarsholm (ed.). Harare: Baobab Books, 1991, pp. 115-24.

Mao, Zedong. *Quotations from Chairman Mao Tsetung* [*The Little Red Book*]. Peking: Government of the People's Republic of China, 1966 [1947].

— *On Guerrilla Warfare*. Chicago: Chicago University Press, 2000 [1937].

Marks, Shula and Richard Rathbone (eds). 'The History of the Family in Africa'. Special issue, *Journal of African History*, 24, no. 2 (1983).

Martin, David and Phyllis Johnson. *The Struggle for Zimbabwe: The Chimurenga War*. London: Faber and Faber, 1981.

Martin, Faan. *James and the Duck: Tales of the Rhodesian Bush War (1964–1980): Based on the Truth. The Memoirs of a Part-Time Trooper.* Central Milton Keynes: AuthorHouse, 2007.

Mauch, Carl. *The Journals of Carl Mauch: His Travels in the Transvaal and Rhodesia, 1869–1872*, E. Burke (ed.). Salisbury: National Archives of Rhodesia, 1969.

Mawere, Abraham, and Ken Wilson. 'Socio-Religious Movements, the State and Community Change: Some Reflections on the Ambuya Juliana Cult of Southern Zimbabwe', *Journal of Religion in Africa*, 25, no. 3 (1995), pp. 252-87.

Maxwell, David. *Christians and Chiefs in Zimbabwe: A Social History of the Hwesa People.* Edinburgh: Edinburgh University Press, 1999.

— *African Gifts of the Spirit: Pentecostalism and the Rise of a Zimbabwean Transnational Religious Movement.* Oxford: James Currey, 2006.

Mbembe, Achille. 'At the Edge of the World: Boundaries, Territoriality, and Sovereignty in Africa', *Public Culture*, 12, no. 1 (2000), pp. 259-84.

— *On the Postcolony.* Berkeley, CA: California Press, 2001.

M'buya. *A Little Leaven.* Salisbury: Christian Literature Association of Rhodesia, 1975.

McDermott-Hughes, David. *From Enslavement to Environmentalism: Politics on a Southern African Frontier.* Seattle, WA: University of Washington Press, 2006.

McGregor, JoAnn. *Crossing the Zambezi: The Politics of Landscape on a Central African Frontier.* Woodbridge: James Currey, 2009.

McLaughlin, Janice. *On the Frontline: Catholic Missions in Zimbabwe's Liberation War.* Harare: Baobab Books, 1996.

McNally, Richard. *Remembering Trauma.* Cambridge, MA: Belknap Press of Harvard University Press, 2003.

Medick, Hans. 'Zur politischen Sozialgeschichte der Grenzen in der Neuzeit Europas', *SOWI*, 20, no. 3 (1991), pp. 157-63.

Menzies, William. *An African Samuel Smiles.* n.p., n.d. [1956].

Meyer, Birgit and Peter Pels (eds). *Interfaces of Revelation and Concealment.* Stanford, CA: Stanford University Press, 2003.

Mitchell, Laura. *Belongings: Property, Family and Identity in Colonial South Africa (An Exploration of Frontiers, 1725–c.1830).* New York: Columbia University Press, 2009.

Mitchell, Timothy. *Colonising Egypt.* Cambridge: Cambridge University Press, 1988.

Mitchell, W.J. Thomas. 'Imperial Landscape'. *Landscape and Power*, W.J. Thomas Mitchell. (ed.). Chicago, IL: University of Chicago Press, 1994, pp. 5-34.

Moorcraft, Paul. *Fireforce: One Man's War in the Rhodesian Light Infantry.* Boulder, CO: Paladin Press, 2007 [1988].

Moorcraft, Paul and Peter McLaughlin. *The Rhodesian War: A Military History.* Barnsley: Pen and Sword, 2008 revised ed. [1982].

Moore, David. 'Zimbabwean Peasants: Pissed on and Pissed off', *Southern African Review of Books*, 4, no. 6 (1994), pp. 5-6.

Moore, Donald. 'Subaltern Struggles and the Politics of Place: Remapping Resistance in Zimbabwe's Eastern Highlands', *Cultural Anthropology*, 13, no. 3 (1998), pp. 344-81.

— *Suffering for Territory: Race, Place, and Power in Zimbabwe.* Durham, NC: Duke University Press, 2005.

Moore, Donald and Richard Roberts. 'Listening for Silences', *History in Africa*, 17 (1990), pp. 1-7.

Moore, Sally Falk. 'Explaining the Present: Theoretical Dilemmas in Processual Ethnography', *American Ethnologist*, 14, no. 4 (1987), pp. 727-36.

Morna, C. 'Schutzdörfer in Zimbabwe für RENAMO-Opfer', *IZ3W*, no. 159 (1989), p. 55.

Morris, Errol. *Standard Operating Procedure.* New York: Penguin Press, 2008.

Morrison, Toni. *Paradise.* New York: Knopf, 1998.

Moyana, Henry. *The Political Economy of Land in Zimbabwe.* Gweru: Mambo Press, 1984.

Mozambique Company. *Handbook of the Mozambique Company: Province of Manica–Sofala.* London: William Clowes, 1893.

Mtisi, Joseph. *Origins and Development of Tea Outgrowers* [sic] *Schemes in Colonial Zimbabwe.* Economic History Seminar Paper. Harare: University of Zimbabwe, 1993.

— 'Green Harvest: The Outgrower Tea Leaf Collection System in the Honde Valley, Zimbabwe'. *Delivering Land and Securing Rural Livelihoods: Post-independence Land Reform and Resettlement in Zimbabwe*, Michael Roth and Francis Gonese (eds). Centre for Applied Social Sciences: Land Tenure Centre, University of Wisconsin/Madison, 2003, pp. 57-80.

Mudenge, Stan. *A Political History of Munhumutapa c.1400–1902*. Harare: Zimbabwe Publishing House, 1988.

Mugabe, Robert. *The Third Chimurenga: Inside the Third Chimurenga*. Harare: Government of Zimbabwe, Ministry of Information, 2001.

Mukonyora, Isabel. *Wandering a Gendered Wilderness: Suffering and Healing in an African Initiated Church*. New York: Lang, 2007.

Munro, William. *The Moral Economy of the State: Conservation, Community Development, and State-Making in Zimbabwe*. Athens, OH: Ohio University Centre for International Studies, 1998.

Muringai, Elvis. 'The Socio-Economic Impact of Concentration Camps on the Peasantry During the Second Chimurenga: The Case of Madziwa Area 1974–1980'. BA (Hons) thesis, University of Zimbabwe, 1985.

Nagl, John. *Learning to Eat Soup with a Knife: Counterinsurgency Lessons from Malaya and Vietnam*. Chicago, IL: University Chicago Press, 2002.

Ncube, Welshman. 'Released from Legal Minority: The Legal Age of Majority Act in Zimbabwe'. *Women and Law in Southern Africa*, Alice Armstrong (ed.). Harare: Zimbabwe Publishing House, 1987, pp. 193-209.

Nelson, Diane. *A Finger in the Wound: Body Politics in Quincentennial Guatemala*. Berkeley, CA: University of California Press, 1999.

Newitt, Malyn. 'The Portuguese on the Zambezi: An Historical Interpretation of the Prazo System', *Journal of African History*, 10, no. 1 (1969), pp. 67-85.

— *Portuguese Settlement on the Zambezi*. London: Heinemann, 1973.

— 'Drought in Mozambique 1823–1831', *Journal of Southern African Studies*, 15, no. 1 (1988). pp. 15-35.

— *A History of Mozambique*. Bloomington, IN: Indiana University Press, 1995.

Nhongo-Simbanegavi, Josephine. *For Better or Worse? Women and ZANLA in Zimbabwe's Liberation Struggle*. Harare: Weaver Press, 2000.

Nkiwane, Solomon (ed.). *Zimbabwe's International Borders: A Study in International and Regional Development in Southern Africa*. Vol. 1, *Zimbabwe, Mozambique, Namibia, and South Africa*. Harare: University of Zimbabwe Publications, 1997.

Nora, Pierre. *Les lieux de mémoires*, vol. 1-3. Paris, Gallimard, 1984-1992.

Nordstrom, Carolyn. *A Different Kind of War Story*. Philadelphia, PA: University of Pennsylvania Press, 1997.

— *Shadows of War: Violence, Power, and International Profiteering in the Twenty-First Century*. Berkeley, CA: University of California Press, 2004.

— *Global Outlaws: Crime, Money, and Power in the Contemporary World*. Berkeley, CA University of California Press, 2007.

Nugent, Paul. 'Arbitrary Lines and the People's Minds: A Dissenting View on Colonial Boundaries in West Africa'. *African Boundaries: Barriers, Conduits and Opportunities*, A.I. Asiwaju and Paul Nugent (eds). London: Pinter, 1996, pp. 35-67.

Nyajeka, Tumani Mutasa. *The Unwritten Text: The Indigenous African Christian Women's Movement in Zimbabwe*. Mutare: Africa University Press, 2006.

Nyambara, Pius. 'Ethnic Identities and the Culture of Modernity in a Frontier Region: The Gokwe District of Northwestern Zimbabwe, 1963-79'. *Movements, Borders, and Identities in Africa*, Toyin Falola and Aribidesi Usman (eds). Rochester, NY: University of Rochester Press, 2009, pp. 200-25.

Obama, Barack. *Nobel Peace Prize Lecture*. Stockholm: Nobel Foundation, 2009.

O'Gorman, Eleanor. *The Front Line Runs through Every Woman: Women and Local Resistance in the Zimbabwean Liberation War*. Woodbridge: James Currey, 2011.

Ogot, Bethwell. 'Rereading the History and Historiography of Epistemic Domination and

Resistance in Africa', *African Affairs* 52, no. 1 (2009), pp. 1-22.

Olick, Jeffrey and Joyce Robbins. 'Social Memory Studies: From "Collective Memory" to the Historical Sociology of Mnemonic Practices', *Annual Review of Sociology*, 24 (1998), pp. 105-40.

Palmer, Robin. *Land and Racial Domination in Rhodesia*. London: Heinemann, 1977.

Pandey, Gyanendra. *Routine Violence: Nations, Fragments, Histories*. Stanford, CA: Stanford University Press, 2006.

Pankhurst, Donna. 'Post-Wars Backlash Violence Against Women: What Can "Masculinity" Explain?' *Gendered Peace: Women's Struggles for Post-War Justice and Reconciliation*, Donna Pankhurst (ed.). New York: Routledge, 2008, pp. 293-320.

Pankhurst, Donna and Susan Jacobs. 'Land Tenure, Gender, and Production: The Case of Zimbabwe's Peasantry'. *Agriculture, Women, and Land: The African Experience*, Jean Davidson (ed.). Boulder, CO: Indiana University Press, 1988, pp. 202-27.

Payne, Lee. *Unsettling Accounts: Neither Truth nor Reconciliation in Confessions of State Violence*. Durham, NC: Duke University Press, 2nd ed. 1999.

Pélissier, René. *Naissance du Mozambique: Résistance et Révoltes Anticoloniales (1854–1918)*, 2 vols. Orgeval: Pélissier, 1984.

Peterson, Derek. *Creative Writing: Translation, Bookkeeping, and the Work of Imagination in Colonial Kenya*. Portsmouth, NH: Heinemann, 2004.

— 'Morality Plays: Marriage, Church Courts, and Colonial Agency in Central Tanganyika, ca. 1876-1928', *The American Historical Review*, 111, no. 4 (2006), pp. 983-1010.

Phimister, Ian. *An Economic and Social History of Zimbabwe 1890–1948: Capital Accumulation and Class Struggle*. London: Longman, 1988.

— 'Rethinking the Reserves: Southern Rhodesia's Land Husbandry Act Reviewed', *Journal of Southern African Studies*, 19, no. 2 (1993), pp. 225-39.

Portelli, Alessandro. *The Battle of Valle Giulia: Oral History and the Art of Dialogue*. Madison, WI: University of Wisconsin Press, 1997.

Pratten, David. *The Man-Leopard Murders: History and Society in Colonial Nigeria*. Bloomington, IN: Indiana University Press, 2007.

Presler, Titus. *Transfigured Night: Mission and Culture in Zimbabwe's Vigil Movement*. Pretoria: University of South Africa Press, 1999.

Prestholdt, Jeremy. *Domesticating the World: African Consumerism and the Genealogies of Globalization*. Berkeley, CA: California University Press, 2008.

Proudfoot, Lindsay and Michael Roche (eds). *(Dis)Placing Empire: Renegotiating British Colonial Geographies*. Aldershot: Ashgate, 2005.

Raeburn, Michael. *Black Fire! Accounts of the Guerrilla War in Zimbabwe*. Harare: Mambo Press, 1986 [1978].

Ranchod-Nilsson, Sita. 'Gender Politics and National Liberation: Women's Participation in the Liberation of Zimbabwe'. PhD thesis, Northwestern University, 1992.

Ranger, Terence O. 'Revolt in Portuguese East Africa: The Makombe Rising of 1917', *African Affairs*, no. 2. St Antony's Papers, no. 15, pp. 54-80. London: Chatto and Windus, 1963.

— *Revolt in Southern Rhodesia 1896-7: A Study in African Resistance*. London: Heinemann, 1967.

— 'African Politics in Twentieth-Century Southern Rhodesia'. *Aspects of Central African History*, Terence O. Ranger (ed.). London: Heinemann, 1968, pp. 210-45.

— 'Connections Between 'Primary Resistance' Movements and Modern Mass Nationalism in East and Central Africa', Part I, *Journal of African History*, 9, no. 3 (1968), pp. 437-53.

— 'Connections Between 'Primary Resistance' Movements and Modern Mass Nationalism in East and Central Africa', Part II, *Journal of African History*, 9, no. 4 (1968), pp. 631-41.

— *Peasant Consciousness and Guerrilla War in Zimbabwe: A Comparative Study*. London: James Currey, 1985.

— *The Invention of Tribalism in Zimbabwe*. Gweru: Mambo Press, 1985.

— 'Bandits and Guerrillas: The Case of Zimbabwe'. *Banditry, Rebellion and Social Protest in Africa*, Donald Crummey (ed.). London: James Currey, 1986, pp. 379-86.

270

— 'Taking Hold of the Land: Holy Places and Pilgrimages in Twentieth-Century Zimbabwe', *Past and Present*, 117, no. 1 (1987), pp. 158-94.

— 'Missionaries, Migrants and the Manyika: The Invention of Ethnicity in Zimbabwe'. *The Creation of Tribalism in Southern Africa*, Leroy Vail (ed.). London: James Currey, 1989, pp. 118-50.

— 'Afterword: War, Violence, and Healing in Zimbabwe', *Journal of Southern African Studies*, 18, no. 3 (1992), pp. 698-707.

— 'The Invention of Tradition Revisited: The Case of Colonial Africa'. *Legitimacy and the State in Twentieth-Century Africa: Essays in Honour of A H.M. Kirk-Greene*, Terence O. Ranger and Olufemi Vaughan (eds).London: Macmillan, 1993, pp. 62-111.

— Review of *Zimbabwe's Guerrilla War: Peasant Voices*, by Norma Kriger, *African Affairs* 93, no. 370 (1994), pp. 142-4.

— 'Protestant Missions in Africa: The Dialectic of Conversion in the American Methodist Episcopal Church in Eastern Zimbabwe, 1900–1950'. *Religion in Africa: Experience and Expression*, Thomas Blakely, W. van Beek, and D. Thomson (eds). London: James Currey, 1994, pp. 273-313.

— *Are We Not Also Men? The Samkange Family and African Politics in Zimbabwe 1920-64.* London: James Currey, 1995.

— 'Violence Variously Remembered: The Killing of Pieter Oberholtzer', *History in Africa*, 24 (1997), pp. 273-86.

— *Voices from the Rocks: Nature, Culture and History in the Matopos Hills of Zimbabwe.* Oxford: James Currey, 1999.

— 'Nationalist Historiography, Patriotic History and the History of the Nation: The Struggle over the Past in Zimbabwe', *Journal of Southern African Studies*, 30, no. 2 (2004), pp. 215-34.

Reid-Daly, Ron. *Selous Scouts: Top Secret War*, as told to Peter Stiff. Johannesburg: Galago, 1982.

Renan, Ernest. 'What is a Nation? [1892]'. *Nation and Narration*, Homi Bhabha (ed.). London: Routledge, 1990, pp. 8-22.

Rennie, John. 'Christianity, Colonialism and the Origins of Nationalism among the Ndau of Southern Rhodesia 1890–1935'. PhD thesis, Northwestern University, Evanston, IL, 1973.

Reno, William. *Warlord Politics and African States.* Boulder, CO: Lynne Rienner, 1988.

— *Warfare in Independent Africa.* Cambridge: Cambridge University Press, 2011.

Reynolds, Pamela. 'Children of Tribulation: The Need to Heal and the Means to Heal War Trauma', *Africa*, 60, no.1 (1990), pp. 1-38.

— *Traditional Healers and Childhood in Zimbabwe.* Athens, OH: Ohio University Press, 1996.

Richards, Paul. *Fighting for the Rain Forest: War, Youth and Resources in Sierra Leone.* Portsmouth, NH: Heinemann, 1996.

Riches, David. 'The Phenomenon of Violence'. *The Anthropology of Violence*, David Riches (ed.). Oxford: Basil Blackwell, 1986, pp. 1-27.

Ricoeur, Paul. *Memory, History, Forgetting.* Chicago, IL: University of Chicago Press, 2004.

Rosenfeld, Gavriel. 'A Looming Crash or a Soft Landing? Forecasting the Future of the Memory "Industry"', *Journal of Modern History*, 81, no. 1 (2009), pp. 122-58.

Roth, Michael, and Charles Salas. 'Introduction'. *Disturbing Remains: Memory, History, and Crisis in the Twentieth Century*, Michael Roth and Charles Salas (eds). Los Angeles: Getty Trust, 2001, pp. 1-13.

Rupiya, Martin. 'A Political and Military Review of Zimbabwe's Involvement in the Second Congo War'. *The African Stakes of the Congo War*, John Clark (ed.). New York: Palgrave, 2002, pp. 93-105.

Rutherford, Blair. *Working on the Margins: Black Workers, White Farmers in Postcolonial Zimbabwe.* London: Zed Books, 2001.

Sachikonye, Lloyd. *The State and Agribusiness in Zimbabwe: Plantations and Contract*

Farming, Leeds Southern African Studies Series, no. 13. Leeds: Leeds University, 1989.

Sadomba, Zvakanyorwa. *War Veterans in Zimbabwe's Revolution: Challenging Neo-Colonialism and Settler and International Capital*. Woodbridge: James Currey, 2011.

Sahlins, Peter. *Boundaries: The Making of France and Spain in the Pyrenees*. Berkeley, CA: University of California Press, 1989.

Said, Edward. 'The Clash of Ignorance', *The Nation* (22 October 2001), p. 11.

Scahill, Jeremy. *Blackwater: The Rise of the World's Most Powerful Mercenary Army*. New York: Nation Books, 2nd ed. 2008.

— 'The Secret US War in Pakistan', *The Nation* (21 December 2009), pp. 11-18.

Scarry, Elaine. *The Body in Pain: The Making and Unmaking of the World*. New York: Oxford University Press, 1985.

Schacter, Daniel. *Memory Distortion: How Minds, Brains, and Societies Reconstruct the Past*. Cambridge, MA: Harvard University Press, 1995.

— 'Memory Distortion: History and Current Status'. *Memory Distortion: How Minds, Brains, and Societies Reconstruct the Past*, Daniel Schacter (ed.). Cambridge, MA: Harvard University Press, 1995, pp. 1-43.

— *Searching for Memory: The Brain, the Mind, and the Past*. New York: Basic Books, 1996.

— *The Seven Sins of Memory: How the Mind Forgets and Remembers*. Boston, MA: Houghton Mifflin, 2002.

Schama, Simon. *Landscape and Memory*. New York: Vintage Books, 1995.

Scheper-Hughes, Nancy. *Death without Weeping: The Violence of Everyday Life in Brazil*. Berkeley, CA: University of California Press, 1992.

Schlichter, Henry. 'Travels and Researches in Rhodesia', *The Geographical Journal*, 13, no. 4 (1899), pp. 376-91.

Schmidt, Elizabeth. 'Farmers, Hunters, and Gold-Washers: A Re-evaluation of Women's Roles in Precolonial and Colonial Zimbabwe', *African Economic History*, 17 (1988), pp. 45-80.

— 'Negotiated Spaces and Contested Terrain: Men, Women, and the Law in Colonial Zimbabwe, 1890–1939', *Journal of Southern African Studies*, 16, no. 4 (1990), pp. 622-48.

— 'Patriarchy, Capitalism, and the Colonial State in Zimbabwe', *Signs*, 16, no. 4 (1991), pp. 732-56.

— *Peasants, Traders, and Wives: Shona Women in the History of Zimbabwe, 1870–1939*. Portsmouth, NH: Heinemann, 1992.

— 'Top Down or Bottom Up? Nationalist Mobilization Reconsidered, with Special Reference to Guinea (French West Africa)', *American Historical Review*, 110, no. 4 (2005), pp. 975-1014.

— *Mobilizing the Masses: Gender, Ethnicity, and Class in the Nationalist Movement in Guinea, 1939–1958*. Portsmouth, NH: Heinemann, 2005.

Schmidt, Heike. *Muredzwa Superwoman: Mapping Areas of Female Power in the Mutasa Mamboship, Eastern Zimbabwe*. Institute of Commonwealth Studies Collected Seminar Papers. London: Institute of Commonwealth Studies, 1993.

— '"Penetrating" Foreign Lands: Contestations Over African Landscapes. A Case Study from Eastern Zimbabwe', *Environment and History*, 1, no. 3 (1995), pp. 351-76.

— 'Healing the Wounds of War: Memories of Violence and the Making of History in Zimbabwe's Most Recent Past', *Journal of Southern African Studies*, 23, no. 2 (1997), pp. 301-10.

— 'Entangled Memories: *Bindung* and Identity'. *Unraveling Ties: From Social Cohesion to New Practices of Connectedness*, Yehuda Elkana et al. (eds). Frankfurt and New York: Campus, 2002, pp. 199-212.

— 'Colonial Intimacy: The Rechenberg Scandal, Homosexuality and Sexual Crime in German East Africa'. 'Masculinity and Homosexuality in Germany and the German Colonies, 1880–1945', Daniel Walther and Clayton Whisnant (eds). Special issue, *Journal of the History of Sexuality*, 17, no. 1 (2008), pp. 25-59.

— 'The Maji Maji War and its Aftermath: Gender, Age, and Power in South-Western Tanzania, c. 1905–1916', *International Journal of African Historical Studies*, 43, no. 1 (2010), pp. 27-62.

— "'A Deadly Silence Predominated in the District": The Maji Maji War in Ungoni'. *Maji Maji: Lifting the Fog of War*, James Giblin and Jamie Monson (eds). Leiden: Brill, 2010, pp. 183-219.

— 'Who is Master in the Colony? Propriety, Honor, and Manliness in German East Africa'. *German Cultures of Colonialism: Race, Nation, and Globalization, 1884–1945*, Geoff Eley and Bradley Naranch (eds). Durham, NC: Duke University Press (forthcoming).

Schoffeleers, Jan. 'Introduction'. *Guardians of the Land: Essays on Central African Territorial Cults*, J. Schoffeleers (ed.). Gwelo: Mambo Press, 1978, pp. 1-46.

Schwartz, James. *Conflict on the Michigan Frontier: Yankee and Borderland Cultures, 1815–1840*. DeKalb, ILL: Northern Illinois University Press, 2009.

Scott, James. *Weapons of the Weak: Everyday Forms of Peasant Resistance*. New Haven, CT: Yale University Press, 1985.

— *Domination and the Arts of Resistance: The Hidden Transcript of Subordinate Groups*. New Haven, CT: Yale University Press, 1990.

— 'Domination, Acting, and Fantasy'. *The Paths to Domination, Resistance, and Terror*, Carolyn Nordstrom and JoAnn Martin (eds). Berkeley, CA: University of California Press, 1992, pp. 55-84.

— *Seeing Like a State: How Certain Schemes to Improve the Human Condition Have Failed*. New Haven: Yale University Press, 1998.

Scott, Peter. 'Migrant Labor in Southern Rhodesia', *Geographical Review*, 44, no. 1 (1954), pp. 29-48.

Seidman, Gay. 'Women in Zimbabwe: Postindependence Struggles', *Feminist Studies*, 10, no. 3 (1984), pp. 419-40.

Shack, William. 'Introduction'. *Strangers in African Societies*, William Shack and Elliot Skinner (eds). Berkeley, CA: University of California Press, 1979, pp. 1-17.

Shadle, Brett. *'Girl Cases': Marriage and Colonialism in Gusiiland, Kenya, 1890–1970*. Portsmouth, NH: Heinemann, 2006.

Shaw, Rosalind. *Memories of the Slave Trade: Ritual and the Historical Imagination in Sierra Leone*. Chicago, IL: Chicago University Press, 2002.

Shetler, Jan. *A History of Landscape Memory in Tanzania from Earliest Times to the Present*. Athens, OH: Ohio University Press, 2007.

Shostak, Marjorie. *Nisa: The Life of a !Kung Woman*. Cambridge, MA: Harvard University Press, 1981.

Shropshire, Denis. 'The Mifananidzo of the Mutasa Dynasty'. *Man*, 30 (1930), pp. 4-5.

— 'A Journey in Mashonaland', *African Affairs*, 51, no. 202 (1952), pp. 52-61.

Soper, Robert. *Nyanga: Ancient Fields, Settlements and Agricultural History in Zimbabwe*. London: British Institute in East Africa, 2002.

— *The Terrace Builders of Nyanga*. Harare: Weaver Press, 2006.

Spear, Thomas. 'Neo-Traditionalism and the Limits of Invention in British Colonial Africa', *Journal of African History*, 44, no. 1 (2003), pp. 3-27.

Spierenburg, Marja. *Strangers, Spirits, and Land Reforms: Conflicts About Land in Dande, Northern Zimbabwe*. Leiden: Brill, 2004.

Standard Swahili-English Dictionary. [ed. Frederick Johnson]. 1939. Reprint, Oxford: Oxford University Press, 1990.

Staudt, Kathleen. *Violence and Activism at the Border: Gender, Fear and Everyday Life in Ciudad Juárez*. Austin, TX: University of Texas Press, 2008.

Stewart, Pamela and Andrew Strathern (eds). *Landscape, Memory and History: Anthropological Perspectives*. London: Pluto Press, 2003.

Stier, Oren Baruch and Shawn Landres (eds). *Religion, Violence, Memory, and Place*. Bloomington, IN: Indiana University Press, 2006.

Stoler, Ann Laura and Frederick Cooper. 'Between Metropole and Colony: Rethinking a Research Agenda'. *Tensions of Empire: Colonial Cultures in a Bourgeois World*, Ann Laura Stoler and Frederick Cooper (eds). Berkeley, CA: University of California Press, 1997, pp. 1-56.

Storry, J.G. 'The Settlement and Territorial Expansion of the Mutasa Dynasty', *Rhodesian History*, 7 (1976), pp. 13-30.

Sutton, John. 'Irrigation and Soil-conservation in African Agricultural History: With a Reconsideration of the Inyanga Terracing (Zimbabwe) and Engaruka Irrigation Works (Tanzania)', *Journal of African History*, 25, 1 (1984), pp. 25-41.

Tonkin, Elizabeth. *Narrating Our Pasts: The Social Construction of Oral History*. Cambridge: Cambridge University Press, 1992.

Trimble, Michael. 'Post Traumatic Stress Disorder: The History of a Concept'. *Trauma and Its Wake. Vol. 2. The Study and Treatment of Post-traumatic Stress Disorder*, Charles Figley (ed.). New York: Brunner/Mazel, 1985, pp. 5-14.

Tripp, Aili Mari. *Women and Politics in Uganda*. Madison, WI: University of Wisconsin Press, 2000.

Tropp, Jacob. *Natures of Colonial Change: Environmental Relations in the Making of the Transkei*. Athens, OH: Ohio University Press, 2006.

Trouillot, Michel-Rolph. *Silencing the Past: Power and the Production of History*. Boston, MA: Beacon Press, 1995.

Truett, Samuel. *Fugitive Landscapes: The Forgotten History of the U.S.-Mexico Borderlands*. New Haven, CT: Yale University Press, 2006.

Truett, Samuel and Elliott Young, 'Making Transnational History: Nations, Regions, and Borderlands'. *Continental Crossroads: Remapping U.S.–Mexico Borderlands History*, Samuel Truett and Elliott Young (eds). Durham, NC: Duke University Press, 2004, pp. 1-32.

Tungamirai, Josiah. 'Recruitment to ZANLA: Building up a War Machine'. *Soldiers in Zimbabwe's Liberation War*, Ngwabi Bhebe and Terence O. Ranger (eds). London: James Currey, 1995, pp. 36-47.

Turner, Frederick. 'The Significance of the Frontier in American History (1893)'. *History, Frontier, and Section: Three Essays by Frederick Jackson Turner*. Albuquerque, NM: University of New Mexico Press, 1993, pp. 59-91.

— *The Frontier in American History*. New York: Henry Holt, 1920.

Ucko, Peter and Robert Layton. 'Introduction: Gazing on the Landscape and Encountering the Environment'. *The Archaeology and Anthropology of Landscape: Shaping your Landscape*, Peter Ucko and Robert Layton (eds). London: Routledge, 1999, pp. 1-20.

United States, Department of the Army. *Counterinsurgency Field Manual*. Chicago, Il: Chicago University Press, 2003.

Vail, Leroy and Landeg White. *Capitalism and Colonialism in Mozambique: A Study of Quelimane District*. London: Heinemann, 1980.

Vambe, Lawrence. *An Ill-Fated People: Zimbabwe Before and After Rhodes*. London: Heinemann, 1972.

Van Allen, Judith. '"Sitting on a Man": Colonialism and the Lost Political Institutions of Igbo Women', *Canadian Journal of African Studies*, 6, no. 2 (1982), pp. 165-81.

Van Onselen, Charles. 'The Reconstruction of a Rural Life from Oral Testimony: Critical Notes on the Methodology Employed in the Study of a Black South African Sharecropper', *Journal of Peasant Studies*, 20, no. 3 (1993), pp. 494-514.

Vansina, Jan. *Oral Tradition as History*. Madison, WI: University of Wisconsin Press, 1985 [1965].

Vaughan, Megan. 'Household Units and Historical Process in Southern Malawi', *Review of African Political Economy*, no. 34 (Dec. 1985), pp. 35-45.

Vines, Alex. *Renamo: Terrorism in Mozambique*. London: James Currey, 1991.

Waldorf, Lars. 'Remnants and Remains: Narratives of Suffering in Post-Genocide Rwanda's Gacaca Courts'. *Humanitarianism and Suffering: The Mobilization of Empathy*, Richard Wilson and Richard Brown (eds). Cambridge: Cambridge University Press, 2009, pp. 285-306.

Warhurst, Philip. *Anglo-Portuguese Relations in South-Central Africa 1890–1900*. London: Longmans, 1962.

— 'A Troubled Frontier: North-Eastern Mashonaland, 1898–1906', *African Affairs*, 77, no.

307 (1978), pp. 214-29.

Weinrich, Anna. *Black and White Elites in Rural Rhodesia*. Manchester: Manchester University Press, 1973.

— 'Strategic Resettlement in Rhodesia', *Journal of Southern African Studies*, 3, no. 2 (1977), pp. 207-29.

Wendel, Tobias. *Mami Wata oder ein Kult zwischen den Kulturen*. Münster: Lit, 1991.

Werbner, Richard. *Tears of the Dead: The Social Biography of an African Family*. Edinburgh: Edinburgh University Press, 1991.

— 'Introduction: Beyond Oblivion. Confronting Memory Crisis', *Memory and the Postcolony: African Anthropology and the Critique of Power*, Richard Werbner (ed.). London: Zed Books, 1998, pp. 1-17.

— '"Smoke from the Barrel of a Gun": Postwars of the Dead, Memory and Reinscription in Zimbabwe'. *Memory and the Postcolony: African Anthropology and the Critique of Power*, Richard Werbner (ed.). London: Zed Books, 1998, pp. 71-102.

West, Michael. *The Rise of an African Middle Class: Colonial Zimbabwe, 1898–1965*. Bloomington, IN: Indiana University Press, 2002.

Weule, Karl. *Negerleben in Ostafrika: Ergebnisse einer ethnologischen Forschungsreise*. Leipzig: Brockhaus, 1908.

Wheeler, Douglas. 'Gungunyane the Negotiator: A Study in African Diplomacy', *Journal of African History*, 9, no. 4 (1968), pp. 586-7.

White, Luise. *Speaking with Vampires: Rumor and History in Colonial Africa*. Berkeley, CA: University of California Press, 2000.

— 'Precarious Conditions: A Note on Counter-Insurgency in Africa after 1945', *Gender and History*, 16, No. 3 (2004), pp. 603-25.

— '"Heading for the Gun": Skills and Sophistication in an African Guerrilla War'. *Comparative Studies in Society and History*, 51, no. 2 (2009), pp. 236-59.

White, Luise, Stephan Miescher, and David William Cohen (eds). *African Words, African Voices: Critical Practices in Oral History*. Bloomington, IN: Indiana University Press, 2001.

Wigen, Kären. *A Malleable Map: Geographies of Restauration in Central Japan, 1600–1912*. Berkeley, CA: University of California Press, 2010.

Wigglesworth, Tom. *Perhaps Tomorrow*. Harare: Galaxie Press, 1982.

Willis, Justin. *Potent Brews: A Social History of Alcohol in East Africa, 1850–1999*. Columbus, OH: Ohio University Press, 2002.

Wilson, Merna. 'Tea Break', *Skyhost*, 4, no. 3 (1992), p. 33.

Wilson, Thomas and Hastings Donnan (eds). 'Nations, State and Identity at International Borders'. *Border Identities: Nation and State at International Frontiers*, Thomas Wilson and Hastings Donnan (eds). Cambridge: Cambridge University Press, 1998, pp. 1-30.

Winter, Alison. *Memory: Fragments of a Modern History*. Chicago, IL: University of Chicago Press, 2012.

Wirz, Albert. 'Die Erfindung des Urwalds oder ein weiterer Versuch im Fährtenlesen', *Periplus*, 4 (1994), pp. 15-36.

Worby, Eric. 'Maps, Names, and Ethnic Games: The Epistemology and Iconography of Colonial Power in Northwestern Zimbabwe', *Journal of Southern African Studies*, 20, no. 3 (1994), pp. 371-92.

Wright, Marcia. *Strategies of Slaves and Women: Life-Stories from East/Central Africa*. New York: Lilian Barber Press, 1993.

Young, Allan. *The Harmony of Illusions: Inventing Posttraumatic Stress Disorder*. Princeton, NJ: Princeton University Press, 1997.

— 'America's Transient Mental Illness: A Brief History of the Self-Traumatised Perpetrator'. *Subjectivity: Ethnographic Investigations*, João Biehl, Byron Good, and Arthur Kleinman (eds). Berkeley, CA: University of California Press, 2007, pp. 155-78.

Young-Bruehl, Elizabeth. *Hannah Arendt: For Love of the World*. New Haven, CT: Yale University Press, 1982.

WEBPAGES

Rhodesians World Wide, http://www.rhodesia.com/.
United States Department of Veterans Affairs, National Centre for Posttraumatic Stress
    Disorder, http://www.ptsd.va.govt/professional/pages/ptsd-overview.asp.

FEATURE FILMS

Flame. Feature film. Harare: Media for Development Trust, 1996.
The Battle of Algiers. Feature film. Italy and Algeria, 1966.

Index